AF515945

GANGA

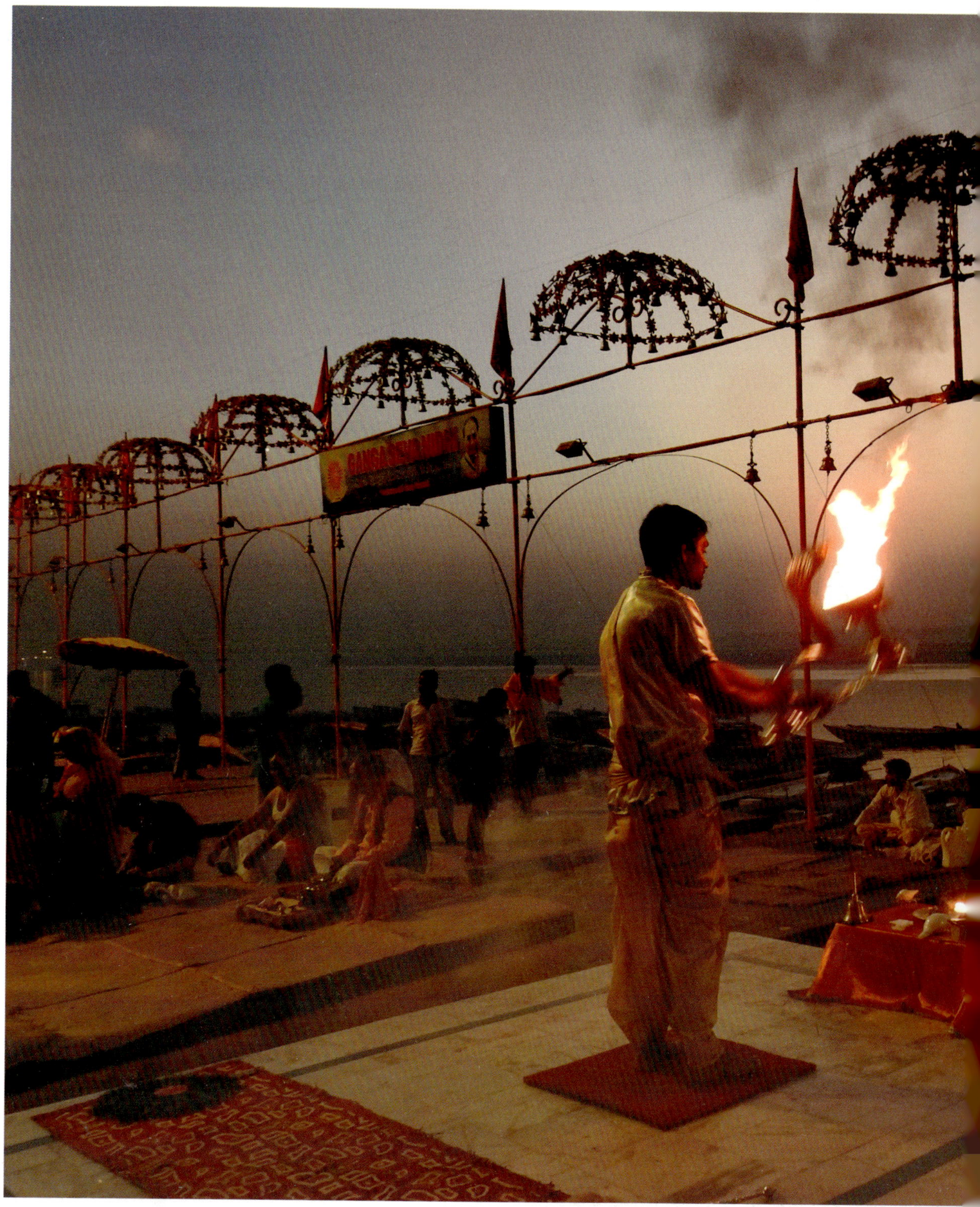

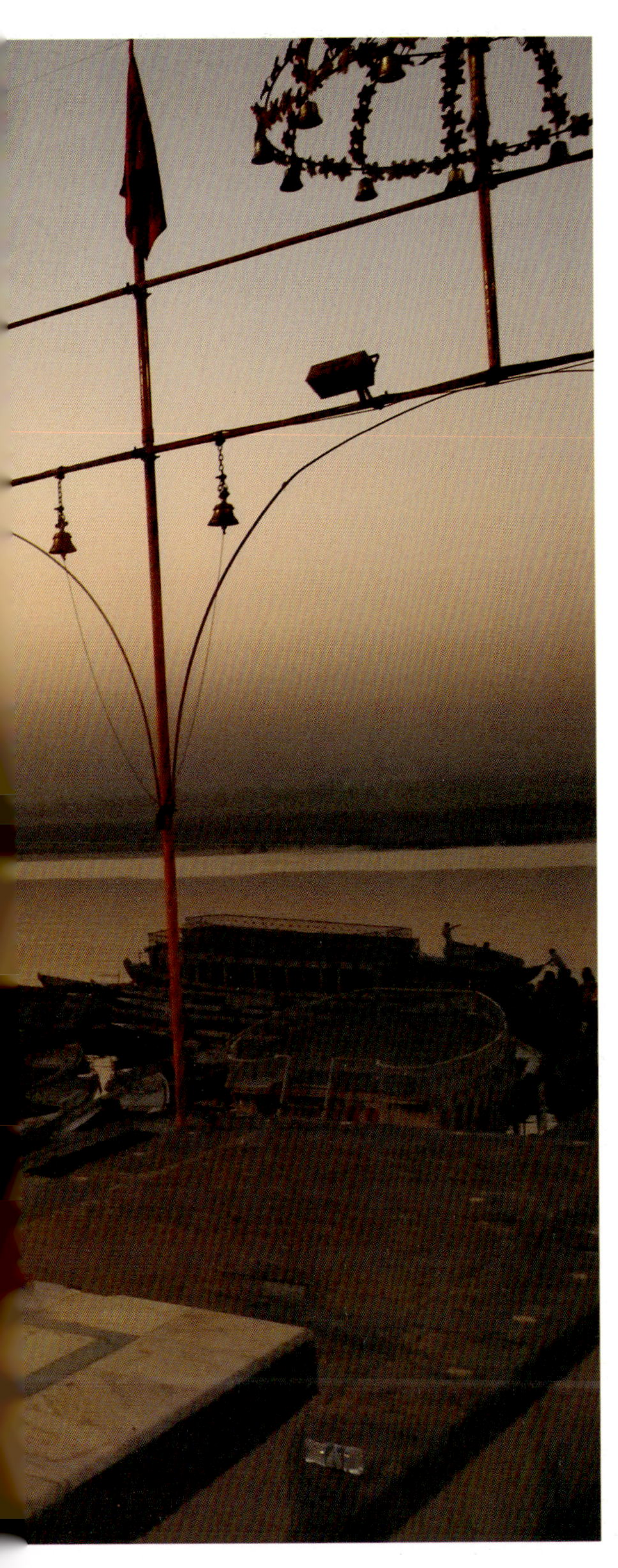

GANGA
AN ENDLESS JOURNEY

CHANCHAL KUMAR GHOSH

Translation by
Sarbani Putatunda

NIYOGI
BOOKS

This book was originally published in Bengali by Ananda Publishers, Kolkata under the title *Ganga Darshan* (2017).

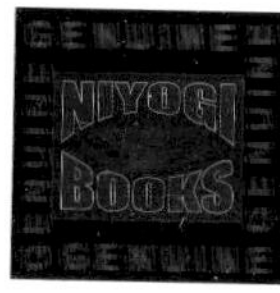

Published by
NIYOGI BOOKS
Block D, Building No. 77,
Okhla Industrial Area, Phase-I,
New Delhi-110 020, INDIA
Tel: 91-11-26816301, 26818960
Email: niyogibooks@gmail.com
Website: www.niyogibooksindia.com

Editor: Sucharita Ghosh
Design: Shashi Bhushan Prasad

ISBN: 978-93-89136-22-7
Publication: 2019

Printed at: Niyogi Offset Pvt. Ltd., New Delhi, India

To my wife Sujata and my brother
Sanjoy whose constant support
helped me complete my journey

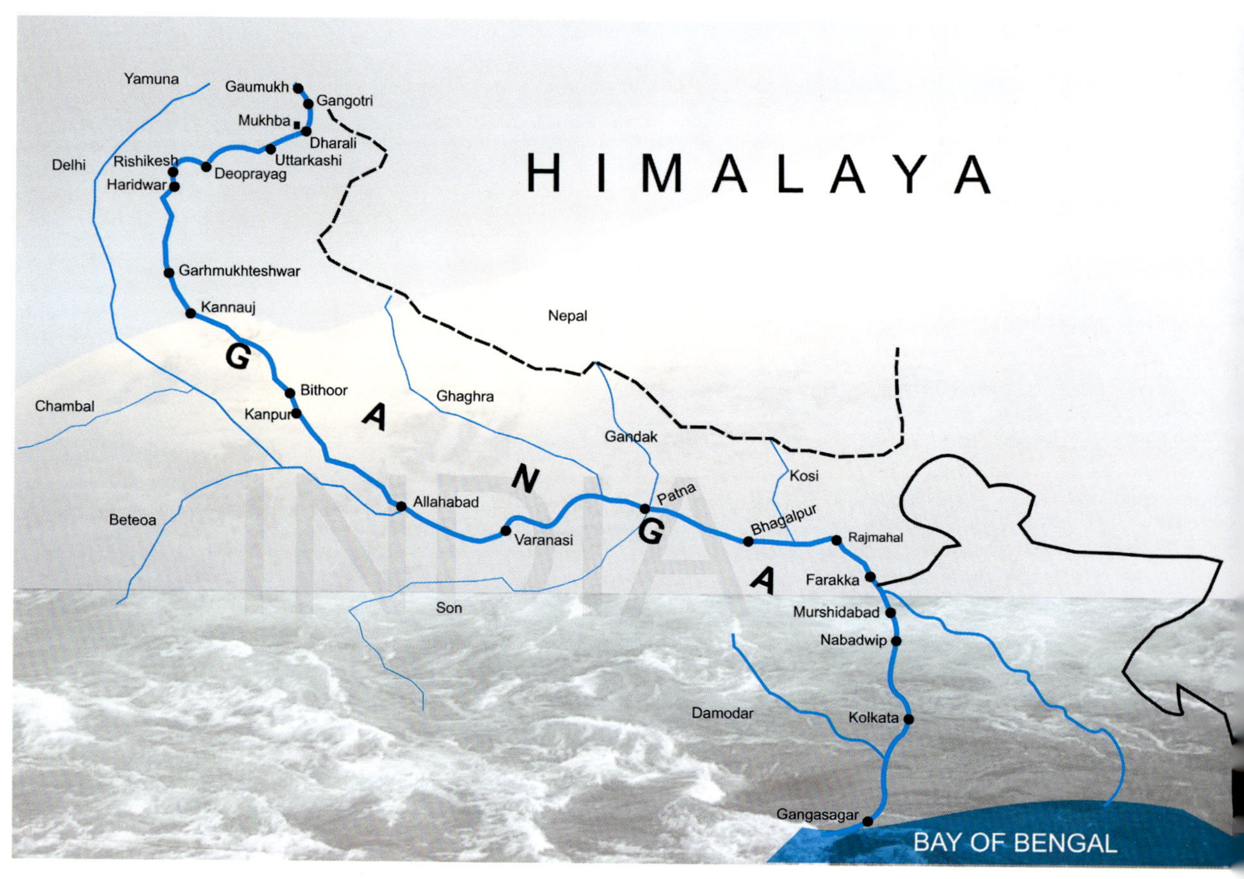
HIMALAYA
Yamuna
Gaumukh
Gangotri
Mukhba
Dharali
Uttarkashi
Delhi
Rishikesh
Deoprayag
Haridwar
Garhmukhteshwar
Kannauj
Nepal
GANGA
Bithoor
Kanpur
Chambal
Ghaghra
Gandak
Kosi
Patna
Allahabad
Beteoa
Varanasi
Bhagalpur
Rajmahal
Farakka
INDIA
Son
Murshidabad
Nabadwip
Damodar
Kolkata
Gangasagar
BAY OF BENGAL

CONTENTS

FOREWORD

I am happy to write the Foreword for *Ganga: An Endless Journey* by Chanchal Kumar Ghosh being published by Niyogi Books.

I am particularly impressed that the author has undertaken a pilgrimage along the Ganga, and written the book as a pilgrim's diary.

My own life has been a pilgrimage for the Ganga, the Himalaya, our beloved Mother Earth. We need to turn to the Ganga to make us all pilgrims on Earth once again, to relearn the values that make us an ecological civilization that have sustained us over centuries – values that we are forgetting.

The Ganga is India's ecological, economic, cultural and spiritual lifeline.

The sources of the Ganga – the lifeline of India – were designated sacred sites in order to protect the Ganga-Him. a, and hence India. The *yatra* to the four pilgrimage centres of Gangotri, Yamunotri, Kedarnath and Badrinath – the *Char Dham* – was meant to connect us culturally and spiritually to these '*Bhu tirth*s' (sacred sites of the Earth). The *Char Dham* yatra would also connect us ecologically to the sources of life, the sources of our rivers, the sources of a civilization's water.

Reading the book took me back to the many places along the Ganga which I have visited since my childhood and the many pilgrimages for the Ganga-Himalaya I have made.

I was born in the forests of the Himalaya, in today's Uttarakhand, which is the source of the sacred Ganga and its tributaries.

Our home is the land through which the Ganga flows – where the Bhagirathi, the Bhilangana, the Mandakini, the Alaknanda join to form the river which has supported our culture and civilization, our agriculture and economy from times immemorial.

I have been engaged in many scientific studies and ecological actions since the early days of the Chipko movement in the 1970s with Sundarlal Bahuguna and Bimla Bahuguna. We did an ecological assessment of the Tehri dam and several other dams on the Ganga. I joined Sundarlalji on the banks of the Bhagirathi for his Tehri Dam Satyagraha. I have undertaken many Ganga *yatra*s for water movements to prevent pollution, privatization and diversion of our beloved Ganga Ma from the early days of the Chipko movement to undertaking Ganga *yatra*s to stop the privatization of Ganga waters by the world's biggest water privatization company – Suez.

Ganga: An Endless Journey describes the pristine beauty of the river, where human carelessness has not destroyed the river, and also the devastation caused by the Tehri dam in the Himalaya and the Farakka barrage in West Bengal. When we treat the Ganga as a mother, have reverence and respect for her as a living being, and follow her ecological rules and laws, she is a river of life. When we violate her integrity, we rob her of her ecological space, her right to flow freely, refuse her her natural route by building dams and barrages, she has the potential to become an 'instrument of annihilation and destruction' – as Haripada Roy of Harinagar village communicated to the author during his pilgrimage. 'We are mortally afraid of the river Ganga,' says Roy.

The transformation of the Ganga from a river of life to a river of death and destruction is because we have forgotten her ecological laws, rules, values, processes. The story of the 'descent of the Ganges' was meant to remind us that the Ganga can be ferocious if we fail to live according to her laws.

The forests of the Ganga catchment are Nature's reservoirs that hold the heavy monsoon downpour with their leaves, soil and roots. As H.C. Reiger, the eminent Himalayan ecologist, reminds us, the myth of the descent of the Ganga is, in fact, an ecological story.

Ganga, whose waves in Swarga flow,
Is daughter of the Lord of Snow.
Win Shiva, that His aid be lent,
To hold Her in Her mid-descent.
For earth alone will never bear
These torrents travelled from the upper air.

The above hymn is a tale of the hydrological problem associated with the descent of a mighty river like the Ganga. Reiger described the material rationality of the hymn in the following words: 'In the scriptures a realisation is there that if all the waters which descend upon the mountain were to beat down upon the naked earth, the mountains would never bear the impact of the torrents ... In Shiva's hair we have a very well-known physical device which breaks the force of the water coming down ... the vegetation of the mountains.'

Forty years ago I joined the Chipko movement as a volunteer.

The women-led Chipko movement started after the 1972 Alaknanda disaster caused by logging in the Alaknanda valley. Women connected the deforestation to landslides and flooding. As they pointed out, the primary products of the forest were not timber and revenue, but soil and water. Forests left standing to protect the fragile Himalayan slopes provide more to the economy than when they are extracted as dead timber.

It took the 1978 Uttarkashi disaster for the Government to recognize that the women were right; when the government had to spend much more on flood relief than the revenues they were getting from timber extraction. In 1981, in response to the Chipko movement, logging was banned above 1,000 metres in the Garhwal Himalaya. Today Government policy recognizes that forestry in the fragile Himalaya has to be conservation forestry – which maximizes the ecological services of the forest by protecting – not extractive forestry.

The Chipko movement, which was initiated to protect the Himalayan forests, was inspired by the sacred and ecological knowledge of the relationship between the forests and water that the story of the descent of the Ganga carries in it. I started my ecological activism with Chipko. The women had come up with the slogan 'What do the forests bear: soil, water and pure air' to replace the slogan of commercial forestry: 'What do the forests bear: timber, resin and revenue.'

After the 1978 flooding of the Ganga, it became clear that water conservation was the first gift of the Himalayan forests. The wisdom of the peasant women of Garhwal is today called the economies of ecosystems. After nearly a decade of Chipko actions, logging was banned in the high Himalaya in 1981. However dams and highways are exempt from this ban, and are becoming a major reason for deforestation in the Himalaya, and they are a continued threat to the Ganga. Without Shiva's hair, her Shakti is too powerful to regulate.

For centuries millions have visited the Ganga, or lived in sacred cities along the Ganga. Their ecological footprint was invisible. Thousands came to the Kumbh, and there was no waste, no pollution. The ocean of people treaded lightly and became one with the Ganga. Our sages came to Rishikesh and Haridwar. In my childhood, Rishikesh was a small settlement but today it is a concrete jungle. The author has cited from Swami Vivekananda's younger brother Mahendranath Dutta's book *Badrinarayaner Paathe* that a mere hundred years ago Haridwar was a village. It is not that there was no congregation of people there. Since time immemorial the entire country gathered at the Kumbh Mela, which the Chipko poet Ghansyam Shailani described as the biggest party on Earth without an invitation, but they never wreaked havoc on the Ganga with their footprint. They treaded lightly.

Pilgrims engage in *tapasya*, and walk with a high ecological consciousness and a very light ecological footprint. Consumers consume nature, natural resources, they consume the Ganga with their demands and the waste they generate, without consciousness of sacred ecosystems where they are, or the ecological impact of their demands. Mass tourism has led to construction on the fragile banks of the rivers. When rivers flood, more damage is caused.

In my childhood old people did the pilgrimage to the *Char Dham* on foot. Along the main arteries we had roads for one-way traffic. Today, while most of the pilgrims still make their Ganga journey with devotion and reverence, the consumers engage in mass tourism and luxury tourism, wanting helicopters and superhighways. Highways mean landslides as mountain slopes are dynamited, and the rubble is thrown down the slope. Landslides create slope instability, with more boulders and debris causing destruction of forests and fields. Less space is left for water; rivers flood more easily. And instead of reaching faster, pilgrims and local people face roadblocks for days on end due to landslides. Having received the gift of living ecologically as a civilization from Mother Ganga over generations, in the last few decades we are being torn away from our ecological and cultural roots, and mindlessly chasing a maldevelopment model which measures how much money flows in commerce, instead of being conscious of how much clean and pure water flows in the Ganga after our visit, and how much waste we create. When we demand more and more luxury hotels, more and more packaged junk food and bottled water, we leave a trail of plastic and aluminium waste wherever we go, including the *Char Dham*. Consumers create waste. A pilgrim expresses reverence, love and gratitude to Ganga Ma for giving us life, sustenance and nourishment, both ecologically and spiritually.

A maldevelopment model based on promoting limitless greed and consumerism is making us blind to nature and culture. In chasing limitless growth, limitless consumption of natural resources, and limitless generation of waste, we are becoming ignorant of the culture of the sacred Ganga and the ecological fragility of the Himalaya. The sacred sets limits. It creates ecological responsibility. Ecological fragility sets limits. These limits are being violated, as rivers are dammed and diverted for electricity, and the pilgrimage to the *Char Dham* is being turned into crass consumerist mass tourism.

Our sacred mountains have sustained local communities and pilgrims for thousands of years because they have been treated with reverence and respect. Today the ecologically fragile Himalaya and our sacred rivers are being ecologically threatened, leading to increasing disasters. The 2013 Uttarakhand disaster which led to 5,000 deaths according to official estimates (20,000 based on the estimate of local communities) and the disappearance of nearly 1,00,000 people is a wake-up call to stop this destruction of the lifeline of our civilization.

The threats to our Mother Ganga or 'Ganga Ma' are many. The Ganga is now threatened at its very source – the Gangotri glacier. Climate change has led to the decline in snowfall and an increase in the rate of melting of snow. From 1935 to 1956, the retreat of the Gangotri glacier was 4.35 metres per year. In the period between 1990 to 1996 it was 28.33 m/yr. The average rate of retreat is 20-38 m/yr. If this retreat continues, the Ganga will become a seasonal river, with major ecological and economic consequences for the entire Ganga basin.

The Himalayan glaciers have already started retreating. The Gangotri glacier, from which the sacred Ganga originates, is retreating at the average rate of 27 metres per year. The Satopanth glacier is retreating at 26.9 m/yr and Dokriani at 15.7 m/yr. Chorabari – which feeds into the river Mandakini – is retreating at 10.2 m/yr. This melting of snow has created the Chorabari Lake (3,960 metres above sea level), also known as Gandhi Sarovar, located about 4 kilometres upstream from Kedarnath town, which is approximately 400 metres long, 200 metres wide, having a depth of 15-20 metres.

On 16 and 17 June 2013, intense and unprecedented rain poured down on the Himalayan range for more than 72 hours. The Chorabari lake burst, leading to its complete draining within 5-10 minutes, as reported by the watch and ward staff of the Wadia Institute of Himalayan Geology (WIHG), who were present at the WIHG camp at Chorabari glacier on 16 June and early morning of 17 June 2013. Usually floods come at the end of a heavy monsoon. In 2013 they came with the first rain. The monsoon came early and the rainfall was far greater than usual.

The heavy rainfall together with melting of snow in the surrounding Chorabari lake washed away the banks of the Mandakini river, causing massive devastation in the Kedarnath valley and surrounding areas. The flood damaged an 18-km stretch of the banks of river Mandakini between Kedarnath and Sonprayag, completely washing away the towns of Gaurikund (1,990 meres above sea level), Rambara (2,740 metres above sea level) and Kedarnath (3,546 metres above sea level). The roads and footpaths between Gaurikund and Kedarnath were also damaged stranding the injured for three days before help arrived. According to local people, more than 20,000 people died in the Uttarakhand disaster of 2013.

But June 2013 was more than a natural disaster. The intense rain in such a short period was typical of the extreme events climate change is bringing. And its impact was aggravated by the hydropower projects under construction in river valleys in Uttarakhand. The 99-megawatt power project at Singoli-Bhatwari, near Augustmuni, being constructed by Larson & Toubro, was a major cause of the devastation in Mandakini valley in 2013. It is one of 12 hydroelectric projects coming up on the Mandakini.

The ecological damage caused by maldevelopment has reduced the capacity of the mountain ecosystem to deal with heavy rain. Climate havoc adds to this vulnerability. The worst landslides occurred where tunnels were being built for these hydroelectric projects. Recklessly blasting the fragile mountains with dynamite for the construction of dams and tunnels has triggered thousands of landslides. When the first rain comes, these landslides fill the riverbed with rubble. There is no space for the water to flow. We are literally stealing the ecological space from our rivers and when they have no space to flow, they *will* overflow, cut banks and cause flooding.

The debris from the tunnels is dumped in the riverbed as well. When the floods carried the debris in the flood waters, the riverbed rose by 20-30 feet at places, the towering river waters washing away homes and villages, schools, roads and bridges, killing the pilgrims as well as local people who were all trapped. Destruction aggravated by ignorance and greed.

This was not a natural disaster. It was a manmade climate disaster. Climate change combined with maldevelopment created the unprecedented disaster. Yet, just before the

Copenhagen Climate Conference, the Government of India issued a report saying there was no impact on India's glaciers. The Kedarnath tragedy shows how heavy the cost of this denial is. We need to recognize that our glaciers are threatened, and melting glaciers will lead to more disasters, greater in their might than what we have seen. Disaster preparedness is the duty of the government. But disaster preparedness needs honest and robust ecological science, and honest and robust participatory democracy.

The Ganga's tributaries are threatened by dams and diversions in the upper reaches and barrages in the plains.

Planners do not see the Ganga and her tributaries as rivers of life. They see them as 20,000 megawatt of hydropower. The 260.5-metre-high Tehri dam, built at Tehri on the confluence of the Bhagirathi and Bhilangana, submerged the ancient capital of Tehri Garhwal, destroyed the lush and fertile fields of the valleys and displaced 1,00,000 people from 125 villages of which 33 were completely submerged. But the displacement due to the dam continues.

At the shore of the reservoir, people were flooded from below and above simultaneously. Fields and homes by the dam shore were submerged as the water level rose from 820 to 835 metres. The authorities of the Tehri hydropower plant were not willing to release excess water from the dam even though the water levels were affecting the surrounding villages. From their point of view, release through the slush gates was spillage. Mooni Devi, who lives at water level, says: 'This used to be such a great place with great farms. The dam builders have turned us all into beggars.'

Ghosh describes how the Ganga water is a stagnant pool above the Tehri dam, and a dying river with hardly any flow below the dam.

Five hundred dams are planned in our region on the Ganga system. A chain of hydroelectric projects have stopped the '*aviral*' flow of the Ganga and in many stretches the Ganga runs dry. The Government of India has been proposing hydroelectric projects on Loharinag-Pala, Pala-Maneri and Bhaironghati on Bhagirathi to tap their hydropower potential. In addition to the already-built Tehri dam and Maneri Bhali-2 dam, a series of dams were planned between Gangotri and Uttarkashi on the river Bhagirathi. The late Swami Gyanswarup Sanand (formerly Dr G.D. Agarwal) had been repeatedly fasting to save the Ganga. It took penance and fasting by today's 'Bhagirath', Prof. G.D. Agarwal, to stop the dams on the Bhagirathi.

In the plains a big threat to the Ganga and the Yamuna is pollution – both from industry and from sewage.

The Ganga is not being treated as a source of life, but as a sink to dump our ever-increasing urban, industrial and plastic waste. Today the Ganga is carrying pollution from 16 large cities, 23 medium-sized cities, 50 small cities all along her 2,525-km route from the Himalaya to Gangasagar. As the author writes, a recent survey conducted on the purity of the Ganga water reported that out of the 2525-km stretch of the river 600 km of the water is unfit for consumption by any living creature. Most of the 2,500 species sustained by the river are gradually dying because of pollution.

And even as billions are poured into cleaning the Ganga and Yamuna through the Ganga Action Plan and the Yamuna Action Plan, the pollution of our sacred river increases because of a combination of corruption and inappropriate technologies.

Industrialization and urbanization have turned our sacred rivers into sinks for pollutants. The Yamuna is clean before entering Delhi. During its 22-km journey through Delhi, it picks up 70% of the pollution of the entire river. All that the Action Plans have done is set up centralized Sewage Treatment Plants (STPs) that do not work, and 70% of all sewage is dumped untreated into the river. The river dies because of pollution; the land dies because it is deprived of rich nutrients. As Sunderlal Bahuguna reminded me, Gandhi called this 'golden manure'. Intelligent zero-waste sewage treatment systems like those evolved at IIT, Kanpur by Dr Vinod Tare would both clean the Ganga and fertilize the soil. We would not be wasting Rs 1,30,000 crores on fertilizer subsidies and thousands of crores on river action plans. Organic farming can be a major action for cleaning the Ganga.

The final threat to the Ganga is privatization. Privatization of water reduces it to a commodity, makes giant corporations owners and sellers of water and ordinary citizens, buyers and consumers. The role of citizens and communities as conservers and caretakers is destroyed. The human right to water, which was recognized by the United Nations in April 2010, is undermined. That is why when the Ganga water which has been brought to Delhi from Tehri was being privatized to Suez through a World Bank project, we built a Citizens Alliance for Water Democracy and told the World Bank and the Delhi government that our 'Mother Ganga is not for sale'. The World Bank project was withdrawn and the privatization stopped.

We need to once again learn reverence for our sacred mountains and rivers. We need to be informed of the latest ecological sciences, not by an obsolete 'development' model which is nothing more than a greed-and-exploitation model that led to the tragic disaster in Uttarakhand. Contrary to what the politicians said, the disaster was clearly manmade, and not a natural disaster. Politicians, decision makers and corporations responsible for causing the disaster through their ignorance and greed, their blindness and shortsightedness, need to take responsibility for the disaster their policies and actions have caused. The 'polluter pays' principle needs to be expanded to cover the scale of ecological devastation we are witnessing. The 2013 disaster should wake us up to the social, ecological and economic costs of destructive policies which have devastated our fragile and beautiful mountain ecosystems. The Himalaya are the youngest mountain system in the world. They cannot bear the violence of deforestation and dam building. They need gentleness and respect. Chipko shook our policymakers out of their slumber which had allowed them to think of forests as timber mines, and woke them up to the ecological functions of the forests in the catchments of our rivers. The 2013 disaster should shake them out of their current slumber where rivers are nothing more than 20,000 megawatts of hydropower. They have to wake up and realise that when respected, our rivers are rivers of life; when violated, they can become rivers of death.

Ghosh's book is a wake-up call to us. As the author reminds us, by our actions, we have transformed our living, cleansing Mother Ganga into a carrier of pollution. Instead of our sins being washed away, we are. If we truly revered Ganga Ma as our Mother, we would not burden her with our sin of pollution and corruption, including the corruption of our faith, our Dharma, which allows us to go in larger numbers to the Ganga to wash our sins, while we extract, divert, and dam more and more of her water, dump more and more pollution into her shrivelling waters. Through his book Ghosh gives a warning – the Ganga will never be cleansed until we cleanse ourselves.

Ganga continuing to flow '*aviral*' (uninterrupted) and '*nirmal*' (clean and free of pollution) is her right. Our ecological and ethical duty as citizens of the timeless civilization the Ganga has given birth to is to prevent her destruction.

I have witnessed the thousands who gather every evening on the ghats in Rishikesh, Haridwar, Varanasi for the Ganga *aarti*. The millions who gather for the Kumbh Mela transcend from noisy chaos to a quiet and peaceful devotion to our Mother.

I believe we have the potential to make a transition from the polluting, careless, industrial, consumerist culture that we are becoming to a culture that lives its faith of reverence for the Ganga, for all our rivers, and our waters. Our spiritual dharma is an ecological dharma – to conserve water, use only what we need, share water as a community, and avoid the adharma or sin of exploiting, wasting, privatizing and polluting our waters, including the Sacred Ganga. As I write the foreword, India is in the midst of a water emergency. If our waters disappear, we will not survive as a civilization.

Ghosh quotes Pandit Nehru who wrote in *The Discovery of India*, 'Ganga, the Sacred river of India has laid the foundation of the heart of our country ... The history of its birth from Gangotri to its history of merging with the sea at Gangasagar, is in reality the true history of India and Indian civilisation. She is our Mother, who has witnessed the various courses of our lives-creation of cities, destruction of kingdoms, cowardice of men, valour of our heroes, tears and laughter, joys and sorrows. The name Ganga resonates in the Indian psyche.'

Our policymakers should read this book to learn lessons for cleaning the Ganga, by cleaning our policies of the polluting influence of greed and commercial contracts, thereby increasing the flow of money while the Ganga shrinks in its flow and purity.

Every citizen should read it for understanding our culture, our sacred geography, our history, and the threat from blind copying of the throwaway culture of waste and pollution that makes us participants in the sin of pollution and desacralization of our sacred Mother.

Children should read it so they are all inspired to be little Bhagiraths, conserving and renewing the Ganga and all our rivers, and through it rejuvenating our ecological civilization so our rivers can sustain us for thousands of years as they have sustained us in the past.

The movement to save the Ganga and its '*nirmal*' (clean) and '*aviral*' (uninterrupted) flow is not just a movement to save a river. It is a movement to save India's troubled soul that is polluted and stifled by crass consumerism and greed, disconnected from its ecological and cultural foundations.

If the Ganga lives, India lives.
If the Ganga dies, India dies.

Dr Vandana Shiva

INTRODUCTION

I still remember the house where we lived in my childhood. It was near the Ramakrishna Math, Belur which stands on the bank of the river Ganga. I also remember whenever my paternal grandmother, a frequent visitor to the Math, would ask me to accompany her there, I would gleefully agree and run along. Once inside the Math premise, I would leave her company and head straight towards the riverbank. Sitting still for hours I would quietly observe the beautiful images floating past me. After all these years I realise how those visits had imperceptibly instilled in me a strange kind of fascination and love for the river.

Since my father had a transferable job, I completely lost touch with the river for several years. After many years, when I returned to the Ganga – my childhood crush – I experienced a number of bereavements. First my grandmother left us. She was cremated on the bank of the river. My tears mingled with the river water. Then, as the years passed by, many of my near and dear ones left us for their heavenly abode on the bank of this very river. Yet, to be honest, each of my visits to the riverbank has reaffirmed my intrinsic connection with her.

I have been toying with the idea of writing about the river for a long time. But the very prospect of documenting her 2,525-kilometre journey, from Gaumukh to Gangasagar, deterred me. Since I could not undertake such a monumentally expensive venture myself, I kept requesting people to assist me in my endeavour. Finally it was my mentor Sri Ranjit Mallick and his wife Smt. Deepa Mallick who volunteered to help. Smt. Deepa Mallick even gifted me her camera and showed me how to handle the equipment.

Finally, one day I left home in search of the route King Bhagirath had taken to bring the Ganga on earth. The pathway itself has a history of its own. It boasts of a rich spiritual heritage. Beginning her journey from Gaumukh the river traverses places like Gangotri, Uttarkashi, Deoprayag, Rishikesh, Haridwar, Bithoor, Kanpur, Allahabad, Varanasi, Patna, Murshidabad, Nabadwip, Kolkata, and finally flows into the Bay of Bengal near Sagar Island.

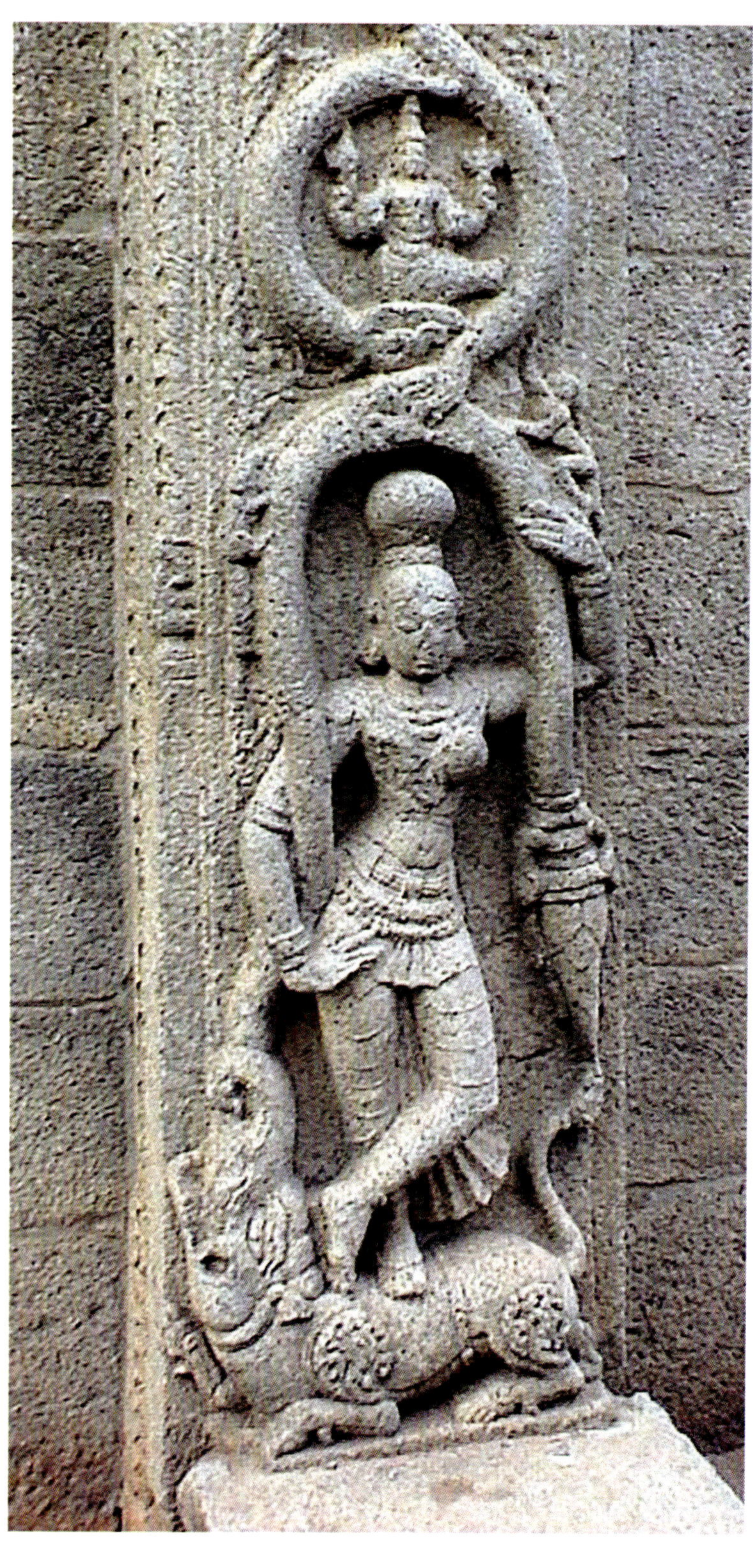

Ganga standing on her *vahana* (carrier), the Capricorn, at Mahabalipuram

I remember, once when Sundarlal Bahuguna (pioneer of the Chipko movement) had asked me, 'Son, what have you acquired while journeying down the banks of the Ganga?' I had spontaneously answered, 'I have been able to comprehend the fact that river Ganga is the quintessence of India.'

'You are right, my son,' he had responded appreciatively. 'To discover the course of the river Ganga is actually visualising the 5,000-year-old history of our nation.'

While tracing the course of river Ganga, I had a strong feeling that the journey was actually helping me to witness the spirit of our country that has flourished on its banks down the centuries. True, a lot has changed over time, yet somewhere there is an invisible thread, linking our present with our past that stretches back several thousand years. There is an invisible cultural continuity somewhere, analogous to the flowing river. Therefore standing on its banks I have always been humbled. The vast expanse of sacred water has appeared to me like an emblem of love, accepting and nourishing everyone. There is an element of universality in her which I find so endearing.

Travelling down the banks of the Ganga I happily clicked numerous photographs. I have done my best to capture the multicoloured life I witnessed over the course of my journey through these images. The responsibility of translating the entire work in English was gladly accepted by Smt. Sarbani Putatunda.

I have been fortunate to come across a cross section of people while journeying down the riverbank. I met ascetics, villagers, teachers, workers in crematoriums, and even scholars. Interacting with them was an enriching experience. True, very often I could not verify the data that was furnished by them, but I retained the beautiful memories associated with the journey. And I present to you these memories.

I am a writer. My vocation is to string my feelings in words and these words are my tribute to the Ganga. It is like floating a lamp in the dark down the sacred river.

Chanchal Kumar Ghosh

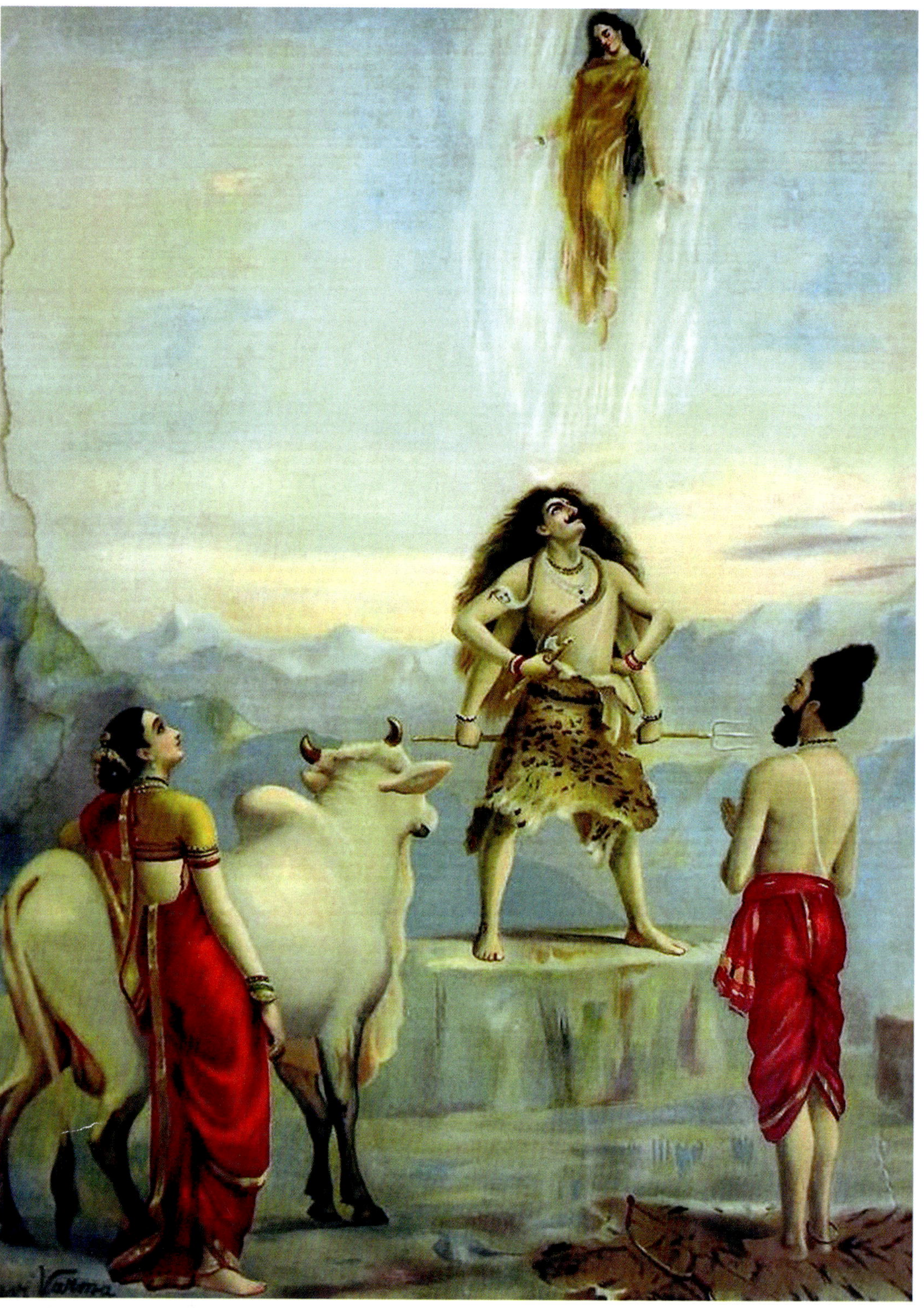

THE STORY OF ORIGIN

For Indians, the Ganga is not simply a river; rather, it is a causeway between heaven and earth. The river has been the source of their existence—both physical and spiritual. Its history spans a few thousand years beginning with the *Rig Veda*. The *Rig Veda* narrates a vivid history of the Indian civilisation that stretched across the banks of river Indus and later branched out to the banks of river Sarasvati. But there is hardly any reference to the river Ganga. At that time, the Ganga had not assumed the importance it did later after the Sarasvati dried up.

To be precise, only three slokas in the entire *Rig Veda* have been dedicated to the river Ganga. The *Rig Veda* is divided into books known as *mandala*s (circles) and in the third *mandala* of the text, the fifty-eighth sloka mentions the existence of river Ganga as river Janhavi. In the sixth *mandala* of the text, the forty-fifth sutra talks about Ganga.

FACING PAGE: *Descent of Ganga* by Raja Ravi Varma

This reference is considered to be rather innocuous by most Indians. And in the seventy-fifth sutra of the tenth *mandala* of the text, the poet categorically offers his prayers to several rivers at one go – Ganga, Yamuna, Sarasvati, Sutlej and Purunchu – requesting them to share his prayer accordingly.

River Ganga was first given her due share of importance in the *Ramayana*. Bhagirath, successor of King Sagar, has been credited as the frontrunner in bringing river Ganga to earth. And Bhagirath actually was the eighth predecessor of Rama. The poet Valmiki has beautifully narrated Bhagirath's herculean task in the *Ramayana*.

The story being repeated over several thousand years has become part of the fabric of Indian psyche—a holy river, descending directly from heaven. It is believed that a mere contact with its holy water rinses all mortal sins. Hence, both the *Ramayana* and the *Mahabharata* sing in praise of river Ganga.

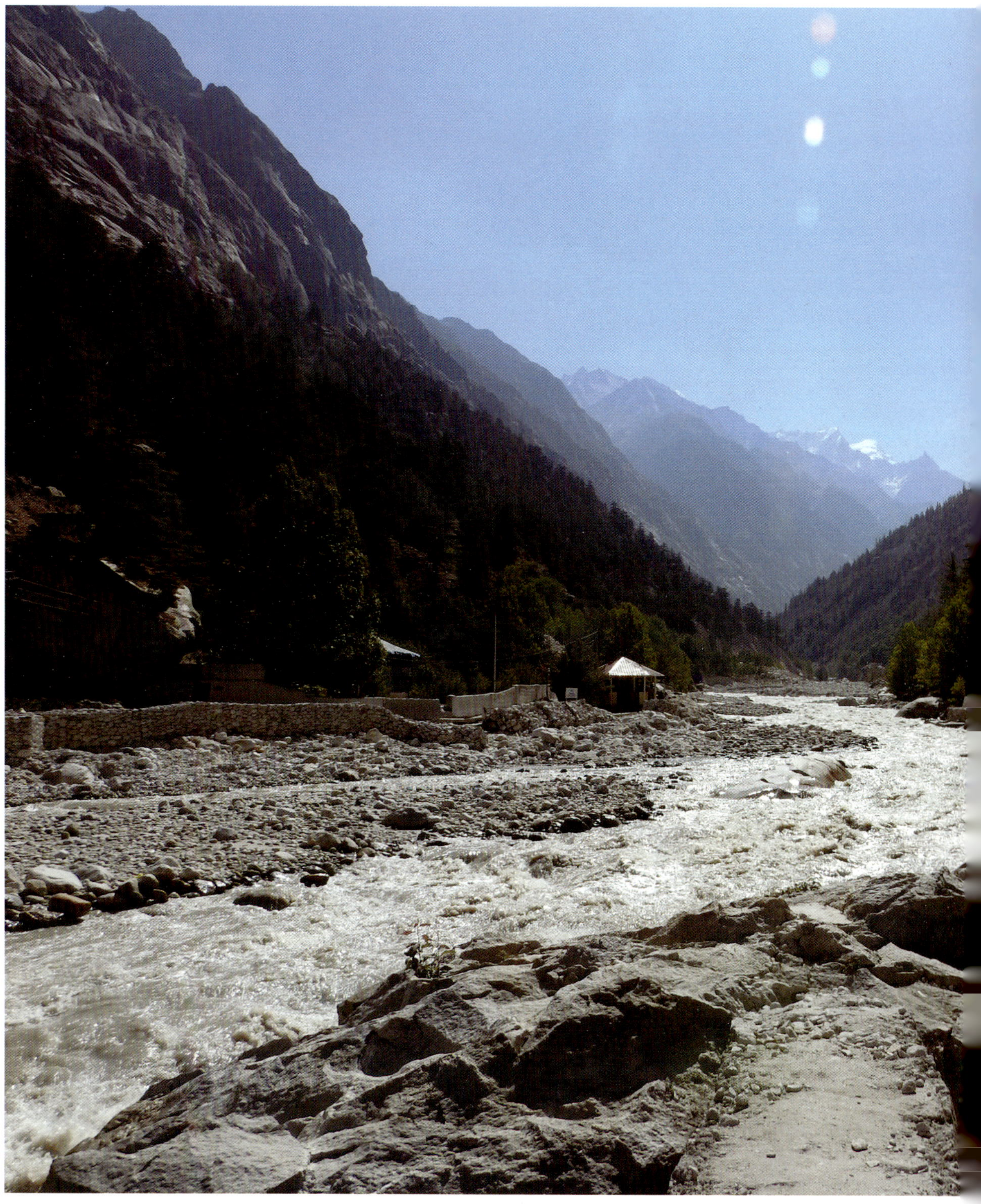

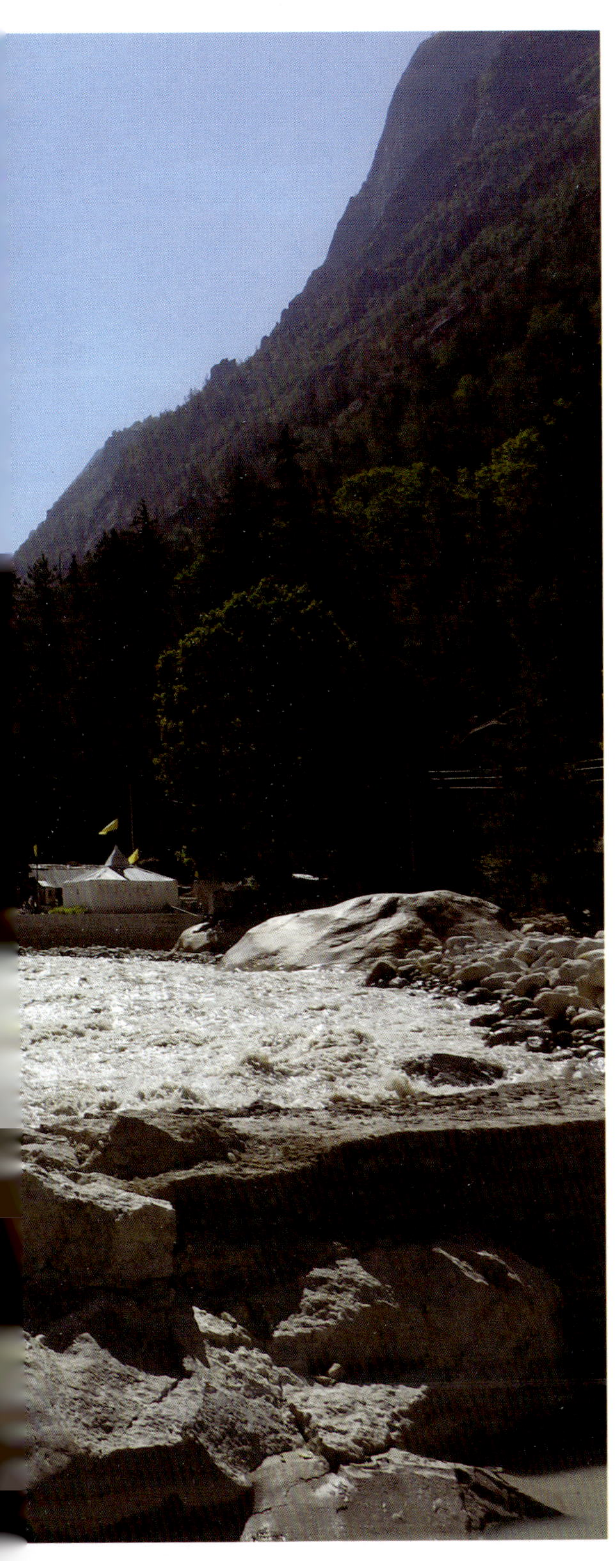

THE BIRTH OF GANGA

Neither the *Ramayana* nor the *Mahabharata* document the origin of the Ganga. The stories that are circulated are actually found in the *Purana*s and in folklores. In fact, there are several versions of it. The most common one is the story of Sage Narada and the *raga*s and *ragini*s.

According to a story from the *Purana*s, one day, as Sage Narada was walking down the paths of heaven he heard a heart-rending cry. 'Who is lamenting in this manner in such an ambience,' he wondered. He walked further down and found a group of crippled men and women crying aloud. Their faces bore marks of immense suffering. Narada was extremely disturbed. 'Who are you,' he asked. 'We are six *raga*s and thirty-six *ragini*s', they replied. Shaking his head in sorrow Narada asked them, 'Why are you suffering like this? Can I help you?' Narada was a real connoisseur of music and so the terrible condition of the *raga*s and *ragini*s disturbed him very much. Coaxed by Narada, one among them suddenly blurted out a strange tale. 'There is a sage called Narada,' narrated the *raga*. 'He considers himself a great singer. But most of his songs are sung out of tune. Listening to his off key songs has turned us into cripples.'

Ganga in the Himalayas

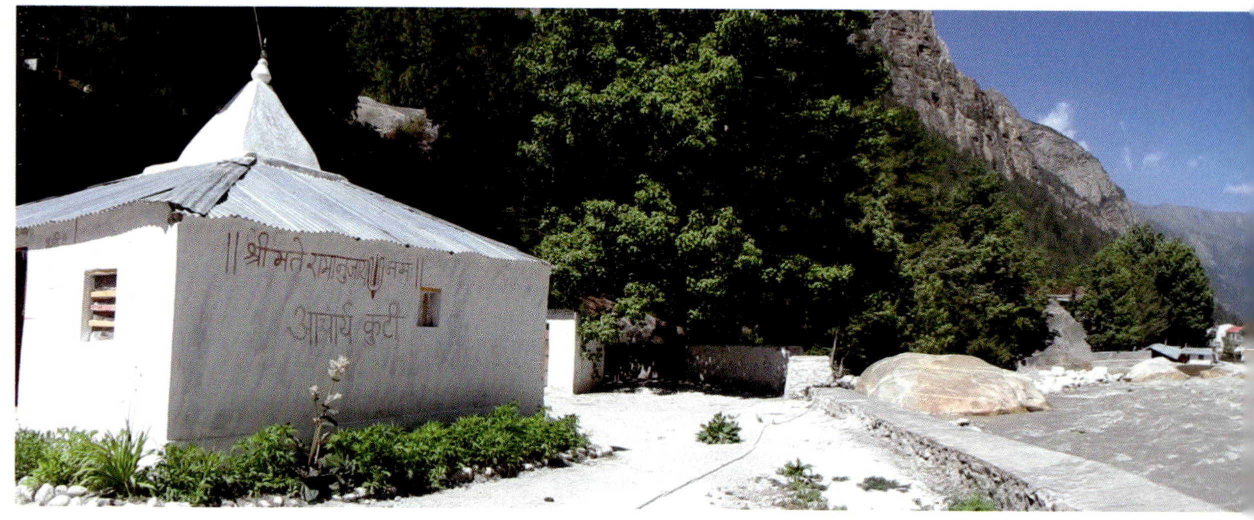

A panoramic view of Gangotri

Narada was taken aback. He prided himself on being the star singer of heaven, but today he learnt that the tunes he sung were totally off the track. Filled with shame and repentance he confessed to the *raga*s and *ragini*s, 'I am sage Narada. Sorry for unknowingly inflicting so much pain upon you all. How can I help you to regain your former selves?'

'Only if Mahadeva [another name for Lord Shiva] sings for us will we regain our former selves,' they replied. So Narada went off to Mahadeva at Mount Kailash, to request him to sing. Filled with shame and repentance, Narada paid obeisance to Mahadeva and narrated to him what he had heard. Mahadeva agreed but on one condition. 'I will sing,' he said, 'provided Brahma and Vishnu agree to be my audience. Only they are capable of appreciating my music.' (Again a possible dig at Narada – neither can he sing nor can he be called a true connoisseur of music!)

So Narada went to Lord Brahma and Lord Vishnu and requested them to be Mahadeva's audience. Both agreed and Mahadeva began his song. His melody flooded the universe and instantly cured the *raga*s and the *ragini*s. In the meantime, Lord Shiva's melody was so overpowering that Lord Vishnu was completely entranced and after sometime droplets of water started dripping from his body. Observing this transformation Lord Brahma held out his divine water pot to contain Lord Vishnu in a liquid state. Naturally the liquid that Lord Brahma collected was nothing but divine water. So when Lord Shiva ended his song and saw Lord Vishnu's metamorphosis, he advised Lord Brahma, 'Since the water you have collected is nothing but Lord Vishnu's

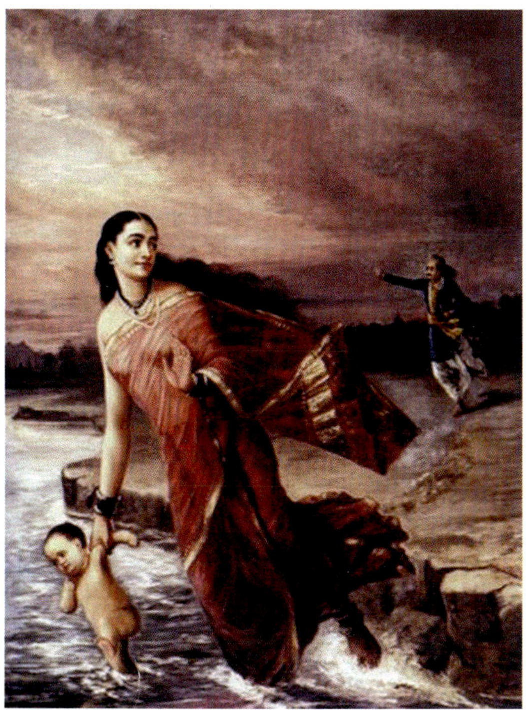

Ganga and Shantanu (1890) by Raja Ravi Varma

bathe in the Ganga, drink its holy water and perform certain religious rites on its bank. He died on the banks of the Ganga and was cremated there.

Finally in the '*Vanaparva*' of the *Mahabharata*, slokas are dedicated in praise of the river Ganga. Furthermore, her banks too will be great pilgrimages, the poet predicts. Even in the *Kaliyuga*, the sloka says, a dip in the Ganga will be considered to be the holiest deed for a man. Just as the sun eliminates darkness from the world, a dip in the Ganga will cleanse men of all sins.

Ganga in the Puranas

Like the *Ramayana* and the *Mahabharata*, many Indian *Purana*s sing praises of the Ganga. In the *Kalki Purana* the sages promise that a dip in the eternal flowing Ganga will ensure eternal heaven to man by cleansing his sins. Ganga, which supposedly originates from the footsteps of God Almighty, is thus praised everywhere. Gods residing in distant hills too love this holy river. Follower of Bhagirath, Ganga shines like a white insignia on the crown of Lord Shiva. Brahma, Vishnu and Shiva worship her as holy, for cleansing sins and ensuring liberation from mortal bondages. Gods and demons worship her as the daughter of Almighty God. Whosoever worships her or even believes in her purity achieves the stature of a sage, and is guaranteed eternal happiness. Whoever serves her cause is bound to be victorious in every walk of life.

The Descent of Ganga

Thence to Jahnu's daughter (Ganga),
there descending
The Himalaya, the heavenly stair
Of Sagaras, but laughing at the frown
On Ganga's face to tug at Shiva's hair:
Her hands as wavelets to his moon extending.

(*Meghadutam* by Kalidasa;
translated by Colin J. Holcombe)

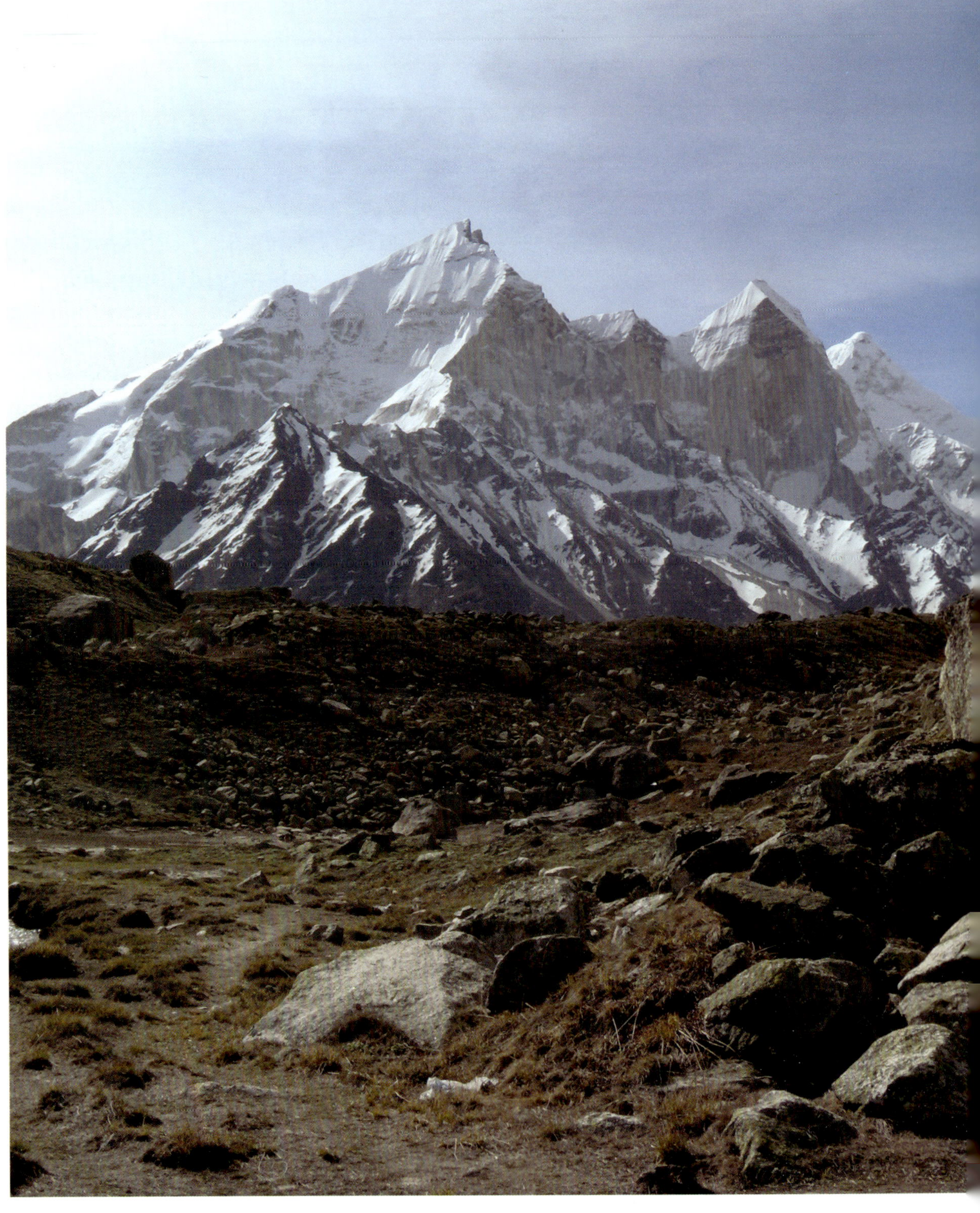

GANGA IN THE HIMALAYAS

GAUMUKH

Surrounded by snow-covered mountains of different heights and sizes like Kirtistamva, Shivalingam, Meru, Bhrigupanth, Satapanth, Chaturangi and Swetavarna from all sides, Gaumukh is a snow-clad cave situated in the heart of the Himalayas. Glaciers of different sizes descend from these peaks and collectively form the Gangotri glacier. At the foot of Gangotri glacier is the Gaumukh cave. The Ganga emerges from this cave.

Chunks of ice come floating by from the dark cave of Gaumukh. These chunks slowly thaw and flow downwards at great speed, thus forming the Ganga. The water, however, appears muddy from afar. For seven months of the year, the entire region remains completely covered with ice. Only during summer, when the ice partially melts, pilgrims visit this sacred spot. Situated at a height of 3,892 km (approximately 14,770 feet) the perilous journey to Gaumukh involves a walk of eighteen kilometres. But the scenic beauty of the place is unparalleled. Since time immemorial people have visited this holy place and offered their prayers to the Ganga.

FACING PAGE: The Bhagirathi group of three peaks in the Himalayas

Ganga has featured in almost all our ancient scriptures – the Vedas, the *Purana*s and epics, the *Ramayana* and the *Mahabharata*. But only recently have people been able to identify both the Gangotri glacier and the Gaumukh cave as its true starting point. In all likelihood these names were attributed much later either by some pilgrims or by some sages who visited these places.

The word 'ga' (originally a Sanskrit word) connotes many things. 'Ga' stands for our sensory perceptions. 'Ga' may also connote mother earth. 'Ga' can also refer to a cow. Just as a cow nourishes us with milk, likewise the fast-flowing water of the Ganga nourishes Indians; hence the name Gaumukh – literally the face of a cow. Gaumukh may

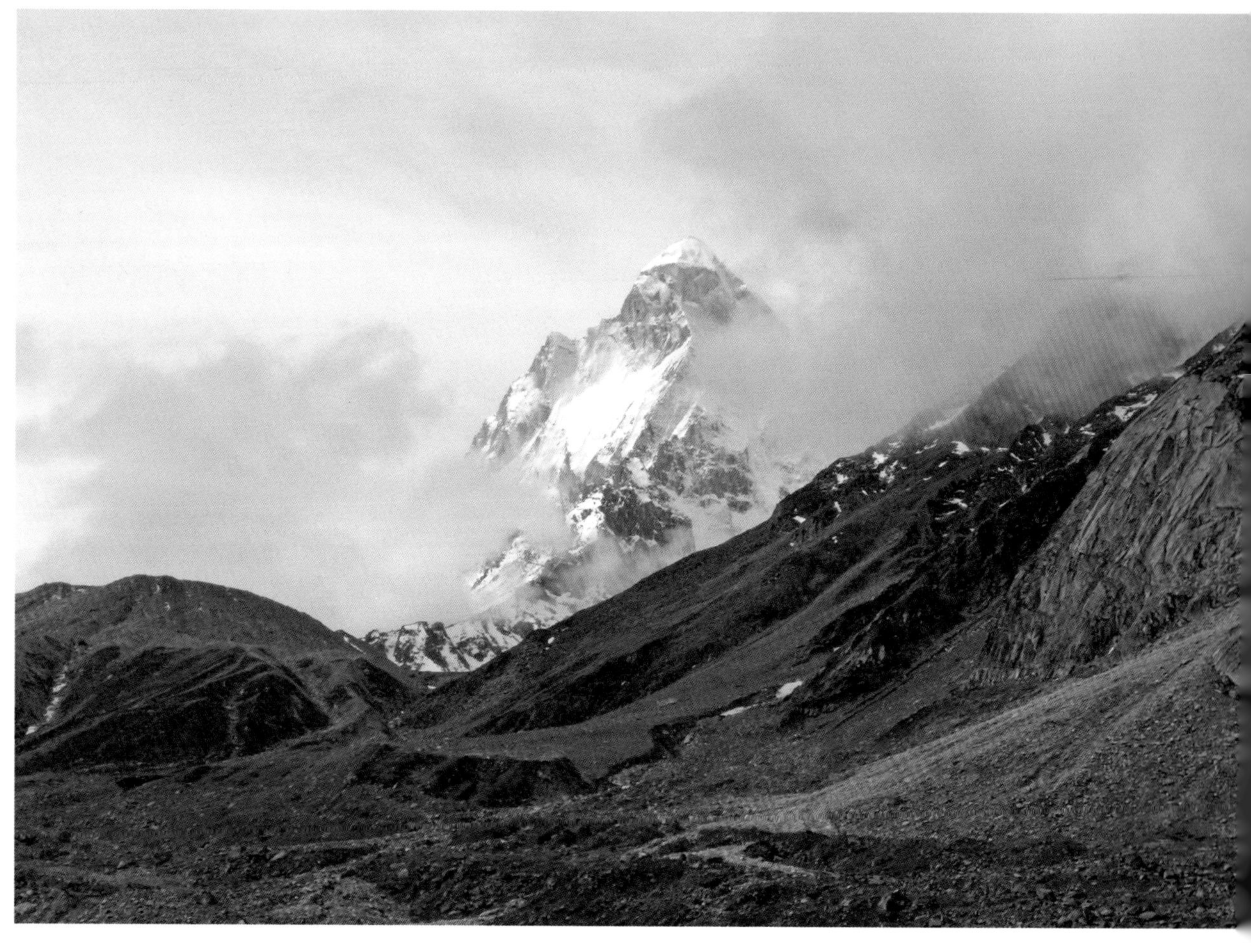

The majestic Shivling peak (6,540 metres), also known as 'Mahadeo Ka Linga'

also mean the place from where Ganga emerges. Interestingly the orientation of the cave Gaumukh keeps changing with the flow of the river. At present the Ganga flows northwards and Gaumukh is oriented accordingly. Gaumukh is situated at the rear-most point of the Gangotri glacier. It is twenty-four kilometres long and about two to three kilometres wide. Only the Siachen glacier is larger than the Gangotri glacier in the Himalayan range.

One has to travel eighteen kilometres on foot along the Gangotri glacier to reach the Gaumukh cave. The journey though not very perilous is extremely tiring. Encircled by the mountainous lush forests, the path is at places very steep and narrow and at places just adequately wide. People unable to walk often prefer riding on horses. There is no well-defined path laid out other than layers of pebbles. But it presents a very picturesque sight. On one side of the path

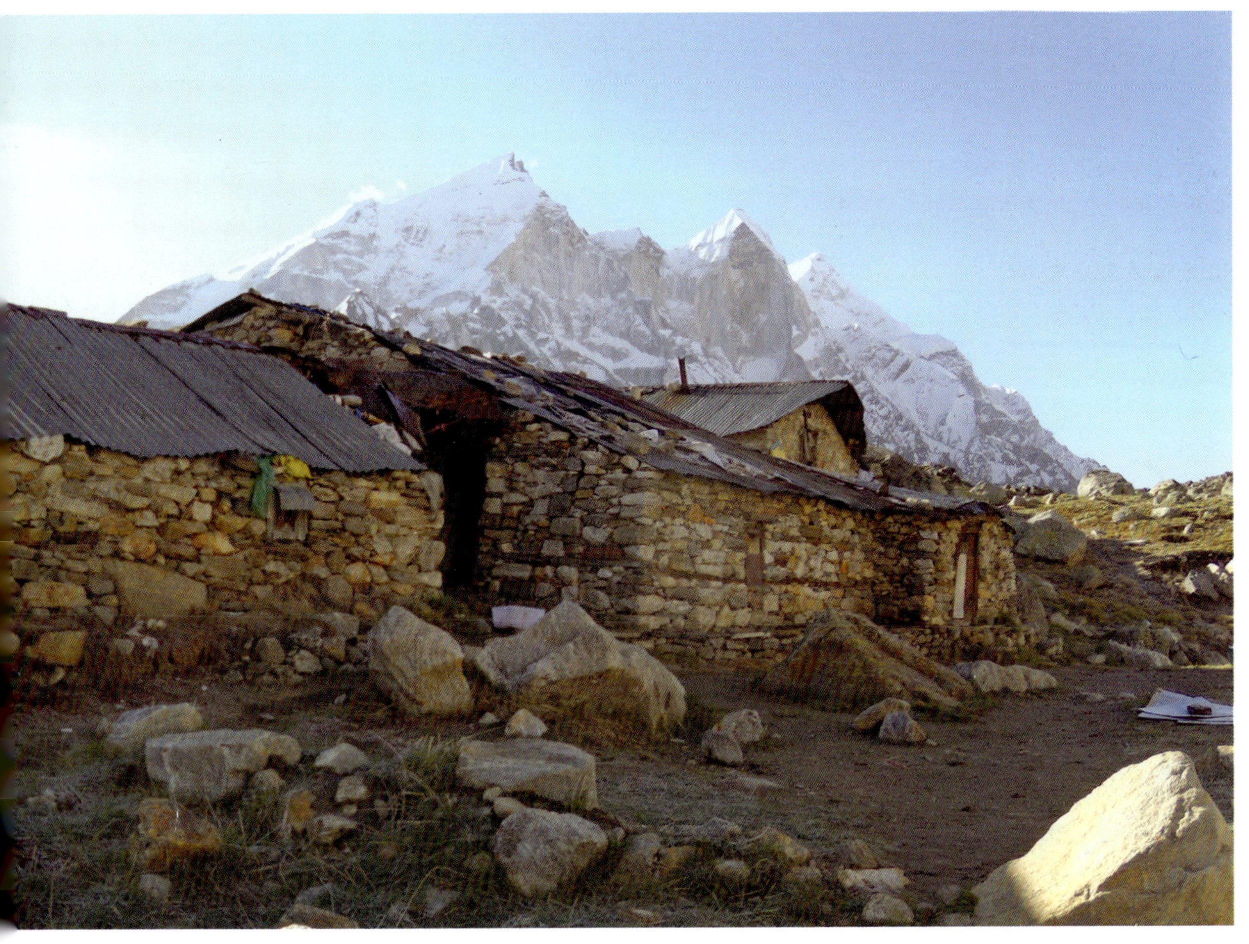

A sadhu's humble abode at the foothills of the Bhagirathi group of three peaks

stand the steep mountain peaks, while on the other side flows the silver-hued Ganga. If one proceeds further, one comes across a series of mountain peaks where ibexes are found in large numbers.

Ten kilometres away from Gangotri is Chiravas, a place full of *deodar* trees and wild mountainous flowers of different shapes and colours. At Chiravas, one frequently comes across waterfalls, flowing merrily down the mountain slopes. Four kilometres from Chiravas is Bhoojvas, also known as Bhojbasa. The place was once full of *bhooj* trees whose leaves (similar to Egyptian papyrus) were used as writing material in ancient India. Now of course there is not a single *bhooj* tree left. The famous Lalbaba Ashram is located here. It's a hermitage set up by a monk lovingly called Lalbaba. He had set up this hermitage to provide shelter to the pilgrims visiting Gaumukh and the Gangotri glacier.

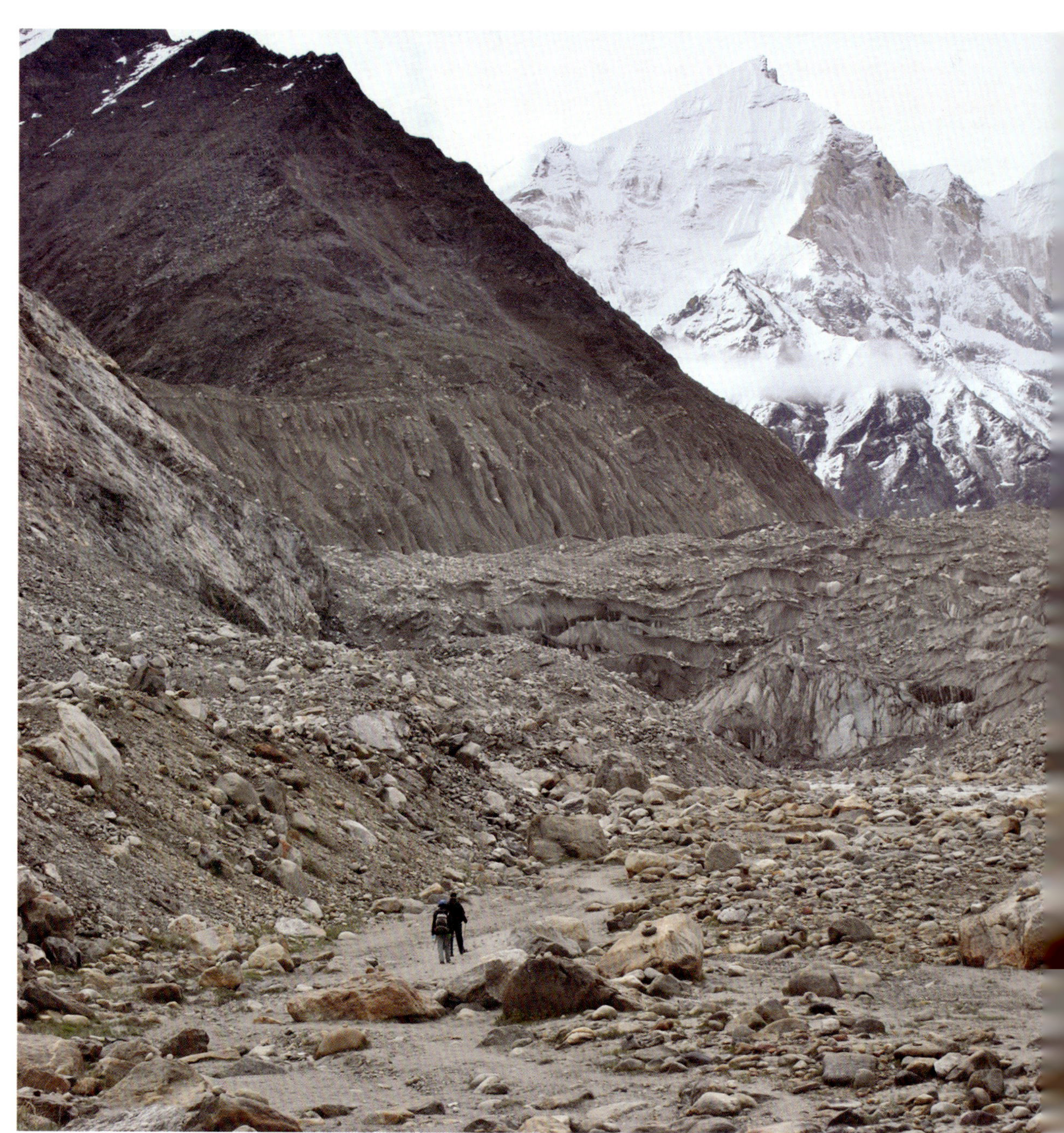

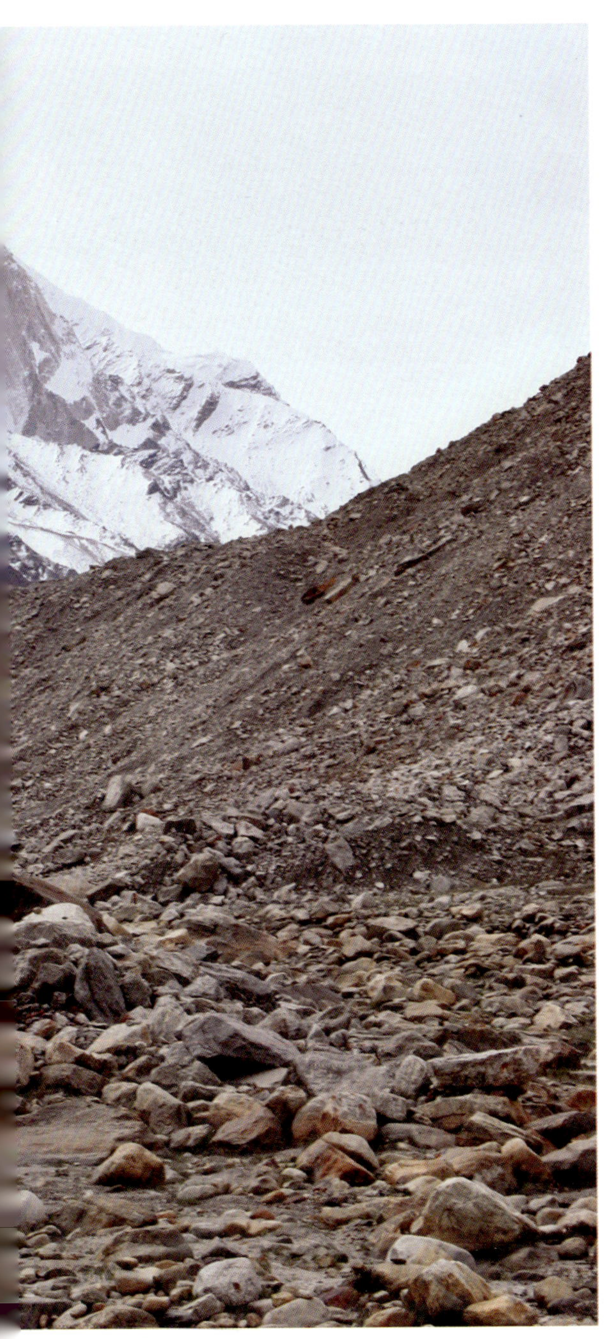

The very concept of a road simply vanishes after this. Boulders and pebbles lie strewn all around for people to walk upon. Gaumukh cave is four kilometres away from here. Whether it be a pilgrim or a stray adventurer, the tranquility of the place immediately captivates a visitor. Ganga here manifests her majestic form. Cutting her path across large chunks of hard rocks, she flows at breakneck speed. The water though ice cold is considered to be the purest of pure, hence ideal for a holy dip. But because she keeps changing her pathway frequently, there is no well-defined bank here for people to use. Yet, people come, bathe, conduct religious rituals and then return to Gangotri.

From a Pilgrim's Diary

It was eight in the morning when I left Gangotri. Since the morning mist had not cleared properly we could not help starting a bit late. Dilip, my porter-cum-guide, accompanied me. Dilip is a local youth of thirty. For the last ten years, he has been ferrying people across these dangerous terrains. I entered the Gangotri temple to pay my obeisance to the deity of mother Ganga. Beside mother Ganga stood the idols of Sarasvati and Yamuna. And in front of them

Gaumukh is a vision here with the Bhagirathi group of peaks shimmering in the distance

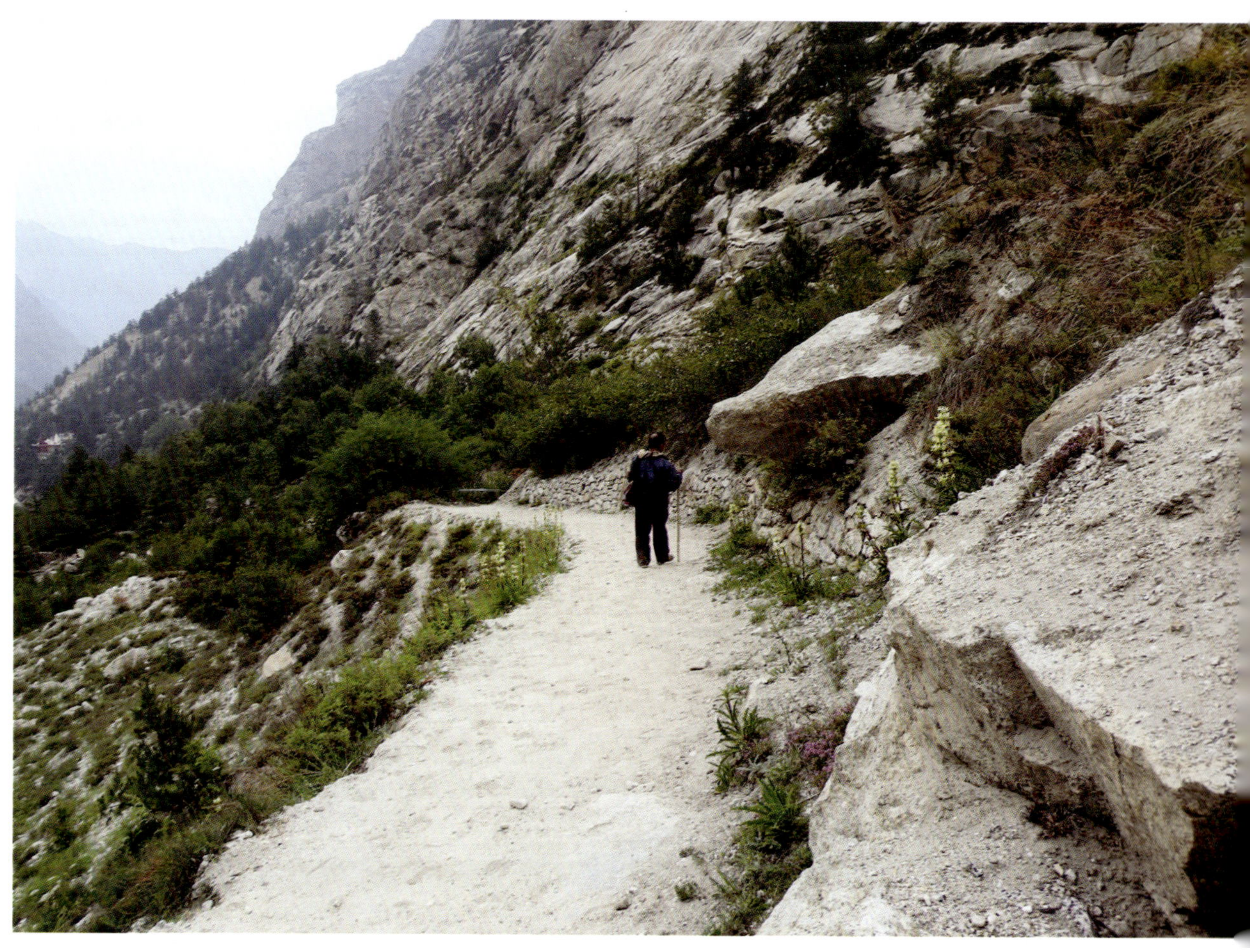

A pilgrim on the way to Gaumukh

was the figurehead of Bhagirath. I worshipped them all. When I told the attending priest about my journey to Gaumukh he blessed me by touching my forehead with a holy flower. A dilapidated staircase rose at the side of the temple leading to a few small rooms. Beside these rooms lay our pathway to Gaumukh. As we mounted the stairs we caught sight of a huge billboard – Gangotri National Park. A few rules written below were expected to be followed while visiting the park. Both Dilip and I were carrying two walking sticks, while Dilip graciously carried my travelling bag. As I glanced downward at the Gangotri valley I found the Ganga tracing her course through pebble-laden terrains. Temples, houses, inns, *deodar* forests and the telephone tower were all visible from there. I took out a map and tried to ascertain the height we had mounted – we were 10,400 feet above the sea level. Huge trees welcomed us as we walked on. 'Don't cars ply down this road?' I asked Dilip.

'No, cars are prohibited by the forest department,' informed Dilip. 'Previously the entire area was a dense forest, inhabited by varied animals. But fifty per cent of the trees have been felled by the local people. And if cars keep plying, these leftover trees too will disappear soon. Furthermore, this road too is not a permanent one. It is in use only for four months a year. No traveller travels down the road for the rest of the eight months.'

We walked on slowly with Ganga flowing on one side of our path. After an hour's walk we saw a range of snow-clad mountain peaks. Dilip told me their names. On our left stood the Marti peak, while in the middle stood the Sudarshan peak; on our right was Theloo. A small turning brought us to a check post where we submitted our permits, procured the previous day, to enter the Gangotri National Park.

On the slopy banks of the Ganga we came across Amritghat Ashram, the hermitage of Sage Gangadas baba. Here, Gangadas baba had spent fifty years of his life, meditating and worshipping the Ganga. On 20 May 2000, he went for his usual ablution to the river and completed his worship. Returning to the hermitage he finished his daily chores and then calmly informed his disciple that it was time for him to depart. They were not to touch his body till everything was over. So saying he quietly sat on the floor of the hermitage and leaned against a stone wall to leave his mortal frame. That was the end of the sage.

We kept walking down the curved path viewing the milestones. After three hours we realised we had walked only six kilometres. We came across a fast-flowing waterfall which ran its course down towards the Ganga. Since the waterfall was pretty wide a tree trunk was laid over it for people to cross. But despite the tree trunk, the journey was pretty scary. I knew if I missed a step I would slide straight down a few hundred metres. Hence, treading on it carefully, I somehow managed to cross over. We had already walked quite a bit and were very tired. A short rest was essential.

We resumed walking and gradually the vast greenery that was accompanying us so far started thinning out. A few visitors rode past us on horses and I couldn't help looking at them enviously. The terrain now turned rough and stony. The little mud that clung to the stones proved extremely slippery. Hence, I walked slowly and carefully with Dilip in front. I looked at him and wondered at his patience. For so many years he has been walking up and down this pathway escorting numerous travellers, as if it was his personal domain. And even the surroundings appeared to greet him as an extended family member. I was really

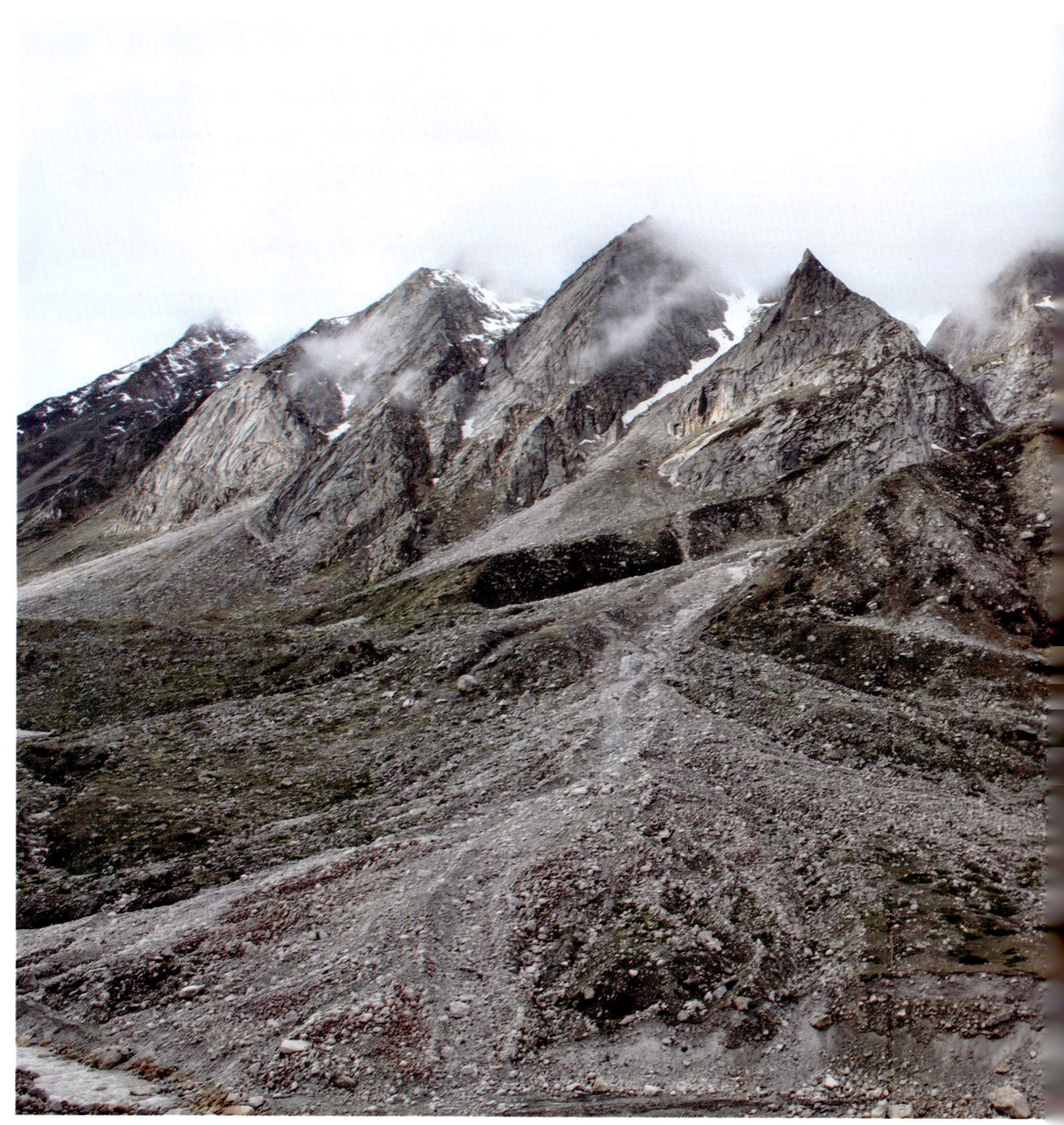

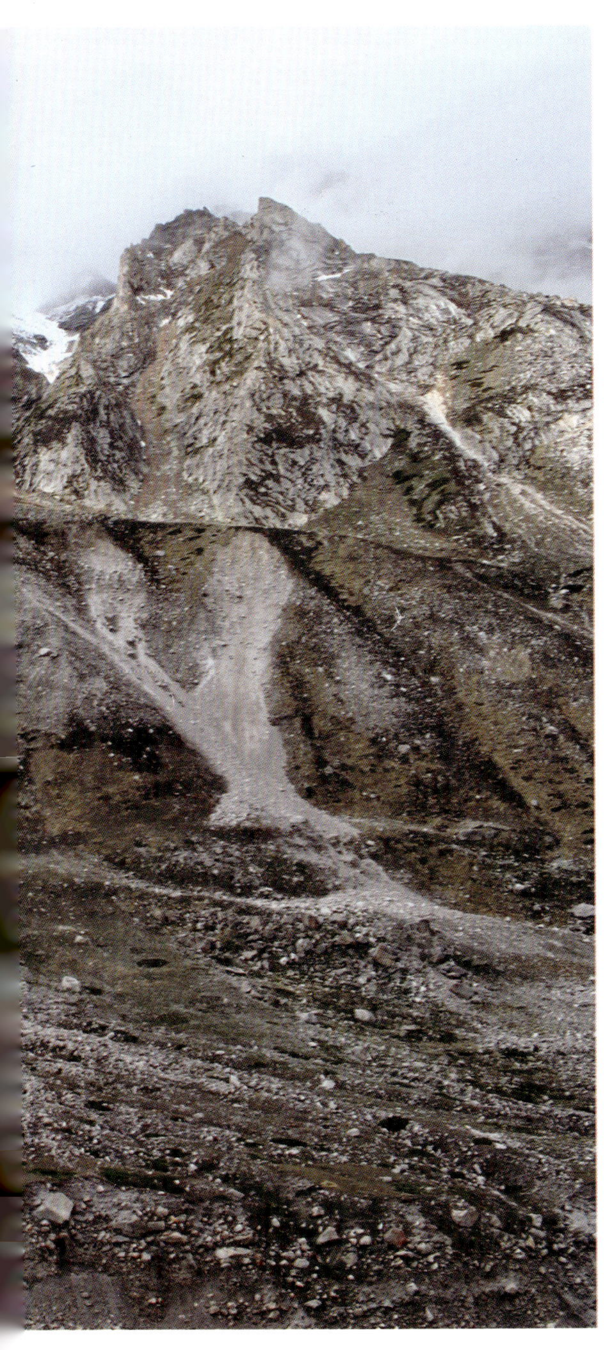

impressed. At times he would break into '*Om Jaya Ganga Mata*' and then walk on. Such unconditional love and faith in the divinity of the Ganga was simply unthinkable. It was as if the Ganga like his mother would help him tide over all adversities.

We came across another turning point and noticed a milestone declaring Chiravas 11,810 feet above sea level. Gangotri was nine kilometres away, while Bhoojvas was five kilometres from there. I asked Dilip the secret behind the name Chiravas. He told me there used to be *chira* forests here. In fact, this was the end point for those trees. Further up *chira* trees cannot thrive; hence the name Chiravas.

Gradually the topography started changing. Till now we had lush green forest trees accompanying us, but from now on nature turned hard, dry and stony. Yet, it was so beautiful. A unique silence prevailed everywhere with only dynamic Ganga making her way merrily down the mountain terrain. The thin riverbank, however, sustained a few green bushes here and there. We came across a large tree which Dilip pointed out saying, 'Babuji, this is a *bhooj* tree. In ancient times people used to make clothes with its bark. They also used it for writing manuscripts,' he added. 'Previously

The narrow and perilous road to Gaumukh

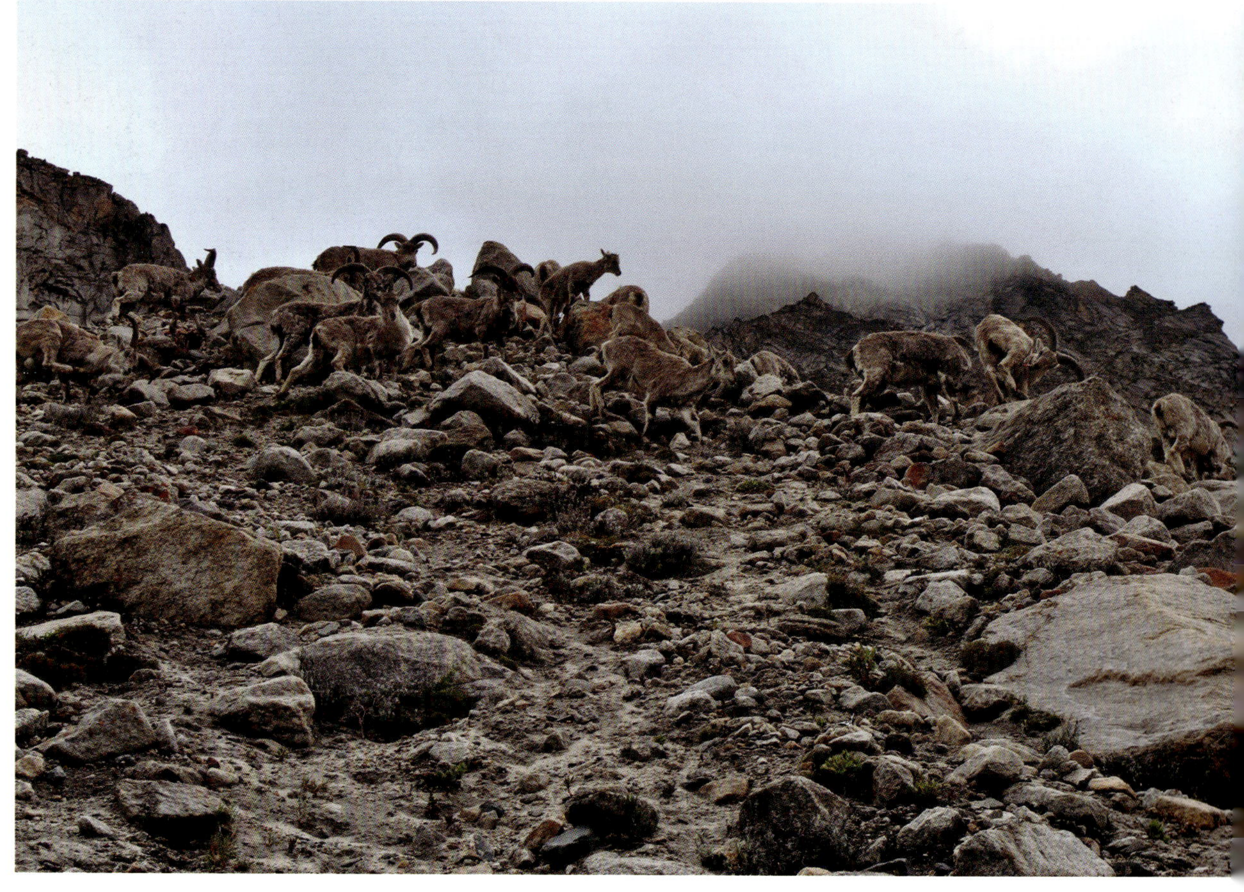

A herd of ibexes. The Himalayan ibex is a symbol of the arid and rocky topography it inhabits

there was a forest of *bhooj* trees here, but people have felled most of the trees. Only a few are left now.'

'Maybe next time when I come,' I said sadly, 'these trees will also disappear. This is how man is destroying nature.' Bhoojvas was just two kilometres from this point, yet my body refused to move further. Glancing at the snow-clad peaks around I felt like staying up there. Dilip, however, tried to encourage me saying, 'Not a long distance, Babuji. Soon we will reach the hermitage of Lalbaba and will be served hot tea and steaming food. You will feel better for sure.'

It was only three pm yet darkness had already started descending down the mountain slopes. It was necessary to hasten our speed. Yet, the little distance that was left to cover proved too much for me. After an immense effort I exerted myself and managed to reach the hermitage. A middle-aged gentleman dressed in ochre robes stood waiting for us. He looked at Dilip and greeted him with a broad smile, 'Welcome,

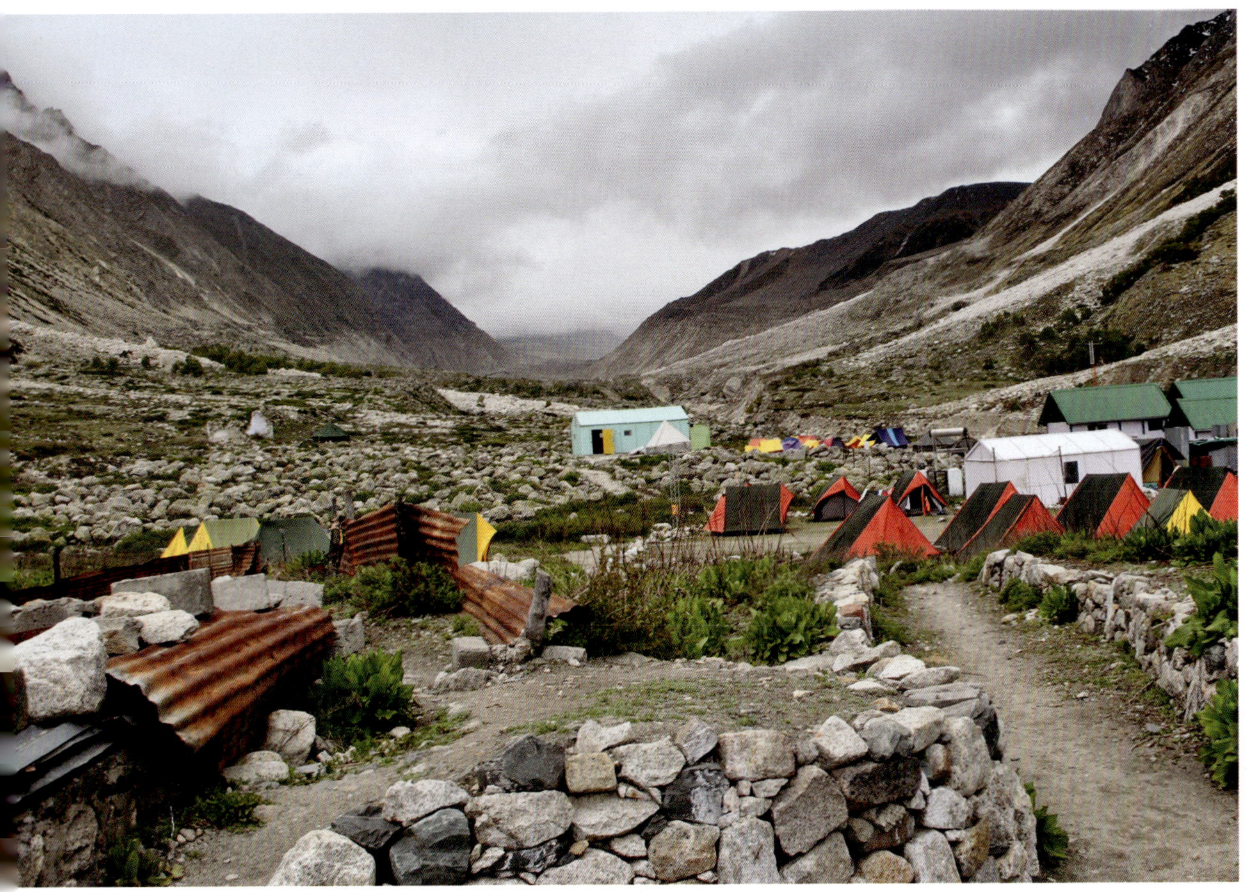

Bhojbasa (3,792 metres) acts as the last point of accommodation for trekkers on their way to Gaumukh

Dilip. I saw you coming from afar. How's everything at home?' Dilip replied, 'Yes, Maharaj, everyone is fine,' while walking into the hermitage. The gentleman then glanced at me and said, 'Please come in. Dilip, take him to that corner room. We do not have any visitors today.'

Crossing an almost dark alley we reached the room. The entire room seemed to be an elaborate bedroom with a sprawling bedstead occupying most of the room. 'You rest here for a while. I will be back soon,' said Dilip. Utterly exhausted, I sunk down into the large bedspread and could not help closing my eyes. After a while someone came up to me with a cup of steaming tea and called aloud, 'Do get up and have your tea. You will feel better.' I opened my eyes and found the ochre-robed gentleman standing with an aluminium mug full of tea. It tasted bitter, but after a sip or two I felt refreshed. Immediately afterwards another person walked in with a plate full of piping hot hotchpotch.

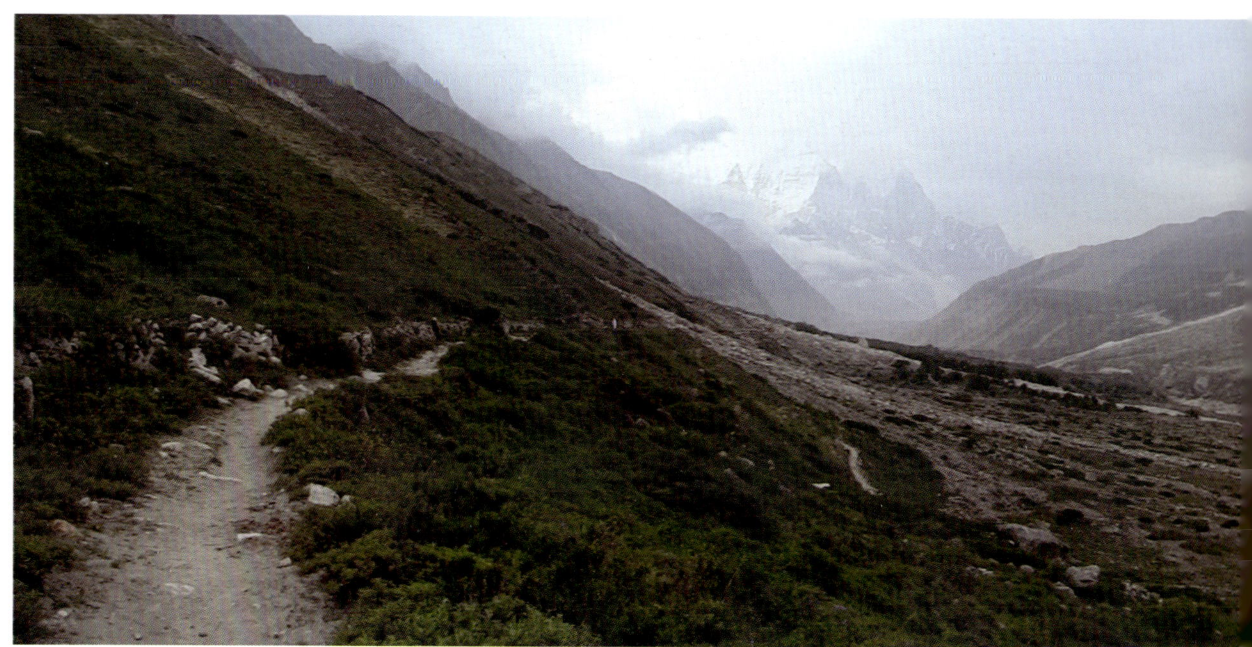

ABOVE: A panoramic view of Bhojbasa – this scenic undulating valley is at a trekking distance of 14 kilometres from Gangotri

FACING PAGE: Gaumukh, birthplace of the Ganga

As the night advanced, the temperature kept dipping. I could not help slipping into the blankets immediately after a plateful of hotchpotch.

'Good morning.' The ochre-robed gentleman's greeting woke me up next morning. 'Hope you have a very good day too,' he added.

We left the hermitage after breakfast. It was a bit misty around us and visibility was poor. We took the southern-most road from the hermitage to reach the southern side of Gaumukh. Since the Ganga by then had turned southwards from Gangotri, we too had to take the south-facing path to get a glimpse of her. As per records, several glaciers have slipped down from different peaks of the Himalayas to form the second-largest glacier of India – the Gangotri glacier. And the Gangotri glacier melted to create the Ganga.

I asked Dilip whether we would be able to step down to the Gangotri glacier. He shook his head and said, 'The entire glacier is covered by layers of sand and stones. You can hardly see anything from above. But you will notice several cracks here and there, which are very deep. It is very risky to step into those cracks. The undercurrent of the submerged Ganga will pull you down and carry you away to the land of the unknown,' he warned. 'But till Gaumukh the path is not as perilous as the one after that.'

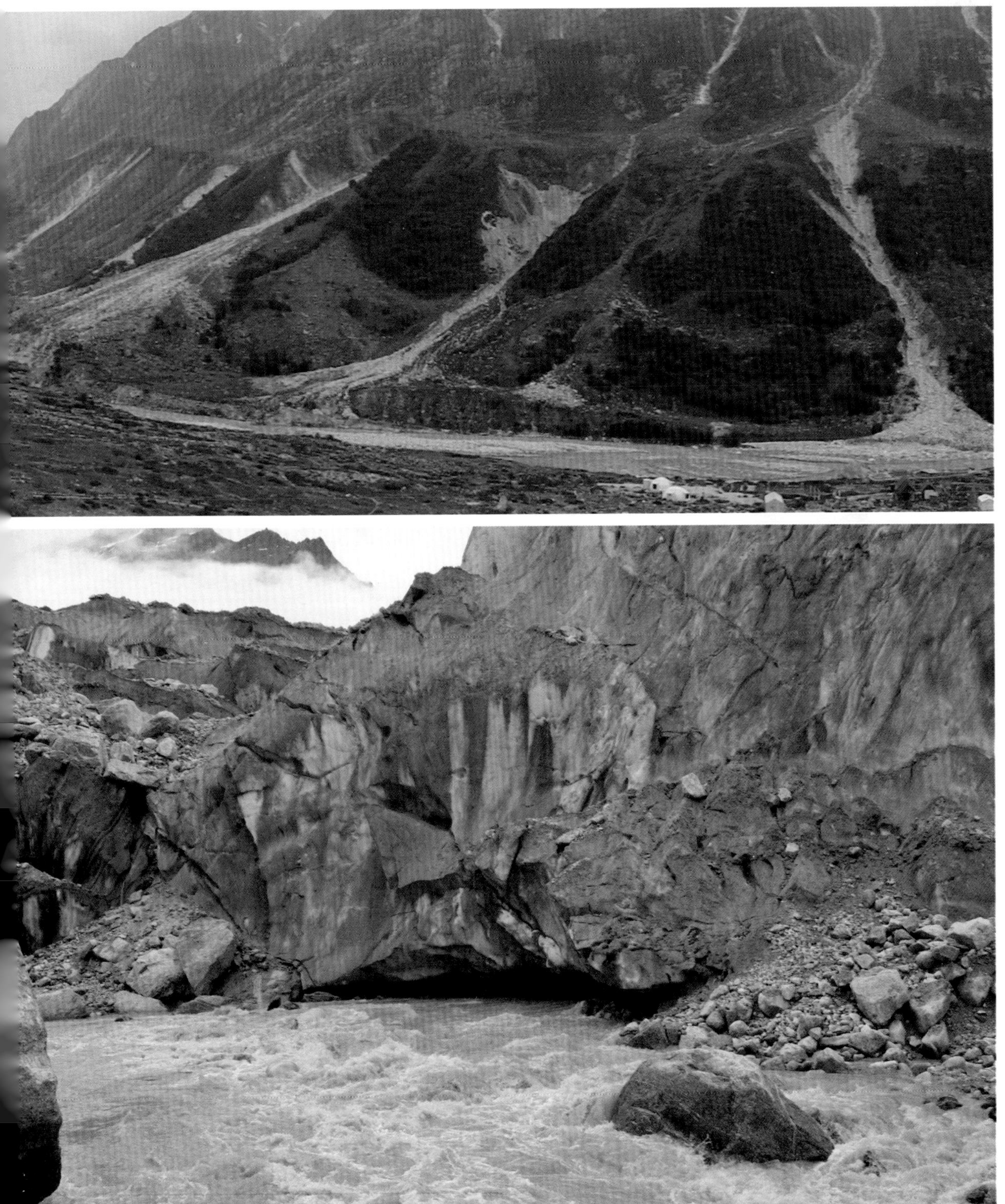

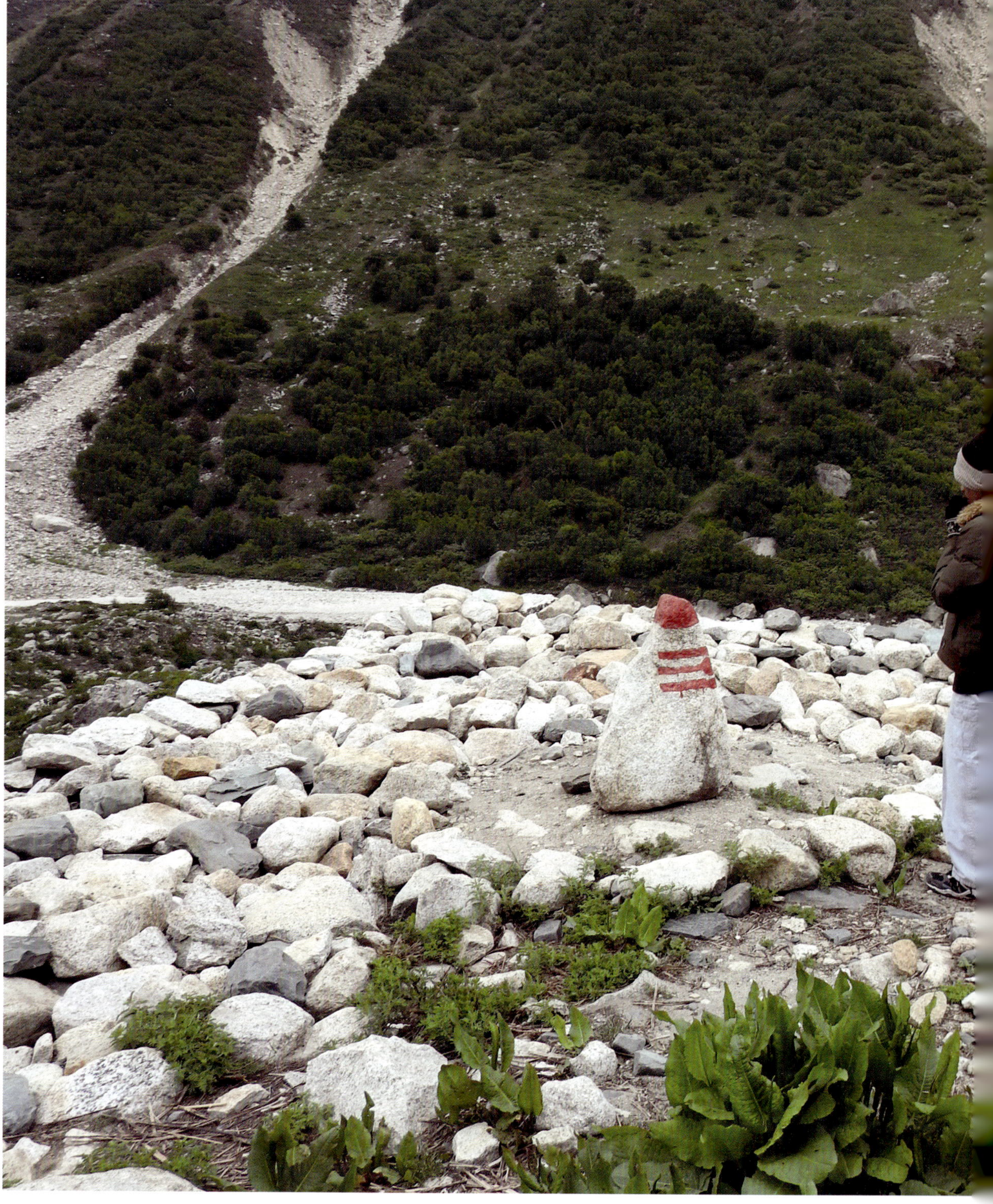

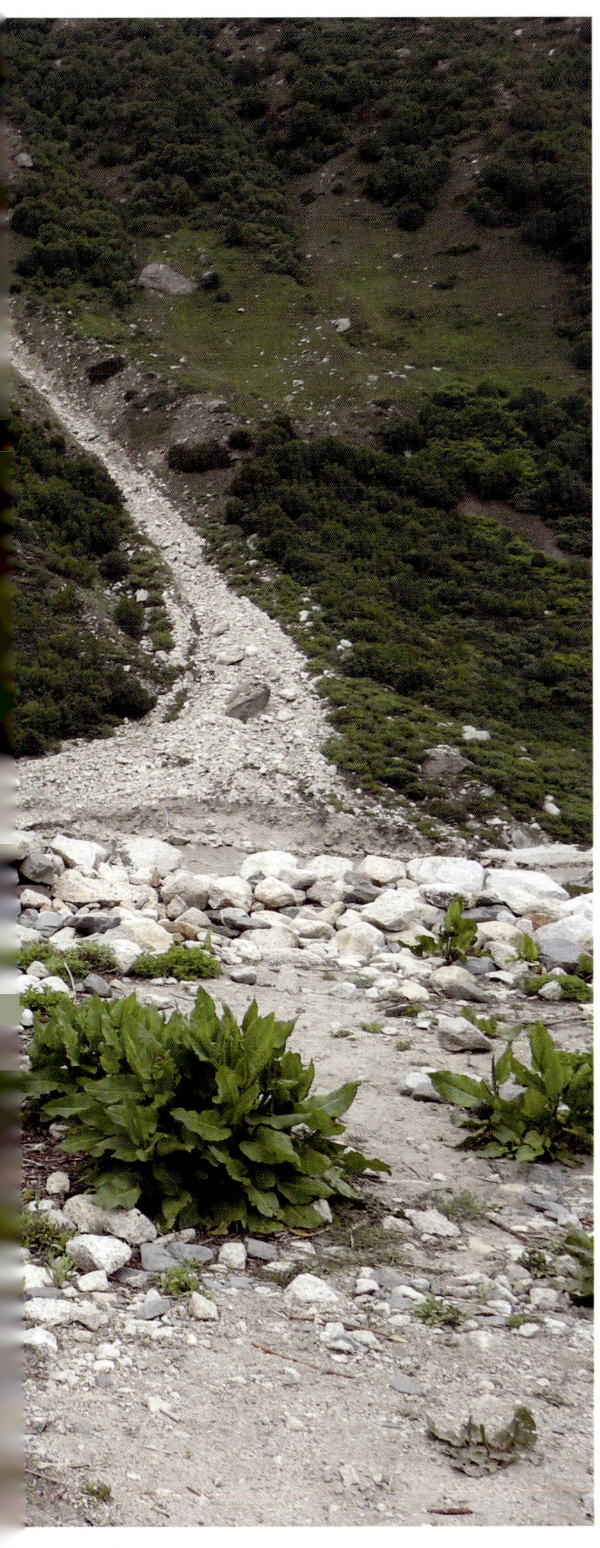

Suddenly Dilip called out, 'Look there stands the Shivling peak.' The ethereal sight transfixed me. There stood the peak in full glory, all radiant and majestically reflecting the rays of the morning sun. According to the *Purana*s this peak is supposed to be the abode of Lord Shiva. And significantly the peak does resemble the crest of a temple. I could well visualise the figurehead of Lord Shiva meditating there on the topmost point of the mountain. We kept walking mesmerised. There was, however, no well-defined path laid out for us. Some small puddles created by the waterfalls coupled with ditches here and there, were all we had before us. 'Be careful,' Dilip kept warning, 'follow me.' It was an utterly barren and stony terrain and we practically had to jump our way forward. I was getting increasingly tired and badly wanted to rest, when I saw three young men walking our way. They met us and by way of cheering us hailed, '*Om Jaya Ganga Mata*.' I asked, 'How far is it?' Dilip raised his hand and pointed ahead, 'Just a few steps, we have almost reached.' The very thought that we had done it invigorated me, and I resumed walking. After a few minutes I could see from a distance the opening of the Gaumukh cave. The Ganga was gushing out with great force. '*Om Jaya Ganga Mata*,' cheered Dilip lifting his

Paying obeisance to the Shiva Lingam near Bhojbasa

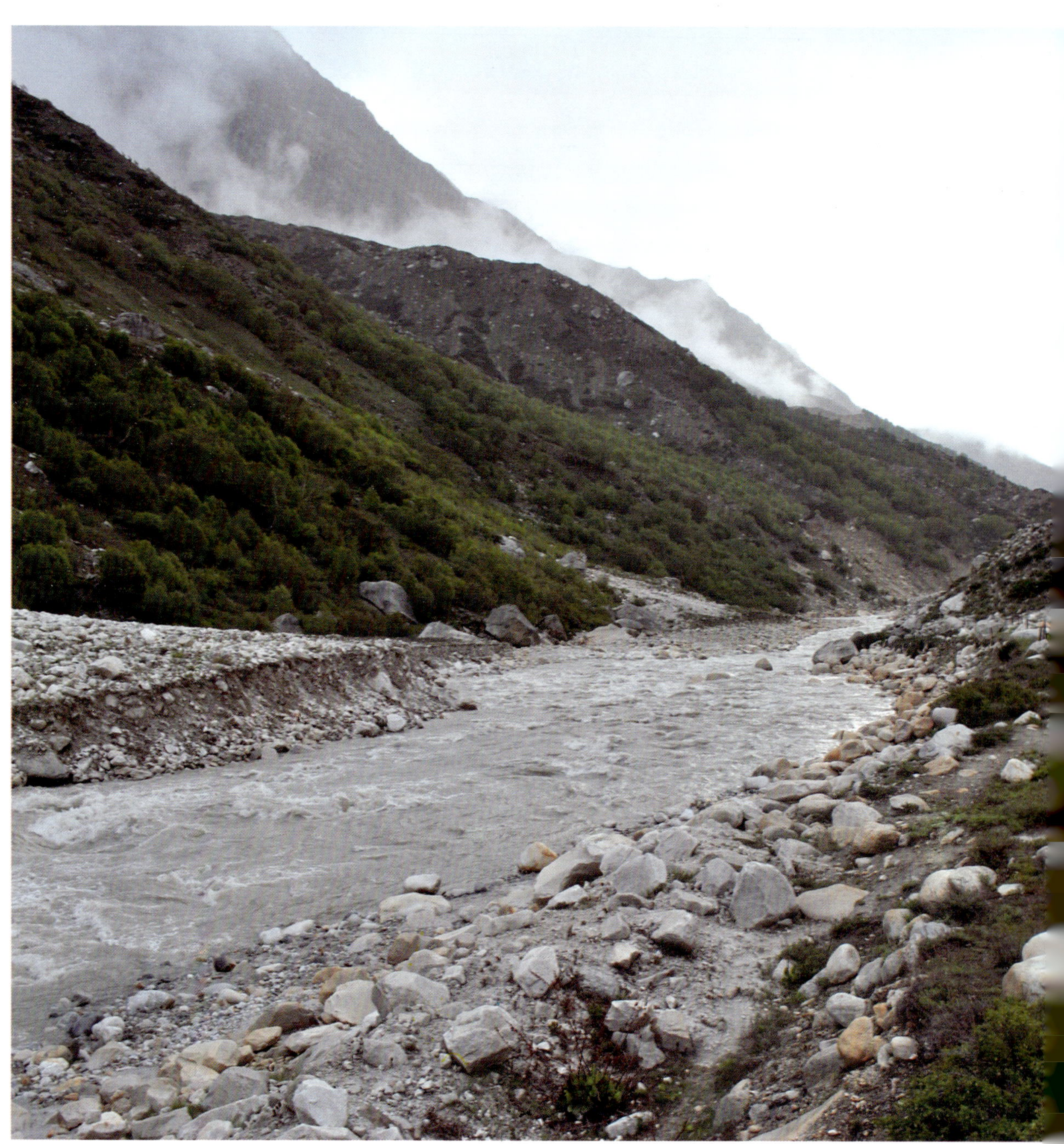

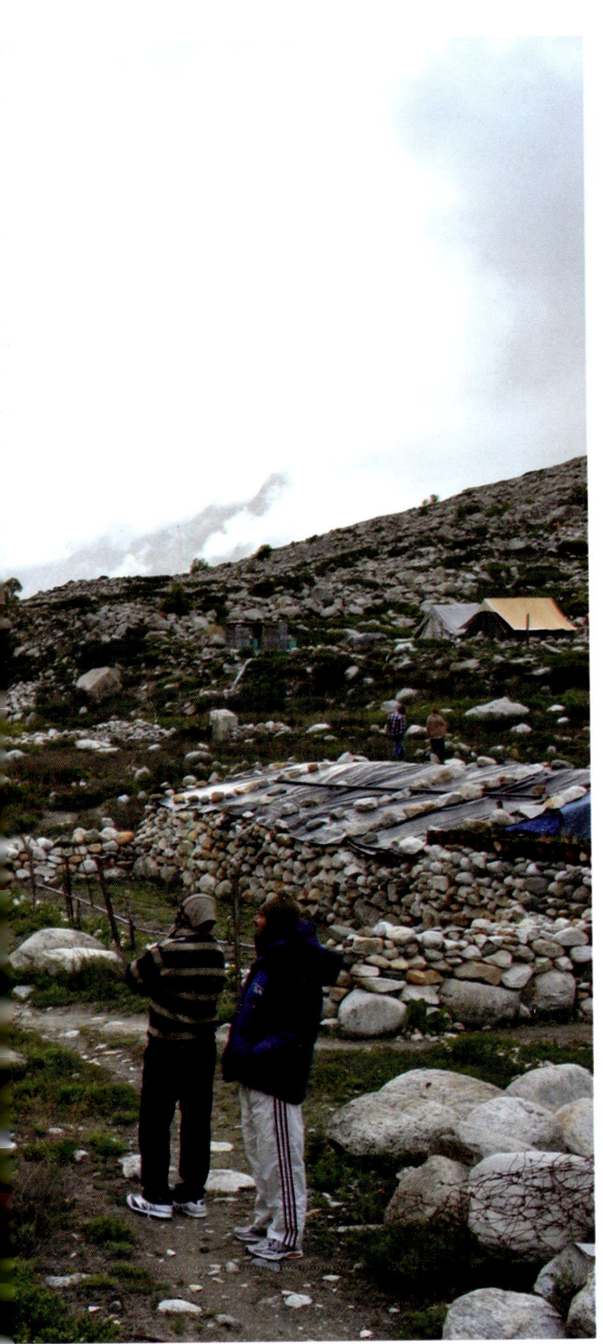

arms heavenward. Fatigue and exhaustion seemed to have vanished and I nearly ran towards my goal. Jumping across a large piece of rock I stood at a distance of some fifty or sixty feet from the cave. It had a greenish hue and water was emerging from its opening at a tremendous speed. The upper wall of the cave was almost twenty-five feet high. The entire scene appeared to me like a child emerging from her mother's womb – the cave being the womb and Gangotri glacier being the mother. For some mysterious reason the cave has been named Gaumukh – the mouth of a cow. There is hardly any similarity between the two. Or maybe thousands of years ago the opening of the cave did resemble the mouth of a cow – who knows. Human voices shook me out of my stupor and I found those young men bathing in the ice-cold water of the Ganga. A sannyasi sat at a distance chanting Shankaracharya's *Gangastotram*:

Devi Sureswari bhagawati Gange
Tribhuvana tarani tarala tarange
Sankara mouli nivasini vimalay
Mama Matirastang tava padakamalay

(O Goddess Ganga! You are the divine river from heaven, you are the saviour of all the three worlds, you are pure and restless, and

The Ganga near Gaumukh, the place where the river emerges from the snout of the Gangotri glacier you adorn Lord Shiva's head. O Mother! May my mind always rest at your lotus feet.)

The amazing sight captivated and enchanted me.

GANGOTRI

Gangotri is one of the four pilgrimages of the Himalayas. The name Gangotri itself is very suggestive. Here the river Ganga changed her course towards the north. So it got the name Gangotri (*Ganga Uttari*).

According to the *Purana*s, King Bhagirath had walked all the way to Gangotri from his kingdom Ayodhya and had meditated for a thousand years to liberate his ancestors from the curse of the sage. In the process he had brought benediction to mankind by bringing down Ganga from heaven.

The first temple dedicated to Ganga is located here; surrounded by sky-scraping mountain peaks and *deodar* trees. The natural beauty of the place is unparalleled. In the middle flows the fast-paced Ganga. A marble temple stands on her bank. Previously there was no temple here for people to worship. So men worshipped a stone that lay here. It is said that King Bhagirath sat on that very stone and sanctified it by meditating for a thousand years. In fact, it is the local priests of the temple who claim that King Bhagirath

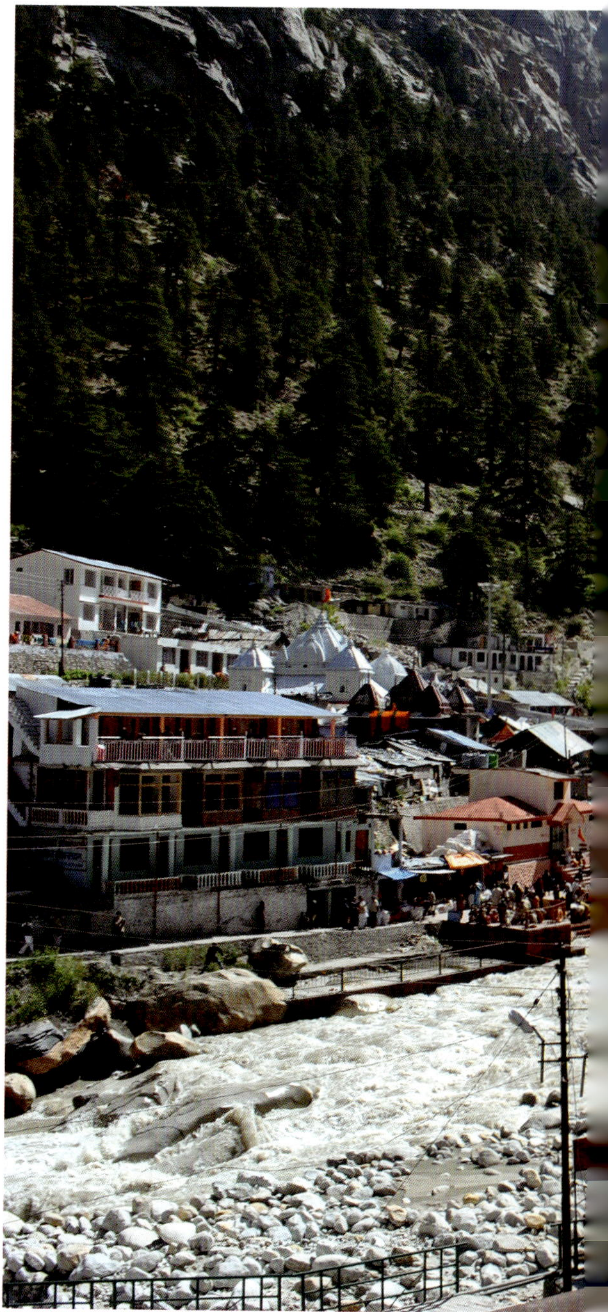

The Ganga flowing through the village of Gangotri

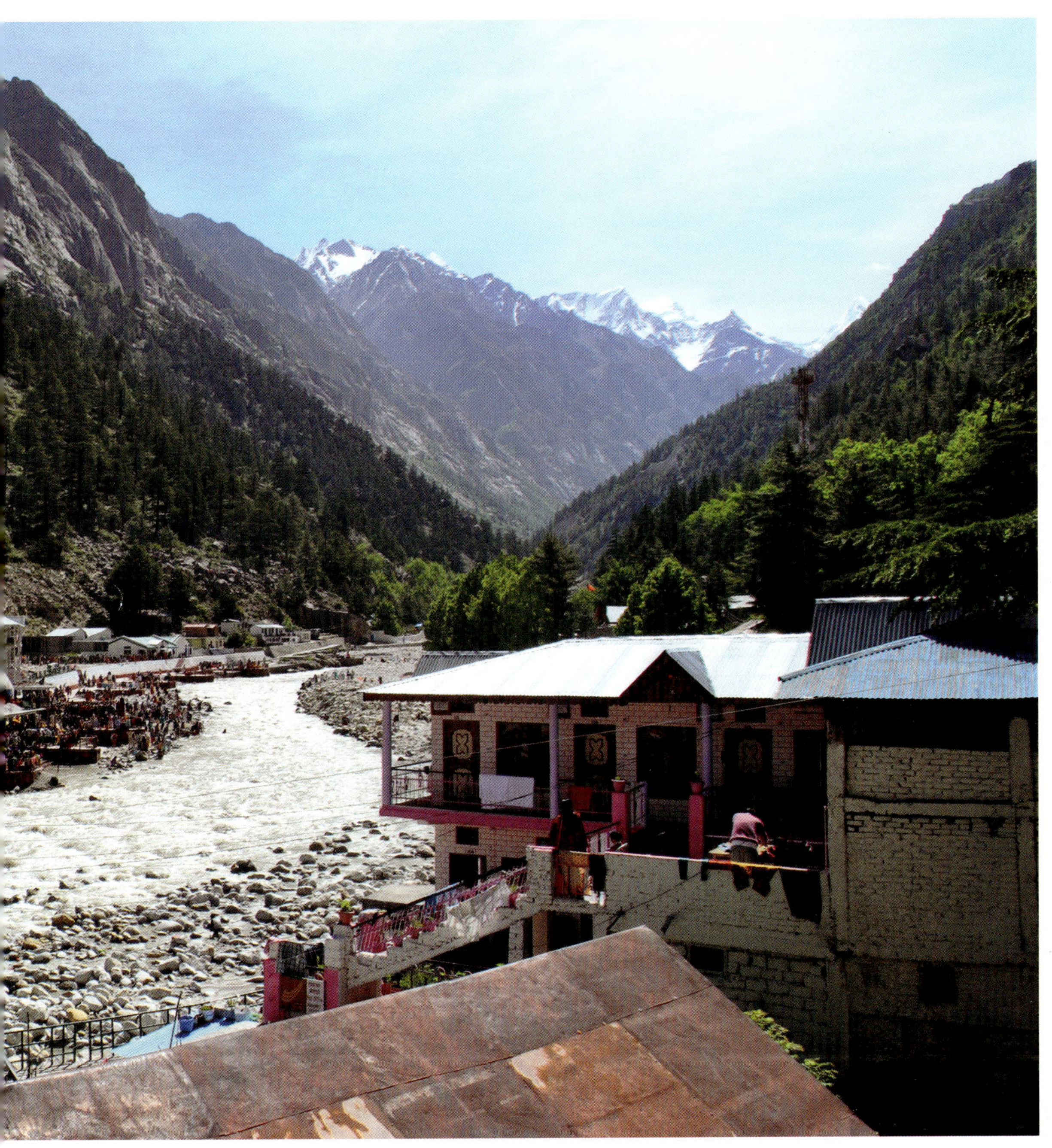

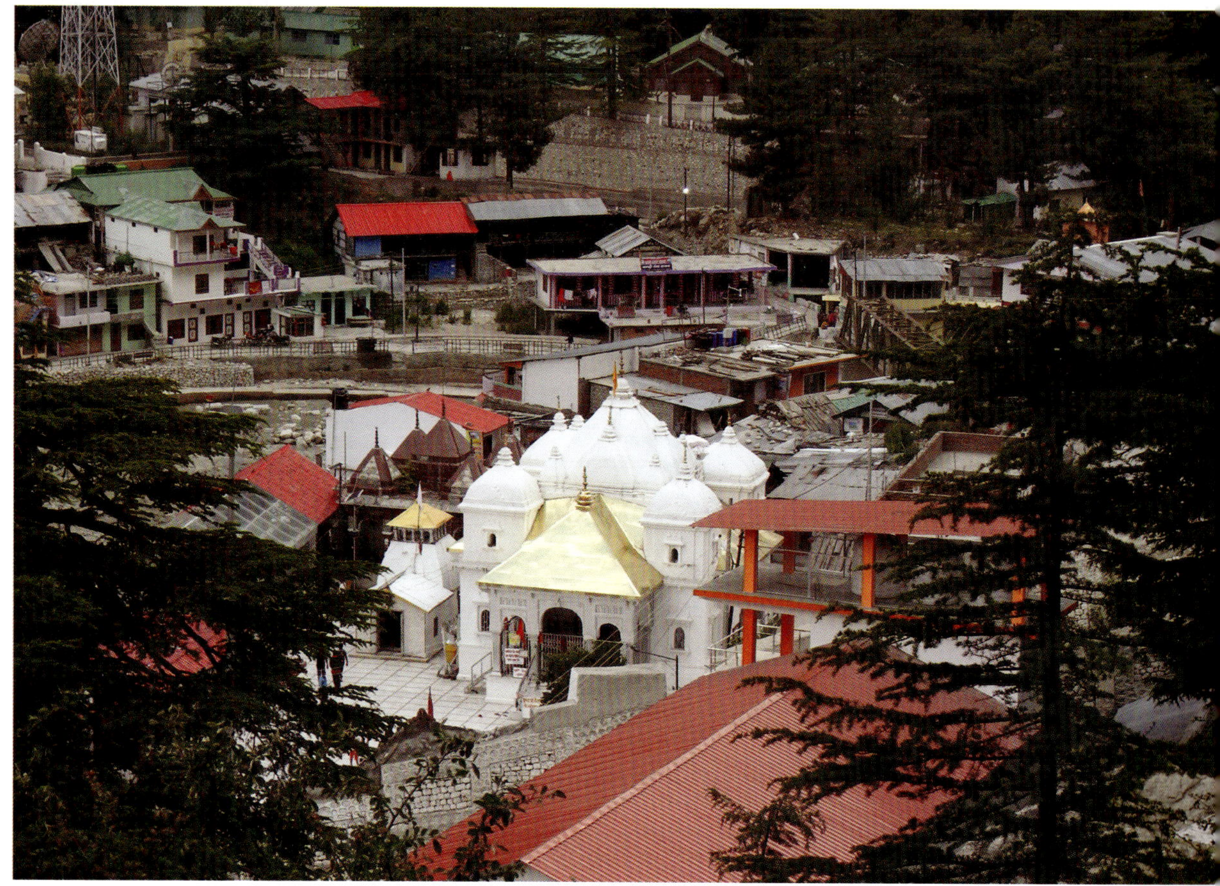

The village of Gangotri and the Ganga temple surrounded by Himalayan *deodar* trees

sat on the stone to conclude his penance and meditation; there is no historical record of these happenings.

Gangotri temple stands at the foot of Bhairav-jhap mountain. In ancient times the place was ruled by the kings of the Tehri dynasty. In the north was the town Boo, presently part of Himachal Pradesh. The southern part of the region was connected to Tibet. There is, however, no historical evidence of any temple existing here prior to the end of the eighteenth century. The first temple that was constructed here was by Daulatrao Sindhia, the king of Gwalior. In 1803 an earthquake decimated it. Even the priests abandoned the site. Then in 1813, a Gorkha captain, Amar Singh Thapa, set up a small structure for worship and brought back the absconding priests. He also brought back the stone which was worshipped in the past. But even that structure got destroyed. The present temple was constructed by the king of Jaipur. The five domes of the temple indicate the influence of Muslim

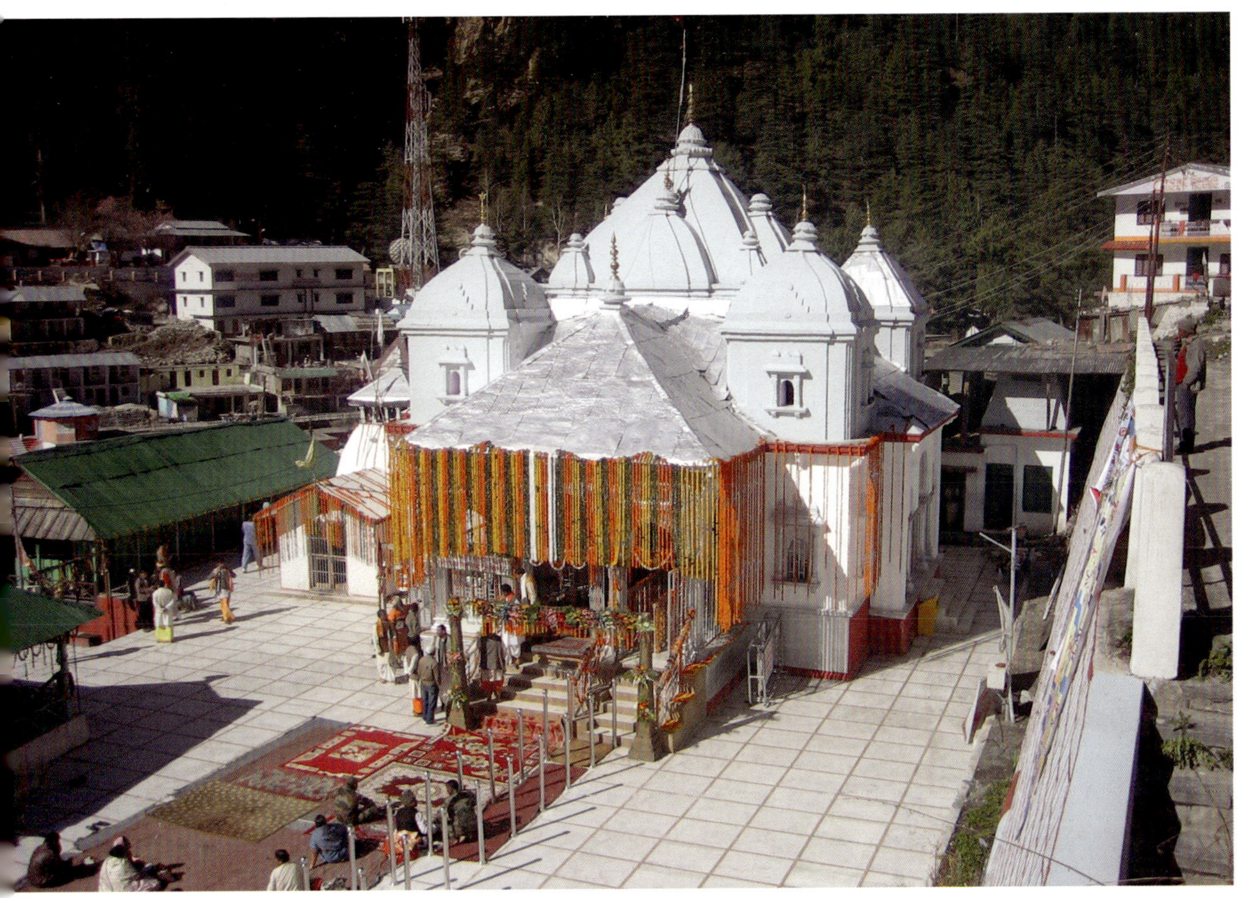

Gangotri temple decorated with flowers on the auspicious day of Akshaya Tritiya (mid summer). On that day the temple opens after staying closed all winter

architecture. In the inner sanctum sanctorum stands the idol of river Ganga. On her right stands the idol of river Yamuna. On her left stands river Sarasvati. In front is the image of Bhagirath. The temple is closed for six months every year because the entire terrain is then covered with thick layers of snow. Then on Akshaya Tritiya, that is midsummer, the door of the temple is opened for public viewing. Priests and pilgrims start flocking here from Akshaya Tritiya itself.

From a Pilgrim's Diary

By evening our bus journey ended at Gangotri. The place was filled with chants of '*Om Jaya Ganga Mata*'. While alighting I unconsciously echoed '*Om Jaya Ganga Mata*'. I found a narrow path in front of me. On two sides of it stood several shops crammed with buyers. A few steps from there I found a sloping lane leading to the river. A hanging bridge stood at a distance. After walking a few steps I stopped short as I espied a few

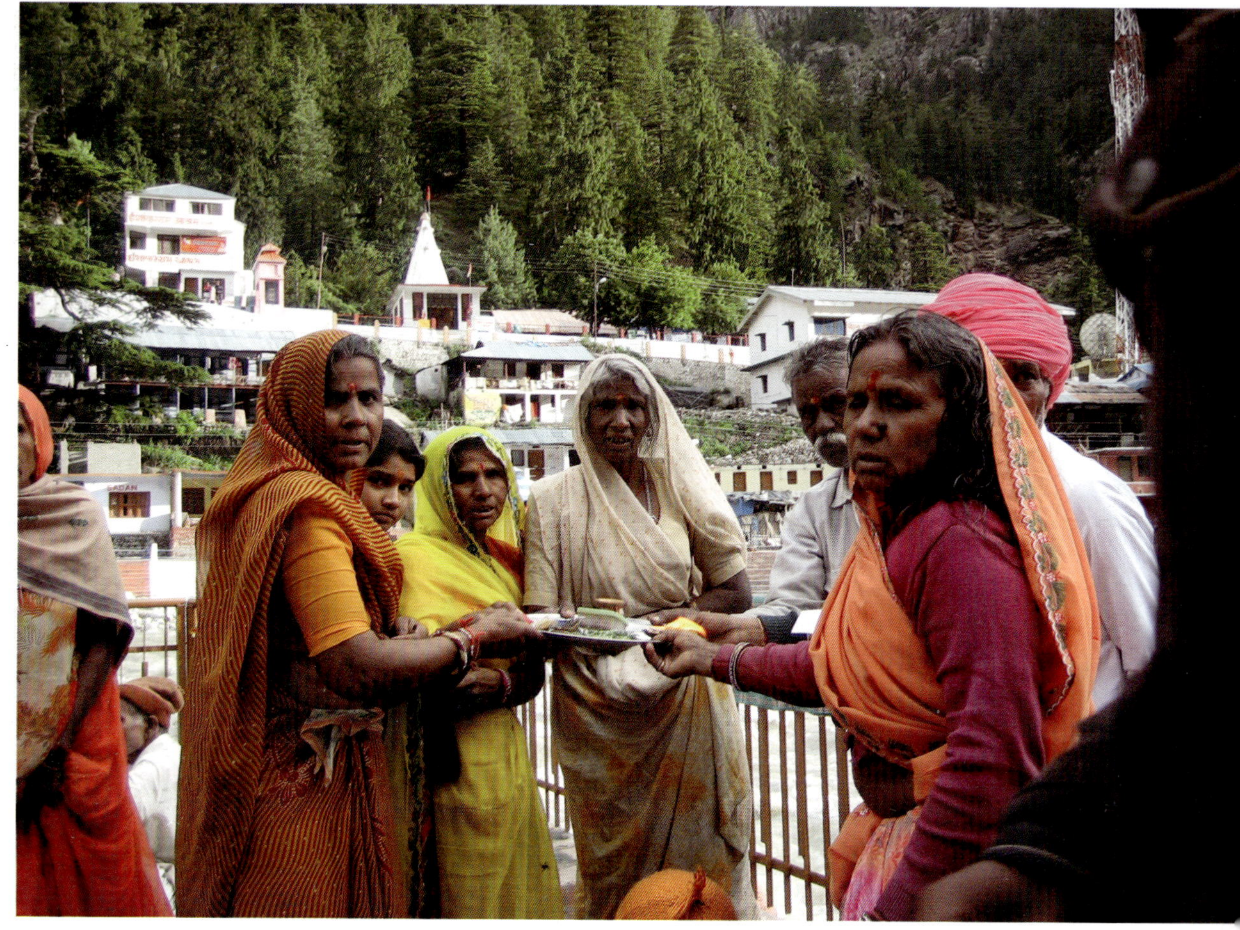

Pilgrims from Bihar at Gangotri

large stone boulders down which flowed the roaring Ganga, with several mountain peaks guarding her zealously on two sides. The temple stood on her expanded bank. Ignoring the ice-cold water men were bathing in the river. There were hotels and hermitages on the slopes of the mountains. *Deodar* forests were visible on the highest point of these mountains. Several unnamed snow-clad mountain peaks stood before us. Later on, however, I came to know the name of this mountain range – Sudarshan. The sight of the radiant rays of the setting sun shining upon these mountain peaks was fascinating.

I crossed the bridge and walked forward and found the Kedar Ganga. There was another bridge there. Crossing it I found a narrow path which led me to a government guest house. The path continued further down leading me to several hermitages. An old hermit was walking down the path while

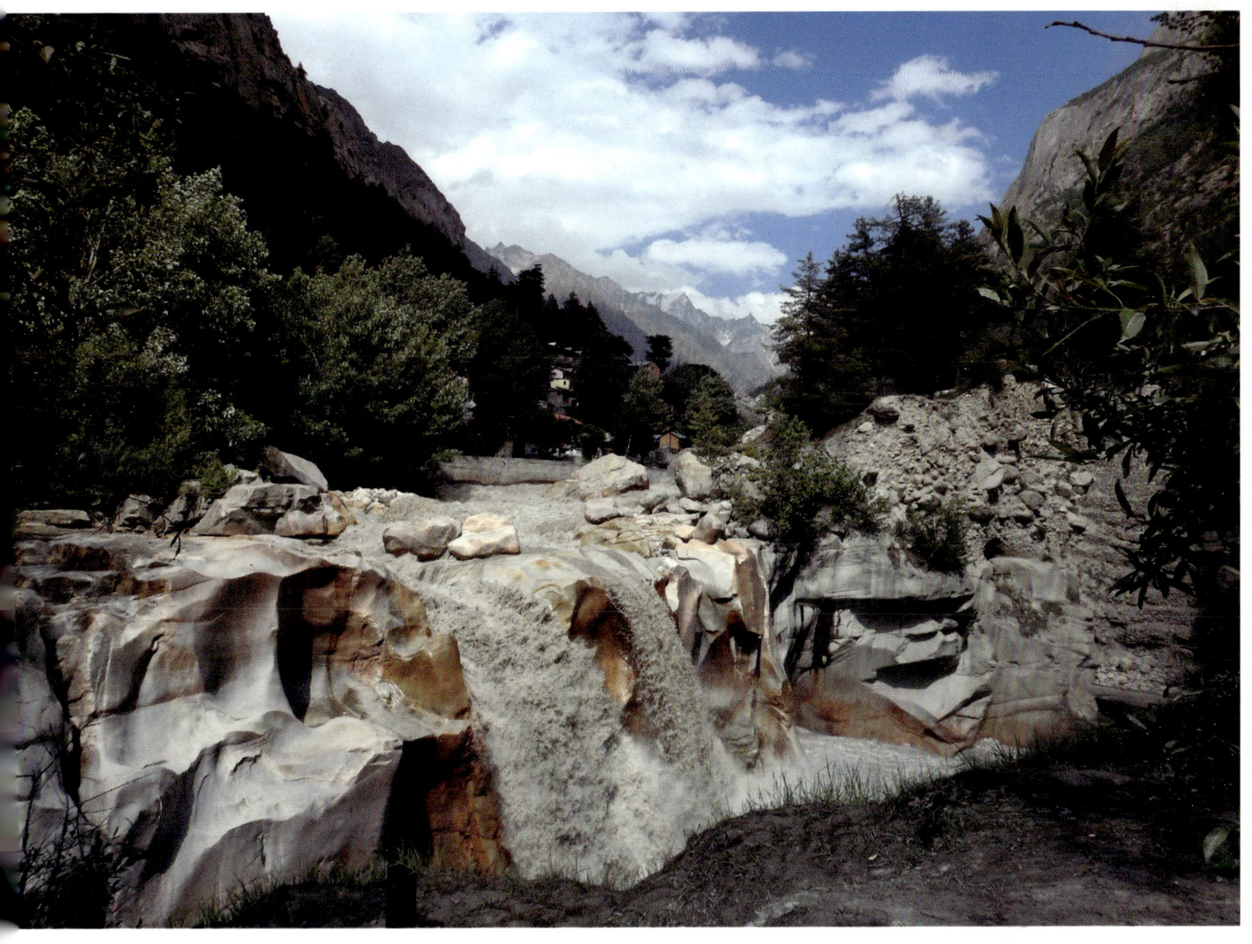

The waterfall at the confluence of the Ganga and Kedar Ganga is named Suryakund. Here radiant rays of the sun have created multiple rainbows

I was loitering. He glanced at me and greeted me with '*Hari Om*'. The voice was tinged with divine tranquility.

I crossed a turning point which came my way, and suddenly stopped short. The sight I beheld was simply breathtaking; the confluence of Kedar Ganga and Ganga and their combined majestic flow over a large stony boulder. The resulting waves, immense in size, acted as a natural spring, sprinkling water droplets on all sides. Added to it, the radiant rays of the setting sun created multiple rainbows. Legend has it that Lord Shiva installed himself here to restrict the onslaught of the roaring Ganga. The river thus fell upon his head and this checked her massive flow. In fact, the constant surging of the water over the stones at the confluence have resulted in crisscross patterns resembling the matted

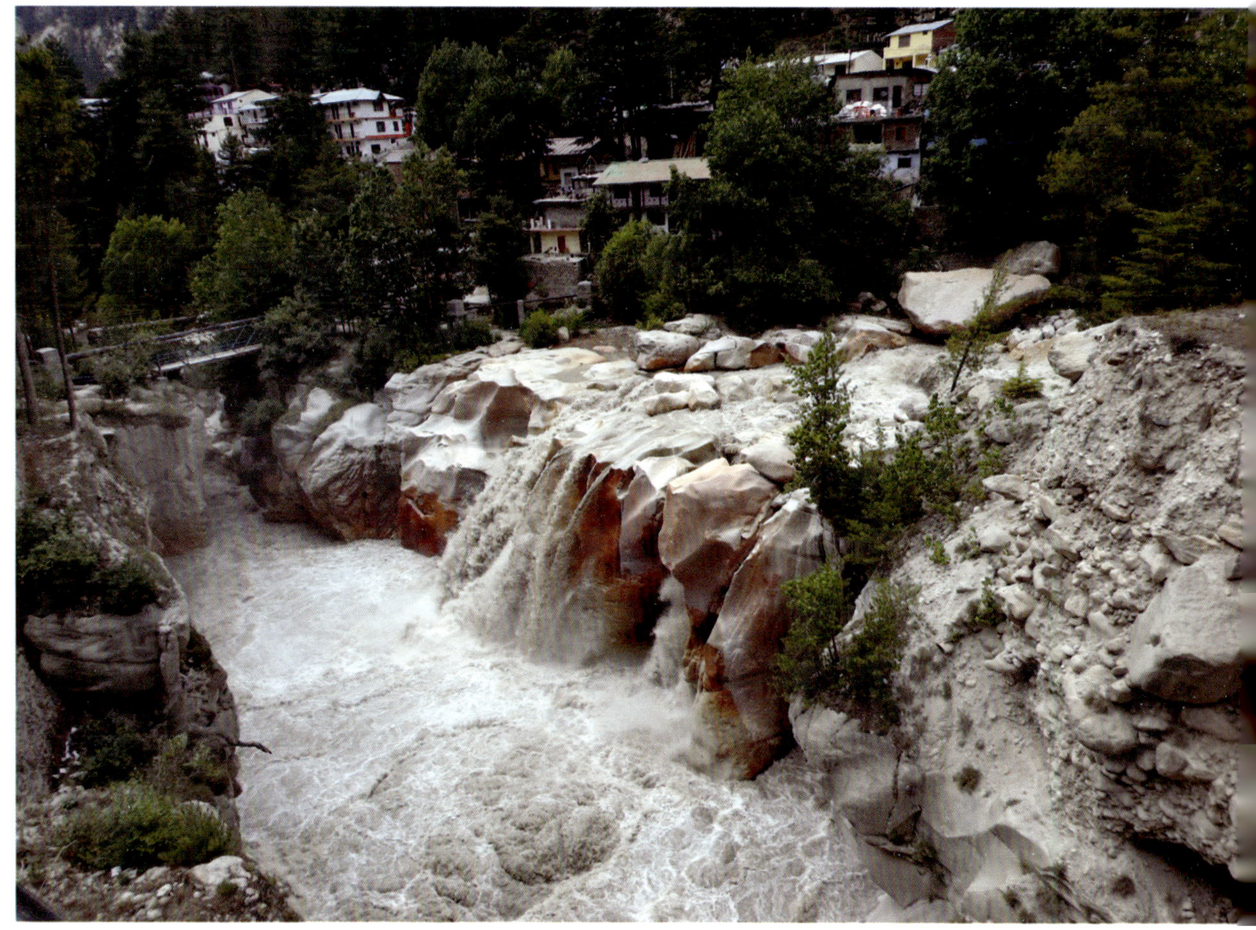

The rush of the river gushing through a gorge is like a presence – ceaseless and immeasurable

hair of Lord Shiva. Instantly a question plaguing me since my childhood arose in my mind. 'Oh River, from where have you come?' Maybe there was a scientist of yore who was also troubled by a similar question. And the answer that he got was – 'from the matted hair of Lord Shiva' – who knows.

A priest had mentioned 'Bangali baba' to me while travelling back from Gaumukh. 'He is a different kind of soul,' I was told, 'who is devoid of all material cravings. He prefers living alone, avoiding human company. Yet, when people visit him he showers them with blessings. And strangely enough, ignoring the terrible cold, he resides here throughout the year.' I walked up to the hermitage that I had been directed to and found a young priest sitting on the courtyard of the hermitage. On enquiry he said that Bangali baba lives just behind the hermitage. Crossing a broad courtyard and bypassing a wooden temple, the young gentleman led me

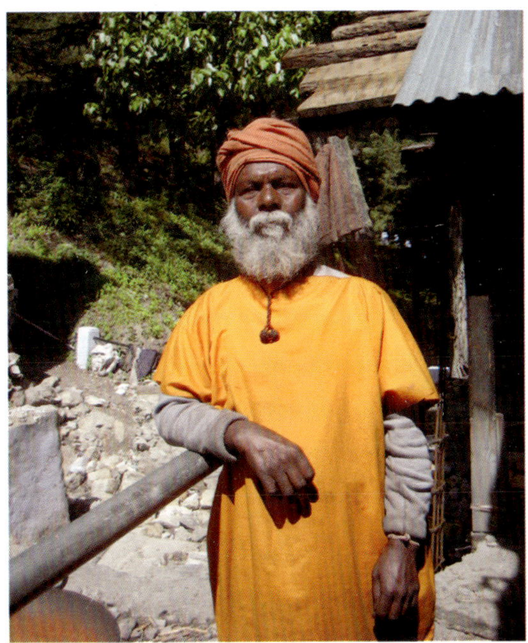

A hermit known as 'Bangali baba' has been living at Gangotri for the last thirty years

to his room. It was a humble structure of wood with a tin ceiling. A large quantity of dry wood was stacked at one corner of the courtyard. The surroundings looked very worn out. The small wooden door of the room opened as Bangali baba walked out. There was really nothing remarkable about him. He looked a commoner to me. The priest introduced me to him and he greeted me softly, 'May you be blessed.'

We silently looked at each other for a while. The modest surroundings of the room seemed ideal for a man like him. Slowly I struck up a conversation. 'How long have you been here?' I asked. 'When I left home I was twenty years old. For the next thirty years I travelled and then came and settled here. It's almost thirty years from now,' he answered. 'In which part of Bengal did you reside before coming here?' I asked. He mumbled his reluctance, clearly not willing to talk about his past. 'What is it like here in winter, Baba?' I continued. 'It's pristine white everywhere, my child. At times during heavy snowfall even river Ganga is covered with snow.'

Suddenly I recalled a photograph of Gangotri I had seen in Haridwar – the Ganga covered with snow. 'How do you survive here in this modest building during winter? The temple remains closed and people hardly visit the place at that time!' I exclaimed. 'It's divinely beautiful,' he answered. 'The temple is shut after Deepavali and people residing around pack up their bags and baggage to leave for the plains. Gradually the temperature starts dipping and there are frequent snowfalls. Of course the snow melts in the morning due to the strong rays of the sun. But by January, the entire place is covered in snow.' I paused before asking, 'Do you step out of your hut in peak winter?' He smiled and said, 'Yes, of course, I have to continue the daily chores. I need water and have to go out to the river to fetch it. Even though the river is covered with snow, a subterranean stream of water

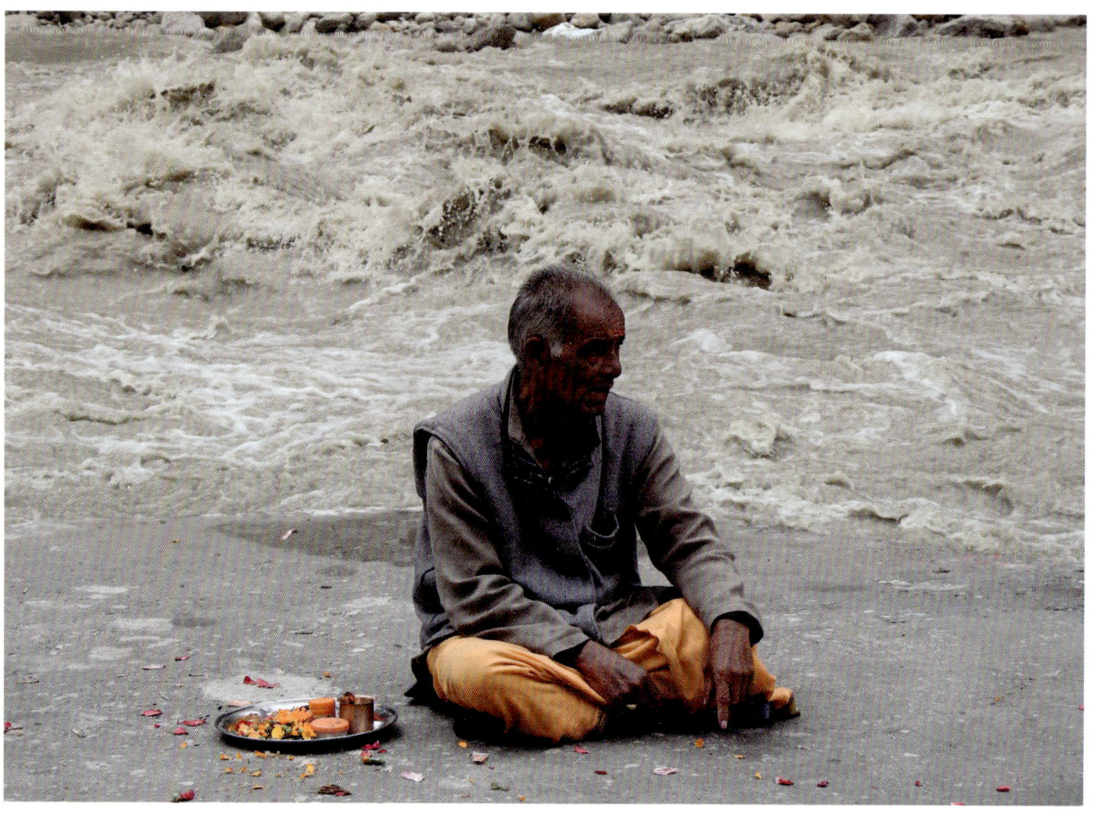

A Brahmin sitting on the bank of the Ganga waiting for devotees

continues to flow. But often the water freezes while carrying it back,' he added. 'What do you do then?' I enquired worried. 'I warm it,' he answered. 'I start a fire with these dry woods and warm the water,' he made it sound a simple affair. 'The people around me leave these woods and also dry food materials for me before they retreat to the plains. That keeps me going.' I couldn't help but ask, 'What do you do when snow piles up outside your hut?' He smiled and said, 'It does and I keep removing it with a shovel. The snow is soft and moveable when fresh and I don't have a problem removing it. But the snows do not remain long. With sunrise they keep melting. In the afternoon the bus carrying passengers arrive at that point and the local hermits come here for small talk. Of course we only talk about the Almighty. Then by evening they go back and I return to my room to continue my studies of the Bhagavad Gita. At times I find pleasure in simply watching the natural beauty of this place.'

'Doesn't the severe winter trouble you?' I asked. He looked at me for a while and slowly answered, 'It's the physical trouble you are talking about? If I keep thinking about physical discomfort when will I think of God? Besides, I protect myself with winter garments, but there are hermits living here who go about stark naked, even during peak winter.'

'Have you met them?' I asked utterly bewildered. 'Yes, of course, I met the great sadhu Krishnashram who lived here till he was one hundred and four years old. People used to look at him in awe when he walked barefoot on the snow. He remained stark naked throughout his life. He used to sit on ice, meditating for hours. Finally the local priests constructed a small cottage for him where he dwelt. But his entire day was spent in meditation. At times he would immerse himself for hours, in the ice-cold water of the Ganga. People would pay obeisance and he would bless them without uttering a word. He would scribble his answer on a slate, for every question that was put to him. People would return gratified. His fame spread far and wide which inspired even a person like Madan Mohan Malaviya to approach him once. Malaviya wanted him to inaugurate the Shiva temple inside the Banaras Hindu University. Krishnashram agreed. When he reached the university, people flocked to see him in person. They showered him with innumerable gifts. But he remained impervious to it all. To him gold was nothing more than a handful of dust. Then a few rich persons approached him with a request to visit their homes. Krishnashram lost his patience and one night, without informing anyone, he left for his favourite destination – Gangotri. He had conquered all physical needs such as hunger and thirst. Severe ailments could not trouble him either. Even after he had crossed his hundredth year, people found him carrying two heavy bucketfuls of water to his cottage every day. The strangest thing occurred once. It was monsoon then. There were landslides everywhere. People found the ceiling of his cottage almost collapsing due to a landslide. They came rushing to request him to step out of his cottage. He refused. Sitting unperturbed he instructed them to leave the place. After the rains when people returned to his cottage they found him in a gravely injured state. Mumbling softly he asked them to carry him to the bank of the Ganga. Doctors came to tend him, but he refused to take their medicines. Then after twenty-two days he woke up completely cured.'

I fell silent. After a few moments I asked Bangali baba, 'Is it possible for worldly people like us to realise God?' He smiled mysteriously. 'God is not a material commodity to be bought in a shop, dear,' he answered. 'He is within you. Why fret about in temples and mosques? Search within yourself and you will realise Him.' Offering me a little bit of *prasadam* he bid me farewell.

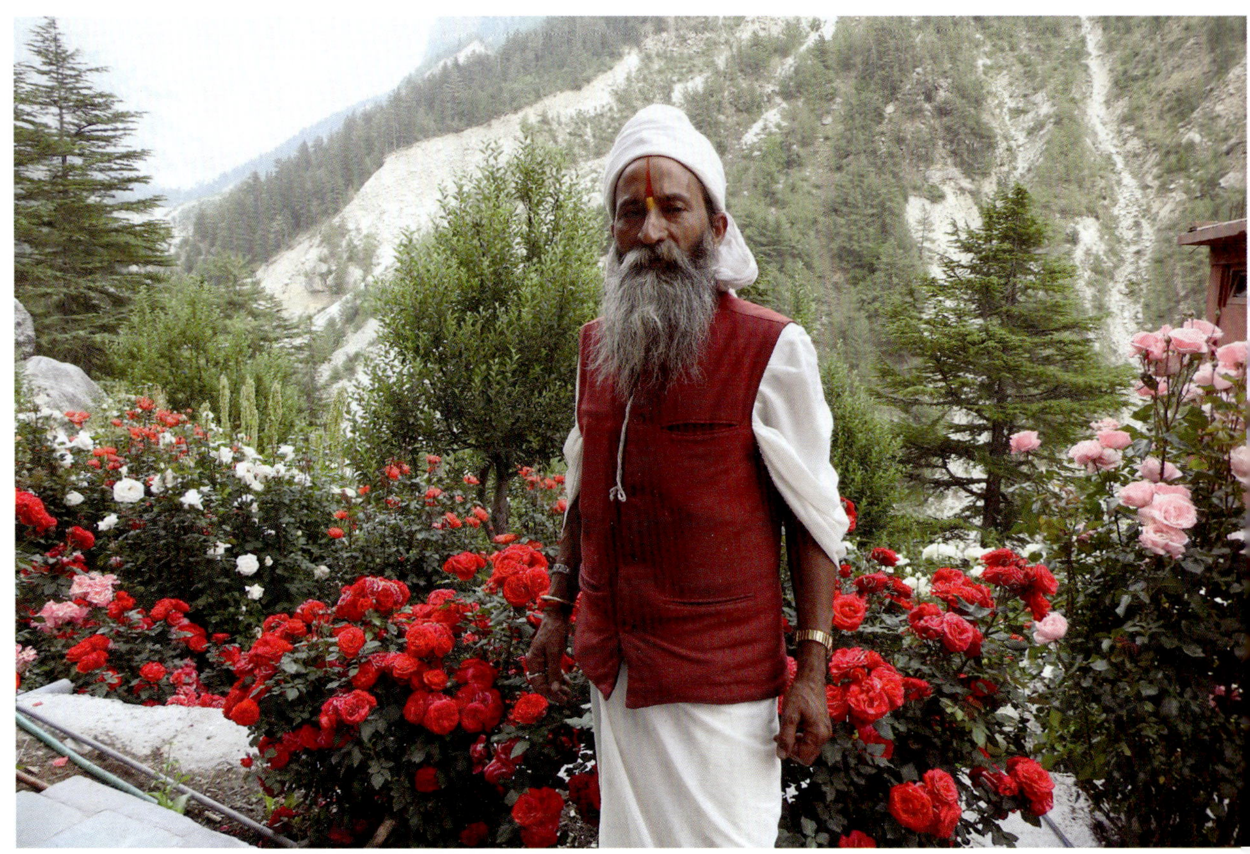

A hermit taking a walk in the picturesque rose garden of Amritghat Ashram

IN SEARCH OF THE GANGA'S ORIGIN

Till the eighteenth century Indians blindly believed that the Ganga actually emerged from the Vinduswarovar. Even the *Ramayana* states that the source of the Ganga was not Manaswarovar but Vinduswarovar. Thus both these lakes became sacred spots for the Hindus. The *Mahabharata* too mentions these two lakes. The five Pandavas on their way to Badarikasram had visited these two sacred spots. People were aware of the existence of Manaswarovar but no one could provide any information about the exact location of Vinduswarovar.

Intrigued by the information about this mysterious Vinduswarovar, men started searching for its exact geographical location. Initially expeditions were undertaken, mostly by foreigners, to trace the existence of Vinduswarovar. Undaunted by the potential hazards of such expeditions and ready to face severe physical hardships, they went about the Himalayas to trace it. Interestingly most of them were Christian missionaries. Their actual interest lay in exploring a route to Tibet, going there, and proselytising the Tibetans. Thus they undertook several expeditions and recorded everything they saw on the way. Their records are invaluable since they provide us with valuable data and also act as guides for future expeditions. Accounts of three Portuguese missionaries – Antonio de Andre, Azvedo and Disderi – can be found in Birendra Nath Sarkar's book in Bengali titled *Gangar Katha*.

In the month of April or May in 1624, Antonio de Andre, a Portuguese missionary, with a team of adventurists, undertook an expedition from Haridwar. They aimed to reach Tibet. They walked along the banks of the Ganga for several days and reached Deoprayag, the confluence of the two rivers Ganga and Alakananda. Perhaps impressed by the high roaring waves of the Alakananda river, Indians had for long presumed that the source of the Ganga lay in the heart of the Alakananda. Antonio de Andre, therefore, firmly bent on reaching Tibet by this route, continued his journey along the banks of the Alakananda. But as he scaled the heights he found the routes turning more and more hazardous. He would often come across pilgrims going to Badrinath. Physically exhausted and severely wounded, yet with radiant faces, they would walk on to reach the Badrinath temple. After a fortnight's walk, Antonio de Andre reached Joshimath – the confluence of Vishnu Ganga and Alakananda. Andre considered the Alakananda to be the Ganga and referred to her as the Ganga in his writings. He also presented the readers a graphic description of the route he was following.

> The mountainous paths are extremely dangerous. In fact there are places where there is nothing called the pathway. Bridges made from ropes are often used to ply from one mountainous terrain to another. Below flows the roaring Ganges. The sight is frightening. Most of the places are covered in deep layers of snow and we have to traverse upon them.

About the mountainous road Andre says,

> Over here the road is dangerous. There's nothing called a path here. One has to depend upon a bridge made out of rope in order to pass from one mountain to another. And down below flows the river with great force. The roaring sound of the river is terrifying. Sometimes one needs to cross heaps of snow as well. The entire mountain range is covered in a thick blanket of snow.

After having travelled for almost a month and a half, Andre reached Badrinath which he described vividly.

> It's a stone temple, which countless pilgrims visit every year. With their arrival the courtyard pulsates with life. There is a hot spring, in front of the temple which flows in several directions. Its water is so warm that its not possible to touch it for long. The water finally gets collected into a cavity, located slightly away from the temple. The pilgrims bathe here expecting to cleanse their sins.

A village called Mana is located a few yards away from Badrinath. Andre bypassed Mana and proceeded towards Tibet. The road was perilous, and the more he advanced the higher were the layers of snow. At times the snow appeared to be knee-deep as well. Andre and his men walked only during the day and after sunset they took shelter under some stony boulders. There were blizzards every evening. To keep themselves warm they would all huddle together. Their limbs would freeze, turn numb and become swollen. Drinking water was scarce so they would chew ice and wait for them to melt in the mouth. Andre provided a detailed description of these hardships they endured during the expedition. 'It's a strange world of dazzling snow. And partial blindness occurs if we look at the mountains for long. Gradually we were all losing our eyesight and it was growing increasingly difficult to proceed forward.' Yet, they walked on till they reached a large lake. Describing the lake Andre wrote, '… in front of us is a large lake. The lake is the source of the two rivers the Ganges and the Sindhu.' Later he referred to it as Manaswarovar. This is how the lake was known over the centuries. Andre had visited the place in 1624 and published his story in 1626.

In 1631 Azvedo, another Portuguese missionary, started his journey to Tibet from Haridwar. After walking for a few days, Azvedo and his companions reached Deoprayag. Like Andre he too considered the Alakananda to be the actual source of the Ganga. Another seven days' walk took them to Srinagar, the capital of Garhwal. Azvedo's arrival coincided with the funeral ceremony of the ruling king. The king was dead and his queens were being dragged to his pyre for sati. Describing this four-hundred-year-old gruesome practice, Azvedo wrote,

> … a huge pyre of sandalwood was set up on the shore of the Ganga. A large crowd had gathered to view the ceremony. Sixty queens were being prepared for sati. The queens looked

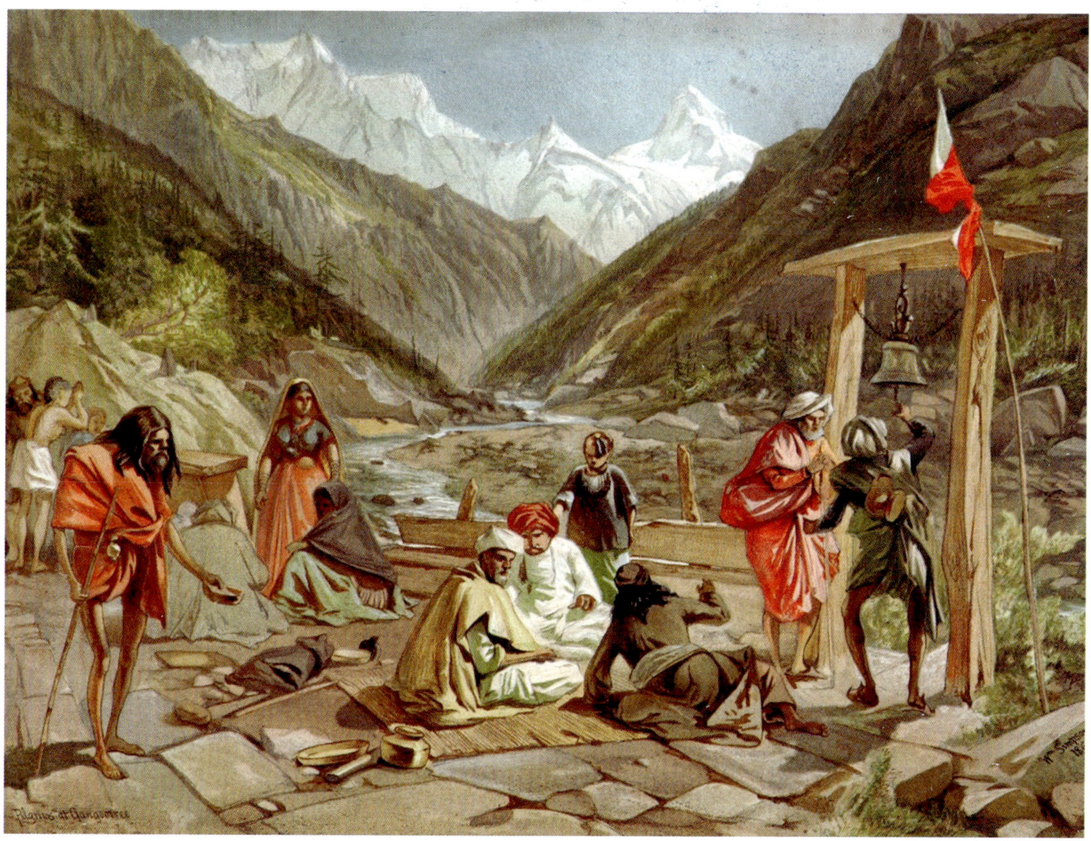

Pilgrimage to Gangotri (1867) by William Simpson

petrified at the thought of being burnt alive. Yet, they could do nothing since a large number of guards cordoned them off. Large drums and cymbals were kept ready while a group of priests stood in front of the pyre chanting mantras, performing the last rites of the king. The moment the pyre was lit a huge uproar arose from the crowd followed by the terrible wails of the queens. Several senior queens started walking round the pyre, yet the moment fire touched their body, they started screaming in pain. Looking at them the rest of the queens too started wailing aloud. Nobody wanted to jump into the pyre, yet, they could not escape because servants of the deceased king caught hold of these miserable ladies and hurled them into

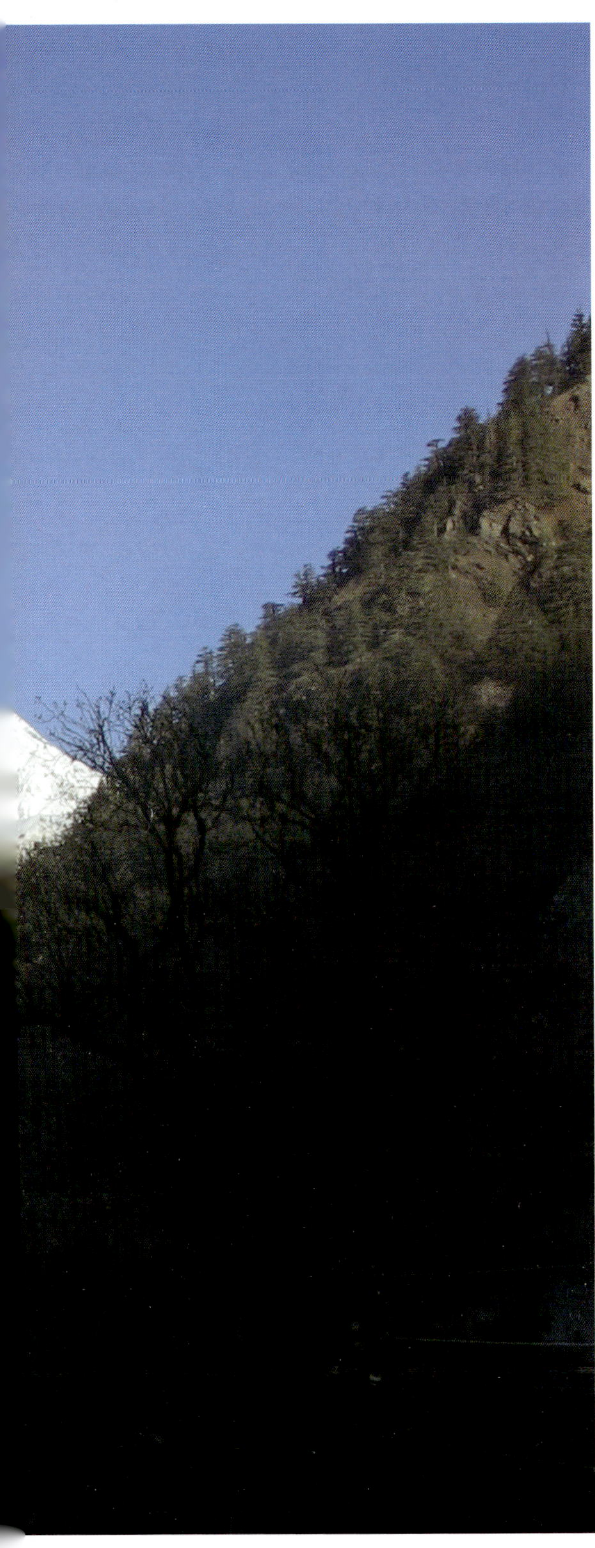

> the blazing fire. Some were beaten up so badly that they fell unconscious. Then their unconscious bodies were tied with ropes and thrown into the fire. Meanwhile the cacophony of drums and cymbals tried hard to drown the wails of these hapless ladies. It was a ghastly sight to behold.

The team continued their journey along the banks of the Alakananda and, after a fortnight's walk, on 31 July 1631, bypassing the Joshimath, they reached the Badrinath temple. They started preparing for their journey to Tibet from here. They crossed Mana and kept walking on the snow-covered paths. Finally after a few days they came across a beautiful lake, which Andre probably too had found previously. 'I am now standing in front of a large lake,' wrote Azvedo.

> The local people consider it to be the origin of both the rivers Ganga and Sindhu. But none of these two rivers are visible, as their paths are covered by chunks of large stones. However, we are able to hear the sound of their roaring waves. The rivers are visible far from here.

Snow-covered mountain near Mukhba village surrounded by dense *deodar* forests. The locals call this Shree Kantha hill

Father Disderi, another Portuguese missionary, followed the footsteps of Azvedo and went in search of the origin of the Ganga. In 1725, having travelled to places like Haridwar, Deoprayag, Srinagar and Badrinath, he reached a large lake surrounded by mountains. 'There is a large lake in front of me,' wrote Father Disderi.

> According to our guide, it takes quite a few days to complete a tour round the lake. People here consider it to be the origin of the Ganga. Another river has originated from the other side of the lake, which is known as Sindhu. This river flows down to Kashmir via Tibet. Scores of pilgrims here come to bathe in this lake. They believe it to be holy.

Though all three missionaries mentioned above primarily intended to visit Tibet for proselytising, they nevertheless made sincere efforts to trace the origin of the river Ganga. The documents of their journey left behind for us, even though full of contradictions, are geographically very important. The documents assisted men who later undertook similar expeditions. Another important explorer's name ought to be mentioned here. He was a royal messenger, sent by Emperor Akbar to trace the origin of the Ganga. But his name is forgotten and there is no written record of his journey. All these explorers however unanimously claimed that Manaswarovar was the real origin of the Ganga, and river Alakananda was the real Ganga.

In 1767 Major James Rennell was appointed as the first surveyor-general of the East India Company's dominions in Bengal. And it was Rennell who first tried to ascertain the exact geographical features of our country. He undertook the task of making a thorough survey of the Ganga. His area of survey however was restricted to four states only – Bengal, Orissa, Bihar and Uttar Pradesh. He worked for four years and then wrote, '… even though there are many rivers in the world which are larger and longer than the Ganga, yet, Ganga is unique for her diverse traits.' He drew a map of the Ganga where he cited Manaswarovar as its source. The map was published in 1790. Later data collected from different sources proved that Rennell's map was incorrect. So the task of drawing a correct map of the Ganga fell upon three people – Lt Webb, Capt. Raapper and Capt. Hayerse.

In April 1808 Webb, Raapper and Hayerse collected a group of men and began their journey from Haridwar. They however did not follow the path of river Alakananda. They walked along the banks of the Ganga and after ten days reached

Uttarkashi. Uttarkashi was then a large village and was also the last point of human habitation. They walked for another seven days and reached Bhatwari. They found a few families living at Bhatwari. The journey so far was hard, yet the journey beyond Bhatwari proved impossible. The steep mountainous paths proved dangerous. At times they had to crawl their way up as walking was out of the question. And below these mountainous paths lay the ever-flowing, ever-roaring Ganga. A moment's indecision would lead them to death. A few hours of inhuman effort, however, finally brought them to the mountain top. Then it was time for them to alight. While descending with a few tribals they came across two waterfalls.

The journey proved very challenging and all the members of the team were utterly exhausted. So Lt Webb decided to call off the expedition. He collected information from the local people and returned home. Describing his experience Lt Webb wrote in a letter,

> We reached Bhatwari on 27th. I collected all possible information from the local people. Inaccessibility of the roads made us decide to leave our luggage with the villagers. Next day as the sun rose we begun our journey. Two local men accompanied us. We could barely walk a few miles that day as we were utterly exhausted. A leader amongst us warned about the impassibility of the roads ahead. So we were forced to return. Had it been possible to proceed further, we would have carried on, despite all dangers. Moreover my companions too were not very keen on proceeding further. Frequent change of weather, scorching sunlight during the day, and extreme cold at night deterred most of us. Some amongst us fell ill. To proceed forward ignoring these deterring factors meant – proceeding toward certain death. We gave up our plans, but collected a lot of information about both Gangotri and the origin of the Ganga from a local person at Bhatwari. Every day he collects water from the Ganga and sells it at a high rate. He informed us that Gaumukh is far off from Gangotri and the entire stretch is covered with snow. No definite source of the Ganga can be traced other than a narrow trickle of water coming out of the cave of Gaumukh. Neither does Gaumukh resemble the face of a cow. From his statement I realised that we were actually sixteen to eighteen miles away from Gangotri. And it was impossible

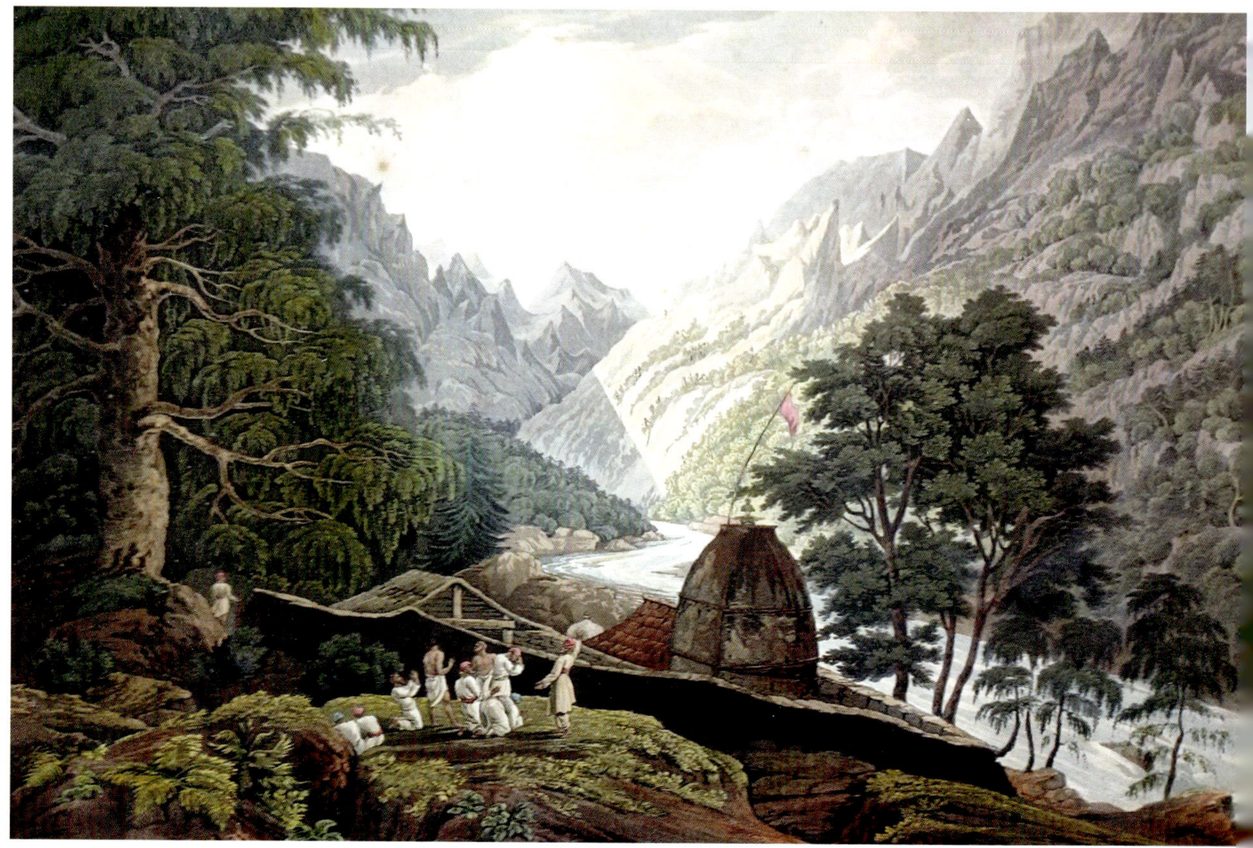

Old Gangotri Temple (1820) by James Baillie Fraser

> for us to identify the exact source of the Ganga without visiting the place. (Capt. Raapper, 'Narrative of Survey for the Purpose of Discovering the Sources of Ganges,' *Asiatick Researches*, Vol. XI, 1818.)

This was the first record of the actual source of the river Ganga – the Gaumukh cave. Prior to it, no one could ascertain the exact origin of the river Ganga.

Another foreign explorer who reached Gangotri and wrote a detailed account of his experience was James Baillie Fraser. He was born in Scotland in the year 1783. Even though he was employed in various professions, his primary love was painting. In 1813 he came to Calcutta and joined the British Army. And as an army man he went to the Himalayas to fight a battle against the king of Nepal. After the battle was fought he spent time exploring the origins of both the rivers Ganga and Yamuna. His love for exploration was coupled with his desire to paint. So in July 1815 he reached Gangotri. Fraser wrote of his experiences,

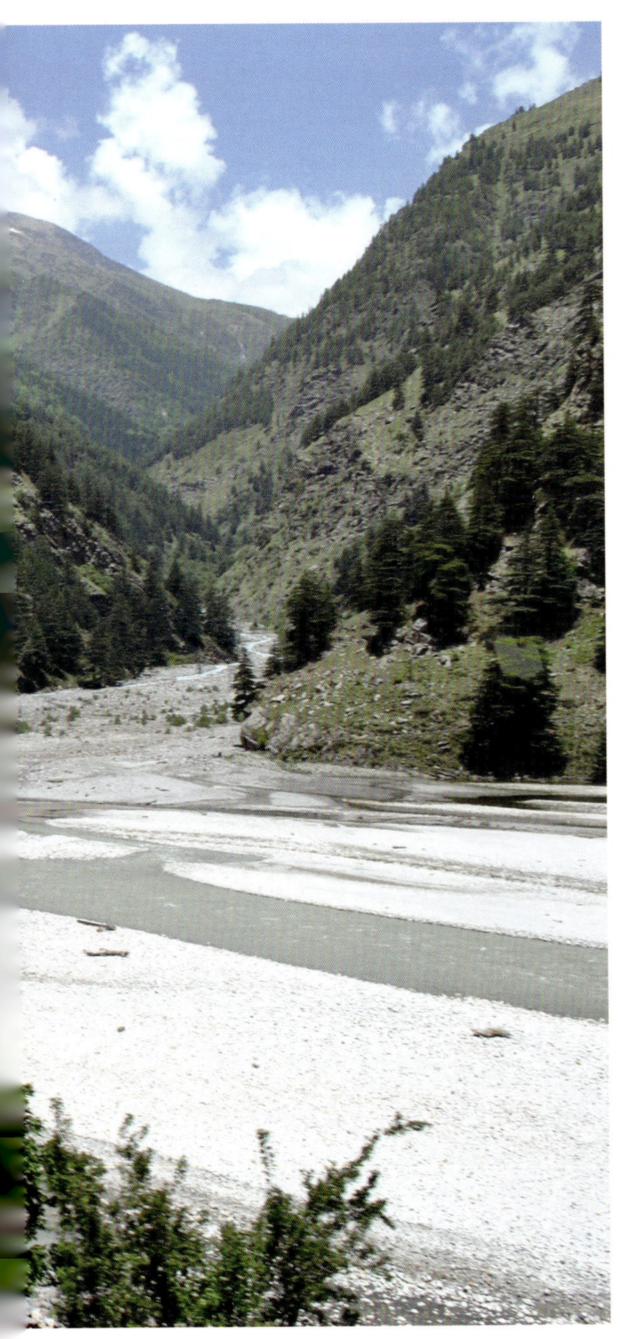

Math and reached Haridwar. From there he undertook a journey towards Tibet and reached Gangotri instead. He published his experiences, 'Three years in Tibet', serially in a journal. Later the series was collected and published in the form of a book.

> I left Bhatwari and reached Gangotri after four days. The last village on the way to Gangotri was Dharasu. Gangotri is about twenty-five miles from this place. After covering half the distance, I came to Bhairava Jhola. Here pilgrims heading to Gangotri offer prayers to the Ganga before proceeding further. On the way there is just a *chatti* or shop and a small temple. After reaching Bhairav Ghati, I lost my way. Here another stream, the Bhot-Ganga, meets the main stream of the Ganga. I wandered a little, but finally managed to return to the correct route after sometime.
>
> As I proceeded along the road to Gangotri, the grandeur of the Himalayas began to unfold before me. The huge mountain range, which looked like a tortoise, all white with snow, rose before me. The Bhagirathi

The Ganga near Dharali village. In the past the road to Dharali was so narrow that only one person at a time could walk down to reach Gangotri and Gaumukh was running down sharp bends of this mountain. Its gurgling waters incessantly appeared to chant 'Hara' 'Hara' – the name of Lord Shiva. Even though the stream of the Ganga is rather narrow at Gangotri, the force with which the water emerges is strong enough to sweep away the hundred white elephants of God Indra. It is perhaps both to cleanse and sanctify the innumerable *Jiva*s (human beings) living on earth that the white waters of the Ganga rush with such rapidity and force. The river Bhagirathi runs between high mountains whose upper slopes are white with snow. Below the snow-clad tops grow the tall pines. On either side of the stream are smooth marble-like white rocks, piled upon one another, resembling a 'Vedic altar'. This panoramic view was so picturesque that I abandoned myself completely to enjoy the heavenliness of the place. I moved from rock to rock, sitting here and there, because I knew that I would never again see such a divine sight. I took in as much as I could the divinity strewn here on the lap of the Himalayas. My senses kept absorbing the quietude and beauty of the place, till my heart brimmed over with joy.

MUKHBA

From Gangotri the Ganga turns southwards to Mukhba. Mukhba is an ancient village and adjacent to it is Dharali. In the ancient times the road to Dharali was such that only one person at a time could walk down it, to reach Gangotri and Gaumukh. It took men almost three days to reach Gangotri from Dharali, traversing a distance of twenty-five kilometres. Now automobiles have reduced the time to just one hour. A few houses, inns and open fields are visible along the way. The Ganga is widest here and flows down quietly. Mukhba is situated right at the end of a hanging bridge. It is said in the *Purana*s that Sage Markandya had once meditated here and hence the name of the village. The village comprises a few wooden huts, scattered here and there. Large apple fields are visible all around. Down the village flows river Ganga while tall insurmountable mountain peaks stand solemnly in front of Mukhba.

Like at Gangotri, right in the middle of the village, there is a Ganga temple, made of white marble. Right after the Deepavali festival, the temple at Gangotri is closed for six months at a stretch because of the inclement weather. So the goddess is brought down here for worship, from Gangotri, for the following six months. Mother Ganga cannot be left alone without being attended upon; hence this procedure

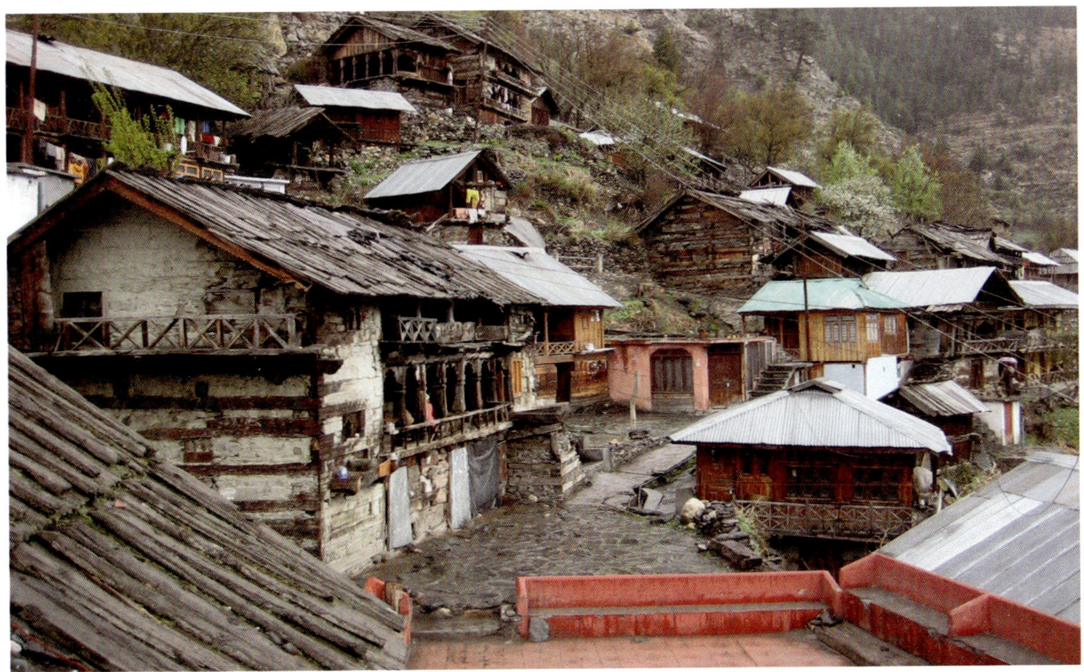

Mukhba village. Interestingly the local inhabitants of Mukhba can trace their ancestry back to Birbhum, West Bengal

of relocating the idol is followed. But for all practical purposes even this village becomes desolate with the advent of winter. And as the temperature plummets the entire region gets covered with thick layers of snow. Only two priests stay back to continue the ritual worship of Mother Ganga. At the end of winter, on Akshaya Tritiya (an auspicious day in the month of May), a long procession of local people carry the idol back, first to Bhairavghat and then finally to Gangotri.

The priests of Garhwal region are Brahmins. But the local inhabitants of Mukhba belong to the Semwal family, who had once hailed from Simolkar village in the Birbhum district of West Bengal. According to local records, seven hundred years ago a group of travellers had undertaken a journey along this dangerous terrain, to reach Gangotri. Most of them died on the way, while a few who survived were unable to return to their village. So they decided to stay back and settle down permanently. They even married the local girls and started families. That's how they lost their previous Bengali identity and became a part of the Garhwal community.

This however is the common story of the entire Garhwal district. Thousands

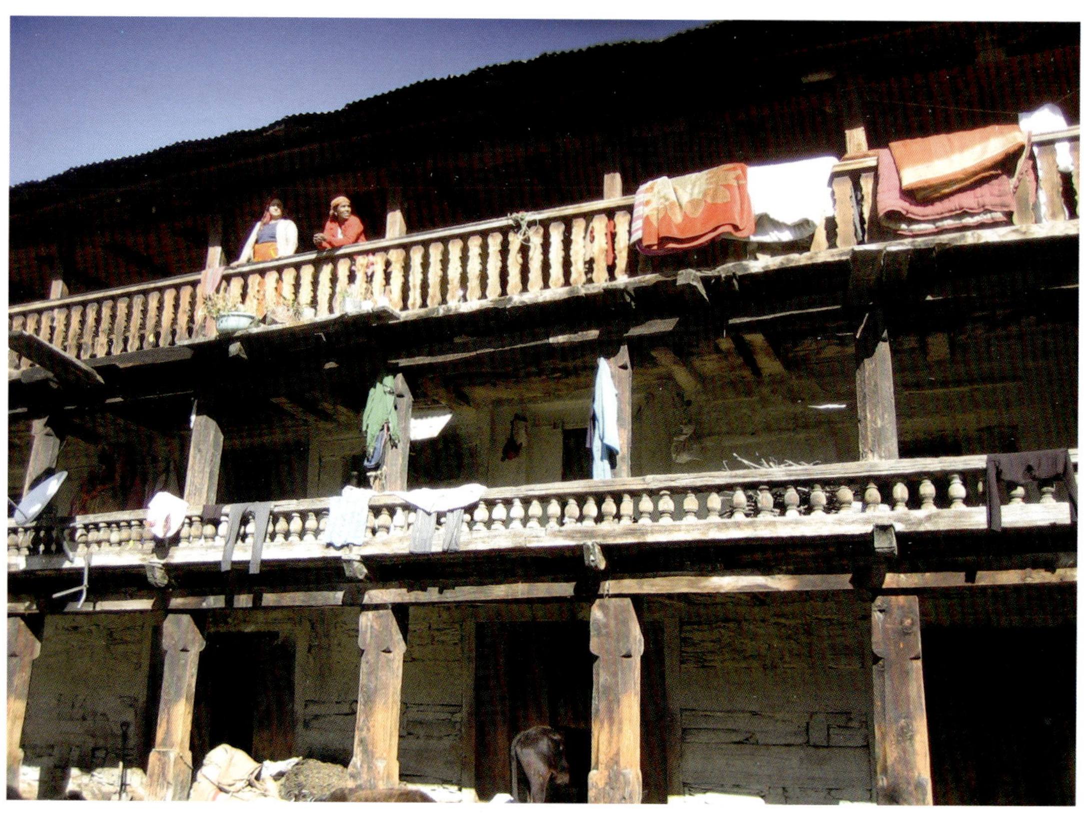

A three-storeyed wooden building at Mukhba, built a hundred years ago

of people from different parts of India – Bengal, Kerala, Maharashtra, Gujarat and Rajasthan – kept visiting Gangotri for multiple reasons and then stayed back to add to the local population. Some came as pilgrims, some came seeking jobs, some came in search of spiritual realisation, while some came to escape their enemies – but finally all of them stayed back renouncing their original tradition and adopting the local way of life.

A hanging bridge across the Ganga becomes visible just a few furlongs from Dharali. And right in the middle of the bridge one gets a panoramic view of the region. Large stretches of sandbanks with a narrow stretch of the Ganga in the middle. Strangely, the thunderous and roaring spontaneity of the river, which one finds both at Rishikesh and Haridwar, is missing. It is all quiet and tranquil out here. The water however is deeper here than anywhere else in the country. One often comes across large tree trunks floating effortlessly in this narrow strip of water, pointing to its depth. There are thick pillars at two ends of the hanging bridge. Thick iron ropes are tied to these pillars to suspend the bridge. On one end of the bridge is Dharali, while at the other end stands a series of mountains. Interestingly to the humble and simple people of Dharali and Mukhba, river Ganga is not a divine deity, but their dearest daughter. They love her and tend her with utmost love and care.

From a Pilgrim's Diary

Dharali, a little hamlet, lies twenty-five kilometres down Gangotri. There are a few houses, shops and motels in the village and in front flows the Ganga. A suspended bridge has been constructed over the river and at the other end of the bridge is another hamlet, Mukhba. I had reached Dharali two days before Akshaya Tritiya, the auspicious day of the temple's reopening. Synchronising the occasion the local shops too had started their business on the day of

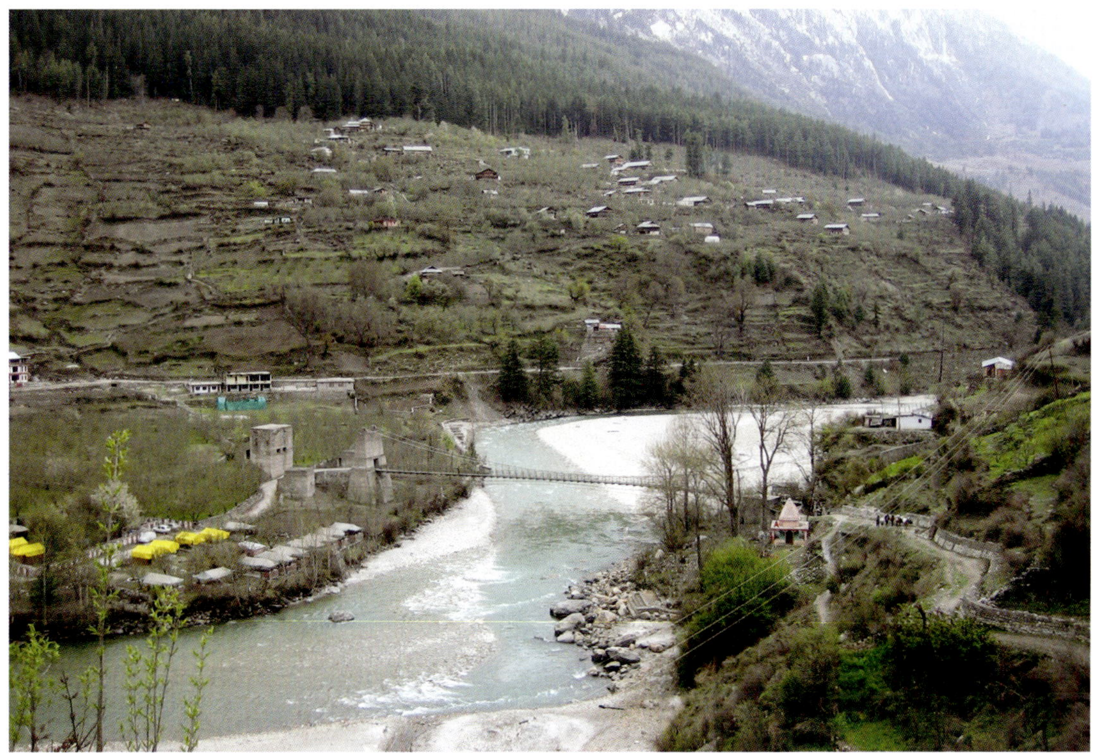

A hanging bridge across the Ganga connecting Mukhba and Dharali

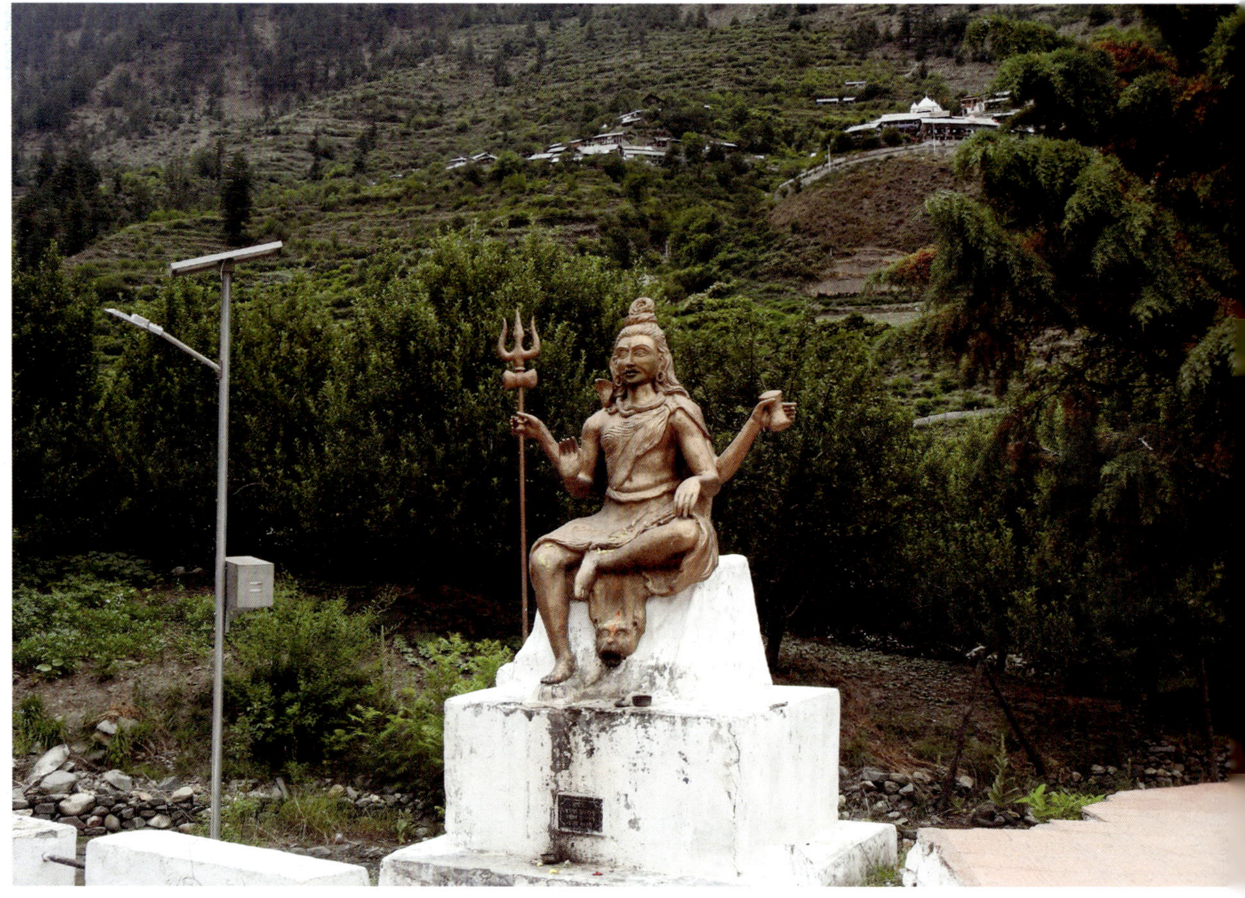

The locals worship Lord Shiva here at Mukhba village (visible on the hilltop). The Himalayas is considered to be Shiva's domain

my arrival. People who had left the hamlet in anticipation of a severe winter had already returned to their old homes.

On this trip I had for company my aged mother, my teacher and his wife. I put them up in a hotel and walked out alone. Peace reigned everywhere. The entire place was soaking in the rain that had just ended. A little away from our hotel I found an apple orchard covered with white flowers. Clearly within a few months the trees would be covered with ripened juicy apples. Fredrick Wilson (1817-1883), a British soldier, had begun this apple cultivation here. First posted at Dehra Dun, he was subsequently transferred to Harshil, a place near Dharali. He came here and possibly fell in love with the place and settled down permanently. It is said that he had procured apple seeds from England to start cultivation. And for commuting he constructed the hanging bridge. Initially local people were scared to step on to the

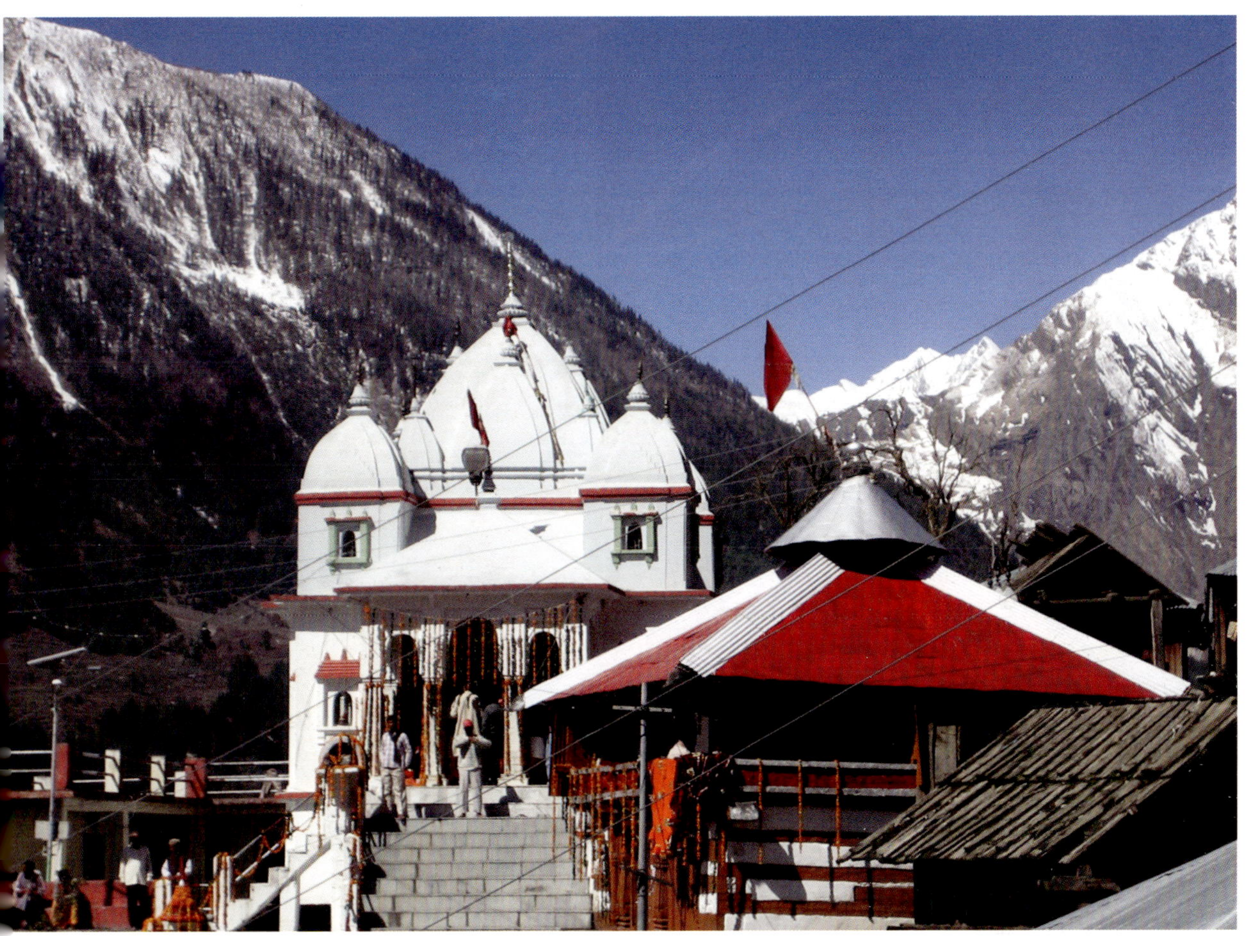

The Ganga temple at Mukhba village

bridge, but Wilson frequently rode on horseback across the bridge for carrying on his commercial transactions. He constructed several bungalows for running his business. He also sought the permission of East India Company to introduce currency for the region. He not only loved the place but also loved the local people. To earn their trust he married a local girl, Raimatta. His second wife too was a local girl, called Sungrami, also known as Gulabi. I heard the story about Wilson from Umaraman Semwal, a local schoolteacher-cum-researcher. As I was crossing the hanging bridge I found him right behind me. When I glanced at him, he smiled and nodded his head, indicating a desire to talk. As we walked along he narrated the above story to me. Mukhba was his native village, but his workplace was at Uttarkashi. He had come home to attend the temple-opening festival. In fact he invited me to his home the following day.

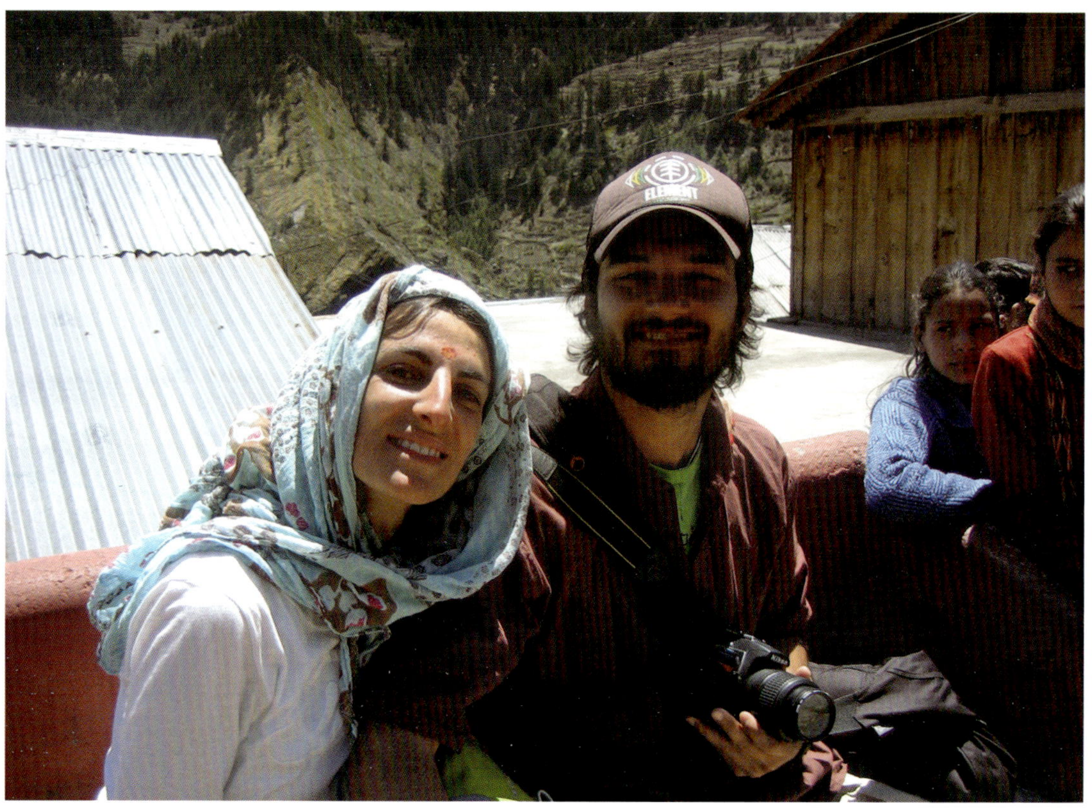

A couple had come from Argentina to watch the temple-opening ceremony festival. This was their second visit

'The local people of these villages maintain two establishments,' informed Semwal. 'During winter they shut down their houses here and migrate to Uttarkashi. The houses therefore remain closed for the following six months i.e. till the end of winter. Then just a day before Akshaya Tritiya, they return here to make a living. Cultivation, priestly duties and running motels are the chief occupations of these villagers. The money they earn during these six months help sustain them year round. But days are changing. The children of the villagers are now refusing to toe the line of their parents. They are pursuing higher studies and opting for jobs elsewhere.'

We were trudging along while conversing and I was soaking in the wonderful natural beauty all around. Below us flowed the Ganga and in front of us lay Dharali. A narrow path twined round the village up the mountain slopes. However our walks were being constantly interrupted, as we had to make way for the donkeys carrying goods up the mountain tops. We could see wooden houses from a distance scattered all around. Most of them were a century old. We proceeded towards the white marble

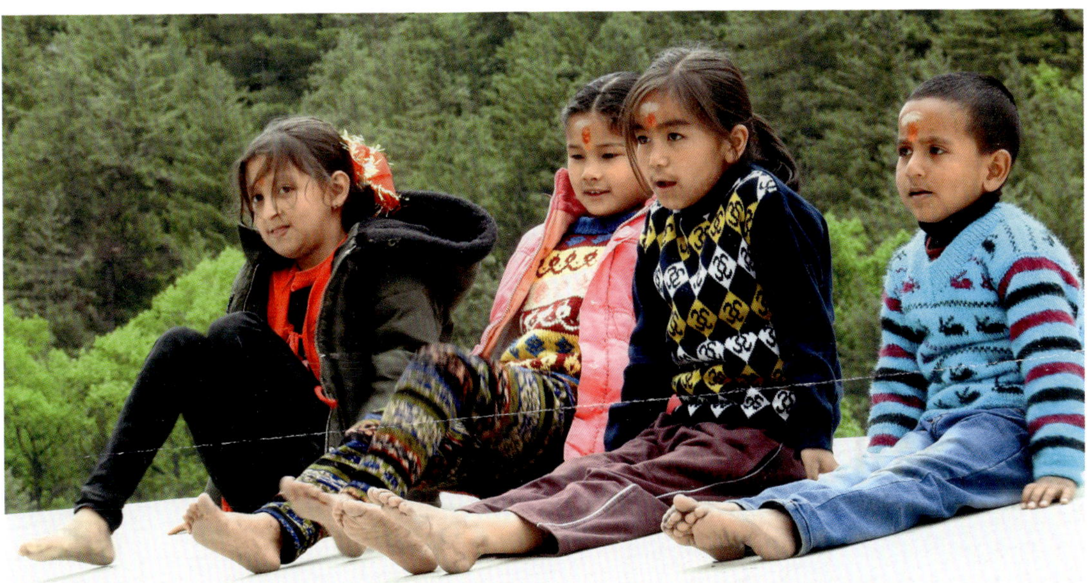

Children in colourful clothes at Mukhba waiting for the festivities to begin

temple, which to me seemed like a replica of the Gangotri temple. But this one was smaller in size. We had to climb a good many steps to reach the courtyard of the temple. The door of the temple however was closed. Adjacent to the main temple was an ancillary wooden structure where dwelt Someswar Mahadev. Mahadeva (Lord Shiva) is the presiding deity in many of the Himalayan villages. A few people had gathered in the courtyard waiting for a meeting. Mother Ganga had been worshipped here for the last six months, and now it was time for her to return to Gangotri. The local people had gathered at the temple courtyard to discuss the nitty-gritty of this journey. The sky being cloudy I felt it risky to tarry longer in this open courtyard and hence left for our hotel.

The loud beating of drums woke me up next morning. As I came out to the balcony I saw a marvellous sight. On my left was the magnificent snow-clad peak of Bandarpuchhya all radiant in the sunlight. I was told this was the source of Yamuna river. The Yamunotri temple stands on its banks.

Later in the morning as I was crossing the hanging bridge I came across a group of hermits walking barefoot. I greeted them with a 'namaste' and then asked, 'Where are you from?' One of them replied, 'We are from Allahabad. We came to Haridwar by train and then walked our way to this place.'

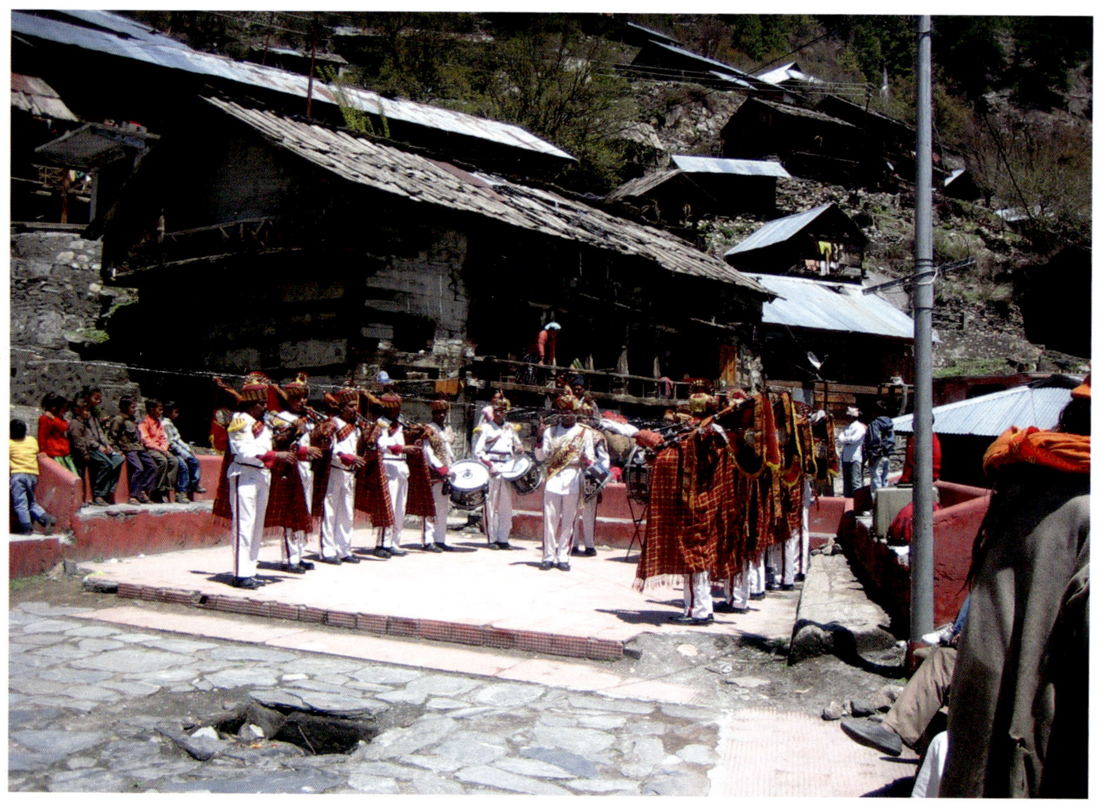

Army troop playing drums and bugle to celebrate the Ganga festival

I was dumbfounded. Previously, when there were no buses or automobiles people were forced to walk here. But now why do they have to walk? Perhaps they had no money to buy bus tickets – I thought to myself. 'People would have given you a lift, had you but asked them,' I suggested mildly.

One amongst them looked at me and said affectionately, 'Right, my son. But down the ages so many spiritual leaders and mythical figures have traversed this route on foot. They neither had cars nor other vehicles for commuting. We just wanted to get the feel of their journey. Perhaps to touch the dust they had touched. Hence we walked the distance.'

Their argument silenced me for good. I walked with them and reached the temple, which was already overflowing with devotees. A troop of army men was waiting for the right moment to play their band. A group of dhoti-clad priests were busy decorating the palanquin that was to carry

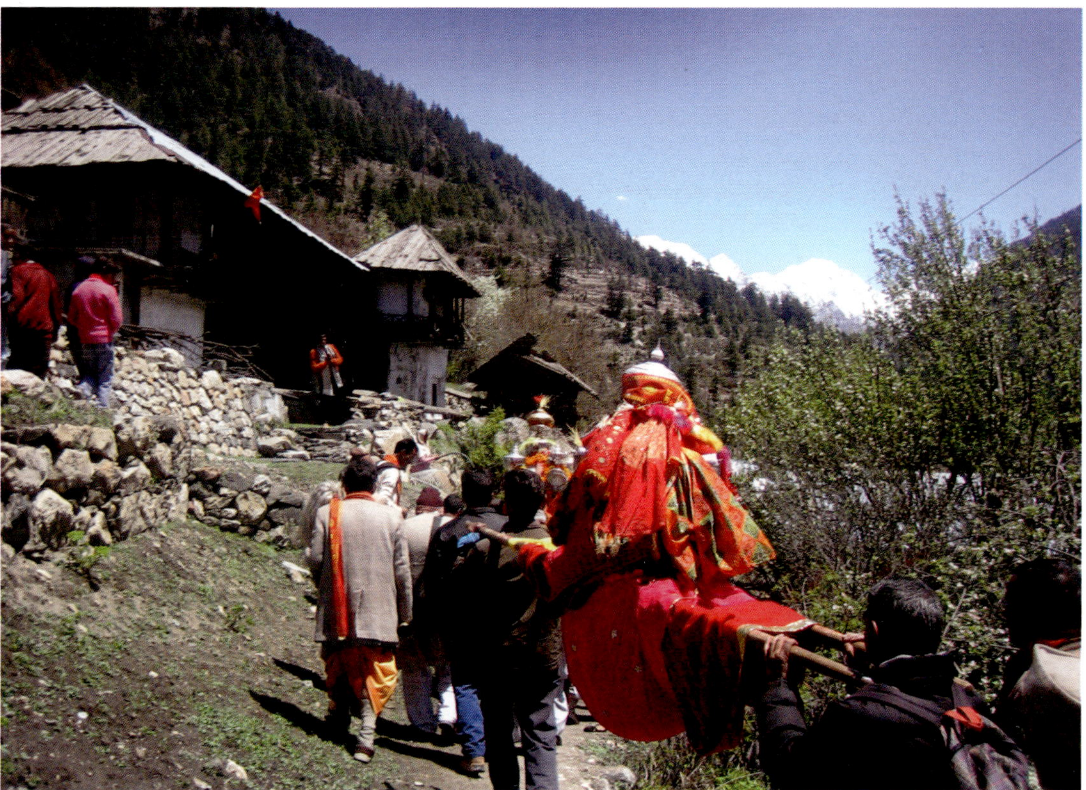

The procession carrying the Ganga idol in a palanquin from Mukhba to Gangotri

the idol of the Ganga back to the Gangotri glacier. The door of the temple, however, continued to remain closed. 'When will the door open,' I asked.

'After sometime, but no outsider will be allowed in,' I was warned. People kept flocking inside. There were journalists, photographers, and a youth from Argentina with his girlfriend. The couple had earlier visited the place and this was their second visit. They kept coming back here because they found the Himalayan range to be unique among mountain ranges. Suddenly the army troop started playing the drums as the priests opened the door of the temple and walked in with the palanquin. A resounding '*Om Jaya Ganga Mata*' arose involuntarily. After a few moments the palanquin was borne out by the priests silhouetted by a deep red cloth. As per rules, the deity would be unveiled on reaching the Gangotri temple. Eight priests bore the palanquin and walked on

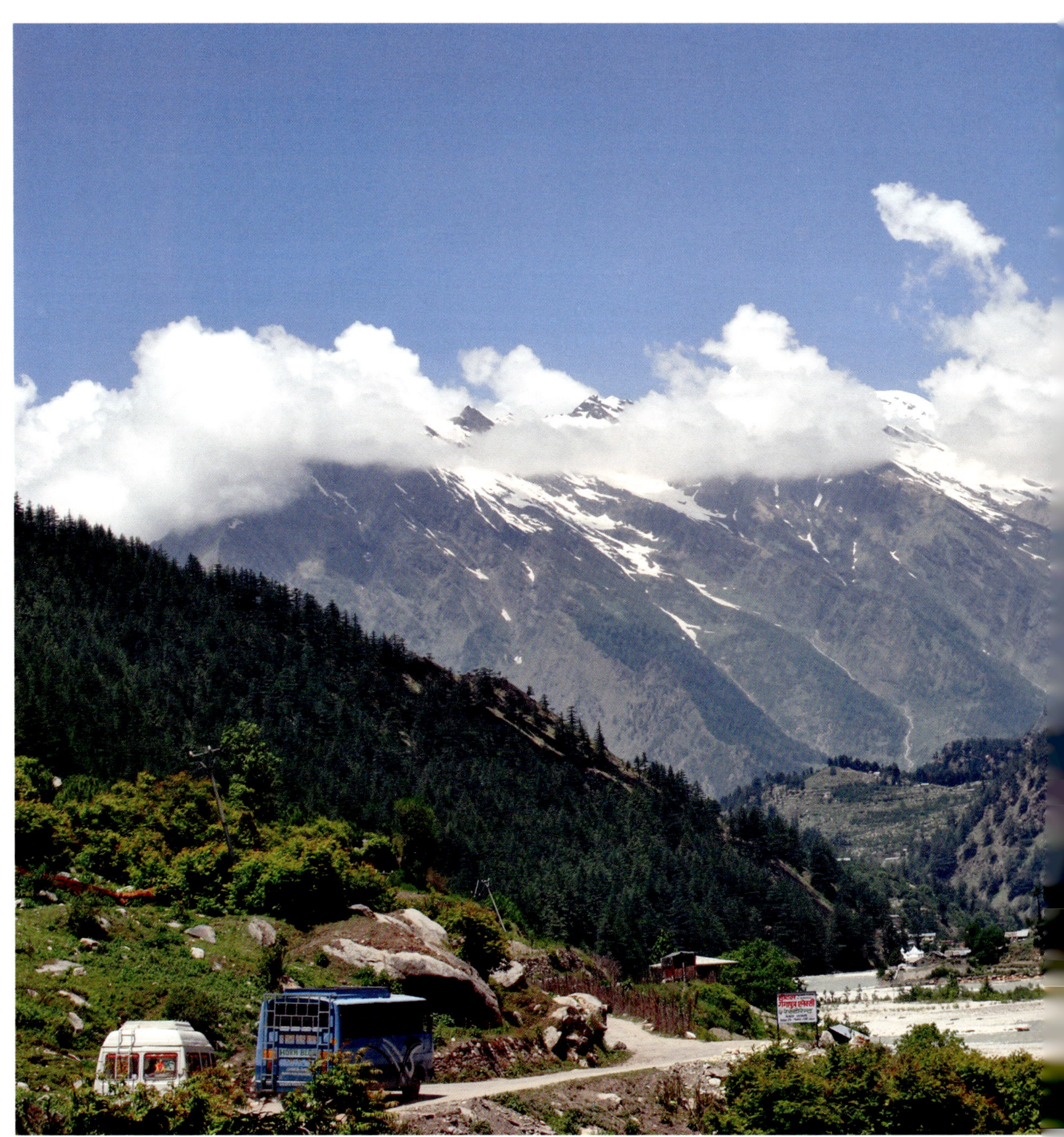

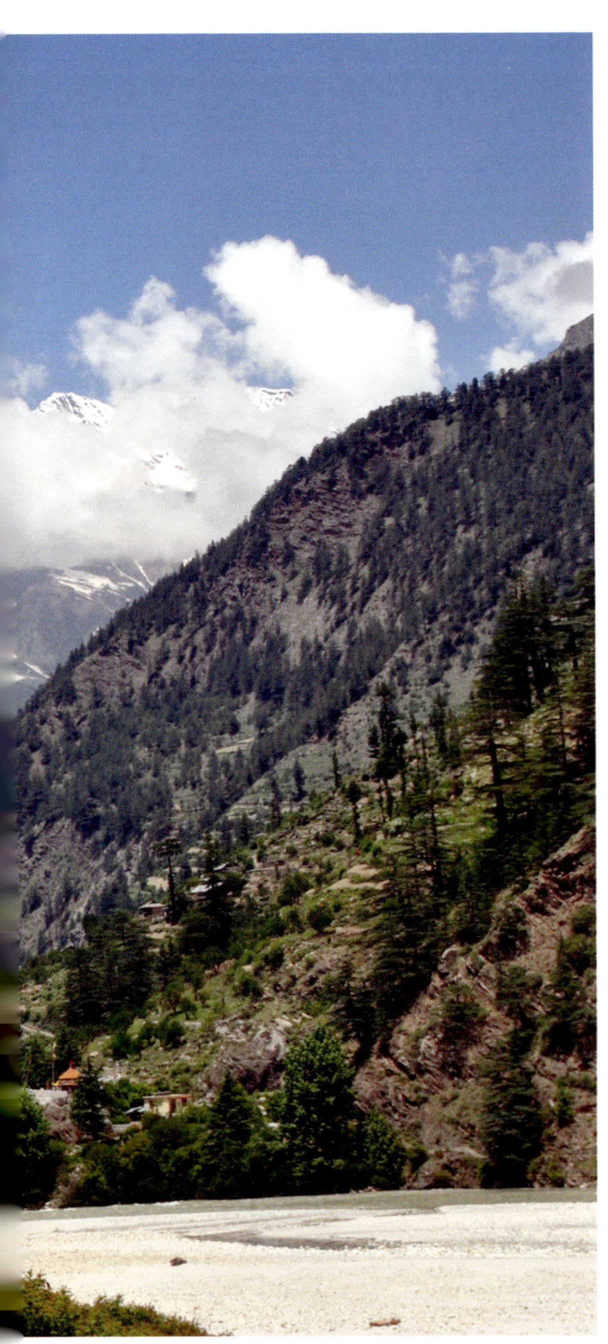

ceremoniously followed by the army band. The local populace followed them. It was a solemn ambience, as if Ganga, their beloved daughter (of Mukhba), was on her way to her in-laws, leaving behind her parental home. The procession kept moving forward with the '*Om Jaya Ganga Mata*' chants resounding at frequent intervals. It was a steep walk down the mountainous path. Umaraman was accompanying me and he informed, 'It's a long walk of twenty-five kilometres and they are going to walk the entire stretch. They will reach Bhairon-ghati by evening, rest for the night and then proceed towards Gangotri next morning. By ten in the morning they will reach the Gangotri temple.' We walked for a mile up to another small temple and then retreated. Only a handful kept walking with the palanquin now.

A car awaited us for the next part of the journey. The route we took was rather dreary. There were no villages waiting to greet us – only a series of steep mountainous paths. After a time we reached the camp of Indo-Tibetan Border Force. This force was formed to protect the Indian border during the Chinese aggression. Even during severe winter months the force remains ever vigilant – zealously guarding the sovereignty of our country. Our car was stopped by an

The road to Gangotri is surrounded by scenic mountains on all sides army official who invited us to lunch. 'Why this sudden celebration?' I asked him.

'The Indian Army likes to celebrate this auspicious day by dining with civilians,' he answered. The army had also arranged for ritual worship when the palanquin would arrive at their camp. Everyone seemed to be waiting eagerly for Mother Ganga's arrival. We, however, journeyed along leaving behind the enthusiastic crowd. After a while we reached the Bhairon-ghati temple. It seemed the temple was protected by Mahadeva's personal bodyguard.

The condition of the roads worsened as we proceeded forward. There were not only large and deep ravines here and there but also loose earth, indicating recent landslides. The Ganga lay far below and was hardly visible. Suddenly after crossing a corner of this perilous path the driver called out '*Om Jaya Ganga Mata*'. We had reached Gangotri.

UTTARKASHI

From Gangotri, the Ganga flows down a distance of hundred kilometres to reach Uttarkashi. On her way she bypasses places like Dharali, Harshil, Jhala, Gungnani, Bhatwari, Maneri and Ganguri. Haridwar is situated further away from Uttarkashi – almost a distance of 176 kilometres. Encircled by a series of mountains Uttarkashi's scenic beauty is unparalleled. It

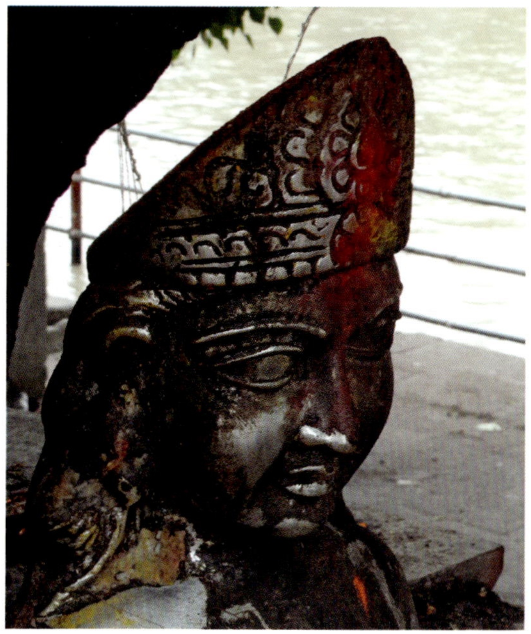

Ganga idol smeared with vermilion near the Ganga ghat at Uttarkashi

is an ancient pilgrimage site, much revered by Hindu pilgrims. In fact like the ancient city of Varanasi, Uttarkashi too has been the homeland of Lord Shiva, for ages. In the days of yore when it was impossible for people to visit Varanasi, they built a second homeland here for Lord Shiva. Uttarkashi has also been mentioned in the ancient *Purana*s. The *Purana*s have predicted that Uttarkashi will survive even when the rest of the world is destroyed. Only then will people acknowledge it to be the true homeland of Lord Shiva. Like Varanasi, Uttarkashi boasts of the confluence of two rivers –

Ashi and Varun – flowing down from two sides. There are several concrete bathing ghats (wharfs) here. And like Varanasi here too the river flows northwards. The central temple of the town is dedicated to Lord Shiva. Though not very old, its exact date of construction is not known. Recounting the happenings of the temple, Sage Tapavan Maharaj observed, 'In Varanasi, Lord Shiva is burdened by loads of flowers and sacred leaves of wood apple, showered upon him by the devotees. But here being free of all those burdens, He remains in a permanent state of meditation.'

Previously there were more than three hundred temples here. Though some have been ravaged, a large number still survives. There are several temples dedicated to Lord Shiva, some dedicated to the Shakti cult, and there is a Kuteswari temple as well. Other than temples there are quite a large number of hermitages too. At one point of time it was considered to be the ideal abode for mendicants who wanted to pursue a spiritual life. According to folklore, Arjuna in the epic *Mahabharata* had battled against Lord Shiva on this very ground of Uttarkashi. The Varnavat mountain at Uttarkashi still bears traces of the house of lacquer, constructed under the orders of the Kauravas, meant to immolate the five Pandavas and their mother Kunti. In ancient times this place was called Barhaat (*Bar* means twelve and *haat* means small market). Historically the place was very important because Tibetan merchants visited it to trade with their Indian counterparts.

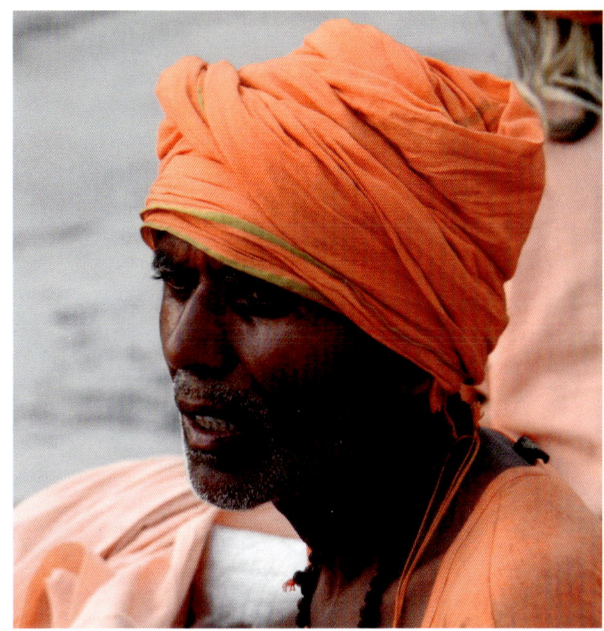

A sadhu waiting by the riverbank at Uttarkashi

A little distance away from Uttarkashi is a place called Ujjli. Large numbers of hermitages have come up here on the bank of the Ganga. The city though has undergone several changes compromising its pristine beauty. Presently it is a densely populated place with a bus stand, schools, colleges, judicial courtrooms and offices. But once you step out of the populated area, you are immediately arrested by the surrounding natural beauty.

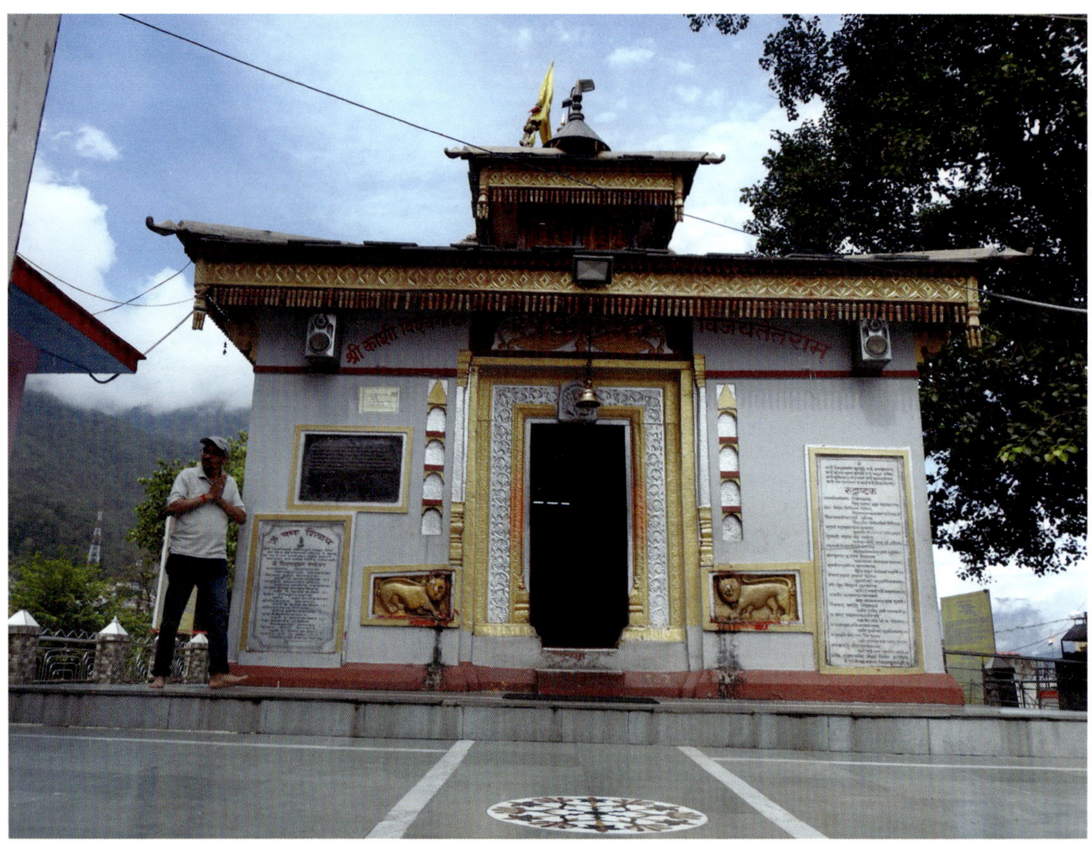

The Viswanath temple at Uttarkashi. This town is also known as the temple town because of its many temples

From a Pilgrim's Diary

Puskhar Rawat's office was a small building located within the marketplace of Uttarkashi. I walked in, one evening, to be heartily received by him. 'I was waiting for you,' he said simply. I looked at this amiable young man in his mid thirties and was taken in by his simplicity. He is a journalist by profession and is presently employed with the newspaper *Dainik Jagran*. He offered me tea from his flask. 'How long will you stay here?' he asked.

'Just for the day. I will have to reach Haridwar tomorrow,' I answered.

'Ok, then let me take you to the Kashi Viswanath temple first. Though Uttarkashi is a small town, there are several temples worth visiting. In fact, previously people used to call this a town of temples,' he remarked.

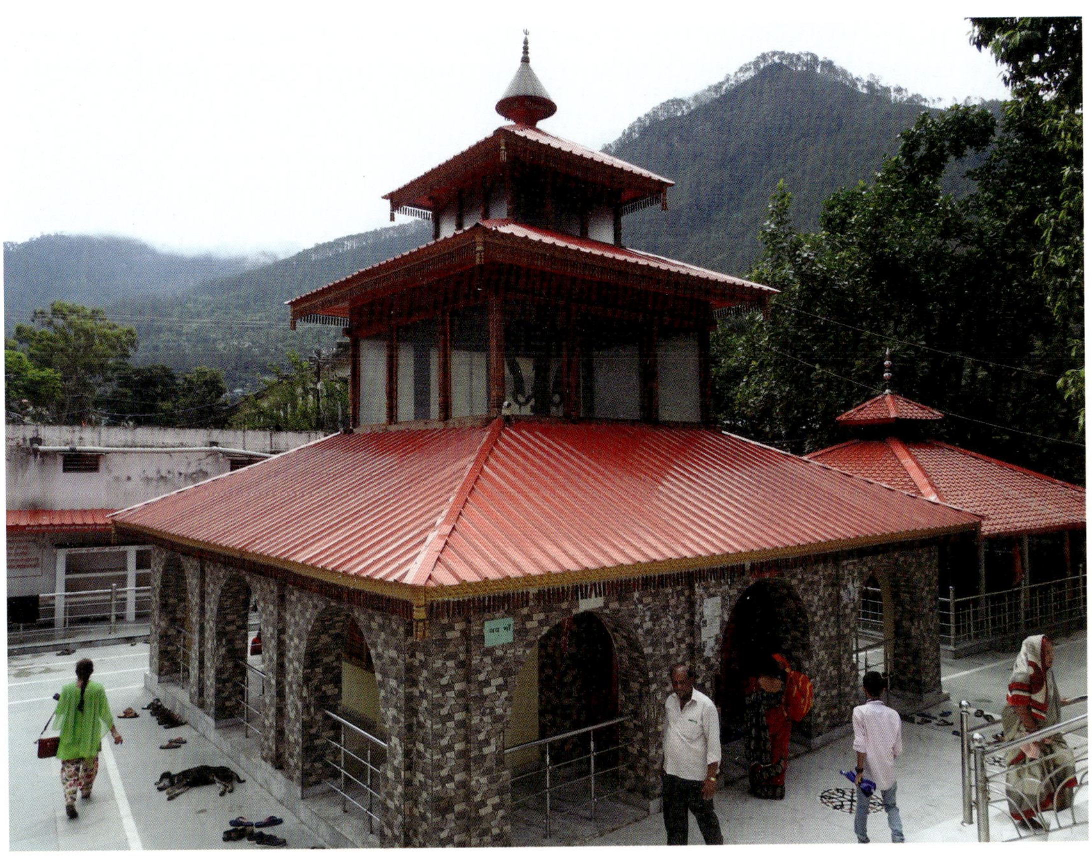

The Shakti temple at Uttarkashi

Both of us walked out of the office, crossed the bazaar and a large playground. The surrounding mountains appeared to me like a necklace adorning the town. A mountain range lay just adjacent to the road we had taken. It is the Varnavat mountain mentioned in the *Mahabharata.* I had read about it. The Kauravas had constructed a lacquer cottage here to burn the Pandavas alive. The cottage is still there. That's how the stories of both our epics, the *Ramayana* and the *Mahabharata,* have intertwined and come down to us.

We reached the Viswanath temple in no time. It is a small temple and not very old. Both of us entered the temple and found a black Shiva Lingam at the centre. Somebody had already been there worshipping the god, for the flowers that were offered lay scattered everywhere. An aged lady sat at a corner meditating. It was evening and slightly dark inside. We sat there for some time soaking in the blissful ambience. After offering our ritual worship to the god we finally left. Right in front of the Viswanath temple stands the Shakti temple. The top of the temple is adorned with a thirty-foot-high trident composed of an alloy of eight metals. According to the existing folklore, Lord Shiva in the guise of a low-caste warrior fought against Arjuna (the famous Pandava of the *Mahabharata*) with this trident. Though old, the trident is clearly rust proof. People consider the trident as ageless as the Shiva Lingam we saw. Amar Singh, a Garhwal army captain, had once tried to remove the trident but despite repeated attempts failed to move even an inch of it. Yet, strangely enough, a bare touch of an innocent child had once set the trident vibrating. People claim to have witnessed this strange happening. I dared not disbelieve the story. Undoubtedly, strange things keep happening around us, for which we have no scientific explanations. This may be something of that sort – who knows.

A few steps away from the temple flows the Ganga. Even though it is neither deep nor very wide here, the speed of the flowing water is considerable. Add to that a constant friction against the submerged rocks and you get a roaring Ganga here. On the other side of the river we found rows of small houses. And behind the human habitation stands a series of mountains covered with dense forest. 'I will be visiting Prabhu-dayalji now. Would you like to come with me?' asked Pushkar.

'Is he a monk?' I asked. 'Not really in the formal sense, but yes in practice he is,' answered Pushkar. Since I wanted to meet Prabhu-dayalji, both of us stepped on to a hanging bridge. I have observed an interesting practice among these people here – they touch the ground before stepping onto a hanging bridge, as if seeking permission from Mother Ganga before stepping on her. I followed Pushkar and touched the ground before stepping onto the bridge. The road we took was along the bank of the river. We came across several small hermitages. After a mile's walk we reached Prabhu-dayalji's residence. It was a small tin thatched structure with a long verandah in front. There was a small flower garden in front of the house. Dressed in immaculate white, the gentleman was sitting on a chair in the verandah. He was bare bodied with a clean-shaven face. He radiated a strange kind of inner peace which instantly arrested my attention. Glancing up at Pushkar he smiled and said, 'Come in, my boy. How are you?'

'Fine. Here is a friend of mine all the way from Kolkata.'

Prabhu-dayalji extended his hand and welcomed me, 'Please come in.'

Then he walked into his room and got two small stools for us. I looked inside his room; it was barely furnished. There was just a cot inside and a few utensils meant for cooking. Other than that there was a small bookcase full of books. His cottage, which closely resembled a hermitage, stood right on the bank of the Ganga. 'How long have you been here?' I asked. 'Four years,' he answered. 'I heard you used to live in Delhi and were well employed. Why did you renounce everything,' I couldn't help asking.

He sat still for some time and then replied, 'True, I was the chief engineer of a large company. I had my wife and children. There was no dearth of money either. My children too were faring well in their studies. Yet, I was not happy with my life. There was a hermitage near my house and a sage lived in it. I would often visit him and listen to his teachings. A few of my acquaintances suggested renunciation of the material world. But I was in a dilemma. Would I be able to adjust to a life of renunciation, I kept wondering? Then one day I renounced everything and walked out of my house. I arrived here and found this cottage. It was occupied by a gentleman who used to be my teacher once. I started living with him and after a time he initiated me. But he did not permit me to become a monk. After having led a busy life in Delhi, I too found it rather difficult to settle down initially. To help me, my teacher would often instruct me to go to the bank of the Ganga and meditate. Gradually I realised I was getting attuned to the ambience of this place. All these years it was my ego that prevented me from enjoying this spiritual bliss and the moment I realised it I experienced a strange kind of detachment from all material objects and pleasures. It was an exhilarating and blissful experience,' he added. 'Aren't you troubled by this loneliness?' I asked perplexed. He smiled at me and said, 'People are constantly afflicted by disturbing noises around them and seem to be unaware of the beauty of quietness. But the beauty of this place is its loneliness. Nature here highlights the universal truth of life. I feel the pulsating presence of the Almighty everywhere. You will be surprised to know that I have spent numerous sleepless nights here looking at the Ganga below and sky full of stars above to comprehend His presence. That's my form of meditation. And when the sun rises with all its golden hue I feel a strange kind of happiness. The sight reminds me of the slokas from the *Rig Veda* –

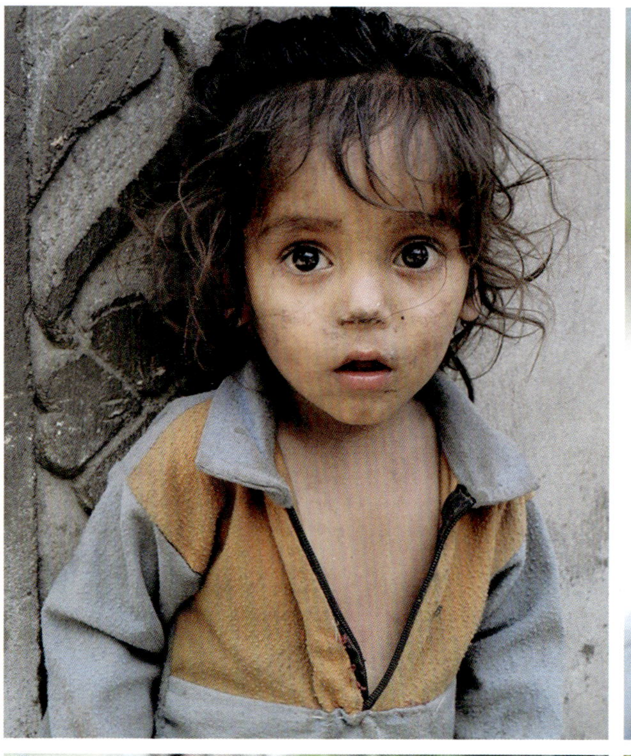

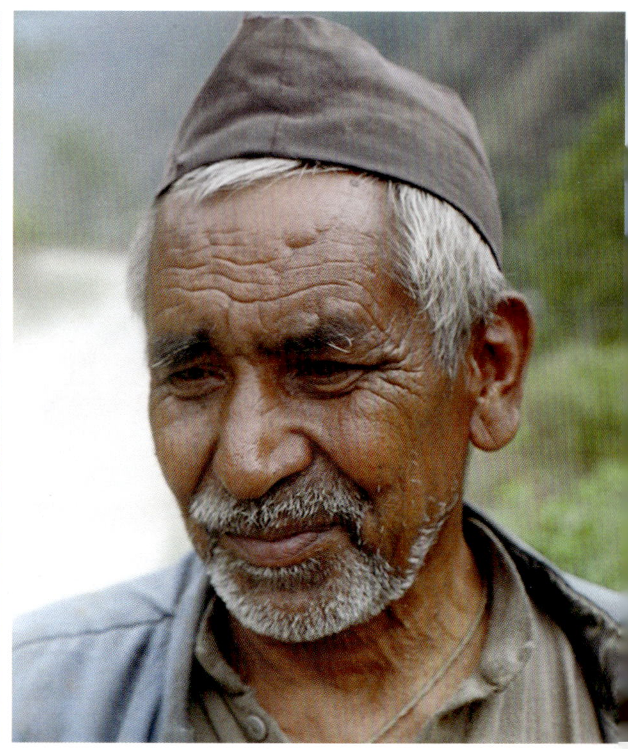

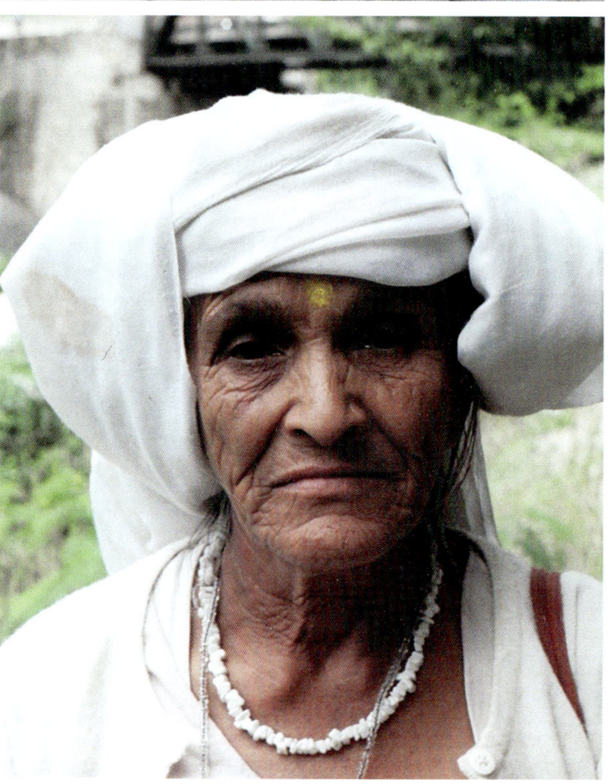

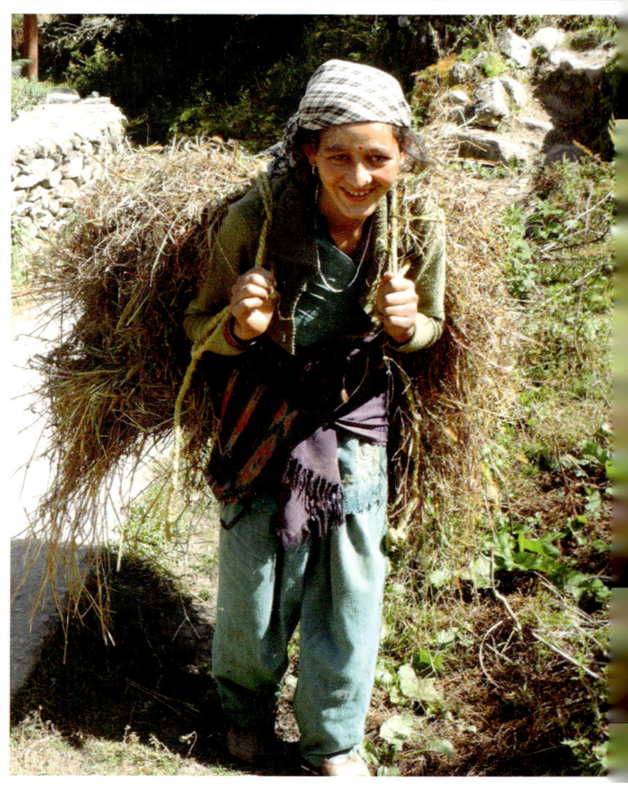

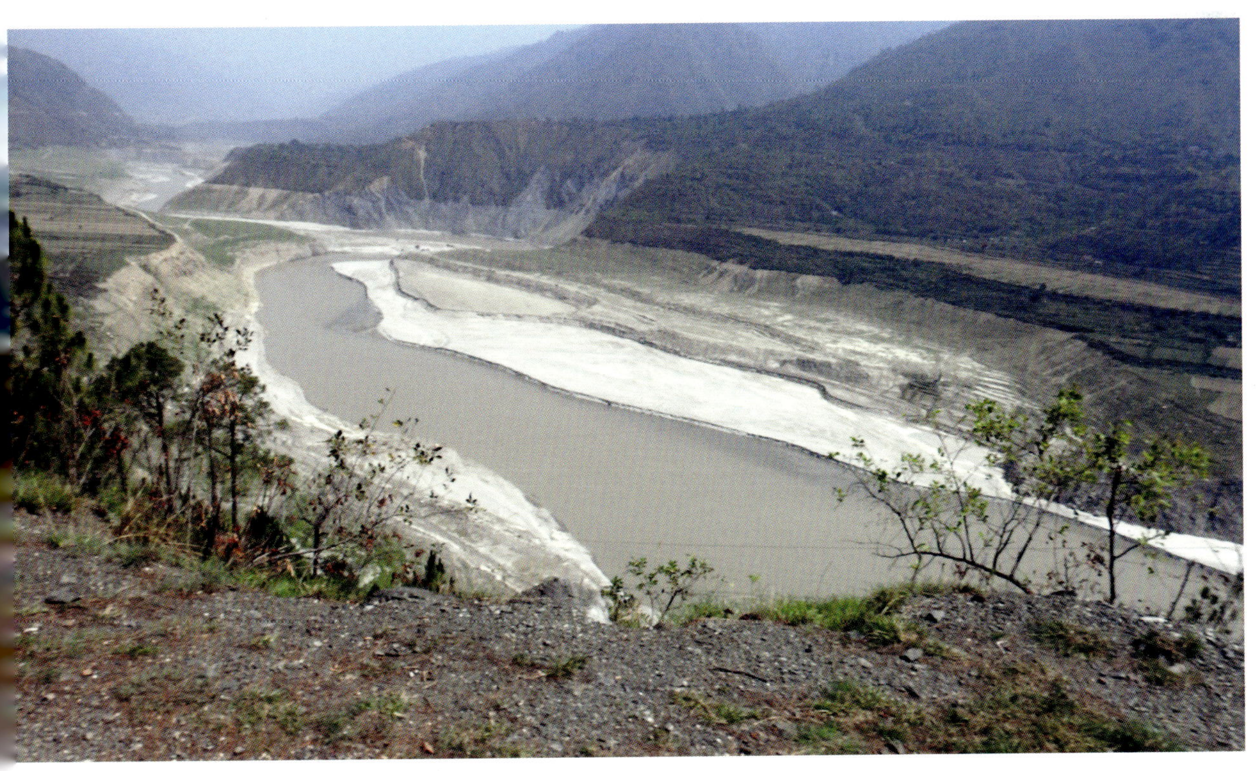

ABOVE: The Ganga near Tehri dam is a lifeless water body bearing no resemblance to the effervescent river

The light is come, amid all lights the fairest; born is brilliance, far-extending brightness.
Night, sent away for Savitar's uprising, hath yielded up a birth-place for the Morning.
The Fair, the Bright is come with her white offspring; to her the Dark One hath resigned her dwelling.
Akin, immortal, following each other, changing their colors both the heavens move onward.
Common, unending is the Sisters' pathway; taught by the Gods, alternately they travel.
Fair formed, of different hues and yet one-minded, Night and Dawn clash not, neither do they travel.
Bright leader of glad sounds, our eyes behold her; splendid in hue she hath unclosed the portals.
She, stirring up the world, hath shown us riches; Dawn hath awakened every living creature.'

(Translation by Ralph T.H. Griffith)

FACING PAGE ABOVE, ABOVE RIGHT AND BELOW LEFT: Different faces of Garhwal
FACING PAGE BELOW RIGHT: A Garhwali woman carrying grass for cattle

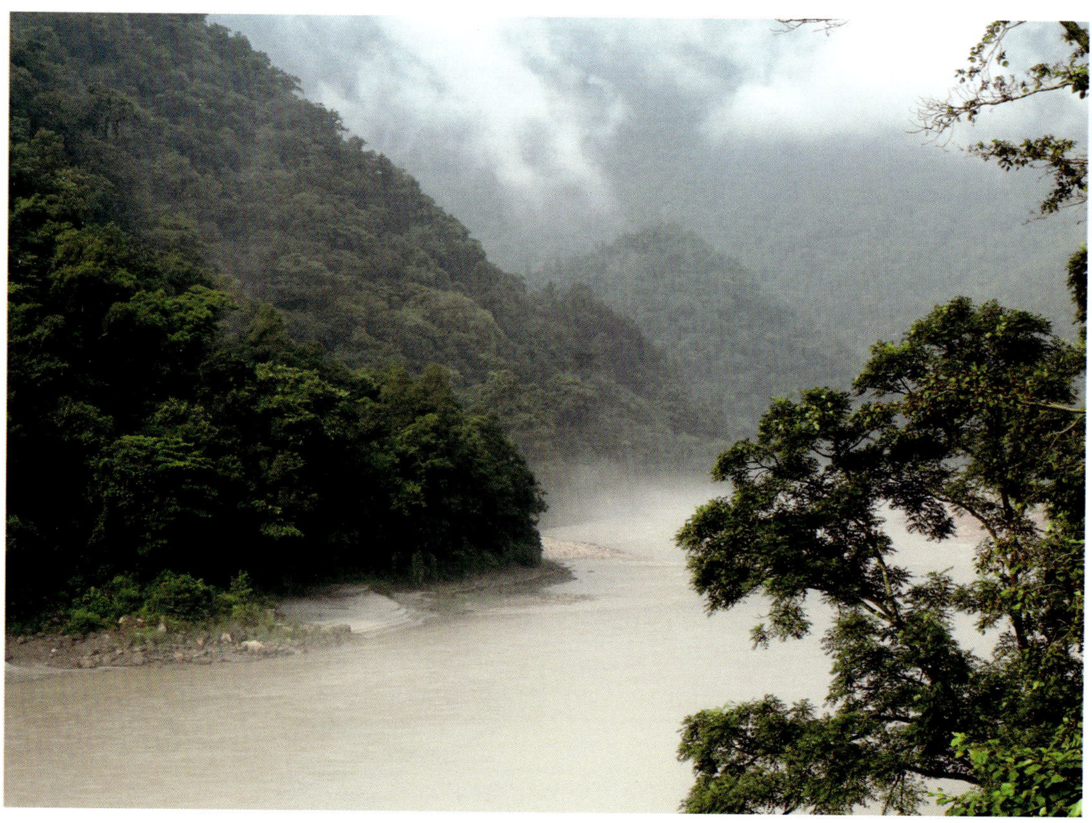

Early morning fog covering the Ganga near Deoprayag

DEOPRAYAG

The confluence of the rivers Ganga and Alakananda is at Deoprayag. Seventy-one kilometres away from Rishikesh, the two rivers merge with one another at Deoprayag. The river that flows down from Gaumukh to Deoprayag is popularly known as the Bhagirathi, but from the confluence onwards the river is known as the Ganga. River Alakananda descends from Badrinath and on reaching Deoprayag loses herself in the ever-flowing and ever-roaring waves of the Ganga. The magnificent sight humbles the beholder. According to old folklores, Sage Devasharma had long practised ascetic rites here, hence the name Deoprayag. Pilgrims down the years have traversed the path of Deoprayag to reach the two most important pilgrimages of India, Badrinath and Kedarnath. A few thousand people live at Deoprayag and a majority of them are practising priests of Badrinath. Religion forms the fulcrum of life for most of the people living here.

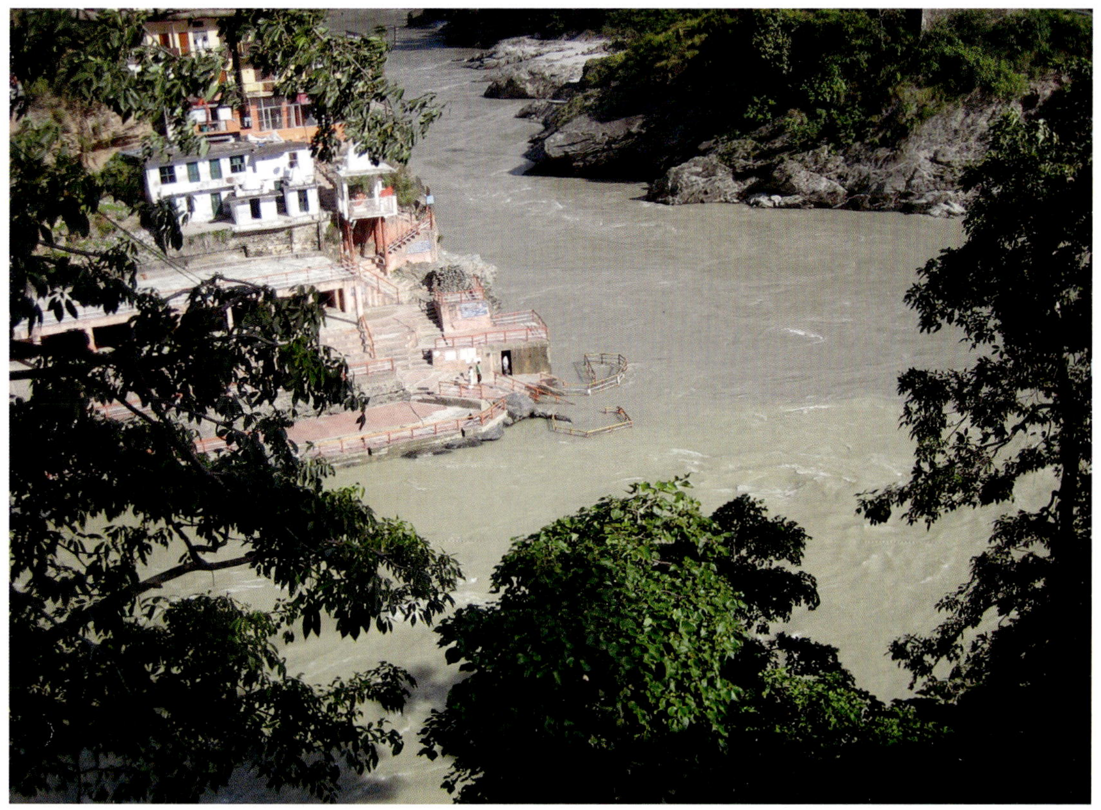

Confluence of the Bhagirathi and the Alakananda at Deoprayag

From a Pilgrim's Diary

A concrete but worn-out staircase with flowers and plants strewn on all sides greeted me when I visited the confluence. Carefully treading the staircase I climbed down to the confluence. There was just a jutting corner of land to stand upon. The sight absolutely mesmerised me. From the right flowed Ganga, swift and ebullient, while on the left was Alakananda. Blue in colour, Alakananda appeared calmer than her elder counterpart. The realisation that she was about to lose her individual identity, merging with the Ganga, may have subdued her a bit.

The merging of two distinctly coloured rivers, ochre and blue, is visible from afar. And the roaring sound of the confluence is audible throughout the place. A stretch has been cordoned off with iron railings, within the confluence itself, for bathers. A strong iron chain is attached to the iron railing for the bathers' safety. A little bit of carelessness might prove hazardous for them, hence these safety measures.

It was a serene afternoon with nobody around at the wharf. I looked up at the sun peeping out over the mountain tops. A monk dressed in a black-coloured robe sat meditating on the courtyard of the nearby Raghunathji temple. The temple stood far above the confluence. It was a small unassuming building with a boundary wall and a small wooden door, leading to the courtyard. A statue of Garuda stood in the courtyard of the temple. In the sanctum sanctorum was the stone idol of Raghunathji, black in colour, with a bow and arrow in his hand. To his left stood his wife Sita Devi while to his right stood his brother Lakshman. I looked inside and found a priest worshipping the idol. A low-powered bulb hung above, heightening the mystic ambience. The moment I stood before Raghunathji and paid my obeisance, the priest came forward and marked my forehead with vermilion.

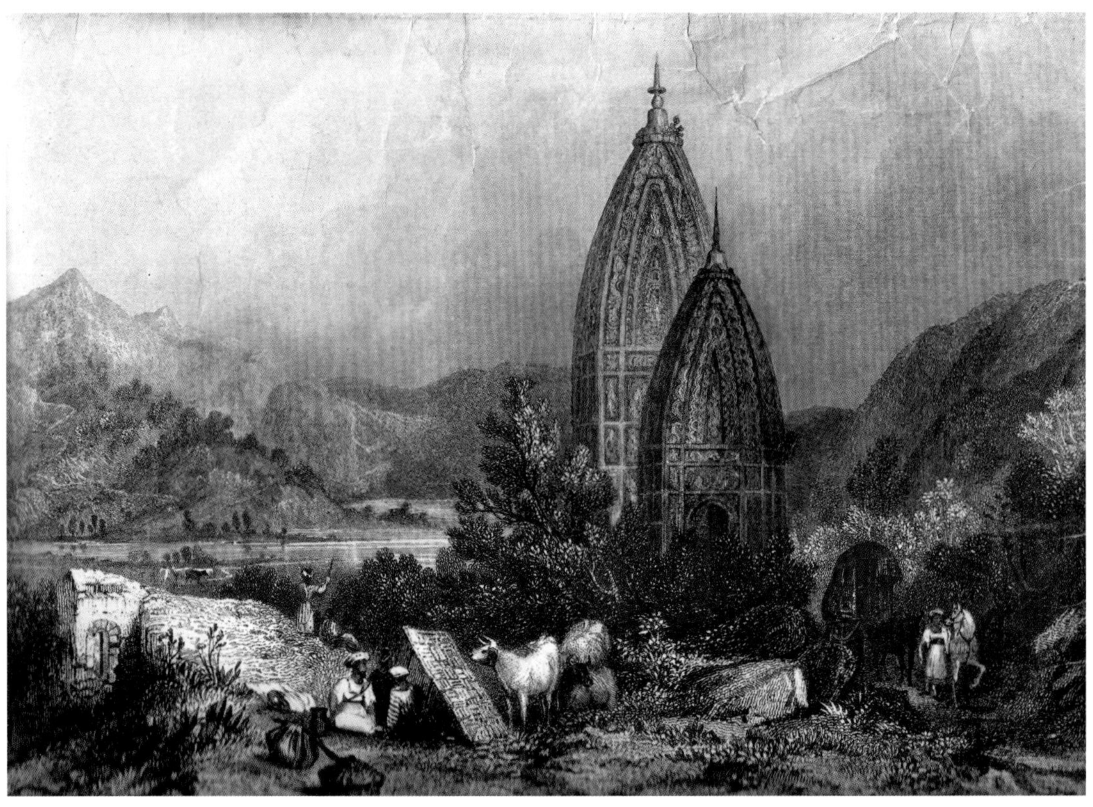

Temples of Mahadeo, in the Shivalic Mountains. Drawn by T.C. Dibden from a sketch by T. Bacon

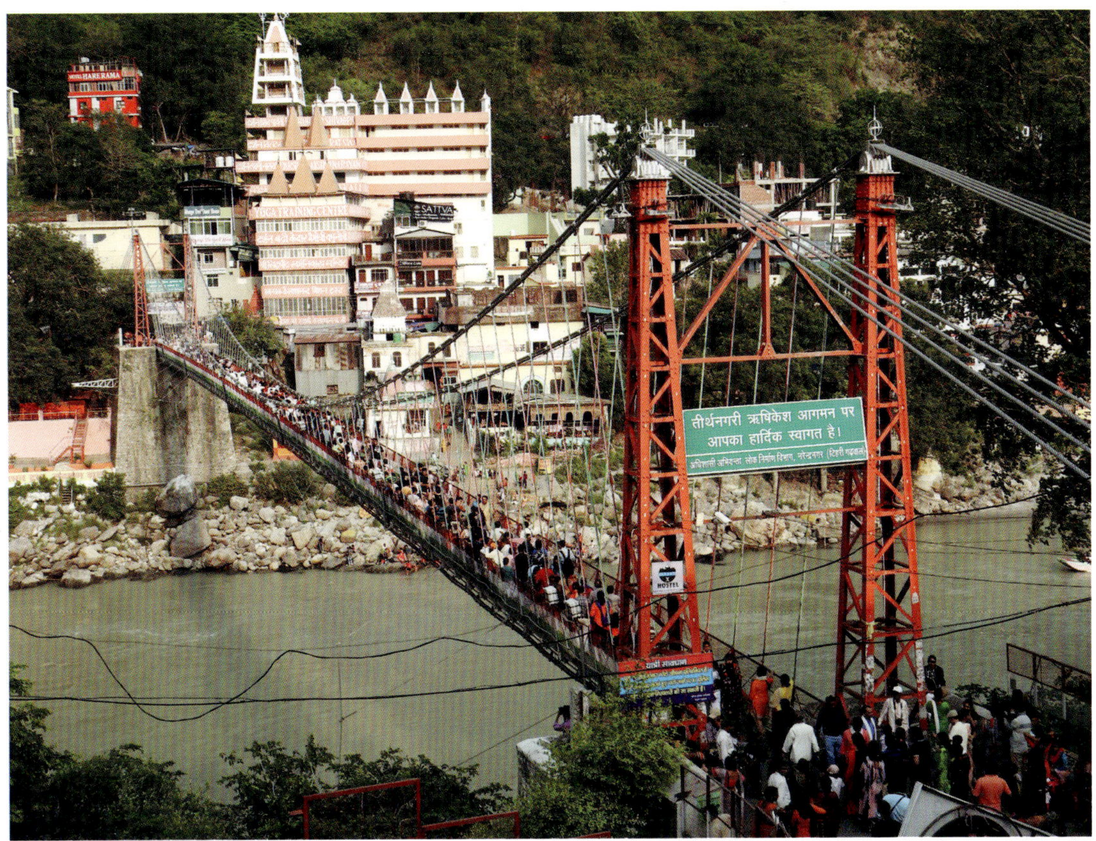

The Lakshman Jhula footbridge over the Ganga is an iconic landmark at Rishikesh

RISHIKESH

The Ganga follows a mountainous route from Deoprayag to reach Rishikesh. Situated on the foothills of the Himalayas, it is considered to be a holy land by the Hindus. According to the *Purana*s, Sage Raibhya had meditated here for a long time. Negating all forms of sensual pleasures he had pursued this spiritual path of appeasing Lord Vishnu. Finally, pleased by his perseverance, Lord Vishnu had granted him a boon. 'You will be considered the greatest of the sages,' Lord Vishnu had said. 'And this place will be named after you. This place will be considered the holiest of holy pilgrimages henceforth.' *Hrishik* means sense and *Ish* means master. The words joined together stand for 'master of the senses'. Lord Vishnu, the presiding god of the senses, therefore prevails here. Sage Raibhya had conquered the calls of his senses and received a boon from Lord Vishnu. Hence the place is named Rishikesh or Hrishikesh.

According to *Baraha Purana,* Sage Devadutta had come to Rishikesh. Mesmerised by the surrounding natural

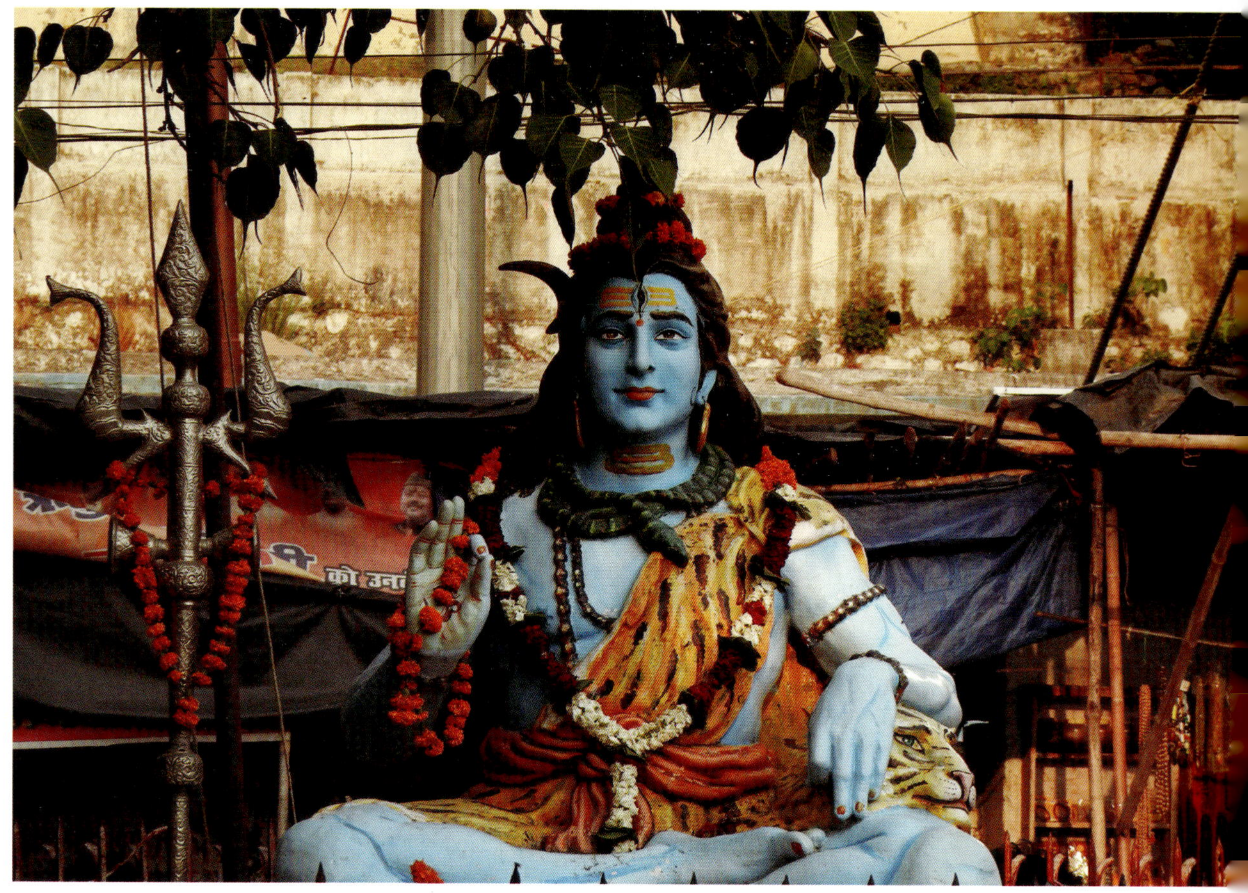

Shiva sitting in benediction, Rishikesh

beauty, he decided to live here in a small cottage and meditate for salvation. Lord Indra, terrified by the seriousness of his prayers, sent a heavenly courtesan to divert him. Allured by the beauty of the lady, the sage stopped praying, gave up ascetic practices and fathered a daughter called Ruru. But Ruru, instead of following the usual path of a human being, decided to complete the course her father had opted for prior to her birth. She started her prayers for salvation. Pleased by her dedication and perseverance, Lord Shiva appeared before her and said, 'What is it you want, my child?' Ruru, who by then had conquered all worldly longings, asked him to bless the land and assist all sages who would visit the place in future, seeking salvation. Lord Shiva blessed her and said, 'Your wish will be fulfilled.' Since then Rishikesh has been considered to be the holy land for all sages aspiring for salvation.

Geographically Rishikesh is an interesting place. The Ganga first touches plain land

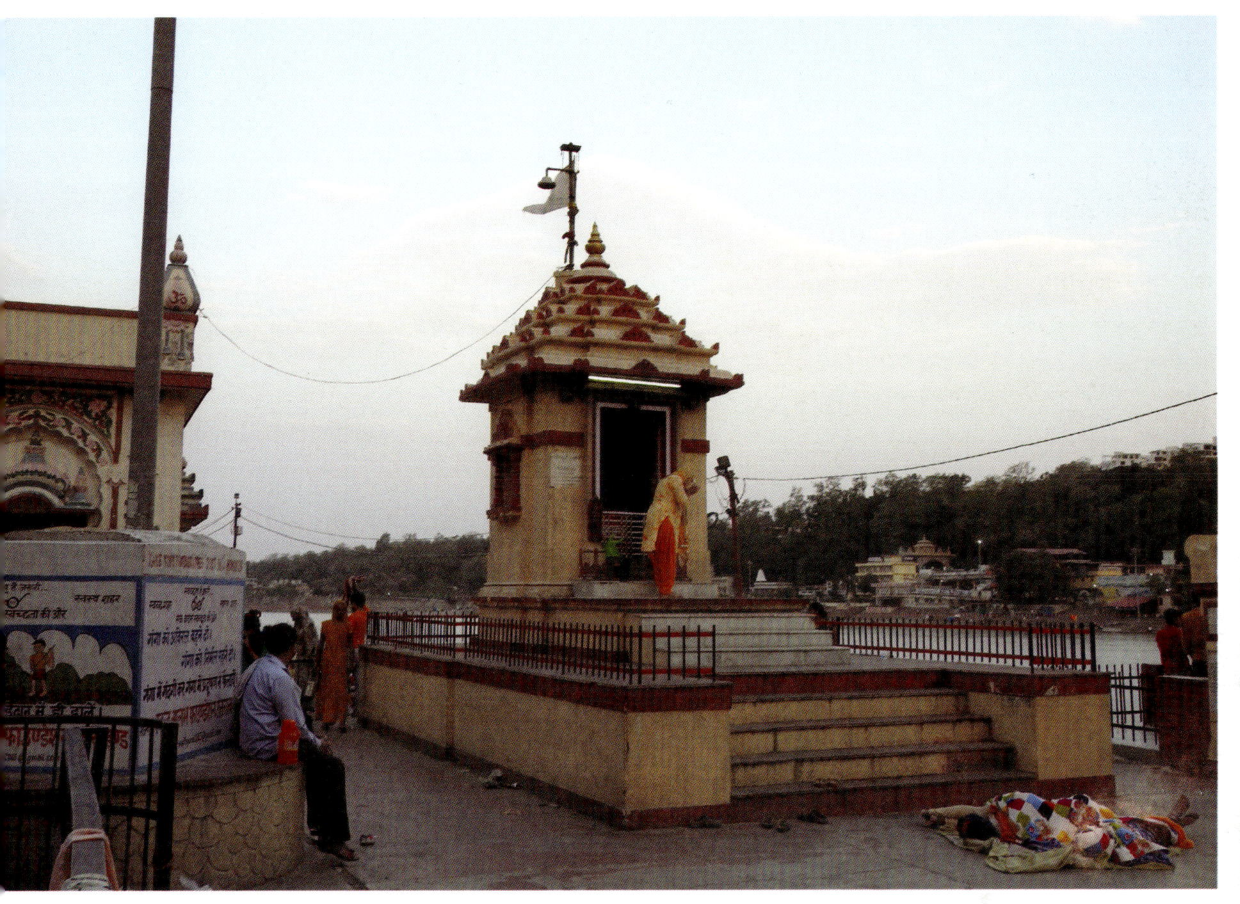

Shiva temple near Ram Jhula, Rishikesh

here even though it is still above the sea level. In the *Mahabharata* the Pandavas visited Rishikesh after their lengthy battle with the Kauravas. After winning the epic battle, the Pandavas came here for a holy dip, to cleanse their sins incurred during the battle. They also offered prayers here to their departed ancestors.

Right from the days of the *Mahabharata,* Indians visit Rishikesh, on their journey to the other Himalayan pilgrimages. In the *Purana*s this place is referred to as heaven, while Kalidasa, the classical Sanskrit poet, terms it a dreamland. At present people call it Garhwal. From here begins the journey to four important Himalayan pilgrimages – Kedarnath, Badrinath, Yamunotri and Gangotri. It is said that even Lord Rama and his brother Lakshman had visited Rishikesh. Numerous sages have visited this land of peace and tranquility.

Unlike Haridwar, Rishikesh is not a congested pilgrimage. Neither has modernity been able to tamper with its

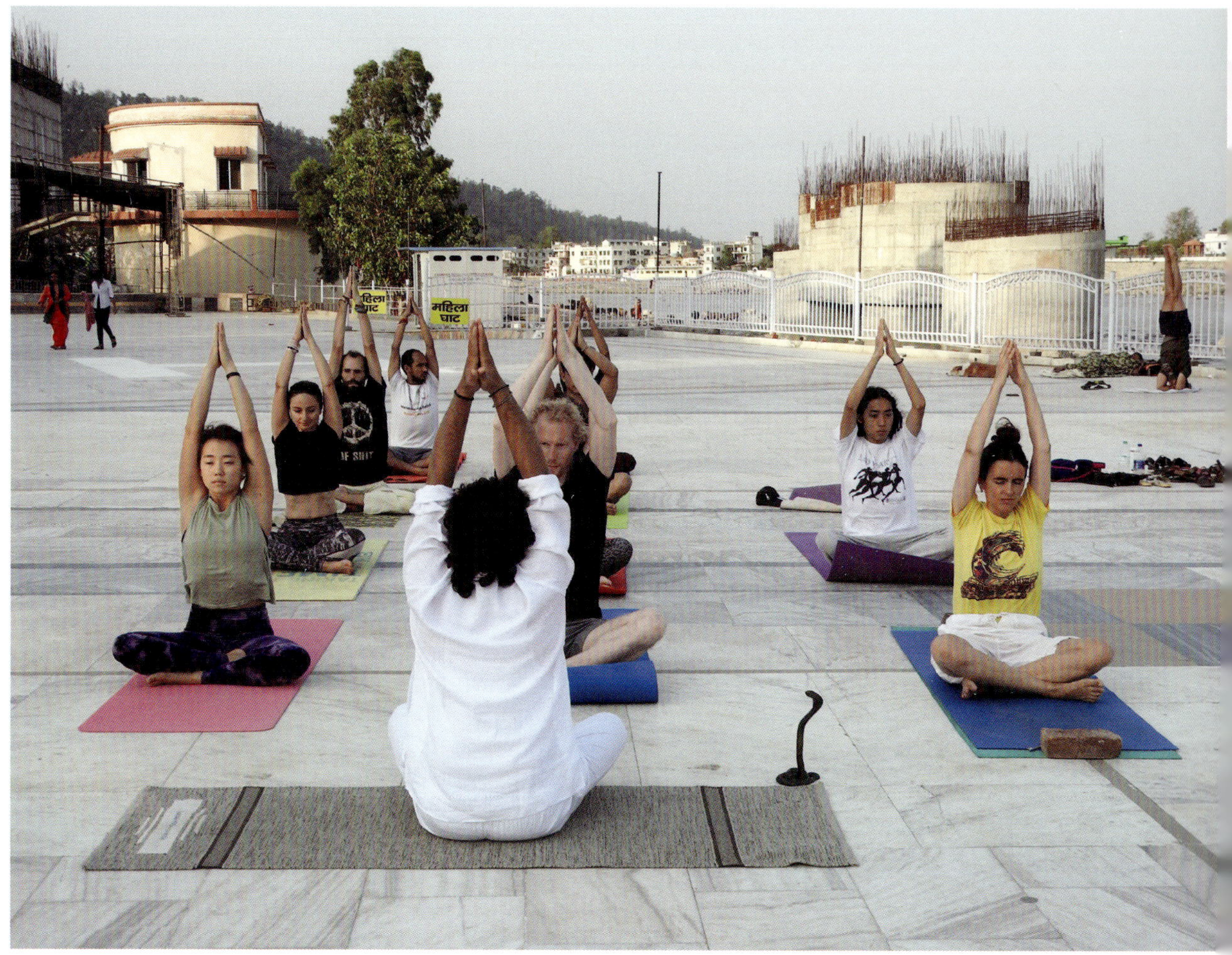

Yoga is a major tourist attraction in Rishikesh

natural topography. One can still feel the pulsating presence of spirituality all around.

There are several old and new temples and small hermitages scattered round Rishikesh. However, one has to cross Ram Jhula, the hanging bridge, to view these hermitages. The water remains transparent throughout the year except during monsoon. Other than being the primary pilgrimage site, Rishikesh is renowned as a centre for learning yoga and meditation. It is acclaimed as the best yoga centre both in India and abroad. People interested in yoga flock here round the year. In 1968, Maharshi Mahesh Yogi's hermitage was visited by the famous Beatles. John Lennon composed his famous 'The Happy Rishikesh Song' here.

All you need to do is say this little word
I know it sounds absurd but it's true

The magic in the mantra will give you the answer
And swallow this that's all you gotta do

Everything you need is here
And everything that's not here is not there
And if there's something missing in this God-
Almighty plan
Could it be you need a woman?

All you need to do is say this little word
I know it sounds absurd but it's true

The magic in the mantra will give you the answer
Just swallow this that's all you gotta do

Everything you need is here
But everything that's not here is not there
And if there's something missing in this God-
Almighty plan
Could it be you need a woman?

Well all you need to do is say this little word
I know it sounds absurd but it's true

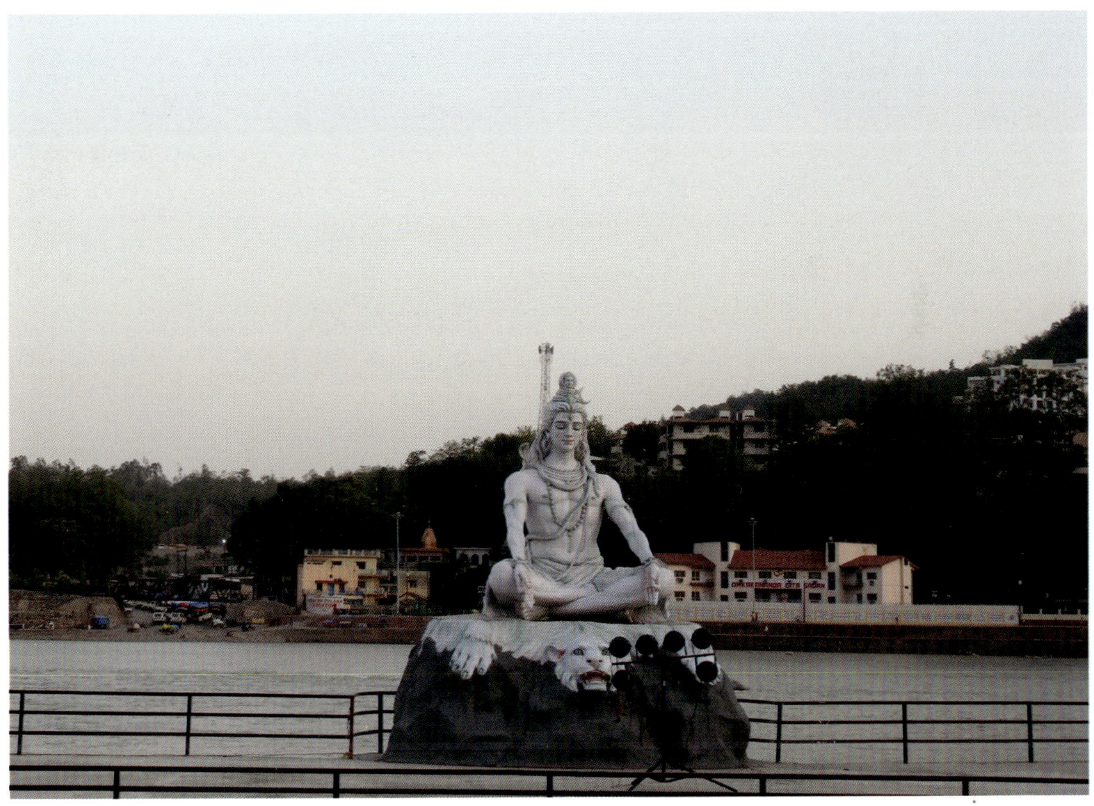

Statue of Shiva in the middle of the Ganga at Rishikesh

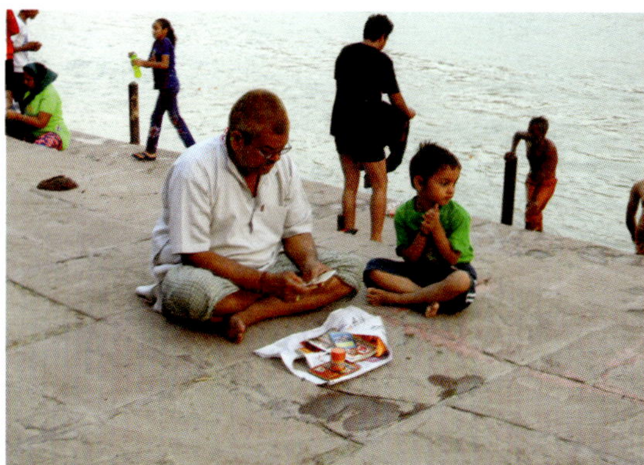

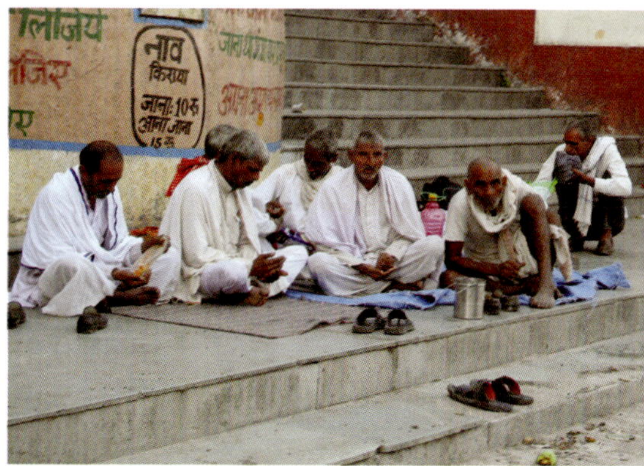

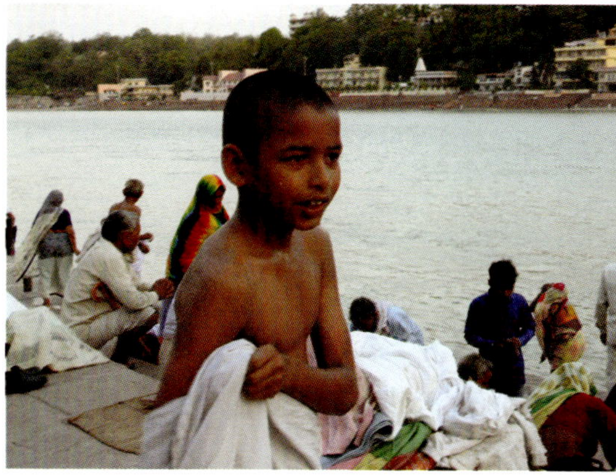

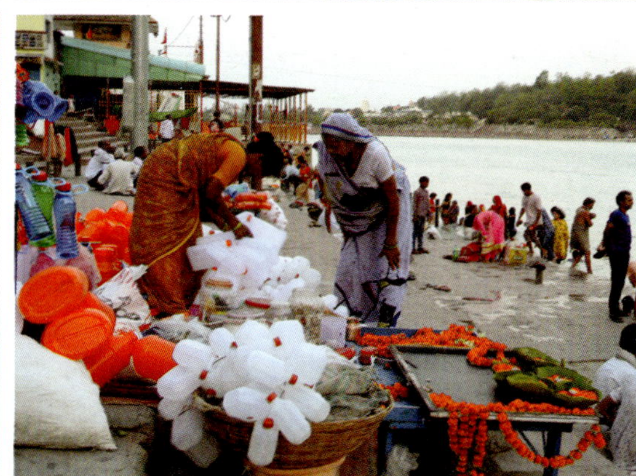

TOP LEFT: Grandfather reading holy books to his inattentive grandchild
TOP RIGHT: Old men chatting at the ghat
ABOVE LEFT: A child changing his clothes after bathing in the Ganga
ABOVE RIGHT: A woman selling water pots for carrying Ganga water

The magic in the mantra will give you the answer
And swallow this that's all you gotta do
Take three times a day after every meal

All you need to do is say this little word
I know it sounds absurd but it's true
The magic in the mantra will give you the answer
And swallow this that's all you gotta do

The place straddles both the ancient and the modern world.

From a Pilgrim's Diary

One evening while walking down Ram Jhula I met a Mataji (female ascetic known as sannyasini) who narrated an extraordinary tale to me. It was a bright evening and I was happily walking on when it started drizzling. I walked on hurriedly trying to avoid the rain. But after a few minutes I realised I had taken the wrong route. Undecided I stood still for a second when the fluttering of a little flag caught my attention. It was flying atop a little cottage. I knew a sannyasini used to live there. So I walked up to it and called out for help. Mataji, dressed in a red robe, with a vermilion mark on her forehead, came out.

'Sorry, Mother, I have forgotten my way to the hotel and have arrived here instead,' I apologised. By then it was raining profusely and I could not turn back. Mataji smiled and asked me to come inside. It was a small barely furnished room with a cot and a few pictures of different deities. She laid a piece of cloth on the floor and invited me to sit. Then we started conversing. After a few words, I realised the depth of scholarship hidden behind this simple get-up. She spoke at length about the origin of the Ganga. Unable to stop myself I asked her, 'Mother, do you really believe in the folklore that the Ganga was brought down to earth by a single human being – Bhagirath?' 'Of course not,' she replied. 'Then how did this story come about?' I persisted. She narrated an interesting tale from the Indus Valley civilisation. 'The people living in the Indus Valley were highly advanced,' she asserted. 'They built beautiful houses, constructed

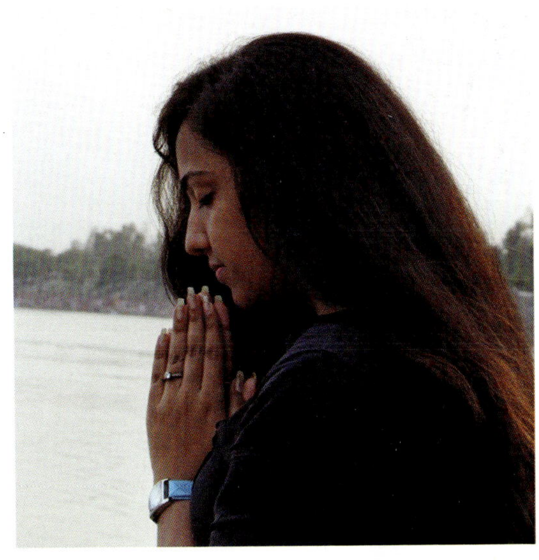

A young girl reciting her prayers on the bank of the river

roads and were highly educated. They could write as well. They could also sing, cultivate, trade with other countries, and were adept in sculpting figures. They were pantheists worshipping different deities. To put it simply, they lived a happy life. But things turned ghastly after a time. Barbaric tribes from the western part of their domain attacked this peace-loving tribe and defeated them. The remaining few left their land and started wandering about. Some of them reached the banks of river Sarasvati.'

'Mother, did river Sarasvati really exist?' I asked in awe. 'Yes,' she replied. 'It originated from the Himalayas and flowed down to Rajasthan, Gujarat and finally merged with the Arabian Sea. The inhabitants of Indus

The waterfront at night, Rishikesh

Valley settled down on the banks of this river. Being wanderers they were utterly helpless. All they could do was appeal to their gods repeatedly: "O Almighty, shower your blessings upon us. Give us wealth, fortune, land, moveable assets and also protect us by destroying our enemies." Their repeated chanting finally took a finite shape in the form of the four Vedas (the Vedic literature) – the *Rig Veda*, the *Sama Veda*, the *Yajur Veda* and finally the *Atharva Veda*.'

'But, mother,' I interrupted, 'our history books tell us that the Aryans who came to India were the original creators of the Vedas.' She shook her head and said, 'The foreigners deliberately propagate such false stories. The barbaric half-civilised invaders, who knew only to kill, destroy and plunder could never compose such divine scriptures. Surely they neither had the requisite poetic skills nor the philosophic bent of mind to compose scriptures such as these. It was our ancient forefathers who composed the four Vedas. So the inhabitants of the Indus Valley settled on the banks of river Sarasvati and once again developed their surroundings. They built houses, cultivated lands and gradually villages and cities came into existence. But nature had her way. Gradually river Sarasvati dried up leaving the banks high and dry. Large areas suddenly became deserts. Unable to bear the hardships these men again wandered off. This time they moved eastward. Finally they arrived on the bank of a small river with crystal clear water surrounded by extremely fertile lands. Large trees provided them shade and shelter. This was the place for them. Again a new

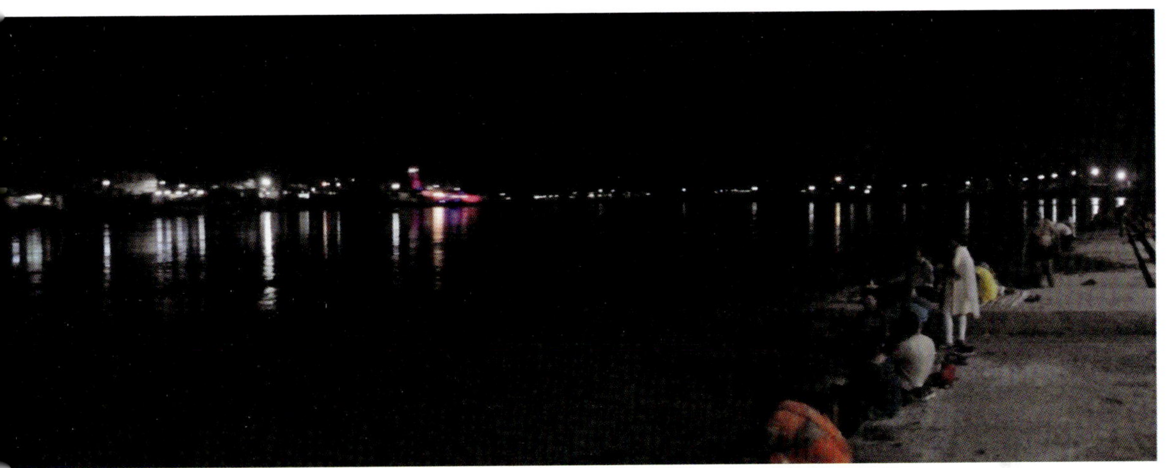

civilisation grew up on the bank of this river. It flourished for quite some time, till men started leading sinful lives. Go[illegible]sness, aberrations and all kinds of sins incurred the wrath of the gods they worshipped. The gods cursed them and once again nature refused to bestow further bounties on them. The scorching sun burnt their plants; the trees died and even the river water turned stale, unfit for drinking. Men and domestic animals cried for water but there was not a drop of pure water anywhere. Then one man in the tribe gave them hope. "There is a large reservoir full of pure water on the foothills of the Himalayas," he assured them. "It descends directly from heaven and is well protected from all sides. If we could only release the water and make it flow towards the plains we shall be saved," he informed.

'Immediately a few among them left and reached the reservoir in no time. The reservoir was large indeed, but was well protected by mountain ranges on all sides. They did not know how to demolish those barriers so they returned home disheartened. A fresh team went forth, but they too returned empty-handed. What could they do other than wait for inevitable death? A senior member suggested, "Let's move away from here. Maybe a new place is waiting for us." "Yes, let's move forward," they cried in unison. It was then that a young man stepped forward. He was called Bhagirath. "How long do we fret about like this?" he asked the rest of the members of his tribe. "What about our old members who are unable to walk?" "Yes, what about them?" they questioned back. "What do we do?" Bhagirath assured them, "I promise to release the water of the reservoir and bring it here. But how many amongst you are willing to accompany me in this venture?" Nobody came forward other than his girlfriend Ganga.

'They travelled for days and reached the reservoir. The sky-scraping mountain ranges did not scare them. On the contrary it increased Bhagirath's determination. "I will certainly release the water and make it flow towards our land. I will detect the weakest point in these mountains and work on it. The water will then revive our barren lands and generate life." Both of them worked day and night to find the weakest point which they could penetrate. It was a tough going. The scorching sun burnt them during the day, while the severe chill froze them at night. They had no food and starved for days together. Yet, they went on searching. Then one day Bhagirath noticed a small crack in between two mountains. He knew he had to work on it and widen the crack to release the water. Single-handedly he started crushing the stone walls. It was an impossible mission. Ganga, unable to bear the sight, came forward to assist him. Then the day arrived when they heard the loud roaring sound of water approaching them. They employed their last bit of strength to break the wall and out flowed the water. Bhagirath being more alert stayed away from the flowing water but poor Ganga could not save herself. Her frail frame was carried away by the gushing water. The water gradually revived the dry barren lands but Bhagirath was inconsolable. A wandering minstrel came to Bhagirath and tried to stem his sorrow. "Why lament, my child? Seek Ganga in this flowing water. Both of you have achieved the impossible and revived the dying land of yours. So cheer up. Remember both your names will remain engraved in the hearts of men till eternity. Sages will sing your praise and even epics will be written eulogising your deed."'

The story transported me to a different world and only after a while did I realise that Mataji had fallen silent. It was already dark and I stood up to leave. Mataji lit a lamp to lessen the encircling darkness. But before I left I had just one question for her. 'Mother, how did you come upon this story?' She remained silent for a while and then replied, 'I read it in a handwritten manuscript. The author is unknown to me. Maybe he too was as great a poet as Rishi Valmiki. Who knows?'

HARIDWAR

Indians consider Haridwar to be the greatest of all pilgrimages. Even though numerous deities like Lord Shiva, Mother Durga, Lord Vishnu and Mother Manasha

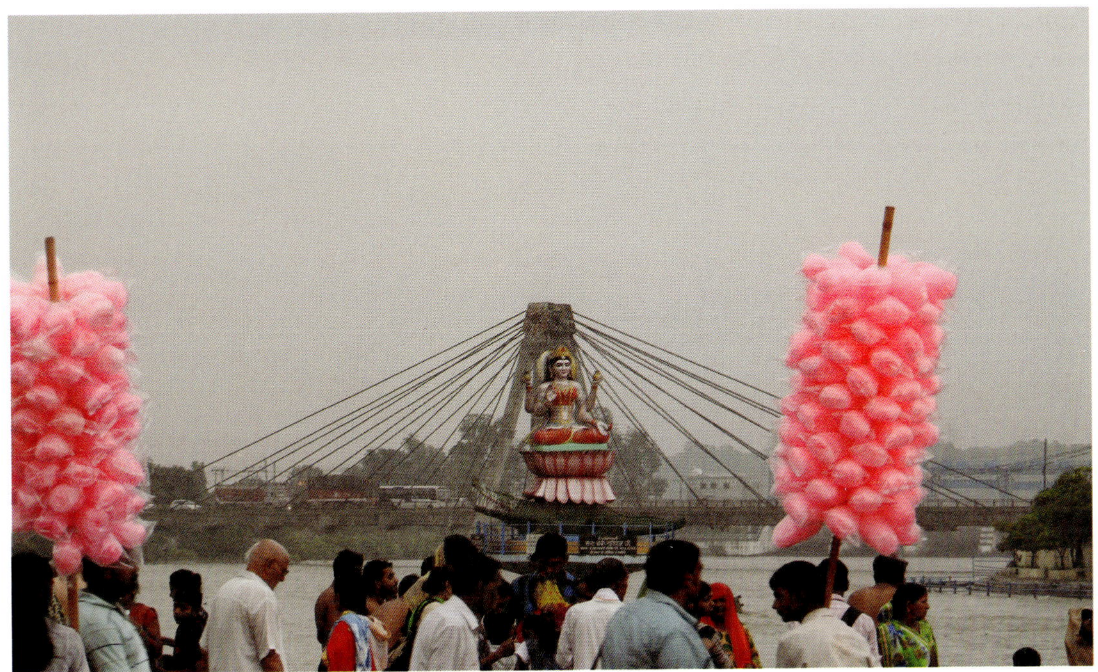

Ganga statue in the middle of the river near Har-Ki-Pauri

are worshipped here, the quintessence of Haridwar is the Ganga and its holy water. The Ganga has found its way to Haridwar from the Himalayas via Rishikesh. Lord Brahma had practised asceticism on the banks of Haridwar; hence, this is considered the most important pilgrimage out of the seven primary pilgrimages of India. The general belief is that both Lord Shiva and Lord Vishnu prevail here at Haridwar. The nerve centre of Haridwar is Har-Ki-Pauri – a wharf for people to bathe at. The shape of Ganga in Haridwar is like a half moon. The renowned Brahmakund, believed to be a replica of Lord Vishnu's footstep, is situated in Haridwar. Down the ages Indians have believed that a dip in the Ganga cleanses men of all mortal sins and Haridwar provides the window to this cleansing. The doctrine seems to have been derived from the Vaishnava philosophy.

From the second to fourth century CE Haridwar was believed to be the gateway to heaven. Even in the *Purana*s, especially in *Padma Purana*, Haridwar is referred to as gateway to heaven. Yet Haridwar finds no mention in the history of the middle ages in India. The first reference to Haridwar as the

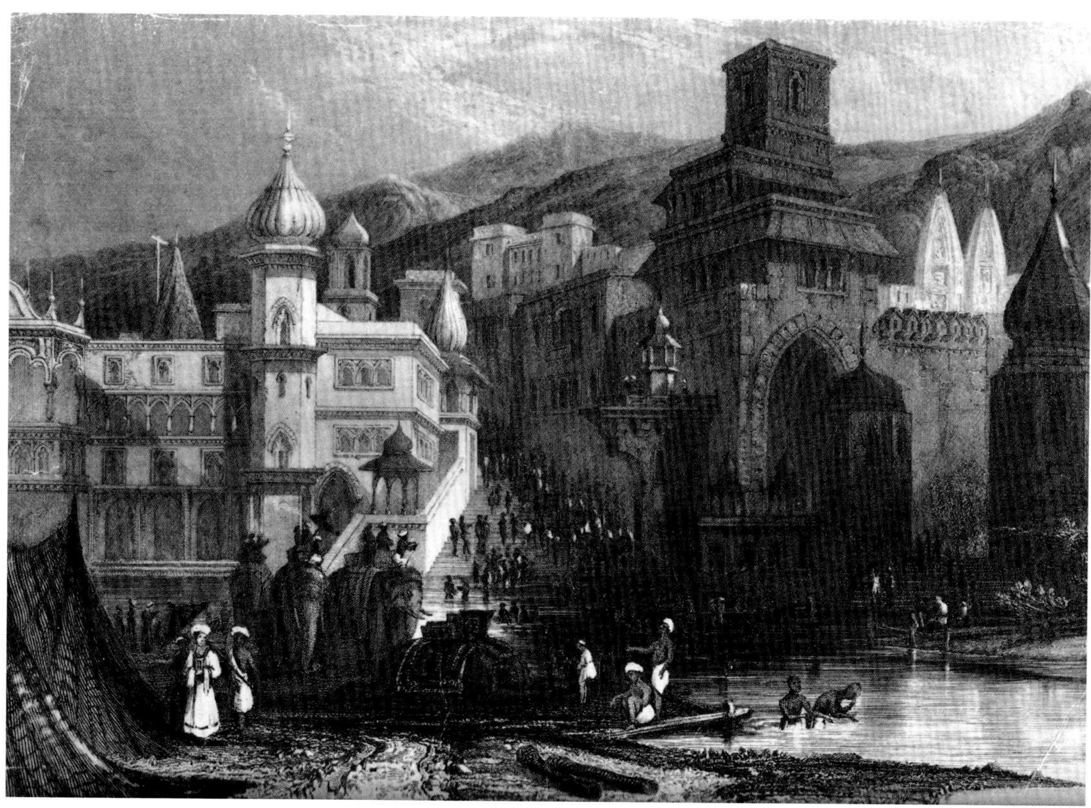

The ghat of Hardwar (1850) drawn by T.C. Dibden

gateway to heaven was found in the ninth-century history written by King Bayook. According to King Bayook, Pratihaar, king of the Gurjar tribe, abdicated his crown to his son and went off to practise asceticism in Haridwar. In Indian history Haridwar has first been mentioned by the Chinese traveller Xuanzang. He came to India 1400 years ago and observed that, 'River Ganga is widest in Haridwar. It flows south-eastwards with tremendous speed. Huge fish-like creatures keep swimming in the fast-flowing river without harming human beings. People here believe that all mortal sins can be cleansed by bathing in the Ganga.' Noted historian Atabi, who had accompanied Mahmud of Ghazni, observed that, 'Indians come to Haridwar to worship the mouth of a cow. They scatter the ashes of cremated people in the water of the Ganga. They also renounce their hair on the bank of the river and turn bald. To the Hindus, Haridwar is as holy as Mecca is to the Muslims.' Traveller Alberuni too had similar observations about Haridwar.

Ironically, when Taimur Lang invaded India, his entry point was the bank of the Ganga in Haridwar. He killed numerous men, women and children within a span of twenty-four hours and then washed his sword in the holy water of the Ganga before saying his evening prayers. During the Mughal rule Haridwar was a district. On its banks stood a fort built by a Rajput king. Emperor Akbar's minister Abu'l Fazl in his *Ain-i-Akbari* mentioned Haridwar and said that most of the people of Haridwar live in a place called Bhogpur. Akbar himself regularly consumed water obtained from Brahmakund. Water was procured for him in large sealed pots from Haridwar and then sent straightaway to Delhi. He carried this water wherever he went. Raja Man Singh had set up a temporary shed on the bank of the Ganga in Haridwar to serve water to the thirsty people. In 1608 during the rule of Emperor Jahangir, an English traveller, Tom Carriet, visited Haridwar to attend the Kumbh Mela. It was supposedly attended by 40,000 people.

It is believed that the present wharfs that exist in Haridwar were constructed by Raja Man Singh. The oldest temple of Haridwar is the Ganga temple. It is said that it was built by Man Singh, though there is no historical record to authenticate the claim.

Near Haridwar is the Sapta Sarovar – seven lakes – a hermitage of Seven Sages. The seven sages who practised asceticism here were – Kashyap, Vashishth, Atri, Viswamitra, Bharadwaj, Gautam and Jamadagni. It is believed, in order to help them practise asceticism undisturbed, Ganga split herself into seven parts. Tranquility still prevails here. The water too is crystal clear. There is a bird sanctuary on the other side which too is very quiet and peaceful, unlike the cacophony of Har-Ki-Pauri. The dawn breaks every day with the sound of monks chanting Vedic slokas.

In the *Mahabharata* we find a reference to this hermitage. King Dhritarashtra spent his final days here with his queen, Gandhari. He would routinely bathe in the Ganga and then conclude his daily worship of the deities. Both of them died here at this hermitage. Presently several hermitages have come up around Sapta Sarovar, yet the prevailing tranquility has not been lost. Haridwar is now a cosmopolitan city but the bank of the Ganga continues to serve as a living continuity of Indian belief in the holiness of both Haridwar and the Ganga.

Haridwar, a Hundred Years Ago

Thomas Daniell's painting of old Haridwar on page 112 is unrecognisable now. The

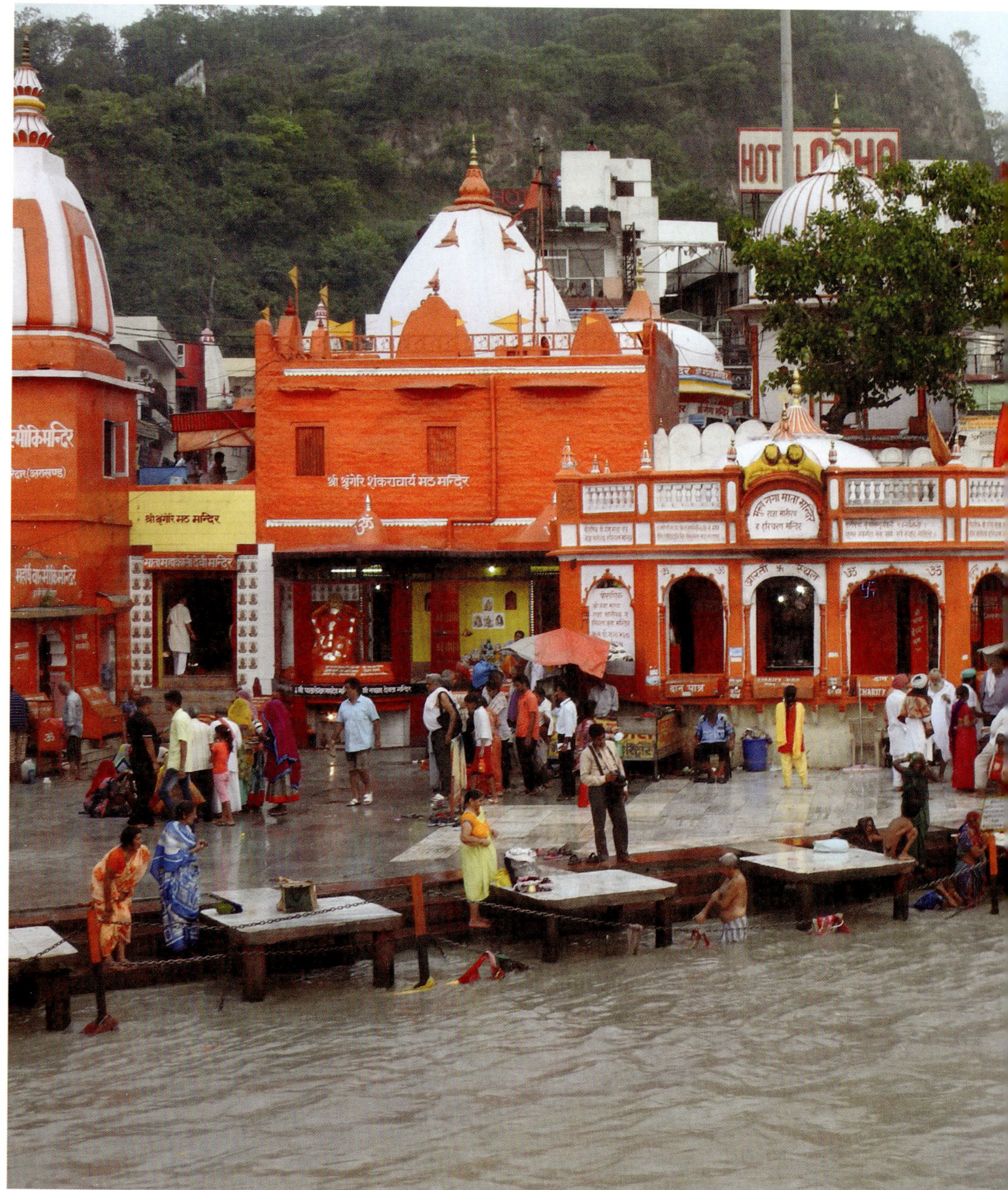
श्री श्रृंगेरि शंकराचार्य मठ मन्दिर

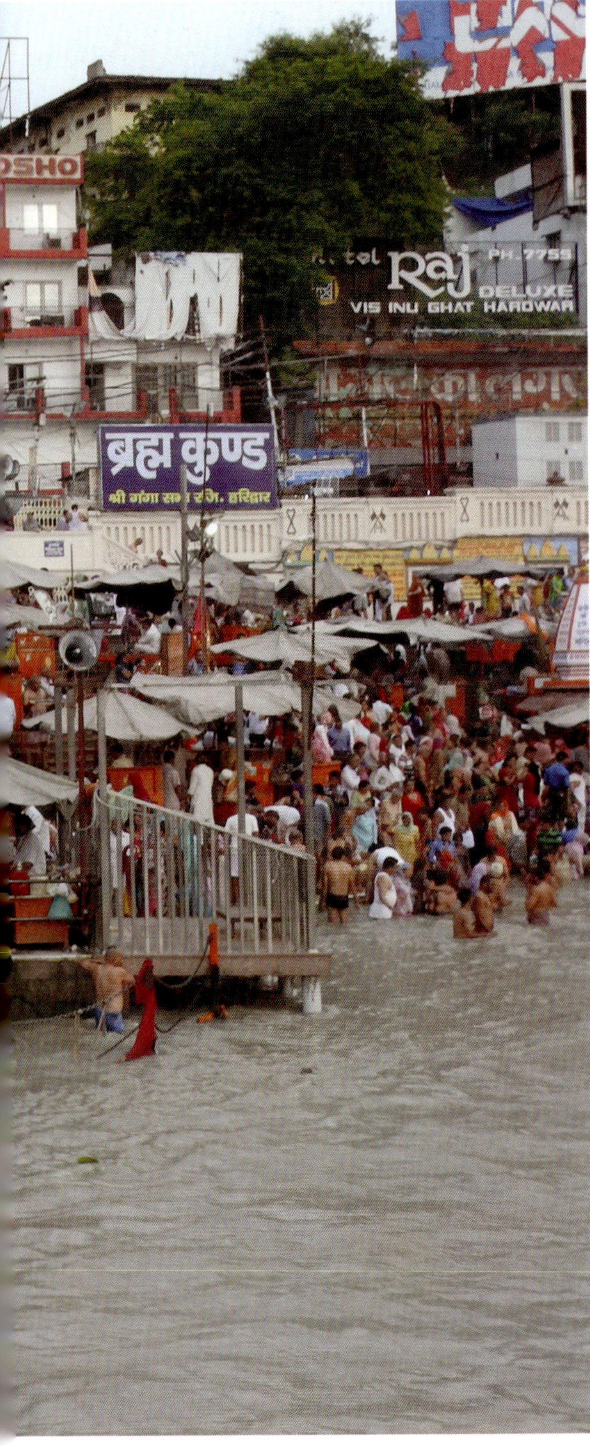

following description was written by Swami Vivekananda's younger brother Mahendranath Dutta (1886-1956) in his book *Badrinarayaner Paathe*:

> My first visit to Haridwar was in the summer of 1894. The route to Haridwar was via Saharanpur by rail. The trains had just started plying the route. But just a few years ago when Swami Vivekananda with his fellow monks, Swami Akhandananda and Swami Abhedananda, visited Haridwar they had to walk all the way from Saharanpur to Haridwar because there were no trains plying. I reached Saharanpur by train via Lucknow and Barreilly and then changed trains for Haridwar. There were no concrete buildings at Laksha, Bali and Kushghat stations. And other than ours (a passenger train) only a dilapidated goods train kept plying the route. The entire rail route comprised dense forests, and passengers were scared of tigers pouncing upon them. And even though we were travelling during the day, our co-passengers appeared vividly scared to even put their hands out of the windows.

The Ganga temple at Har-Ki-Pauri, the iconic ghat of Haridwar

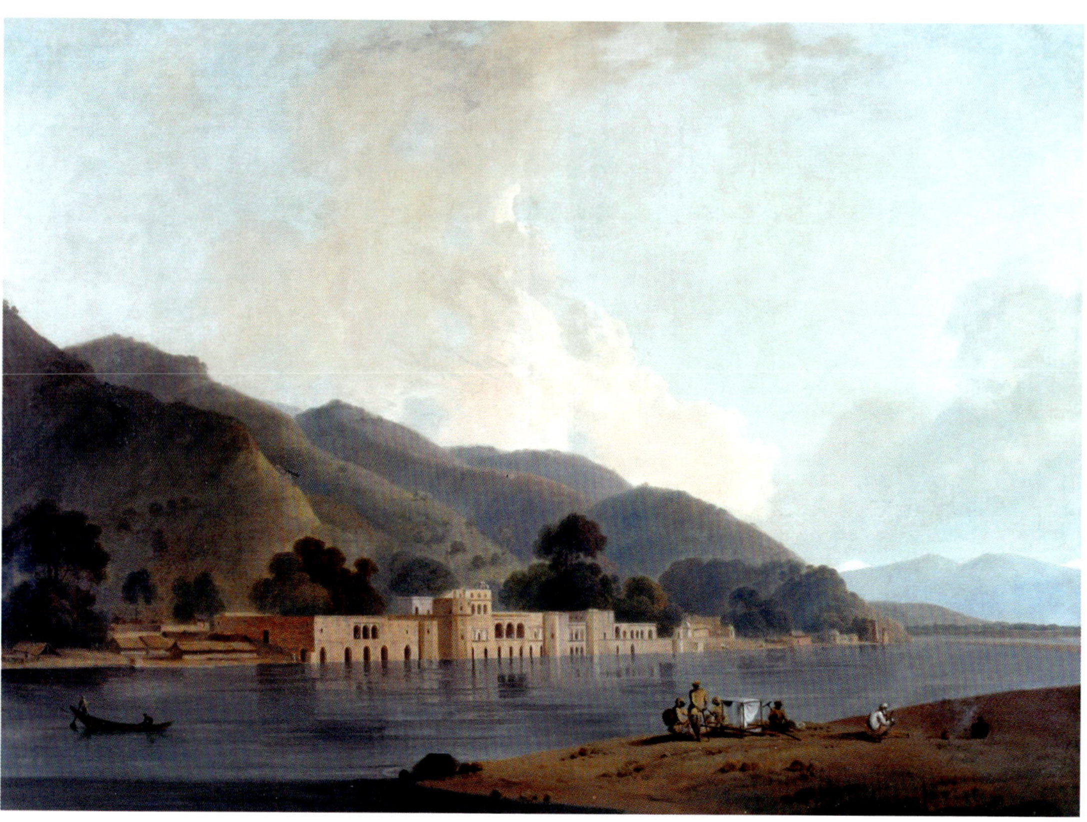

Hurdwar by Thomas Daniell

We reached Haridwar in the evening and found just a few concrete buildings outside the station. Two belonged to the railways while the others belonged to the local priests (*panda*). Just a few metres away from the station was a large warehouse, where local businessmen stored their wares. Nothing was visible outside the station premises except long stretches of sand dunes, and a thin rivulet, resembling a drain, trickling down. A narrow bridge, which stood across this rivulet, was chiefly occupied by the local priests. With sticks in hand they sat upon the bridge waiting for clients. And whenever a traveller approached, they intimidated him, by asking questions about his seven generations. Clearly the sticks were being used to scare the poor visitors who did not co-operate. Since ours was a large group of Bengalis, the scene was slightly different. It was our group who chose the right priest to take us along. Hardly any roads or concrete building were visible for quite some time as we kept walking along the bank of the Ganga. The entire stretch of the road was pebbled and slopping towards the river. So walking became increasingly difficult. Finally we reached the Brahmakund where the priest took us to a house where we were expected to put up. The locality was a combination of dense forest and just a handful of houses. It was growing dark and since there was no electricity, the priest lit a lantern for us.

Having decided to eat only after a dip in the Ganga, I had starved the whole day. So the moment we reached the house I dumped my bags and walked out in search of a wharf (there being no Har-Ki-Pauri then). It was almost dark as I fumbled my way to the Ganga. I took my bath in the ice-cold water and then shivered my way back to the house. Thereafter, I warmed myself and again walked out, this time in search of food. I found only two shops which sold food. Several monks were sitting in front of them. I bought a few fried purees, a few bits of sugar candies and a tumbler full of yogurt. I brought these items home and ate ravenously. The surrounding ambience of the place, however, was not at all congenial and I knew it was impossible for me to put up there any longer. So I walked out for the third time, this time in search of a home. There was a grocery shop near at hand whose owner kindly informed me about another inn nearby. 'There on the hilltop is a new inn coming up. You can perhaps find accommodation there,' he assured. So off I went to the hilltop, found a building under construction. It had already grown dark by then, so I bribed the caretaker-cum-guard and found a room to put up. Gleefully I returned to my former place, collected my bags and baggage and went groping back to the hilltop inn. Later on it was this building that came up as a modern and well-known hotel in Haridwar – Surajmal Inn. Early next morning I went to the Ganga to bathe and meditate for some time. Then I went exploring the place. Unlike the present well-developed city, Haridwar then was a land of forest, hills, temples, a few caves and the Ganga. However, it was the presence of the Ganga that made the city so attractive to the pilgrims.

From a Pilgrim's Diary

This time I came to Haridwar after a gap of thirty years. Undoubtedly things have changed for the better. The road beside Har-Ki-Pauri has been widened and all the old dilapidated buildings demolished yielding place to a series of brand new hotels. More people are flocking, resulting in newer shops here and there. Haridwar has indeed changed.

Since I had put up in a hotel on the bank of the Ganga the cacophony of the bathers woke me up early next morning. Changing my clothes I quickly walked out to find a group of villagers walking towards Har-Ki-Pauri. I asked the senior-most members in the group, 'Where are you from?' The answer was Balia, Uttar Pradesh. 'So you have come all the way from Balia to bathe in the Ganga of Haridwar – but why?'

'That has been our tradition. All our ancestors had visited Haridwar and bathed in the holy water of the Ganga, and we are merely carrying on the tradition.' I was so taken aback that it took me a few seconds to ask why. 'Babuji, as human beings we are constantly committing sins every day. They must all be cleansed before we die. And a dip in the water of Ganga *Maiya* cleanses all our sins,' was his simple answer. His faith and conviction bowled me over and I remained silent.

I remember having asked a monk once, 'Do you really believe that a dip in the Ganga cleanses all our sins?' He had remained quiet for some time and then

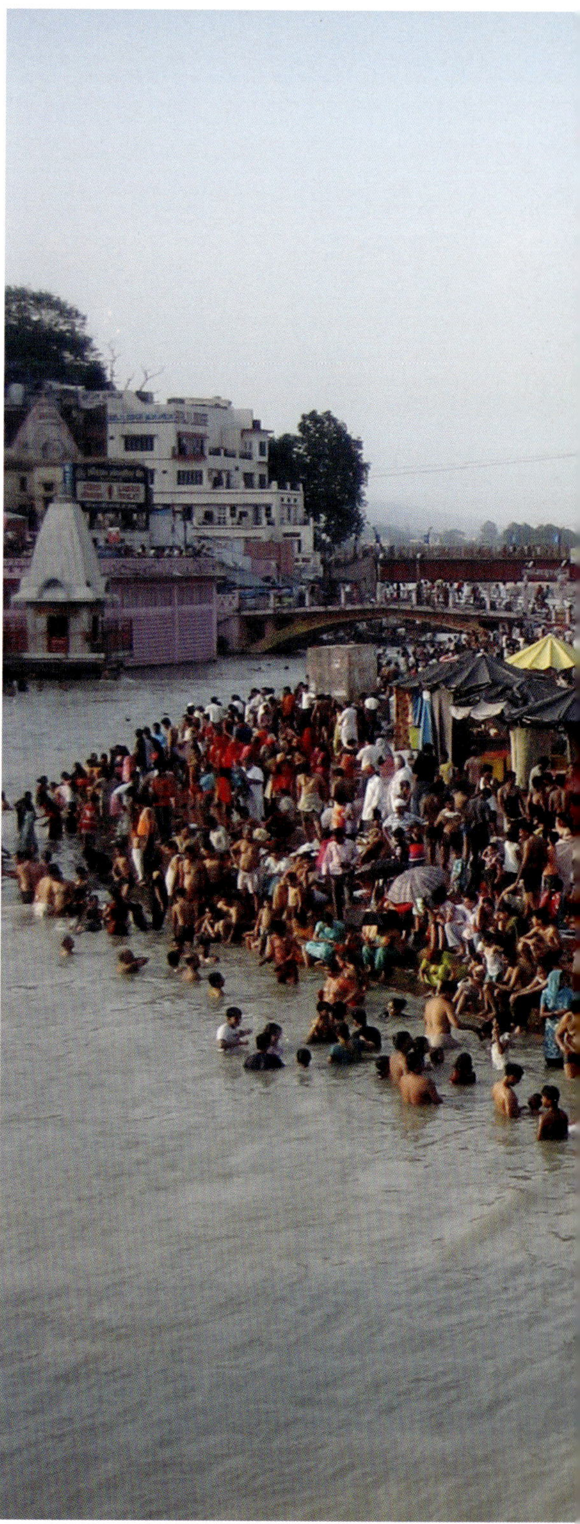

There is a constant stream of devotees at Har-Ki-Pauri, Haridwar

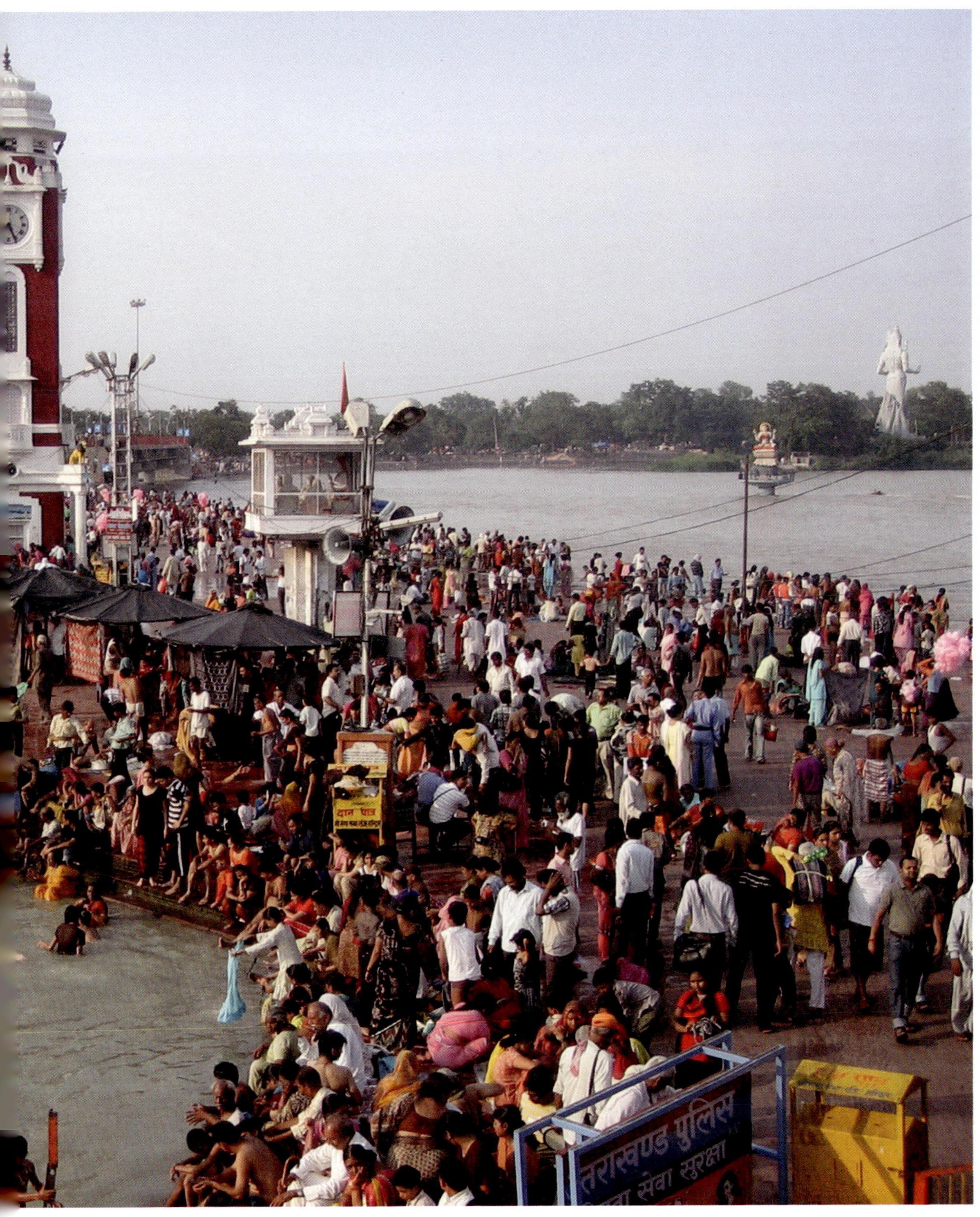
दान पात्र
पुलिस
सेवा सुरक्षा

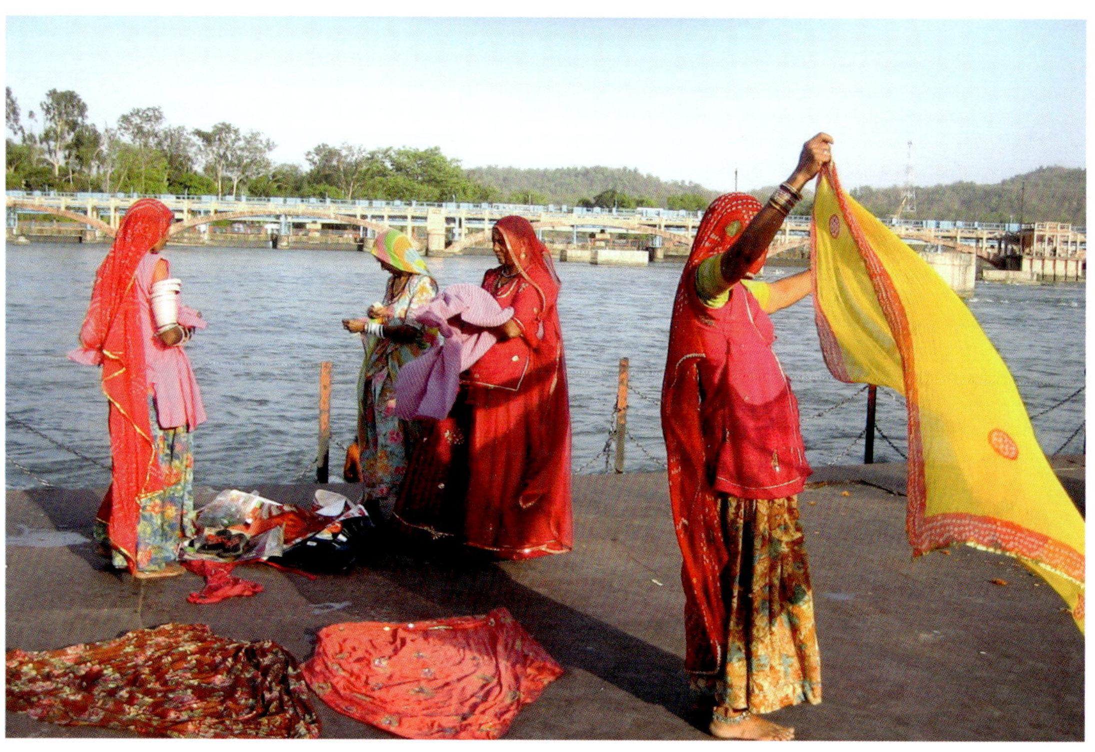

ABOVE: Rajasthani women in colourful attire preparing to take a bath at Har-Ki-Pauri
FACING PAGE ABOVE: A family hailing from Rajasthan getting ready for their ritual baths at Har-Ki-Pauri
FACING PAGE BELOW: Three women absorbed in prayers at Har-Ki-Pauri

answered, 'Look, India is a country deeply immersed in religious beliefs. The tradition is age old – in fact five thousand years old. Our sages had composed scriptures like the Vedas, Upanishads as well as the epics which gradually percolated down to our psyche. While it is true that modern urbanity has reduced our beliefs and convictions to a large extent, yet it has not been lost totally. People still have faith in our scriptures.' 'But do you think the Ganga still retains the promised holiness after having washed the sins of so many sinners?' I asked laughingly. He looked at me seriously and quoted the *Purana*. 'It has been mentioned in the *Purana*s that Ganga while entering earth was blessed by Lord Narayan who told her, "All who dip into your holy water will be cleansed of all sins." This had depressed poor Ganga. "But how will I bear the burden of so many sinners, Lord?" she had asked Narayan. "Listen, my child," Narayan had answered, "not only the sinners, there will be numerous holy men too who will come to you for ablutions. Their holiness will negate the sins of the sinners,"' the monk had answered.

I followed the group of bathers along the narrow road, jostling our way to the bank.

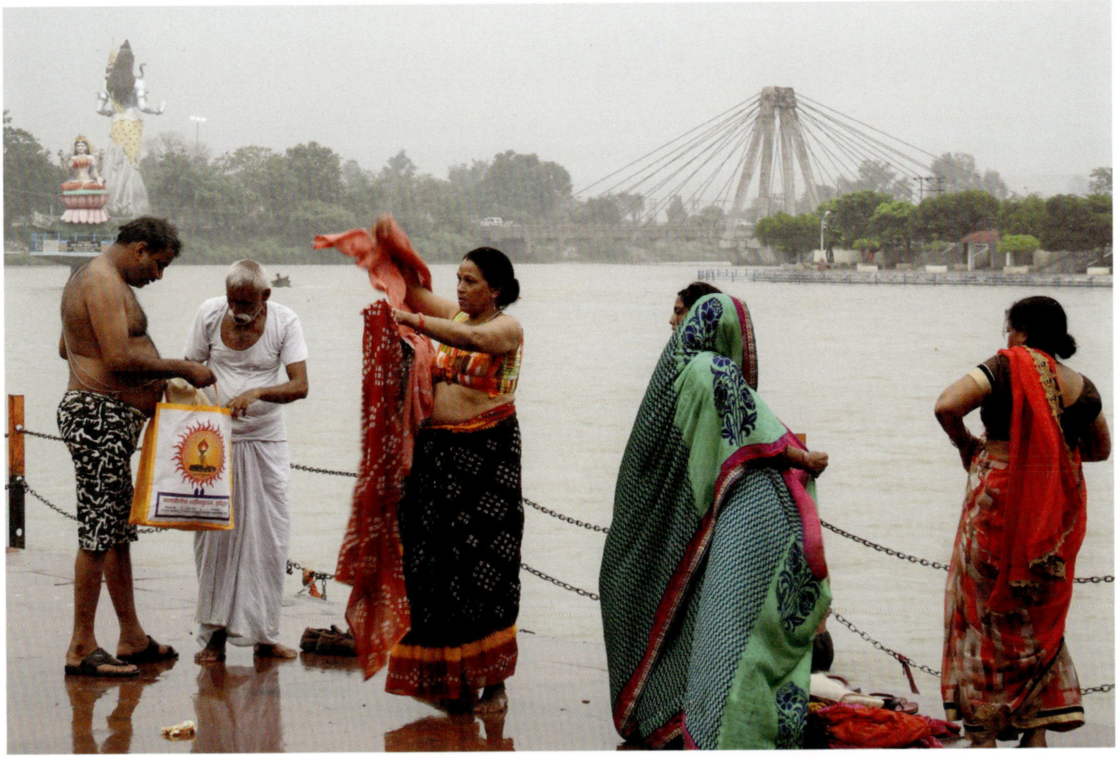

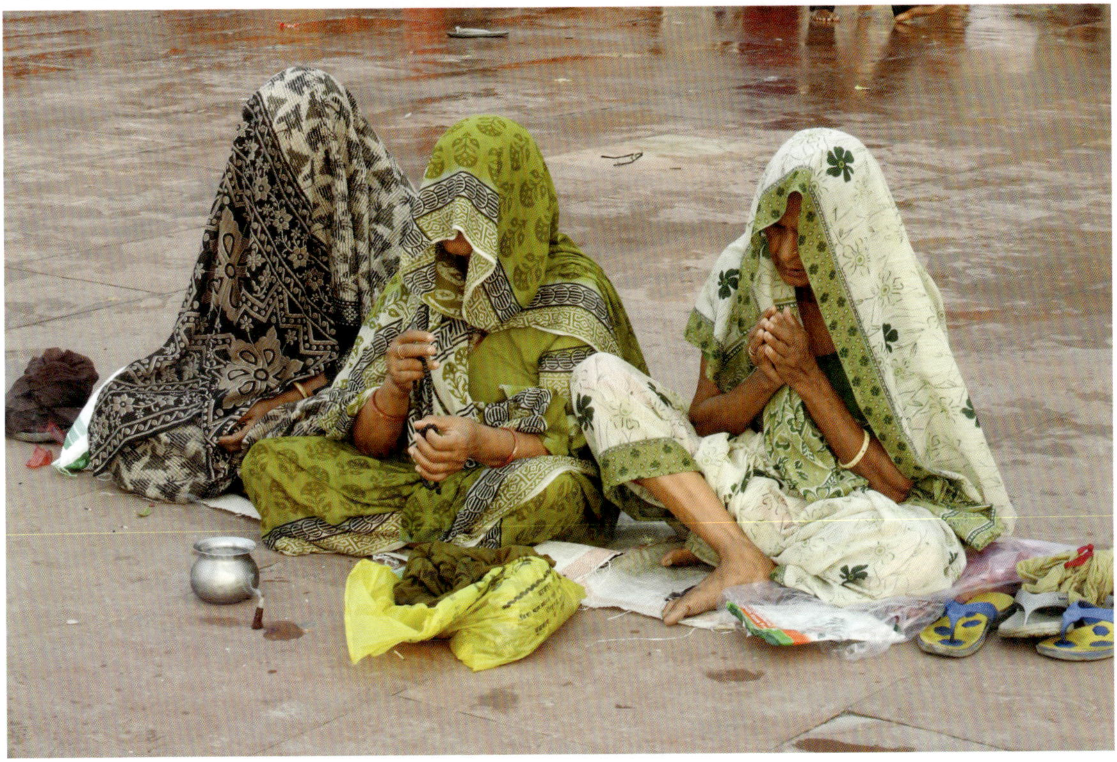

It was early morning yet the wharfs were overcrowded. It was possibly an auspicious day in the almanac, hence the crowd. I fought my way up the bridge and stood on the edge to look at the ever-flowing, ever-loving Mother Ganga. The colourful congregation of devotees and tourists took me back to my first visit to Haridwar.

I clearly remember my first visit to Haridwar. We were a group of five college mates; young and in search of new adventures. We used to spend most of our time on the bank of the Ganga enjoying the natural beauty of the place. Our added attraction however was the bathers, particularly the girls and ladies. One morning sitting idly on the bank we saw a group of women approaching the bank. Their attires suggested that they were from Rajasthan. The wharf that day was particularly empty. Other than us there were no male bathers around. We knew these ladies had come to bathe and so were on the verge of leaving (hesitatingly though). But before we could leave, the ladies, impervious to our presence, started undressing. Stark naked they dived into the river, bathed and then came up to offer their prayers. Only after completing the entire ritual they put on their dresses and left, without even glancing at us. We were stupefied. How could they, we kept wondering. It was only after many years I realised that their gesture was an eye-opener for us, teaching us to appreciate true beauty. For them bathing in the holy Ganga was more important than glancing at a few ogling young men. This conviction is something we Indians have intrinsically imbibed from our ancestors, and no logic can change it.

The sunrays were getting warmer with the passage of time. I got up for a cup of tea. Crossing the bridge I reached a tea stall. A lady was serving tea. I sat on a bench waiting for my cup when I glanced at the two gentlemen sitting opposite me. The younger of the two asked his companion, 'Who do you think is the presiding deity of Haridwar?' The elder one replied, 'Look, Haridwar being considered a holy land down the centuries, I think many gods have tried to establish their supremacy here. Not all have been successful, but more or less everyone has got his or her share.' I laughed aloud and said, 'Really it's something to ponder upon.'

The older of the two turned to me and said, 'On a serious note, I can quote the *Purana*s to prove my point. It is said in the *Purana*s that King Sweta after years of asceticism was able to please Lord Brahma. Lord Brahma blessed him and promised to reside here permanently. Hence, Haridwar is also called Brahmapuri. The wharf where we all bathe, Har-Ki-Pauri, is also known as Brahmakund. Next was Dakshya Prajapati, the successor of Lord Brahma. He came to Haridwar and practised asceticism at length to please Lord Narayan (Vishnu's other name). Lord Narayan came to him and left his footprints at Har-Ki-Pauri. This is the reason behind our deep conviction that Haridwar is indeed the holy land.' The other gentleman, who was silent all the while, next asked him, 'But what about the other deities who are worshipped here?'

The lady served us tea, so there followed a short break in the conversation. After a sip the gentleman continued, 'With Lord Narayan's blessings Dakshya Prajapati became the king of this region. He had a daughter – Sati. Sati's husband was Lord Shiva. Dakshya Prajapati however did not approve of Lord Shiva. So one day he performed a *yajna* where he did not invite Lord Shiva, his son-in-law. Sati was mortified. Unable to bear the insult meted out to her husband, Sati committed suicide. Lord Shiva heard the news and in a frenzy he beheaded Dakshya. The terrified gods in heaven came down to appease Lord Shiva and promised him a place here. From then onwards the name Hardwar came into existence; where *Haar* stands for Shiva. The entire Himalayan range is considered to be the domain of Lord Shiva. Geographically, Haridwar is actually the entry point to the Himalayas. But the followers of Lord Vishnu refused to accept the predominance of Lord Shiva here and they insisted that the name should be modified to Haridwar – *Hari* standing for Lord Vishnu. The fight kept continuing till the English spelling of the name ended the bitter battle. In English this place bears the name "Haridwar" while in Hindi it is spelt as "Hardwar".'

'Wonderful idea!' I exclaimed as both of us clapped in appreciation. The gentleman continued, 'It is Mother Ganga who rules here though. Pilgrims come here primarily to offer prayers to her. They believe her to be the Divine Mother who will listen to them and fulfil their wishes.' True, I reflected, nowhere in the world is a river worshipped thus or is considered to be a mother figure.

As the day advanced I left the tea stall and continued ambling about. I came across another tea stall where a young monk was sitting and sipping his cup of tea. He looked at me and suddenly chanted, '*Om Jaya Ganga Mata*!' Next he stared hard at me and asked in Bengali, 'Where are you from?'

'Kolkata,' I answered.

'Are you a tourist?'

'Not exactly. A wanderer is possibly a better word. I have come here to see, and to learn.'

'Well said,' laughed the monk. 'But is there an end to it?'

Now it was my turn to question him, 'Where do you stay?'

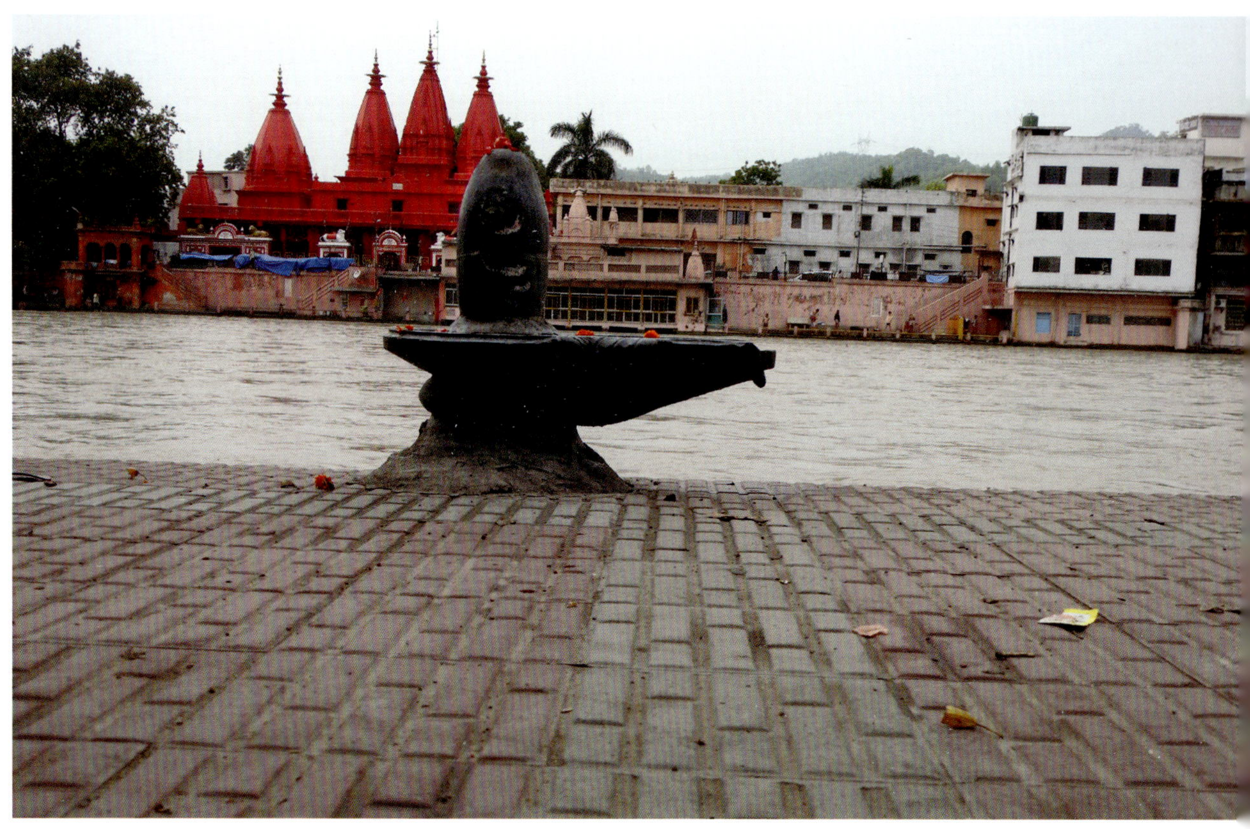

Shiva Lingam on the riverbank at Haridwar. In Sanskrit 'Hara' stands for Shiva whereas 'Dwaar' stands for gate. So Haridwar is literally the gateway to Lord Shiva

'There in that cottage beside Neeldhara.'

'Where is Neeldhara? Never heard of it.'

'There is the road. Just on the other side of it is Neeldhara, the real Ganga.'

'Then what about the river which I see before me? The wharf called Har-Ki-Pauri?'

'Oh that! It is a canal dug by the British.' I was taken aback. All this while I was worshipping only a replica of the true Ganga?

'Let's then go to see the real Ganga,' I said and started walking with him.

Crossing the highway we reached an open space where stood a small cottage. The monk opened the door and invited me in. It was a barely furnished room with a cot and a pile of books upon the cot. Most of them were written in English. There was a small table too where various objects were piled up. There was no electricity and I wondered how he managed to survive here. The monk gave me a small packet of fruits and said, 'Come, let's go to the bank of the Ganga and talk.' The water of Neeldhara clearly is neither fierce nor fast flowing. The water too is not very deep. Looking at the river I asked the monk, 'How long have you been here?'

'Two months ago I visited this place and fell in love with it. The cottage that I live in belongs to another monk. The tranquility of the place has mesmerised me.'

'How long do you plan to stay here?'

'Don't really know. As long as I feel like, I suppose.'

'The place is worth it.'

'That doesn't mean I will love it till eternity. Change is rampant everywhere and this place cannot be an exception.'

'Shall I ask you a personal question? Clearly you are well educated and belong to an affluent family. Then what made you renounce everything and lead a life of an ascetic here?'

He answered unhesitatingly, 'I never thought of becoming an ascetic. I was a student then at the Indian Institute of Technology, Kanpur. A monk from the Ramakrishna Mission came to lecture us. His lecture on Swami Vivekananda impressed me and I started reading the collected works of Swami Vivekananda. After a while I realised the futility of the material world around me. And that is when I decided to leave home in search of something that is everlasting and also tangible.'

'Have you found it?'

'I am still in search of it.'

'But what is it?'

'I really don't know. Had I known what it is my search would end.'

There was a deep conviction in his words which reminded me of an incident I had read long ago. Swami Vivekananda had visited Sri Ramakrishna and had asked him, 'Have you seen God?' Ramakrishna had answered with all sincerity, 'Yes, I have. I have seen God just the way I see you.'

I was deeply impressed. But I didn't want to continue asking personal questions so I changed the subject and asked, 'You were telling me something about the real Ganga. Please continue.'

'Yes, this was the real stream of the river. One hundred and fifty years ago, during British rule, the area was once hit by a severe draught. The Governor General of India decided to divert the course of the river to irrigate the lands on the other side of the river for the farmers. So a canal was dug, and a dam was put across, thus restricting the original course of the Ganga. It's such a pity. Hundred years ago this place was the nerve centre of international trade and commerce. Large ships used to anchor here. Now look around. Large stretches of sandbanks have reduced the river to a mere trickle. Such a sad sight! But enough for today; it's time for you to return to your hotel. You will have to walk a long distance.'

As I was about to leave, I saw a procession approaching the bank. The monk stopped me and said, 'Just wait for some time. It

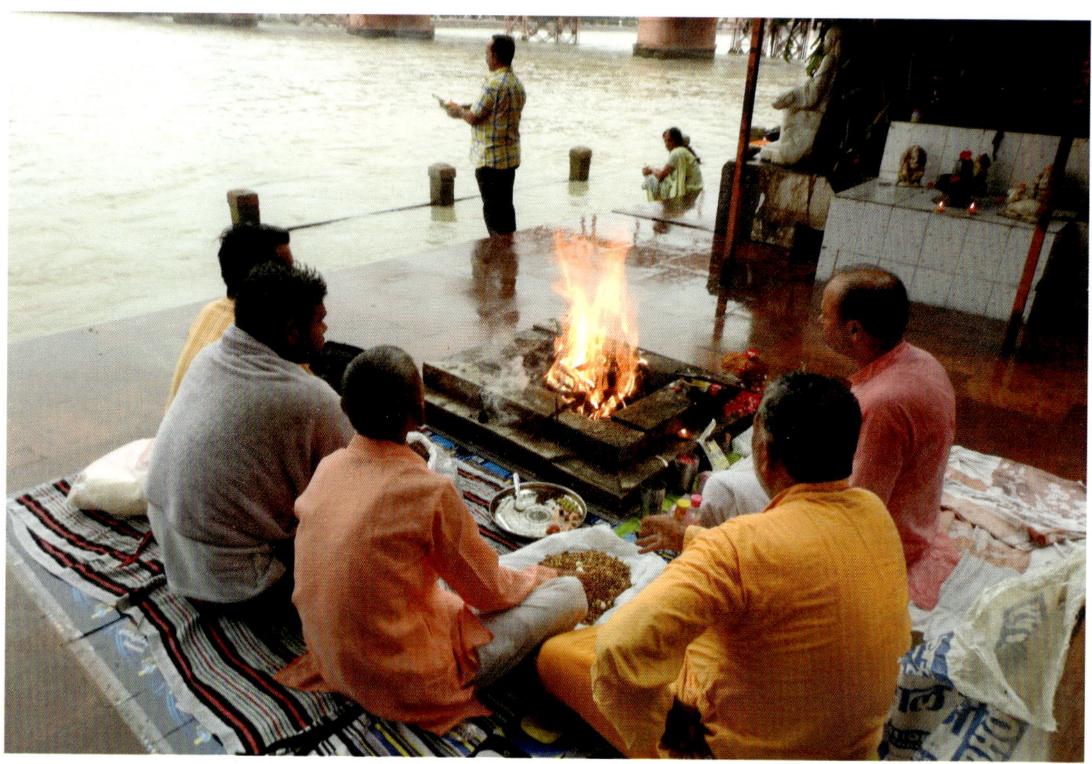

Yajna performed at Birla ghat, Haridwar

seems a monk has left his mortal remains. His last rites will be performed on the riverbank. You wanted to learn more about the diversity of the world, isn't it? Will you go there?'

Cremation was a ritual not unknown to me. I have witnessed it on various occasions. Yet, this was something I had never seen – a monk being cremated. So I accompanied him to the bank of the river. The body of the departed soul was first wrapped up in a shroud and then immersed into the river. All the while they were chanting the name of Lord Rama. Interestingly the body was left in a sitting posture. Everything was over within a short time and the monks left after a holy dip in the Ganga. Shortly afterwards I heard some feminine voices talking and giggling their way home. I glanced at them and realised how life goes on – there is life followed by death and again death followed by life.

It was almost noon and the sun burnt bright just upon the meridian, as I returned to my hotel room. I spent the rest of the day recollecting my experiences.

In the evening I once again visited Har-Ki-Pauri. Devotional songs were being played on the microphone. The sound echoed through the entire place. As always Har-Ki-Pauri was densely crowded. After some time I heard a loud noise of cymbals and saw before me a few priests approaching the bank of the Ganga. Attired in red robes they were all carrying burning lamps mounted on lamp sticks. Immediately devotional songs glorifying the Ganga blared loudly from the microphone and the crowd stood up in reverence. The priests commenced their daily ritual of worshipping the Ganga. It was a marvellous sight – like a festival of lights.

There is another ritual which people observe on a personal level – floating a lighted wicker lamp on the river. It's a way of offering their desires to the Almighty and praying for fulfilment.

Anurag Patel was sitting next to me. He had come from Thailand. Gujarati by

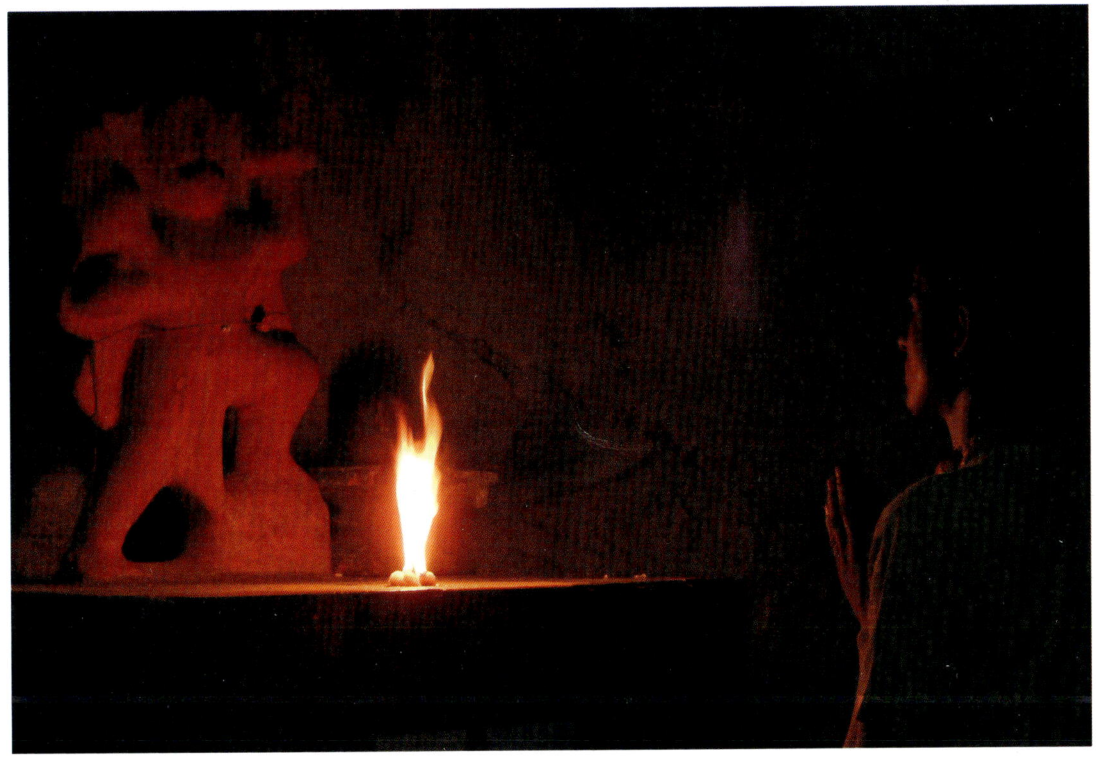

A man worships Lord Hanuman in the lamplit dark temple at Haridwar

birth, Anurag's ancestors were all settled in Thailand. Anurag seemed perfectly at ease with the happenings around us. I turned to him and asked, 'How do you like it? Don't you find it strange?' He just shrugged and said, 'No, I am familiar with most of this.' Then he spoke at length about the rivers of Thailand. There are several rivers in Thailand bearing different names he said. But *my-naam-khan* is attributed to all of them. *My* stands for mother, *naam* stands for water and *khan* stands for Ganga. For the inhabitants of Thailand all rivers are manifestations of the Ganga. Their most famous river however is Mekong. *Me* stands for mother, while *kong* means Ganga. Numerous Thai students come to India every year for pursuing higher studies. They often arrangc rcunions here, which begin at night and are called the Ganga Night.

'But why do they float burning lamps on the river?' I asked Anurag.

Reflecting for a while Anurag recounted a beautiful story. 'Nearly six hundred years

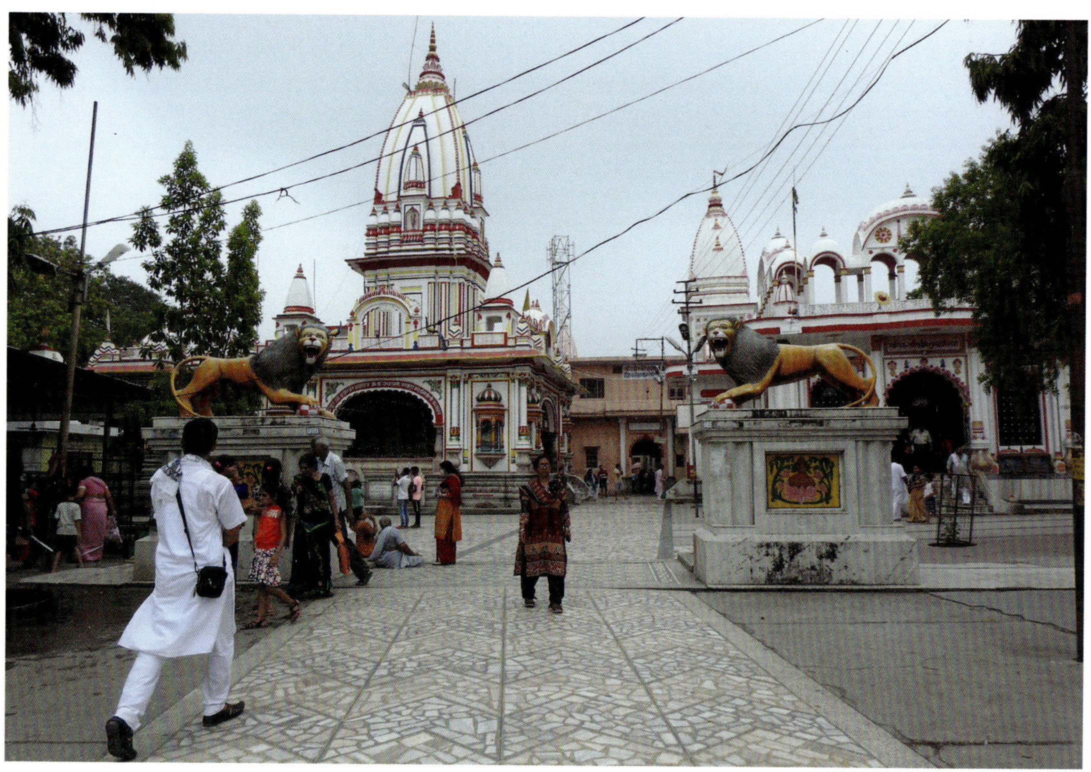

Daksheswara Mahadev temple, Khankal. It is one of the five pilgrimages (*panch tirth*) within Haridwar

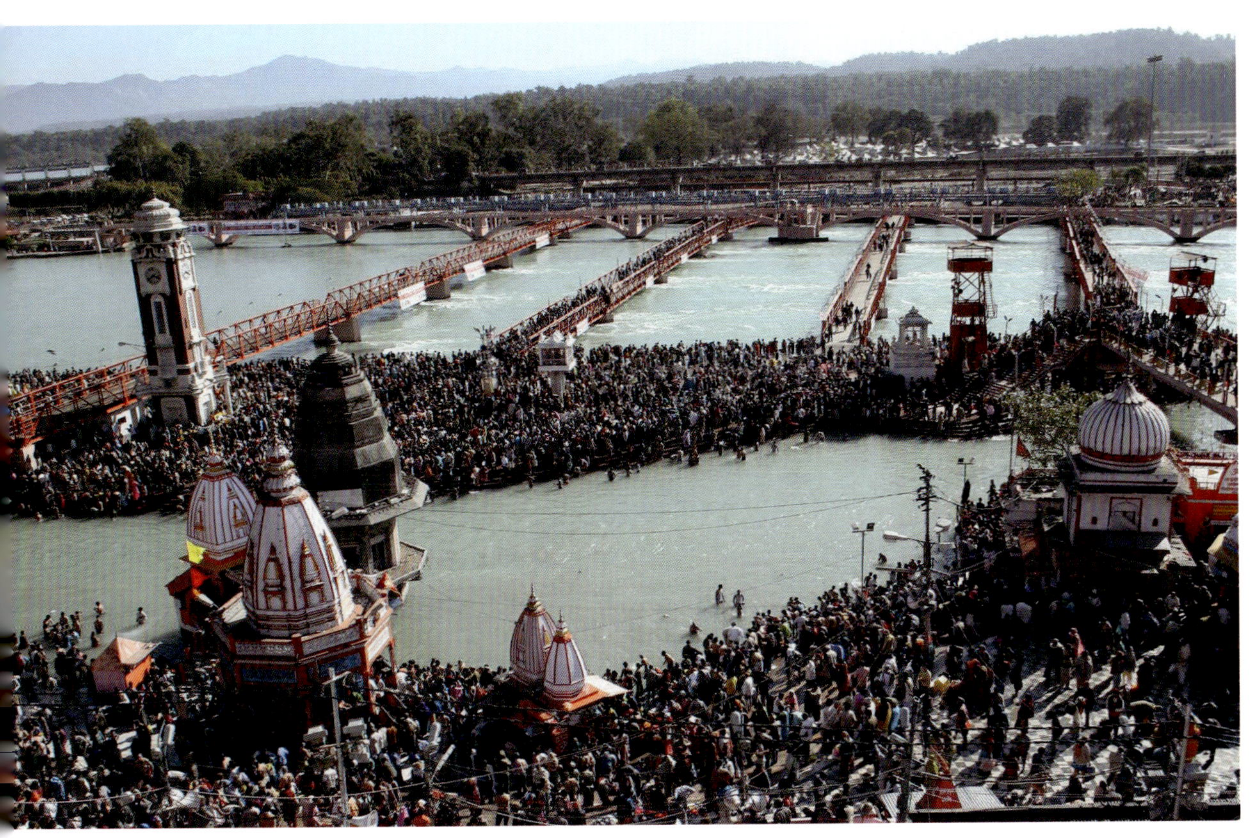

Kumbh Mela, Haridwar, 2010. Millions of pilgrims, devotees and tourists converge here every twelve years to wash away their sins and attain Moksha

ago, King Ruyanda ruled Thailand. He was a Buddhist. There was a Brahmin in his kingdom who had a beautiful daughter named Navamaas. Impressed by Navamaas's beauty the king married her. A few weeks after the marriage, the auspicious Buddhist festival *Kathin* took place. It was customary for the king to visit a Buddhist monastery on that day. Ruyanda wanted his newly wedded wife Navamaas to accompany him but the date collided with another festival – worshipping the Ganga – and so she refused. In the evening she lit a lamp and placed it on a plantain leaf and then floated it on the river. Afraid of displeasing the king she was secretive about it. The leaf floated on the river and finally reached the king's boat. Seeing this strange sight the king started enquiring about it. Navamaas then revealed her secret and the king happily included Ganga worship with the Buddhist festival. From that day onwards the people of Thailand offer burning lamps to their rivers,' concluded Anurag.

So that was the connecting link, I realised.

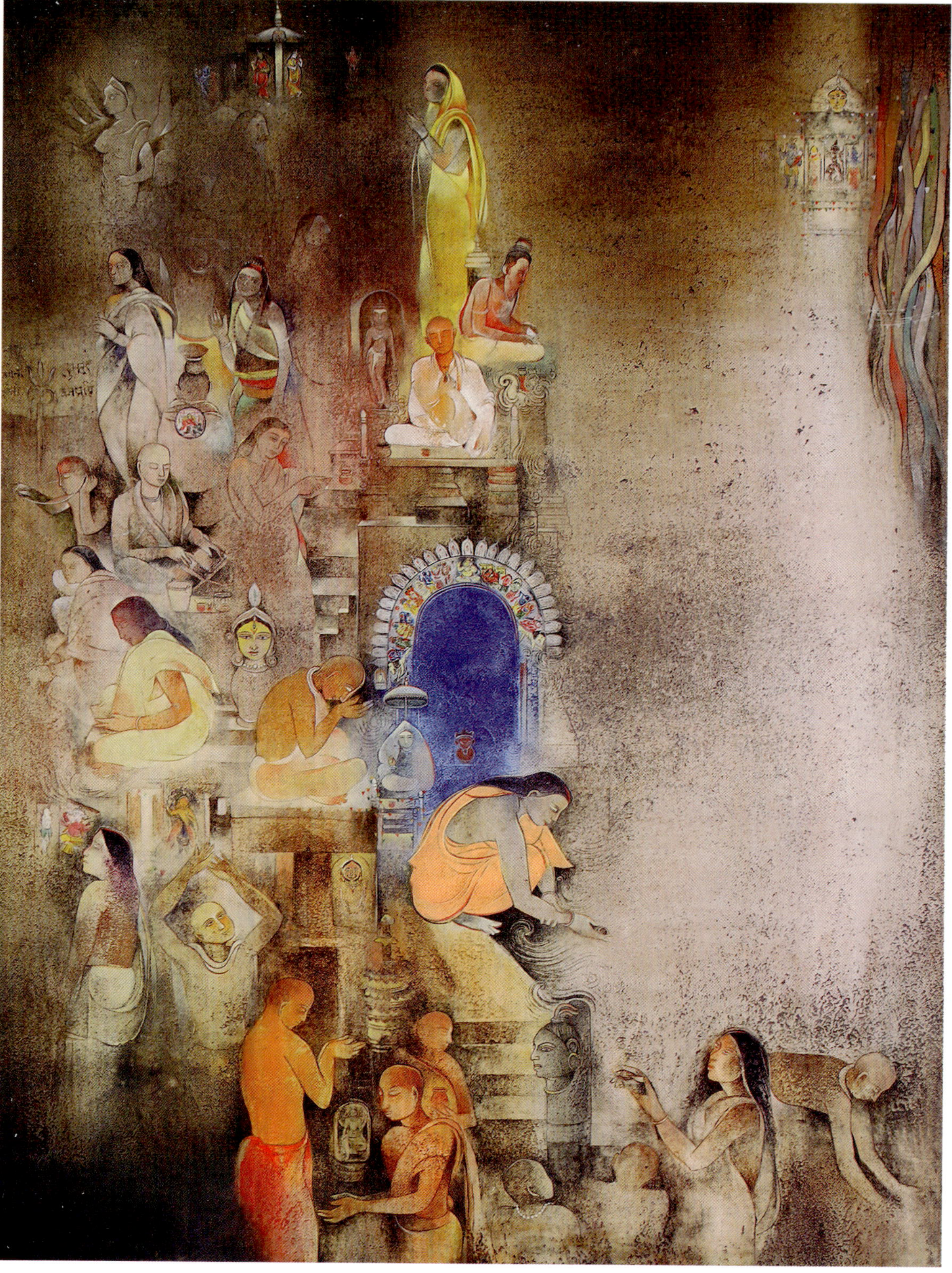

GANGA IN THE PLAINS

GARHMUKHTESHWAR

Forty-seven kilometres from Meerut, and 100 kilometres from Delhi, Garhmukhteshwar is a small hamlet on the bank of the river Ganga. The hamlet is named after Mahadeva or Lord Shiva – Mukteswar is another name for Lord Shiva. There are four Shiva temples here. The place has been reverentially mentioned even in the *Mahabharata*. It is believed that at one point of time the place was a part of Hastinapur. The hamlet is famous for its autumnal fair – Kartick mela. Thousands of devotees flock in search of divine benediction. Other than that another fair too takes place here – Ganga Dussehra mela – which is equally popular and famous. Devotees pay homage to the river Ganga on this occasion. The third festival that is held here is Gadha-ka-mela or donkey festival. Thousands of horses and donkeys are traded in the fair and the bidders come from all parts of the world including neighbouring Pakistan and Bangladesh.

FACING PAGE: Ganga descending with life throbbing on her bank, by Siddhartha Sengupta

BITHOOR

Bithoor is another small hamlet on the banks of the river Ganga. It is twenty-five kilometres north-west of Kanpur. The Ganga is quite wide at Bithoor. The place is a wonderful fusion of spiritual heritage and history. Time appears to have stopped entirely at Bithoor. Innumerable wharfs, old dilapidated mansions, and temples dot the landscape of Bithoor. It is believed temples and houses keep vying in their effort to outnumber one another. Interestingly there are quite a few mosques as well. Thus one hears the tinkling of the temple bells along with the sound of prayers from the mosques simultaneously. Bithoor does not boast of opulence, neither is the place infested with

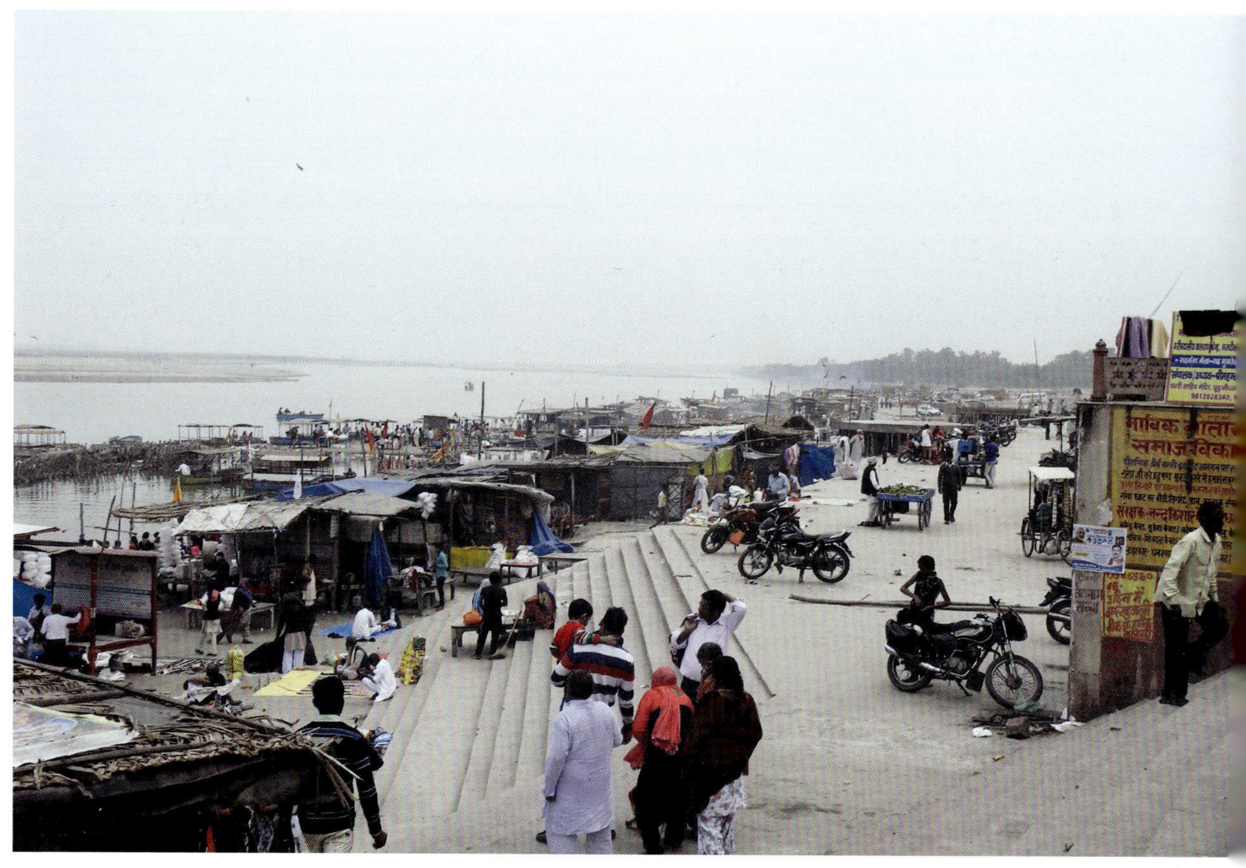

Above: The Ganga ghat at Garhmukhteshwar. Locals call this the Bridge ghat

Facing page above: The Ganga ghat at Bithoor

Facing page below: Relics at the ghat at Bithoor conjuring up the grey past by transporting visitors to another time

pilgrims like Varanasi, yet its tranquility touches the heart of the visitor.

It is said Lord Brahma while creating the world had performed a *yajna* at Brahmavarta (another name of Bithoor). Located on the bank of the Ganga, Brahmavarta also has a temple dedicated to Lord Shiva. Throughout the day pilgrims and devotees keep flocking Bithoor to worship the ruling deities. There is also another story about Bithoor. In the ancient times, Bithoor was known as Utpalaranya. It was then ruled by king Uttanpad. His son Dhruva prayed to Lord Vishnu here at Bithoor and pleased him. The place is now worshipped as Dhruva Tila. It was also inhabited by Sage Valmiki. It is here that Sita, renounced by Lord Rama, gave birth to her twin sons Lava and Kush. At the hilltop is Valmiki's hermitage and Sita kund. The Ganga when viewed from this hermitage looks majestic.

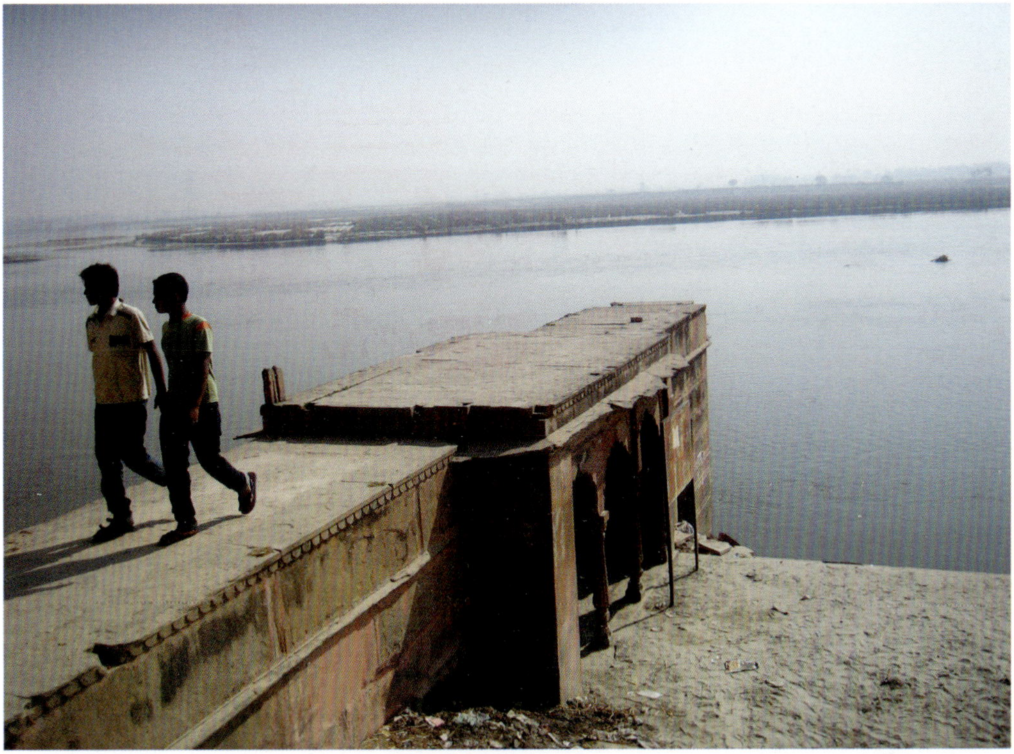

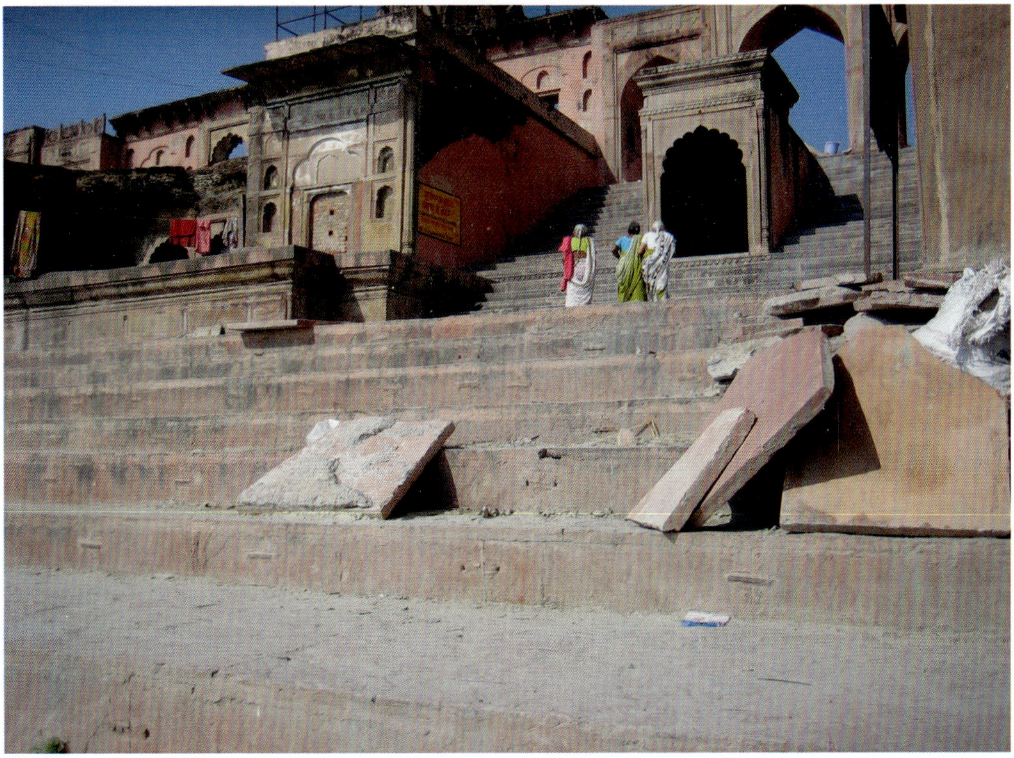

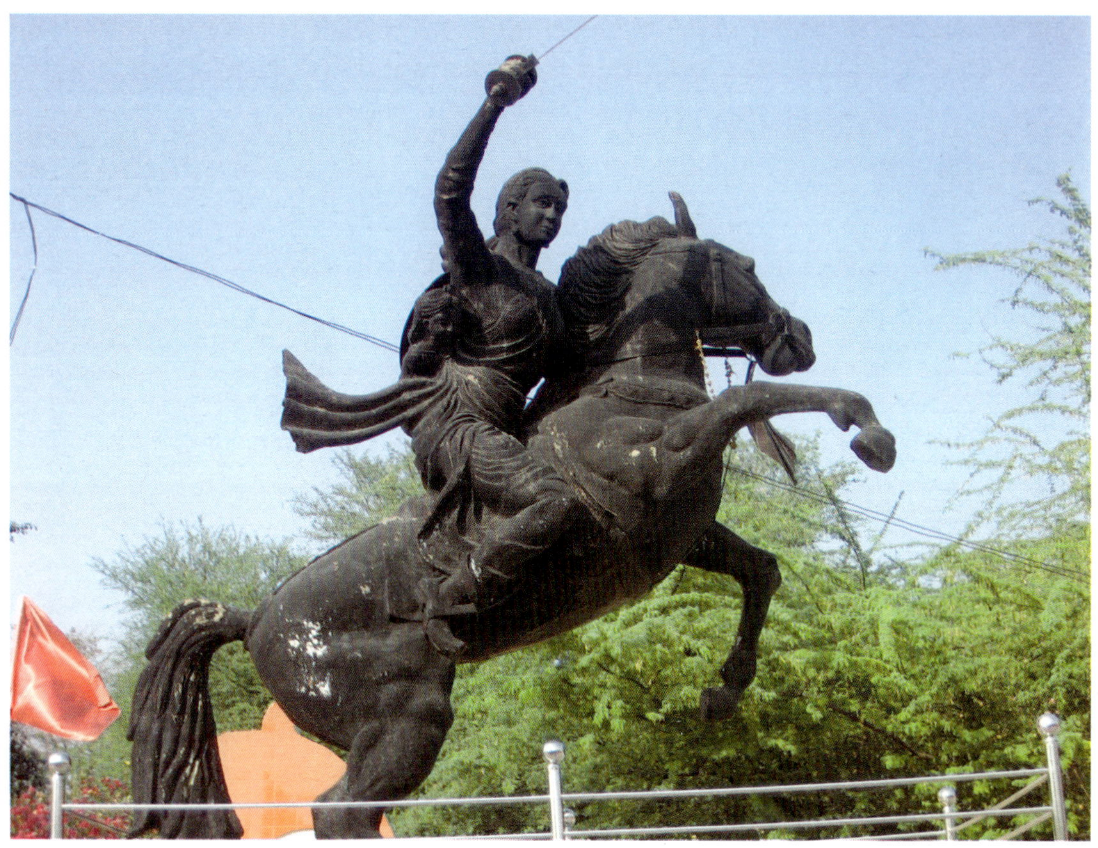

Statue of Rani Lakshmibai of Jhansi. She spent her childhood in Bithoor

Rani Lakshmibai of Jhansi spent her childhood here. The palace of Nana Saheb is situated at Bithoor. But in 1857 during the Sepoy Mutiny, this palace was completely destroyed. At present a park here has been dedicated in the memory of Nana Saheb.

From a Pilgrim's Diary

I was sitting on Golu Mishra's country boat. Ferrying people has been the profession of his ancestors for the last three generations. Consequently, love for the Ganga runs in his blood. Even though some of his ancestors had served the British Army, at one point of time they all had risen against the British imperialists and fought against them. Reclining in the silhouetted portion of the boat Golu kept recounting the stories of his ancestors. But his main preoccupation was the river Ganga. For Golu and his ancestors

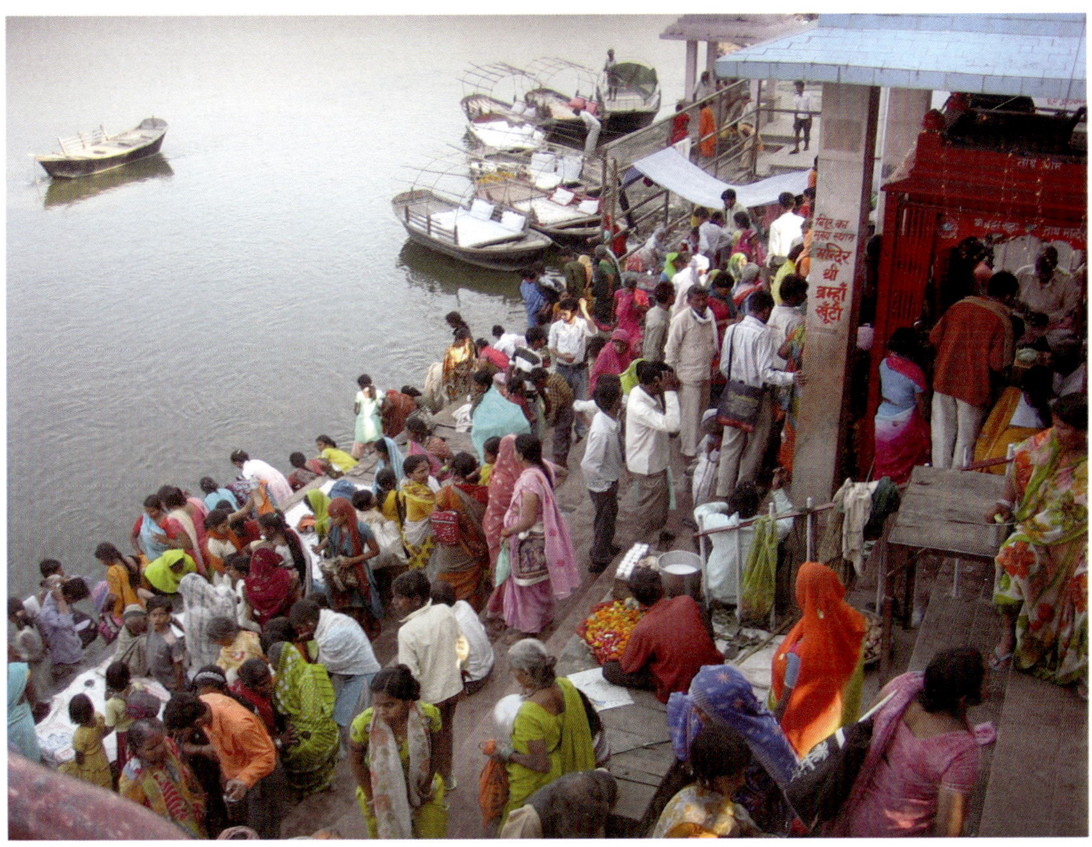

Ganga Dussehra is celebrated at the Brahmavarta ghat, Bithoor

the Ganga is not a mere river. He refers to her as the Divine Mother. Surprised at his address I asked him, 'Why do you call the river Mother Ganga?' He looked at the river quietly for some time and then replied softly, 'You want to know why? Just as a mother suckles and nourishes her child after birth, Mother Ganga keeps nourishing us in all possible ways. The fishermen fish here for their livelihood, the helmsmen steer their boats to earn their living, the farmers draw water from her to irrigate their fields and even after our death, our mortal remains are immersed in this river. So right from our birth till our death we are completely dependent on her and she never refuses to shower her bounty upon us.'

Golu was illiterate yet in his simple way he narrated a profound philosophy to me. I couldn't help admiring him.

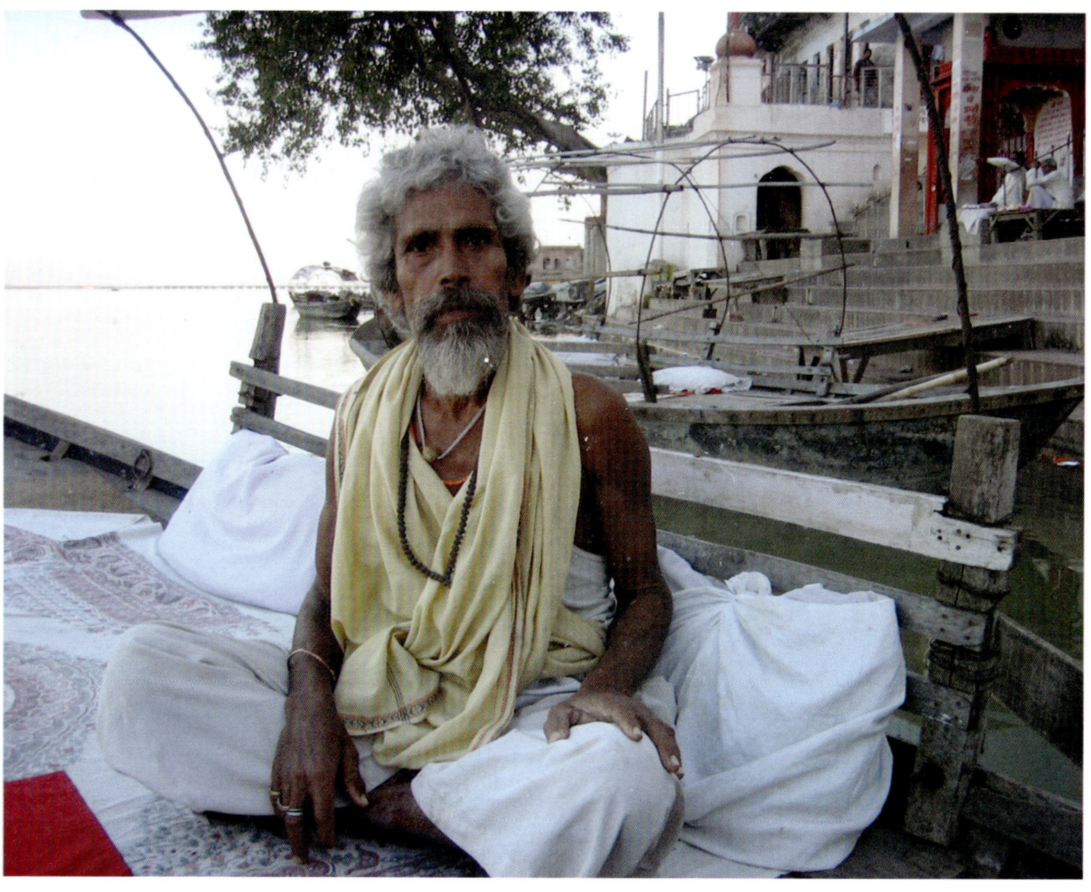

An old boatman waiting for passengers at Bithoor

It was twilight and darkness was fast approaching. The bells of the temples on the bank of the river started ringing, reminding us of the vespers. Soon we could hear the sounds of various devotional songs being played in different temples. Golu sang along and I sat spellbound. It was the same songs I had heard at Gangotri, Uttarkashi, Rishikesh, Haridwar and also Varanasi where the river is considered to be a divine entity – Divine Mother. But at Bithoor it sounded so different!

HOLY GANGA – HOLY WATER

As mentioned earlier, in the *Purana*s Lord Vishnu blesses the Ganga and tells her she will remain pure despite washing off the sins of numerous sinners. The purity of the holy men bathing in her waters will wipe away the sins she will accumulate. Yet in the present century we are really sceptical about the river's capacity to purify everything and everyone. And we are responsible for this sad state of affairs. We have been polluting the river water, right from its source.

What is so Special about the Water of the Ganga?

Blessed by Lord Vishnu, the Ganga has been worshipped as a divine entity down the centuries. Never has the Ganga been treated as just a river. She has been worshipped as a mother figure everywhere. And in return the Ganga has nourished and shaped our religious beliefs, nurtured our heritage and boosted our economic status. Hence, Indians believe that a dip in the Ganga purifies man of all sins. It is therefore hardly surprising that Indians flock to the river on various occasions for a dip in its holy waters.

To be candid our feelings for the Ganga are born more out of our beliefs and emotions rather than any rationale. There is, however, a grain of truth behind the belief that the Ganga purifies everything. The river water has been regarded as the

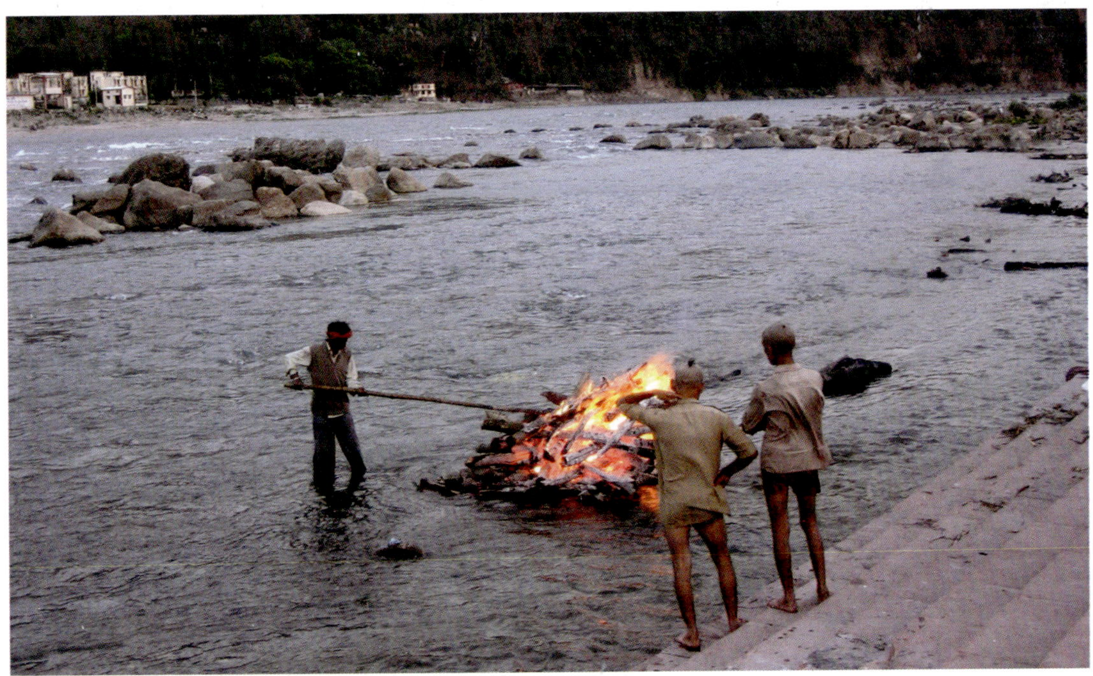

Funeral rites on a scaffold right in the middle of the Ganga in the hope of direct ascension to heaven

ideal drinking water since time immemorial. I remember the words of an old teacher: 'Our village was close to the bank of river Ganga, and my grandmother never drank anything other than the pure water of the Ganga. My father would visit the river every day with a small pitcher to fetch water from the river. The mouth of the pitcher would then be tied with a four-times folded thick piece of cloth, and left to stand for several hours. Once the mud and other impurities settled down at the bottom of the pitcher, the clear water would be poured in a brass container. My grandmother would use this as her drinking water. I was forty years old when my grandmother died. But never in those forty years have I seen her falling sick.'

In the seventeenth century, a French businessman and traveller, Jean-Baptiste Tavernier (1605-1689), wrote about the water of the Ganga in his book *Travels in India*:

> I come to the pagoda of Benaras, which after that of Jagannath, is the most famous in all of India, and of equal sanctity, being built on the margin of the Ganga, and in the town of which it bears the name. The most remarkable thing about it is that from the door of the pagoda to the river there is a descent by stone steps, where there are at intervals platforms and small, rather dark, chambers, some of which serve as dwellings for the Brahmans, and others as kitchens where they prepare their food. For after the idolaters have bathed, and have gone to pray and make their offerings in the pagoda, they prepare their food without anyone but themselves touching it, through the fear they have lest anyone who approached it might be unclean. But above all things, they ardently desire to drink the water of the Ganga, because, as soon as they have drunk it, they believe, as I have said, that they are cleansed from all their sins. Every day large numbers of these Brahmans are to be seen going to the clearest part of the river to fill round small-mouthed, earthen pots, which hold about a bucketful, with this water. When they are full they are taken to the chief priest, who directs the mouth to be covered with a very fine cloth of fire-colour, in three or four folds, upon which he applies his seal. The Brahmans carry this water at the end of a stick, flat like a lath, from which hang six small cords, and to each of them one of these pots is attached. They rest themselves by changing the shoulder frequently, and

they sometimes travel three of four hundred leagues of country with this load, and then sell it, or make a present of it, but only to the richest persons, from whom they expect a liberal reward. Some of these idolaters, when they celebrate any festival – especially when their children are married – drink this water at a cost of 400 or 500 ecus. It is drunk only at the end of the repast, as we drink hypocras or muscat in Europe, each guest receiving a cup, or two, according to the liberality of the host. The principal reason why this water of the Ganga is so highly esteemed, is that it never becomes bad, engenders no vermin; but I do not know whether we should believe what is said about this, taking into consideration the number of bodies which are constantly being thrown into the Ganga.

In practice, sustenance of a large section of people residing on the banks of the Ganga is dependent on the water of the river. They firmly believe that nobody can fall sick by drinking the water of the Ganga. In the ancient times sealed pitchers of the Ganga water were often stored for years together. And the water remained good and pure for long spells of time compared to other waters. We really cannot state specifically whether this happens because of our faith in the water of the Ganga or whether there is some scientific reason behind it.

It has been found on analysis that the water of the Ganga has a purifying agent in it which helps to cleanse other waters as well. Famous doctor-cum-scientist Dr Harrison had once introduced germs of the dreaded cholera into a pitcher full of the Ganga water. After a day he noticed that all the germs of cholera were completely destroyed by the water.

Talking about this cleansing property of the Ganga water, famous American author Mark Twain in his travelogue *Following the Equator* (1897) had once observed,

It has long been noted as a strange thing that while Benaras is often afflicted with the cholera she does not spread it beyond her borders. This could not be accounted for. Mr. Henkin, the scientist in the employ of the government of Agra, concluded to examine the water. He went to Benaras and made his tests. He got water at the mouths of the sewers where they empty into the river at the bathing-ghats; a cubic centimeter of it contained millions of germs; at the end of six hours they were all dead.

He caught a floating corpse, towed it to the shore, and from beside it he dipped up water that was swarming with cholera germs; at the end of six hours they were all dead. He added swarm after swarm of cholera germs to this water; within six hours they always died, to the last sample. Repeatedly he took pure well-water which was barren of animal life, and put into it a few cholera germs, they always began to propagate at once, and always within six hours they swarmed – and were numerable by millions upon millions.

For ages and ages the Hindus have had absolute faith that the water of the Ganga was absolutely pure, could not be defiled by any contact whatsoever thing touched it. They still believe it, and that is why they bathe in it and drink it, caring nothing for its seeming filthiness and the floating corpses. The Hindus have been laughed at, these many generations, but the laughter will need to modify itself a little from now on. How did they find out the water's secret in those ancient ages? Had they germ-scientists then? We do not know. We only know that they had a civilization long before we emerged from savagery.

Yet, at present, we have grave doubts about the cleansing property of the Ganga water. Is it because of our sins or our ignorance? Right from Haridwar to Kolkata, the river water is becoming increasingly polluted due to our negligence.

Industrial Revolution and Pollution

For the last three thousand years India has been dependent on agriculture. Boats and ships have been sailing and fishing has thrived; yet the Ganga continued to retain the power of auto-cleansing. But with the advent of the British imperialists followed by industrialisation the river gradually started losing this aforementioned capacity. Constant release of chemical wastes from different industries like tanneries, paper mills, factories producing pesticides and chemical fertilisers gradually kept increasing the pollution level of the once pure river. Added to it the population explosion has played a vital role in polluting the river water further.

Previously, the pollution level would rise from the plain land of Haridwar, but unfortunately now the pollution seems to have spread to the Gangotri glacier as well. Several years ago only a few fanatic adventurists would visit the Gangotri glacier, but now the footfall has increased manifold. Consequently large numbers of hotels, motels

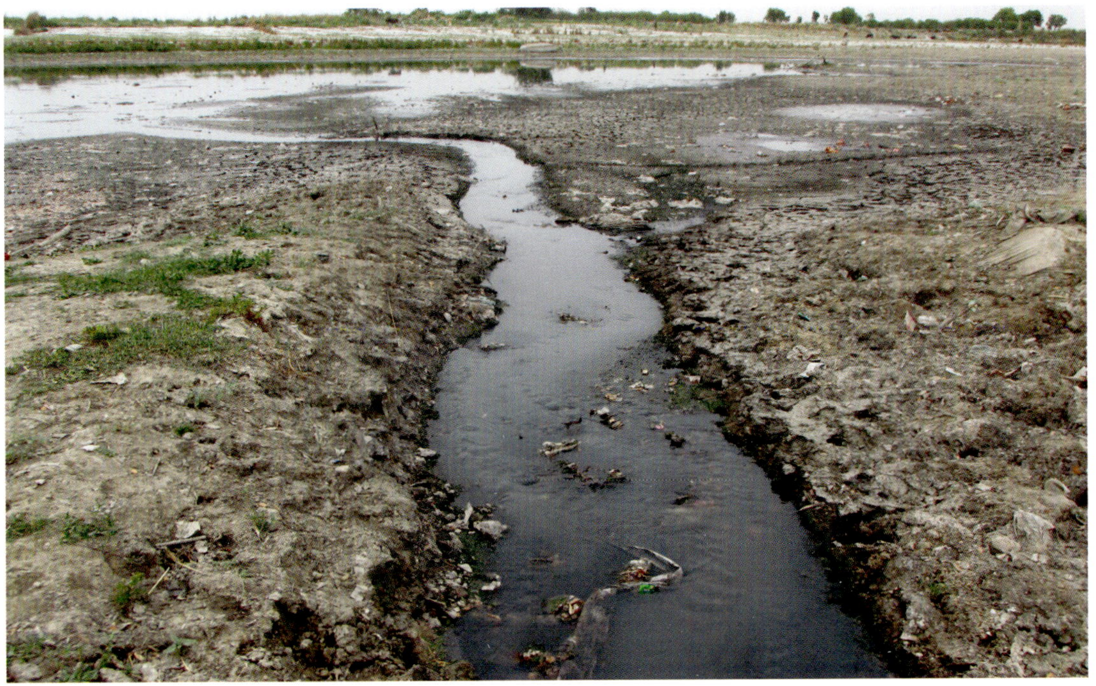

Industrial and urban waste is choking the Ganga. A number of initiatives have been undertaken to clean the river in vain

and inns have started mushrooming. This is the major cause of the growing pollution in that region. Things have taken a turn for the worse after the construction of several dams across the river at various points. Water in those regions has stagnated leading to a rise in the pollution level. The case of Tehri dam can be cited to prove this point. The water adjacent to this dam has stagnated beyond redemption. The local people now term it a lake and not the fast-flowing river Ganga. The long 2,525-kilometre route of the Ganga, from the Himalayas to Gangasagar, is constantly being polluted both by chemical and human wastes.

Presently there are sixteen large cities, twenty-three medium-sized cities, fifty small cities, and several thousand villages situated on the banks of the river. Billions of people living there keep polluting the river on a daily basis. The agricultural lands in these regions further contribute to the river pollution by using chemical pesticides. According to a recent survey, the water of the Ganga which down the centuries has sustained human lives is now proving to be increasingly contaminated because of its growing pollution. At present, drinking the water is potentially dangerous and life threatening too. Bathing in the river does not cleanse a person of her sins any more, rather it increases the risk of her contracting various diseases.

Not just human lives are at risk though. The aquatic animals, insects and other underwater living organisms are also finding the river water to be harmful. A total number of 15 million species of aquatic creatures are found around the world, of which 1 million 27 thousand live in the Indian subcontinent. The Ganga sustains 2,500 of them. But most of these species are gradually dying due to scarcity of oxygen in the water of the river. A recent survey conducted on the purity of the Ganga water reported that out of the 2,525-kilometre stretch of the river, 600 kilometres of the water of the Ganga is unfit for consumption by any living creature. In West Bengal four important fishing spots, Falta, Kolkata, Lalgola and Farakka, are showing a steady decline of fish. Even the supply of the delicious hilsa fish is on the wane. Dolphins which dwelt in the entire stretch of the river are hardly visible now.

Cleansing Power of the Ganga

Despite growing pollution Indians still believe in the cleansing property of the Ganga water. Should we consider this belief to be mere blind faith or is there really a scientific basis behind it? An in-depth study of the Ganga water has revealed that it has a magnificent capacity of auto-cleansing. In fact most of the rivers of the world have this power of auto-cleansing. But in case of the Ganga this power is the highest. Even if the water is stored for an infinite period of time neither can germs grow nor thrive in it. The famous Tagores of Calcutta used to preserve the Ganga water in earthen pitchers for months together and even carried it to London with them.

As mentioned above, nearly all the rivers of the world can clean their waters by a natural process. There are several bacteria, phytoplankton, etc., which kill the disease-creating pathogens by consuming them. In 1985, *The Hindustan Times* reported, 'All rivers of the world have a certain self-purification capacity. Ganga is more powerful than most of them.' But what is it that makes the Ganga so special?

One plausible explanation for this strange property of the Ganga is the height of its source, 12,500 kilometres in the Himalayas. While traversing these mountainous terrains the river keeps absorbing useful chemicals, found in the mountains, which in turn assist it to cleanse itself internally. And in its long course of 2,525 kilometres various electro-chemical reactions take place in the water,

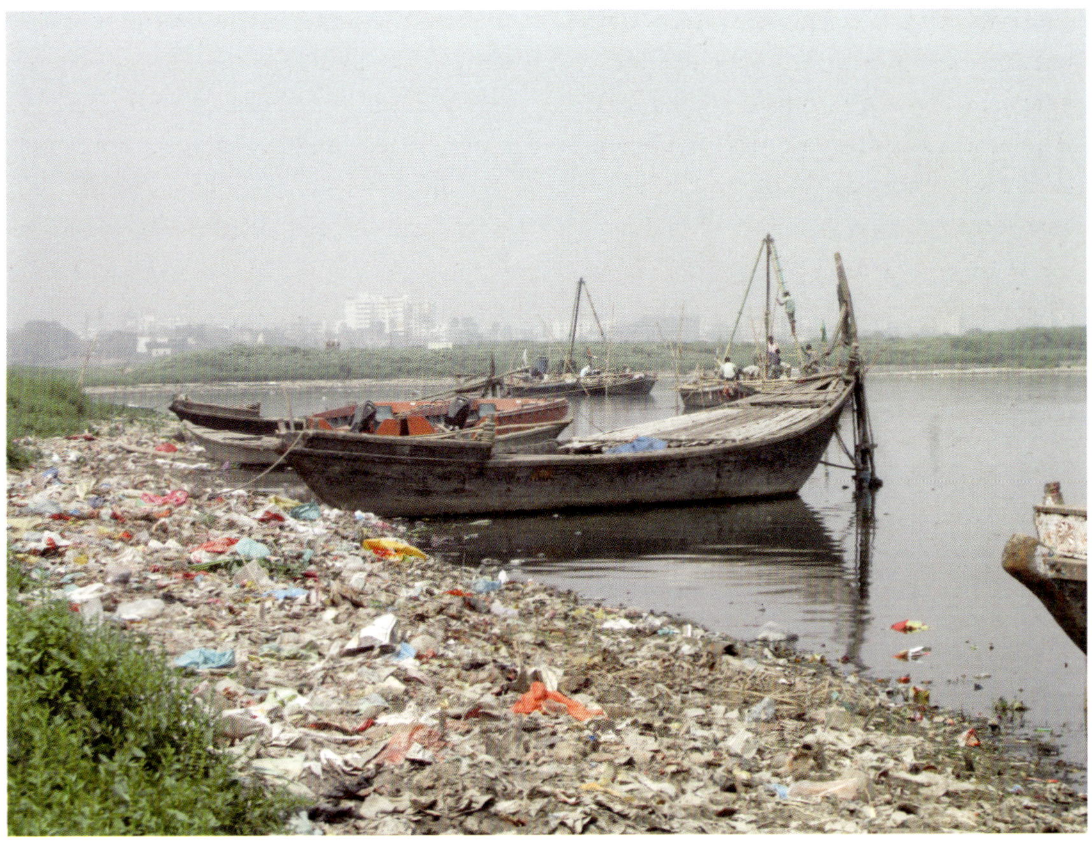

In Patna the riverbank has become a plastic-waste dump

thus deactivating the harmful impacts of elements poured into it. The elements lose their harmful effect and finally settle down on the riverbed. This is how the water of the Ganga is being cleansed down the ages. But at present the quantity of pollutants that are being poured into the river far exceeds its power of auto-cleansing – thus gradually turning it into a polluted water body not fit for human consumption.

KANPUR

From Bithoor the Ganga flows down to Kanpur city – the largest city of Uttar Pradesh. Previously it was known as Kanhapur, named after Lord Krishna (who is also called Kanha). And as the story goes in the *Mahabharata,* Duryodhan had gifted this city to his best friend Karna after whom the city was first named Karnapur. Later on however it was changed to Kanpur.

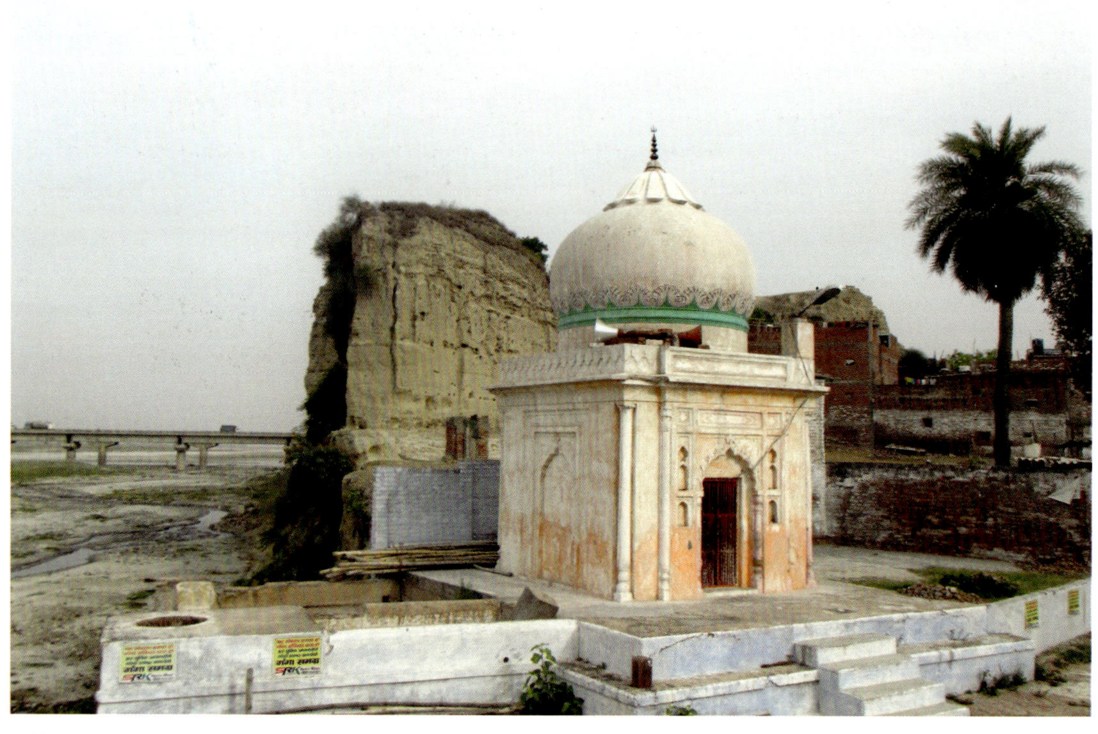

Old ruins of a palace beside a modern temple, Bengali ghat, Kanpur

In 1764-1765 Emperor Buxor of Ayodhya hid in Kanpur after being defeated by the British Army and with British consent he built a fort here as well. But in 1801, after being totally captured by the British, Kanpur lost its age-old heritage and started changing into a modern city. In 1857, during the Sepoy Mutiny, a terrible war ensued between the British Army and the Indian troops led by Nana Saheb. Nana Saheb's battalion was massacred and as revenge, thousands of British men, women and children were killed mercilessly. The history of Kanpur is, therefore, a history of tears and bloodshed.

Kanpur is the largest industrial city of Uttar Pradesh. On one side of the city flows the river Ganga devoid of its effervescence. It is a thin trickle here, analogous to a canal, compared to other places. On the bank stands the temple of Anandeshwar which remains crowded with worshippers right from early morning. Near the temple is the filthy bathing wharf full of flowers, discarded plastic packets and other materials thrown out from the temple. The wharf is cleared every few days by a cleaner who merely collects the huge heap of wastes and dumps it back into the Ganga. Poor Ganga, unable to protest, has to bear this torture on a regular basis. On proceeding further along the bank one comes across a barrage meant to divert the river water to the agricultural fields for irrigation. On the other side of the barrage is a large piece of land, raised out of the river bed, where cultivation is a thriving business. Small boats ply the entire day carrying different agricultural products. The river here has split into thin strips of water bodies for about two miles, indicating that in the near future the river will die a natural death here. And the entire region will be converted into agricultural land. I detected another smaller wharf just after the barrage, where floating decomposed corpses are a common sight during monsoon. The stench of these corpses fills the entire area. According to a local milkman, previously the river had plenty of fish and tortoises who devoured these dead bodies and cleaned the river in the process. But after the construction of the barrage these aquatic creatures have completely vanished leaving the area full of stench and filth.

About a mile north of Kanpur is Jajmou, the oldest leather goods producing centre. There are about 400 tanneries at Jajmou where hides of thousands of cows and buffaloes are tanned daily. Tanning involves chemical treatment of the hides and water, whose wastes are then channelised into the river Ganga. Even though water treatment plants have been constructed here to prevent this growing industrial pollution, yet they are not adequate. National Ganga River Basin Authority and corporation authorities have instructed each tannery to construct individual water treatment plants to stop this growing menace.

However, most of the tannery owners appear impervious to this ruling of the government. The owners and trade union leaders of these tanneries are so powerful, both politically and economically, that the government officials feel scared to inspect their factories and report irregularities to the government. Another important feature of Kanpur is the famous Sisamau drain, where all human corpses and animal carcasses are dumped. Just beside this drain is Bakramundi, a large slum. All waste materials of the slum are cast off into the Sisamau drain which overflows and inundates the entire surrounding areas during monsoon. In other seasons the Ganga is the sole outlet of this filthy drain of Kanpur. According to the local people, the water of the river in this area

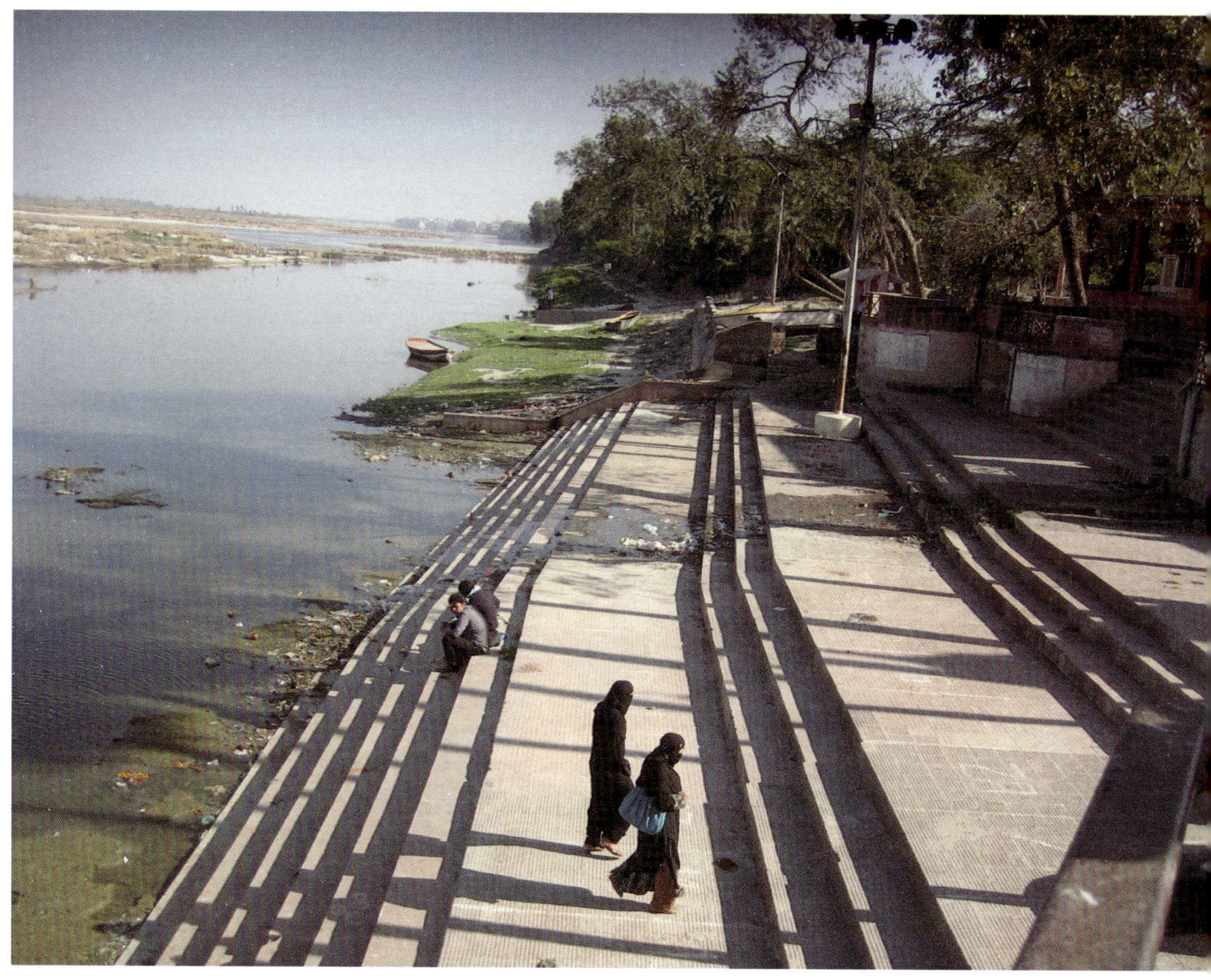

The historic Massacre ghat or the Satti Chaura ghat of Kanpur. Here scores of Englishmen and Indians were butchered during the Sepoy Mutiny of 1857

is so polluted that fish and other aquatic creatures are unable to thrive in it. Even the farmers of the area do not use the water for irrigation. Plants die if watered with the water from the Ganga here. Instead they dig deep wells to draw water and irrigate their fields. As a result the cost of agriculture keeps mounting. However, they have not found any other alternative means to reduce the pollution of the Ganga, particularly in this area.

The Government of India has sanctioned billions of rupees to detoxify the Ganga in Kanpur, but hardly anything is being done. A few preventive measures have been taken but, due to lack of proper implementation, the end result is dismal. Added to it the corrupt businessmen and politicians appear to be more interested in filling their coffers rather than improving the condition of the river. Thus, the Ganga of Kanpur instead of cleansing men of their sins is giving rise to greater sins of corruption.

From a Pilgrim's Diary

I was sitting on the bank of the Ganga at Satti Chaura ghat. The place has witnessed many sad historical events. With me was Sakeel Ahmed, a local schoolteacher. He is an active member of Ganga Banchao (Save the Ganga) Movement. For the last two days while touring different wharfs of the river I saw very depressing sights. Bhairon ghat that stands across the barrage has very little water; and to worsen matters a drain has been connected to it. A half-eaten corpse lay floating in the water. It was such a horrifying sight. I wonder whether such a sight is ever visible in any other part of the world.

Sakeel however tried to assuage my sorrow. 'We are trying our level best. We have approached the politicians and the government officials as well, but despite repeated promises from all of them no steps have been taken,' he said. 'Ganga will never be cleansed,' I replied, 'until we cleanse ourselves.' Sakeel kept quiet for a while and then continued, 'I had read in a journal about the pollution of the river Rhine. It flows down six countries of Europe and is known as the river of love. At one point of time the river had become so polluted that its water was not fit for consumption. So the heads of all the six countries decided to make the Rhine pollution free. Accordingly roads and parks were constructed along its banks and the local people were given the responsibility to look after the workings. Within a span of a few years the Rhine was pollution free. My question is, if a river like the Rhine can be cleansed like this then why not our Ganga?'

'The comparison is fruitless,' I pointed out. 'First of all the length of Rhine is much shorter than Ganga. It's only 1,230 kilometres long, almost half the length of Ganga. Also the entire area of its estuary and banks is about ten million square kilometres compared to Rhine's two million square kilometres. Furthermore, the population residing on the banks of the Ganga is almost ten times more than that of the Rhine. Also the population residing along the banks of the Rhine is conscious about the need of maintaining a pollution-free surrounding. So the question of comparison simply does not arise here.'

Sakeel thought for a few minutes and admitted, 'I agree with that. Yet, my point is, had our authorities implemented the policies properly and included common men in their workings I am sure things would have worked out. Our rules regarding industrial pollution should be more stringent and implemented with due care. That we are tampering with the gift we have received from nature is a national shame. I have approached our next generation, whose minds are yet to be corrupted, and they have volunteered to assist us.'

'Have you started functioning?' I asked. 'Yes, we have. We have approached students from ten schools, four undergraduate colleges, a university and the IITs. And the response is really very positive. Not just the students, even the teachers have volunteered to help us. I believe the power of creation is stronger than the power of destruction.'

I was really impressed by young Sakeel's zeal. And he was absolutely right. In fact, his words reminded me of a recent experience I had while visiting Mathura, another ancient pilgrimage of India. There was the large Lord Krishna temple in Mathura, constructed at his supposed birthplace. Historical records state, the first temple was constructed by Lord Krishna's grandchild Vajranava, which was later extended by Chandragupta Maurya. The temple was then demolished by Sultan Mahmud. The temple was rebuilt only to be destroyed again by Sikandar Lodhi. A new temple came up under the patronage of Veer Singh. Emperor Aurangzeb destroyed it and constructed a mosque there. But after the advent of the British, the present temple came up without a glitch. Despite repeated assaults by barbarians, the existence of the temple could not be wiped out. The same holds true for the Ganga, I feel. If common men come forward with the intention of cleansing its polluting agents, no power on earth can re-pollute our beloved Ganga.

Darkness was fast approaching and it was time for both of us to return home. But before mounting Sakeel's motorcycle, I suddenly caught sight of a young lady and her daughter approaching the river Ganga. She had a wicker lamp in her hand and had come to worship the river. She lit the lamp and performed the usual rites of worship. After that she floated the lamp in the water and sprinkled the holy water around her and left. The sight aroused hope in me. Two opposing forces keep fighting against each other. Here too we were witnessing something of this struggle – a force which wanted to free the Ganga of all pollution; while another, impervious to future happenings, was opposing this positive effort. But finally redemption lay in the hands of the nameless populace who treated the river as their mother. I was reminded of a sloka from the *Rig Veda*:

'With all her eyes the Goddess Night looks forth approaching many a spot: She

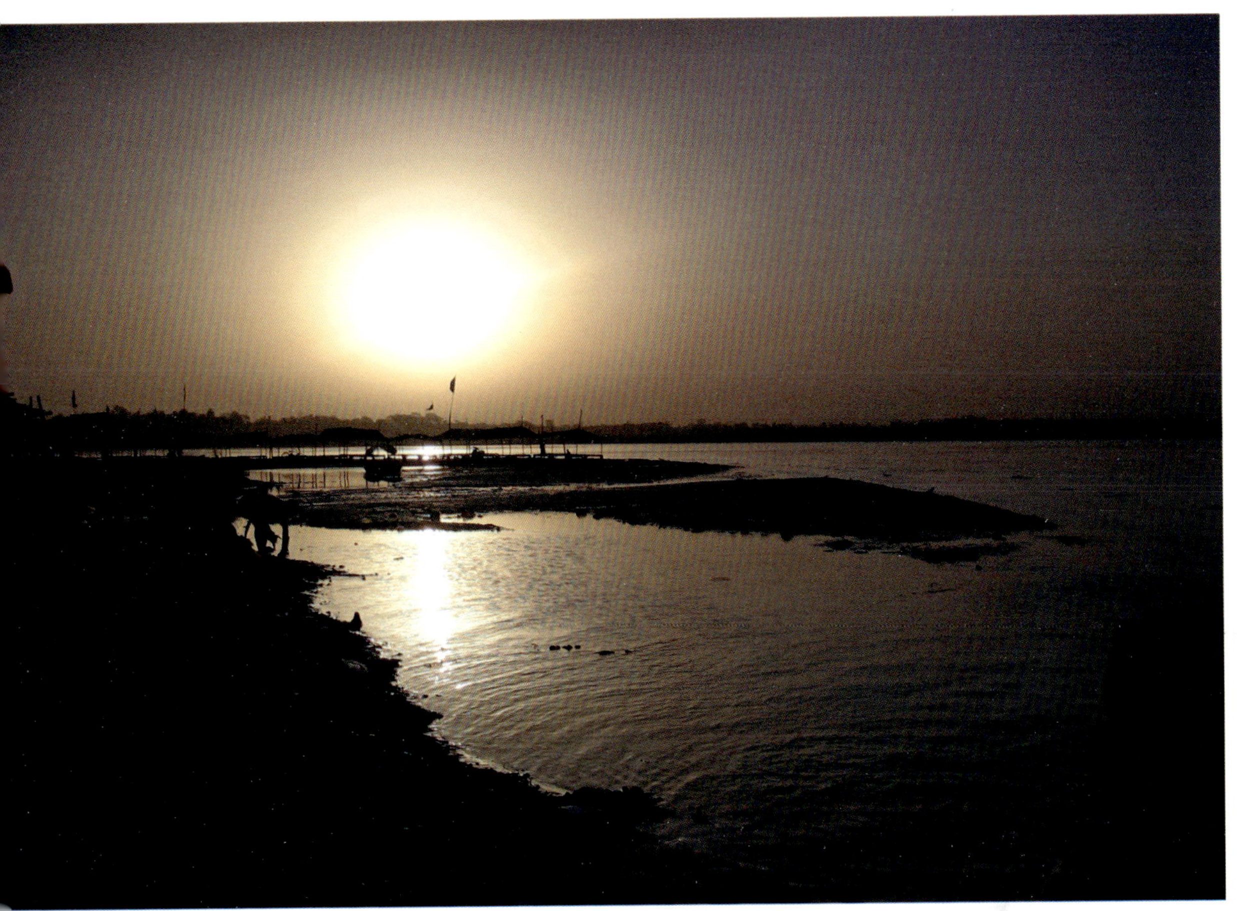

Dawn at Triveni Sangam, Allahabad. Here lies the confluence of the rivers Ganga, Yamuna and the mythical Sarasvati

hath put all her glories on. Immortal, she hath filled the waste; the Goddess hath filled height and depth: She conquers darkness with her light.' (Translated by Ralph T.H. Griffith)

ALLAHABAD

The ancient name of Allahabad was Prayag. Since time immemorial this place was considered holy by the Hindus because it is located near the confluence of the three most important rivers of India: Ganga, Yamuna and Sarasvati (Rig Vedic). Out of the several Aryan colonies Prayag possibly was the most important one. Describing the significance (*Prayag Mahatmya*), an ancient scholar wrote in *Prayag or Allahabad: A Handbook* (1910) that it was the merging point of 'Two noble-born maids – (Ganga and Yamuna – daughters of the ascetic Jahnu and of sun) – wave their white and blue chauris, the woolly tail of the yak.'

In his *Raghuvamsha* poet Kalidasa dwells on this phenomenon. Rama addressing his spouse Sita says,

> Lo! My darling of faultless limbs, how the Ganga mingled in current with the waves of the Yamuna looks! At one place it looks like a string of pearls interspersed with sapphires besmearing neighboring things with their blue luster; while at another place it looks like a garland of white lotuses, the interstices of which are studded with the blue ones. At one place it looks like a flight of white swans fond of Manasa Lake in company with the China geese of dark colors, while at another place it looks like a painting of the earth ornamented with white sandal paste where in the ornamental leaves of the fringes are made of black aloes. At one place it looks like the moonbeam variegated by darkness attached to shade, at another place like a white streak of ornamental clouds with part of the blue sky slightly visible through the chinks; and at yet another, like the body of the God Shiva anointed with cosmetics of ashes and adorned with the ornament of black snakes. (Stanzas 54-57; canto XIII. Translated by Colin J. Holcombe)

In the *Mahabharata* Sage Pulastya narrated how Lord Brahma had conducted a *yajna* here and thereafter the place was called Prayag. There was also the hermitage of Sage Bharadwaj where Lord Rama had put up during his exile to the forests. And after the famous battle of the Kurukshetra, Yudhistira, agonised at the thought of the dead kinsmen and thousands of soldiers, was advised by Sage Markandya to visit Prayag. The visit would not only cleanse his sins but also help him restore his mental peace.

Later, the Chinese traveller Xuanzang on his visit to India described Prayag in the following words:

> The country is five thousand li (1/2 kilometer) in circuit and the capital, which lies between two branches of the river, is also 20 li. The grain products are very abundant and fruit trees grow in great luxuriance. The climate is warm and agreeable; the people are gentle and compliant in their disposition. They love learning and are very much given to hearsay.
>
> There are several Deva temples. The number of heretics is very great. To the south west of the capital, is a stupa which was built by Ashok Raja. Although the foundations have sunk down, yet the walls are more than 100

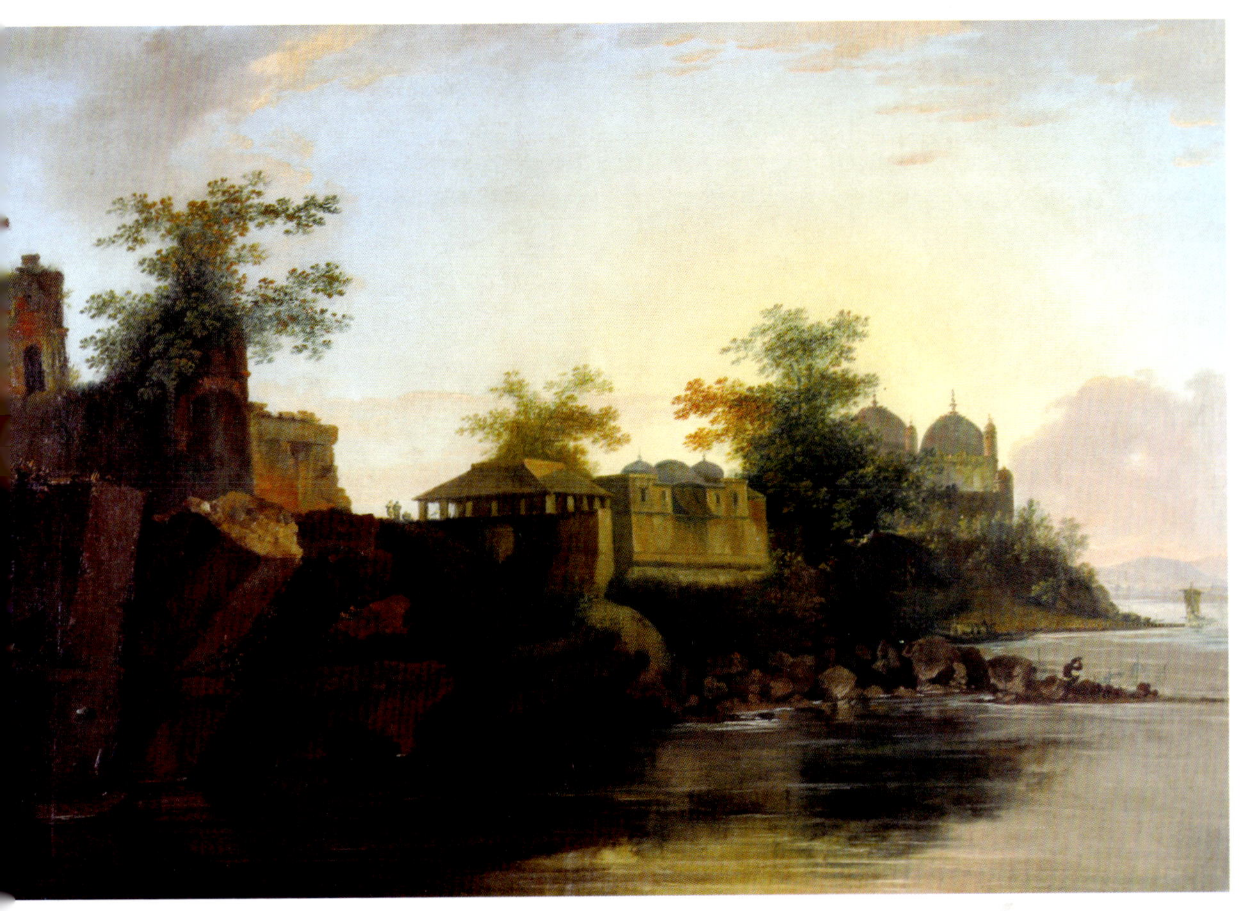

Allahabad fort (curra) near Allahabad by Thomas Daniell

> feet high. Here it was that Buddha discomfited the heretics. By the side of it is a stupa containing hair and nail relics and also a place where he sat and walked. (*Buddhist Records of the Western World* by Samuel Beal)

Rulers of Ikhshakhu dynasty ruled Prayag. They lived in the palace named Illbash, or abode of the gods. Thus, Allahabad comes from the name Illbash. During the reign of Emperor Harsha Vardhana this place of confluence was known as Daanshetra (from where wealth is bequeathed), because every five years he would visit the confluence to distribute wealth from his royal coffer.

Emperor Akbar realising the significance of the place planned to construct a fort here. In 1583 a fort was built here with red-coloured stones. River Yamuna flowed by the side of the fort. The confluence of three rivers is just a few furlongs away. There was the underground temple here and the eternal banyan tree. Many people used to visit the

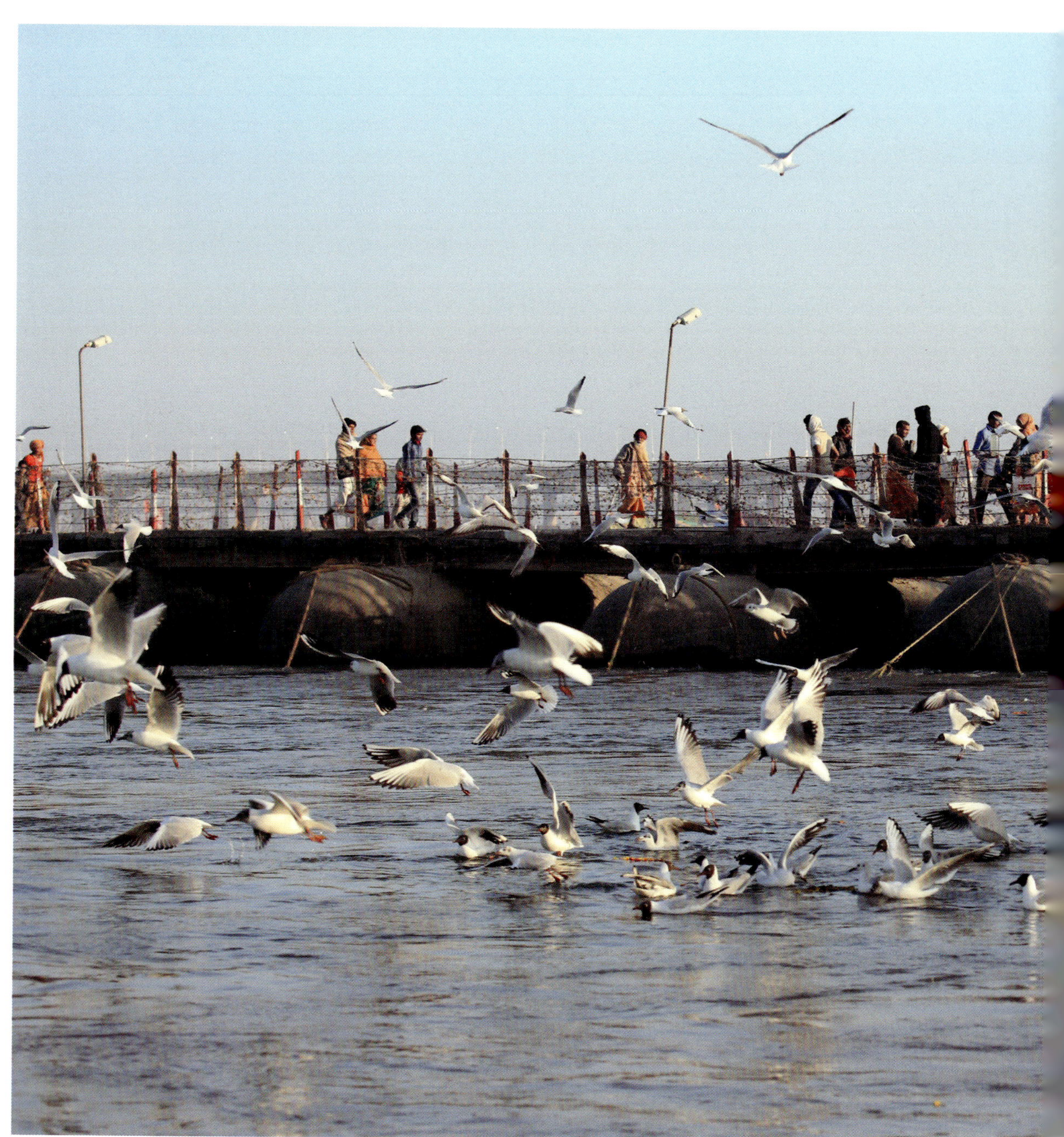

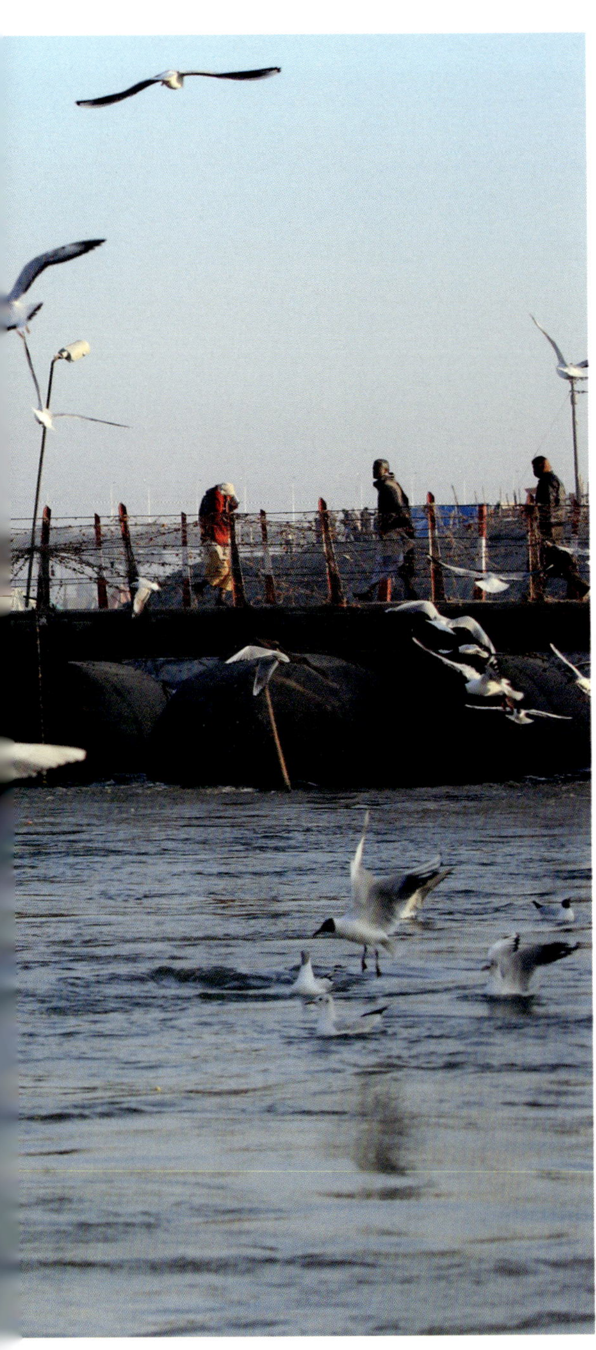

tree and then jump into the Yamuna river and end their lives, expecting to reach heaven straightaway. Later this ancient banyan tree was felled.

Famous artist Thomas Daniell has wonderfully described the fort in the following words:

> This building composed chiefly of freestone, was erected by Emperor Akbar. The pillars are richly ornamented and whole executed in a masterly style. The fort is favorably situated on the point where the rivers Ganga and Yamuna unite. The numerous vessels to be seen on these rivers, particularly on the former, give Great Spirit to the scenery. (*Oriental Scenery,* 1816)

To be precise modern Allahabad came into existence during Akbar's reign. Present Allahabad, now officially renamed Prayagraj, is densely populated. Like Kanpur, Allahabad too channels human wastes to the Ganga. Though much is lost yet, traces of the ancient past become visible during the Kumbh Mela, conducted here every twelve years.

Migratory birds from Siberia fly from the cold Arctic regions to a warmer climate along the Gangetic belt

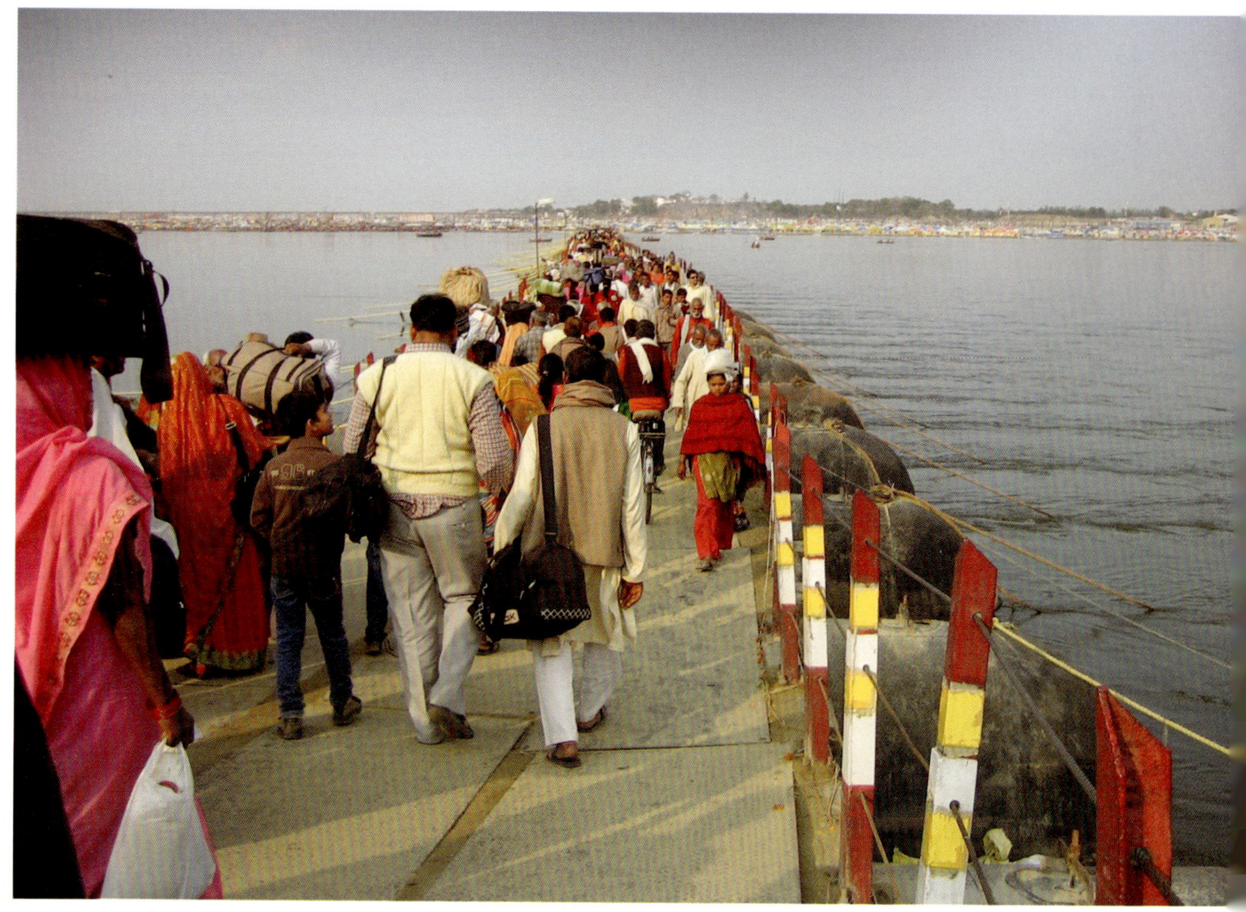

ABOVE: A procession of Kumbh Mela pilgrims cross the Ganga at Allahabad
FACING PAGE ABOVE LEFT: An old man worshipping the Ganga
FACING PAGE ABOVE RIGHT: Joys of childhood
FACING PAGE BELOW: Newlywed couple seeking blessings from Mother Ganga

From a Pilgrim's Diary

Today is the auspicious beginning of the Kumbh Mela. I left the inn in the morning to amble about the mela ground and have a firsthand experience of the mela. The rickshaw could not proceed as the entire fair ground was barricaded by the police with iron rods. The sight of millions of people walking in the fair seemed analogous to the flow of the Ganga. I too merged in the teeming crowd. People from different parts of the country had assembled here, and interestingly it seemed like a melting pot for me. They had all come for a dip in the Ganga to cleanse themselves of sins. The bank of the river overflowed with eager devotees waiting for their turn to take a dip. I could see a barber shaving off the hair of

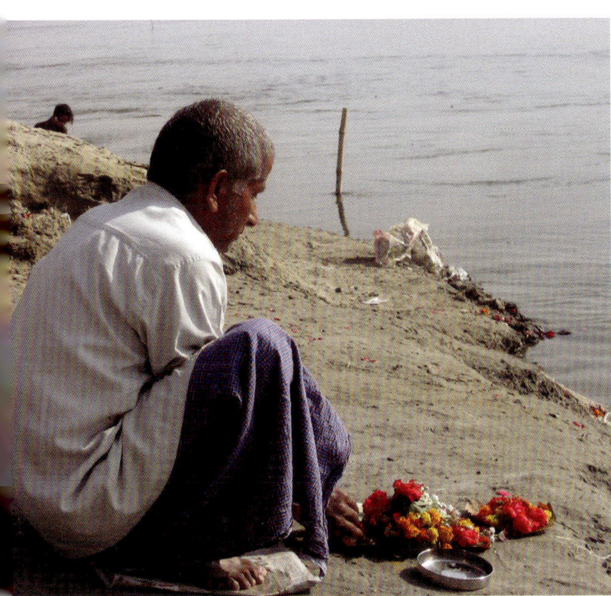

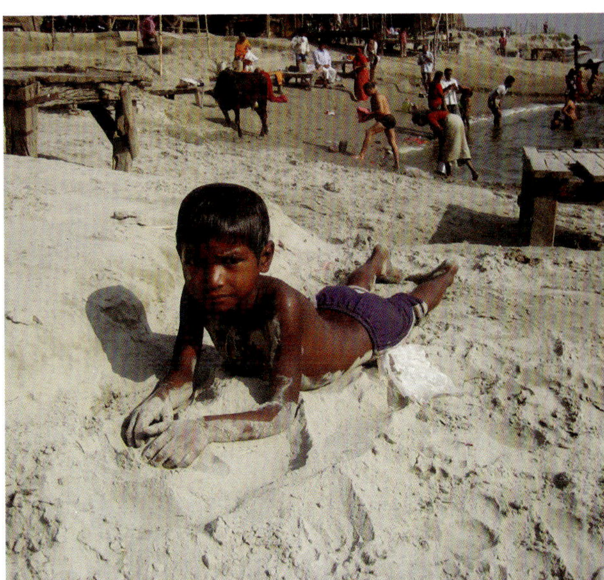

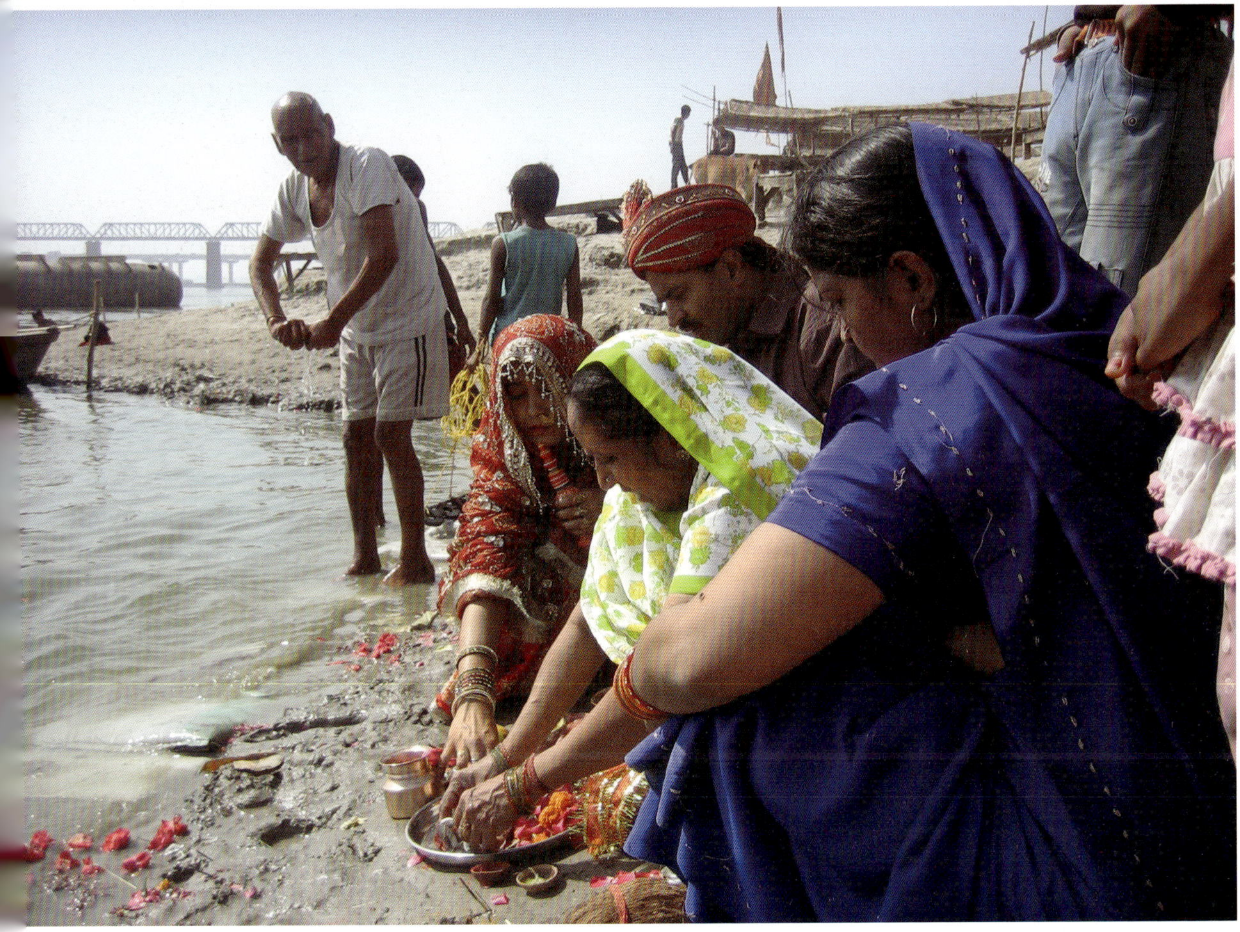

a pilgrim. A few people were selling the holy water of the Ganga. A priest was sitting idle waiting for devotees. A few thugs and ruffians too were loitering about to pounce upon an unsuspecting victim. Everyone had assembled there to make something out of the prevailing situation. I found the young monk of the Ramakrishna order, whom I had met the previous day. I saluted him and he asked, 'So you too have come for the holy dip?'

'I had my share yesterday,' I replied smiling. 'Today I have come to see the fair ground teeming with multicoloured crowds. May I ask you something, Maharaj? What does the word "kumbh" stand for?'

'Kumbh stands for a pitcher,' he replied. 'And mela stands for the ground where people unite. There's another meaning – it is a place where all evil forces are defeated and universal peace is attained. It is a place where men are uplifted spiritually. That is the fundamental message of our ancient religion. Defeat the evil and let holiness triumph. According to the *Purana*s, when the struggle between the gods and the demons ensued for the prized possession of ambrosia, at first a pitcher full of poison emerged from the sea. Since the poison would destroy the entire creation Lord Shiva volunteered to drink from the pitcher full of poison. His throat turned blue because of the poison and he came to be known as Neelkantha (*neel* is blue and *kantha* means throat). Huge amounts of wealth followed the poison and finally came out the pitcher full of ambrosia. Another round of battle followed between the gods and the demons. Both sides wanted to consume the contents of the pitcher to gain immortality. The fierce battle lasted twelve years (twelve days for the gods). In the meantime, Jayanta, son of God Indra, ran away with the pitcher only to be pursued by the demons. Jayanta tired of this marathon took rest at four points on earth. He put down the pitcher while he rested, and on all these four points droplets of ambrosia spilled over. These four points therefore became holy spots for the people. They were all situated on the banks of three different rivers – Nasik situated on the bank of river Godavari, Ujjaini on the bank of river Shipra, Haridwar and Prayag on the banks of river Ganga. These four places thus became famous as four pilgrimages. Every twelve years on an auspicious day and hour (according to the Hindu almanac), a holy dip is advised at any one of these four places, to cleanse men of their sins. It is believed that a dip in the Ganga on that particular day and hour spiritually liberates a person. Hence down the ages Kumbh Mela is considered to be an ideal cleansing festival of various human bondages. In fact Kumbh

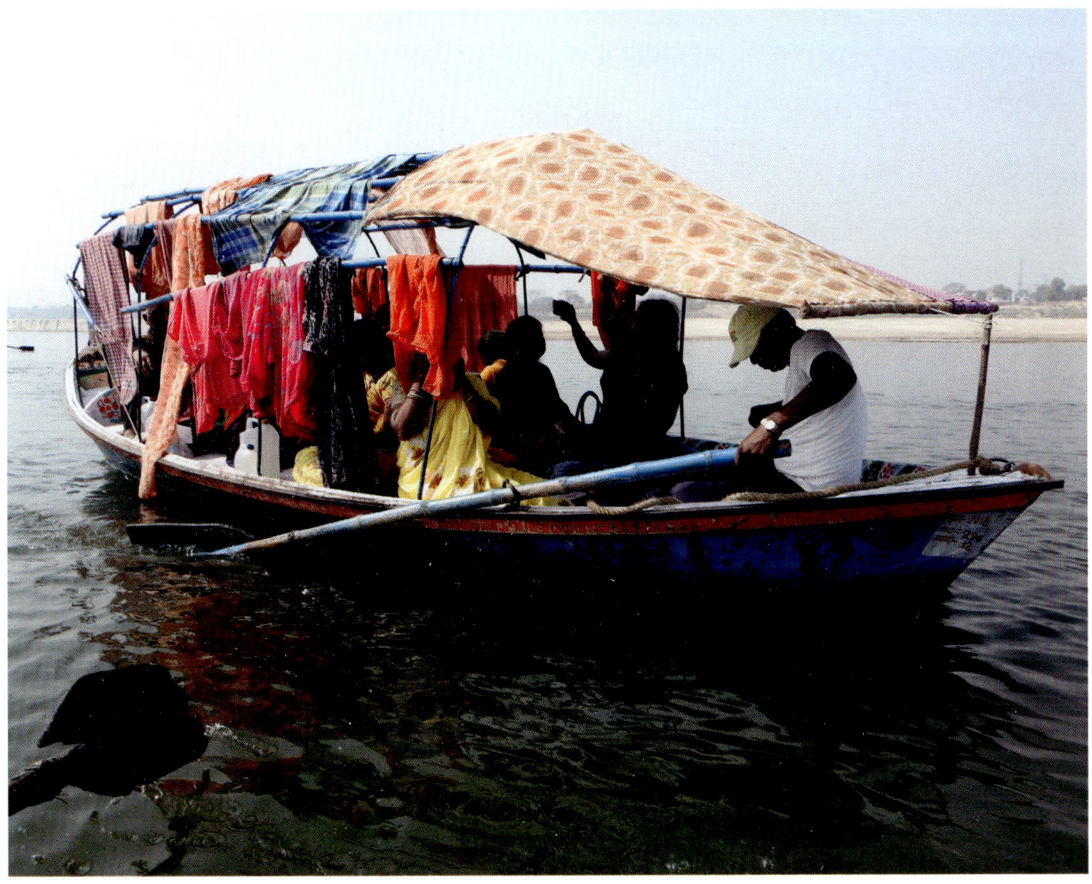

Going back to the riverbank after taking a bath in the Ganga

Mela actually provides a slice of Indian life and heritage.'

'When did the Kumbh Mela start?' I asked, impressed by his interpretation of mythology and history. 'Though the exact date and year is unknown, there is no reason to doubt its ancientness. Kumbh Mela was first mentioned in the travelogue of the Chinese traveller Xuanzang. Xuanzang was a Chinese pilgrim who came to India in 630 CE and spent fifteen years in the country. He visited most of the Buddhist pilgrim sites of India. From his descriptions we have come to know many things about ancient India. Let me read to you what Xuanzang wrote.' The young monk took a book out of his bag and started reading aloud. 'This is what Xuanzang had to say:

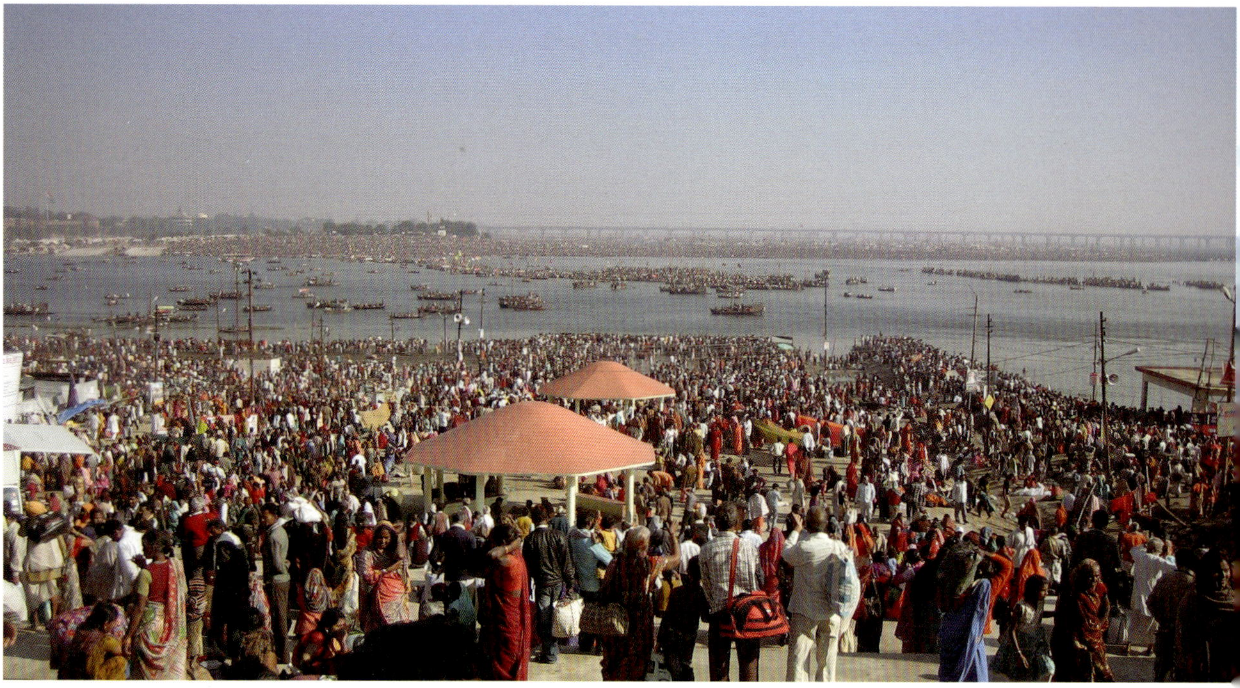

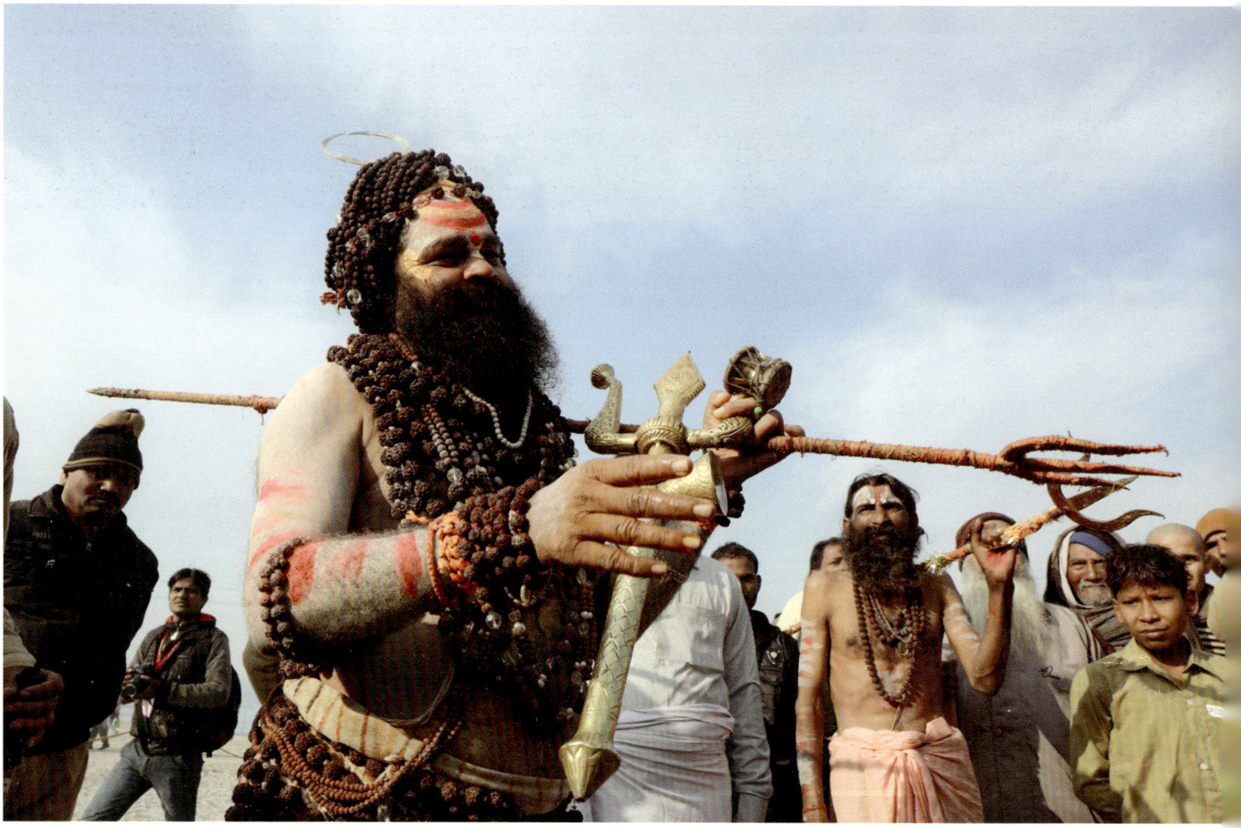

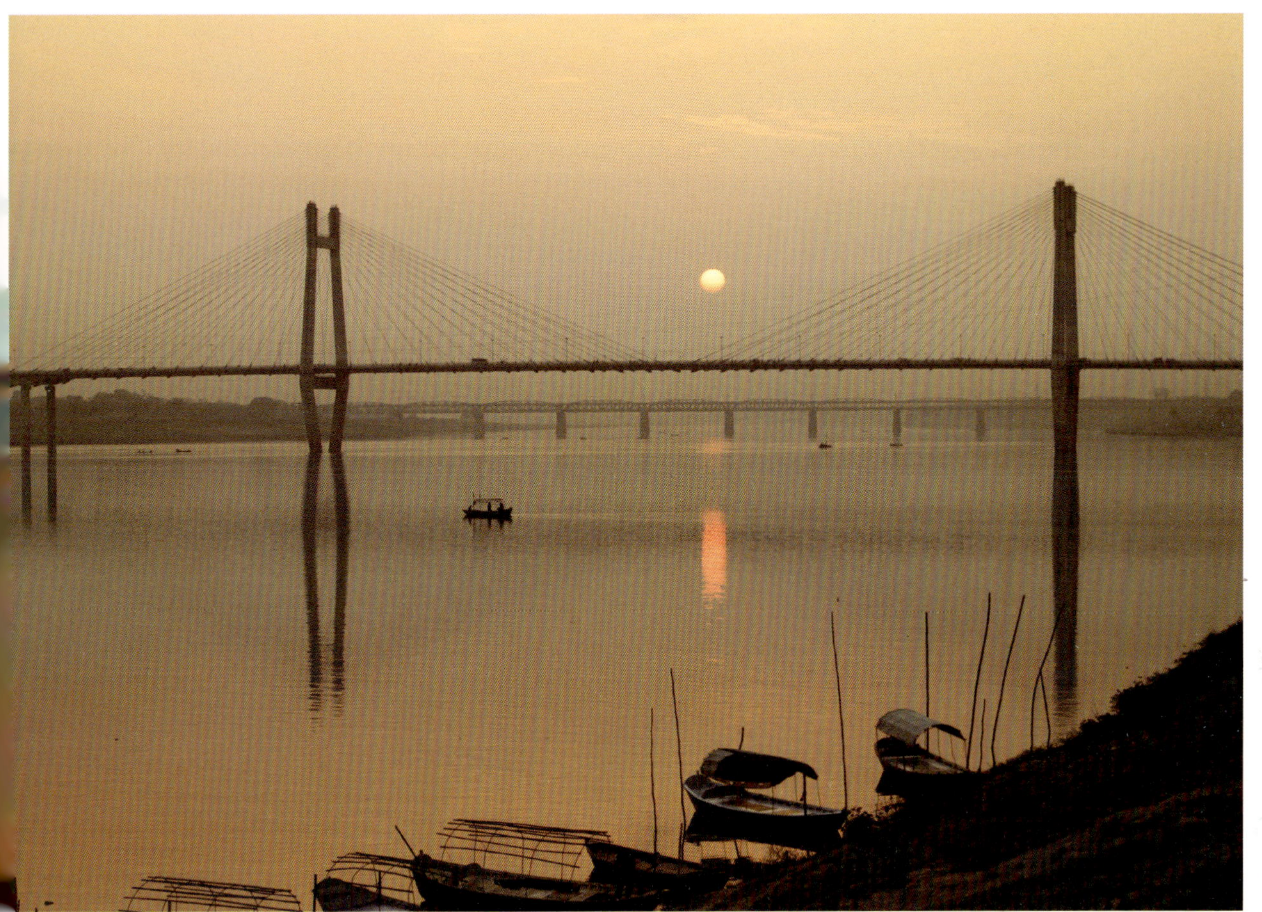

ABOVE: Yamuna bridge, Allahabad

FACING PAGE ABOVE: Kumbh Mela – congregation of pilgrims at the world's largest religious festival

FACING PAGE BELOW: Ash smeared and dreadlocked Naga sadhus wearing rosary beads and armed with tridents are a major draw at the Kumbh Mela

On the east this kingdom borders on the river Ganga, on the north it abuts on a great mountain (Range), through its center flows the river Yamuna. Going about 800 *li* to the east of this river, we come to the source of the river Ganga. This head stream is about three or four *li* in width. It flows south east, and where it enters the sea it is 10 *li* and more in width. The water of the river is blue, like the ocean and its waves are wide and rolling as the sea, the scaly monsters though many, do no harm to men. The taste of the water is sweet and pleasant and sands of extreme fineness border its course. In the common history of the country this river is called Foshwui, or the

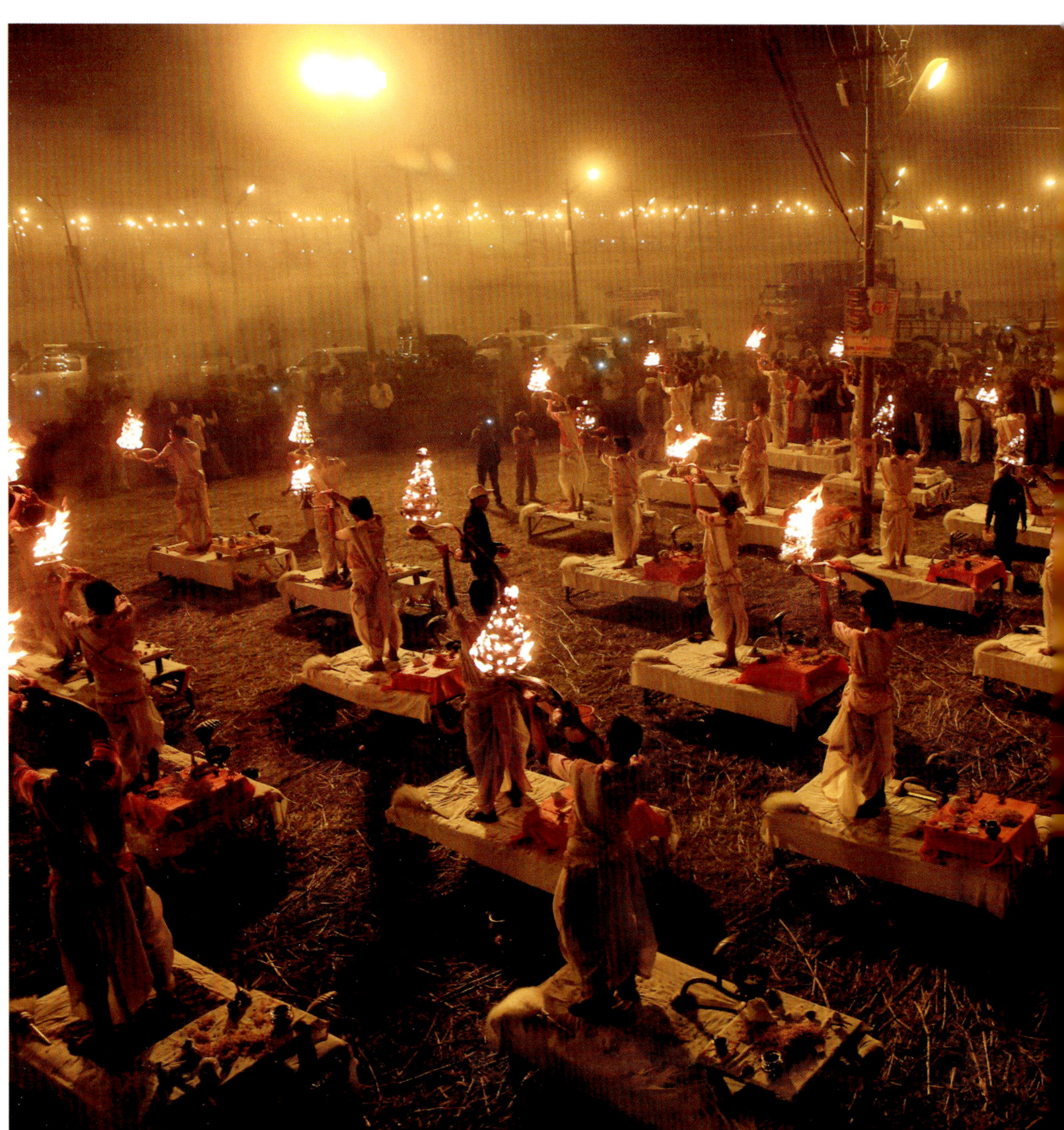

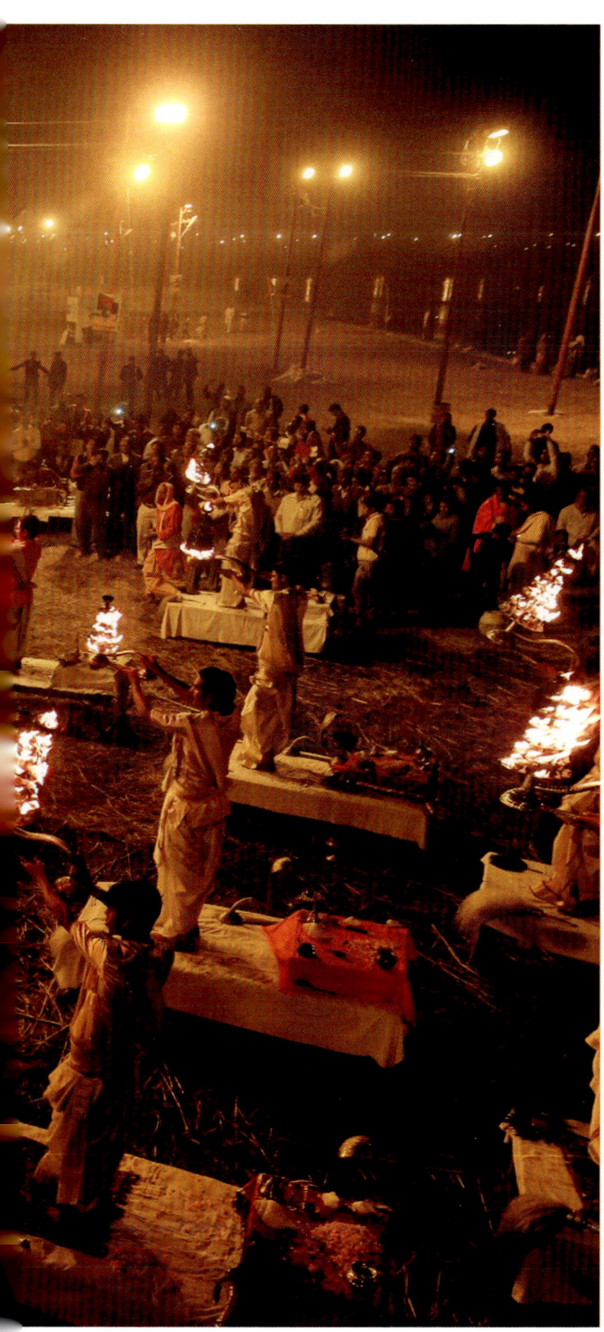

> 'blessed River'; 'those who bathe in it are cleansed from sin;' those who drink its water or even rinse their mouth there from, escape from all dangers and calamities and when they die, forthwith are born in heaven, and enjoy happiness. So the common folk, men and women, are always congregating on the banks of the river.

The monk closed the book and paused. Then he said, 'The present Kumbh Mela was first initiated by Acharya Shankar, to counter the growing influence of the Buddhists and the Jains. It was Shankar who revived the flagging spirit of Hinduism. And in his effort to do so he collected large numbers of Hindu monks and then started the Kumbh Mela. Shankar wanted common men and ascetics to take part in this large fair (mela) to exchange knowledge. The monks would impart spiritual knowledge to the worldly people while the worldly people would learn to practise the art of renunciation. It was not a mere platform for cleansing of sins, that he visualised, but an ideal platform for exchanging ideas as well.'

It was almost afternoon and the crowd was growing bigger and bigger with every passing minute. There was no place to stand

Priests offering evening worship with lighted lamps at Kumbh Mela, Allahabad

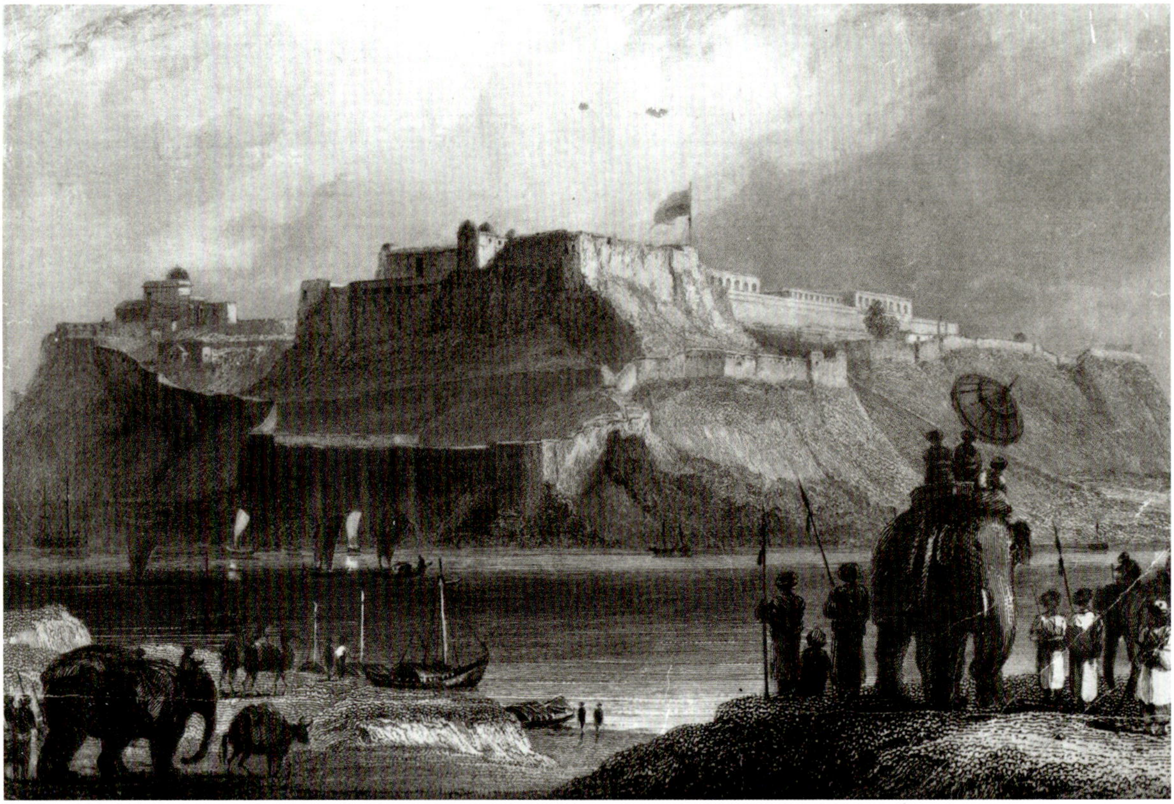

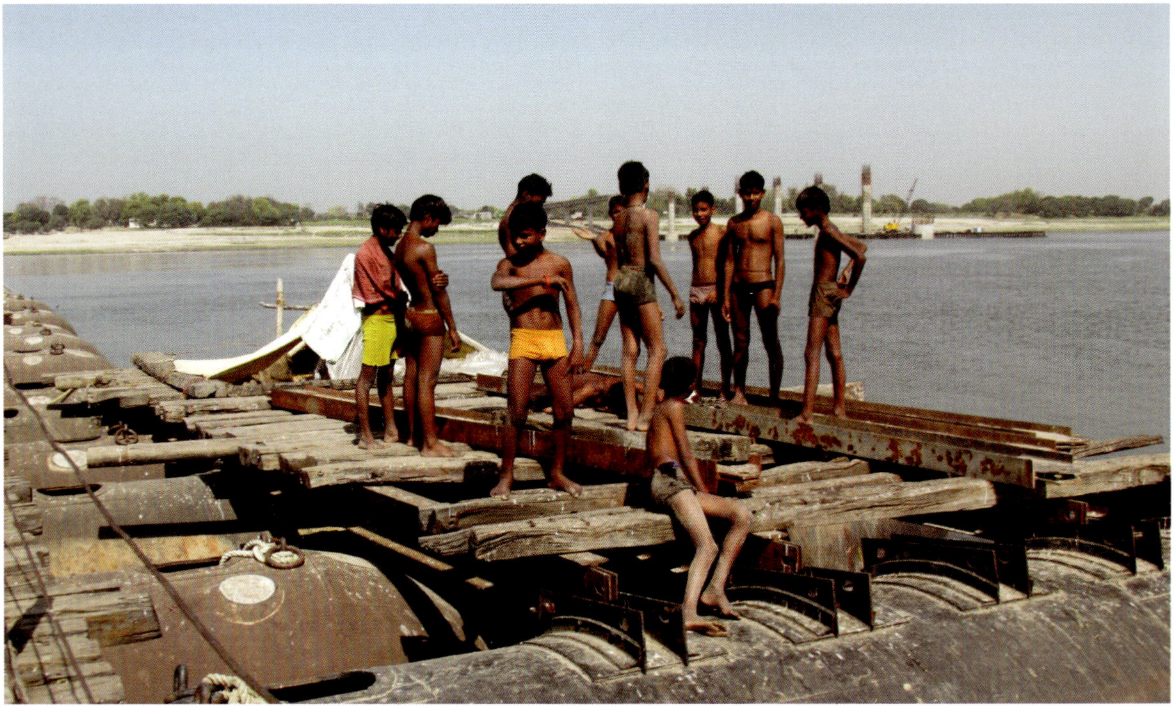

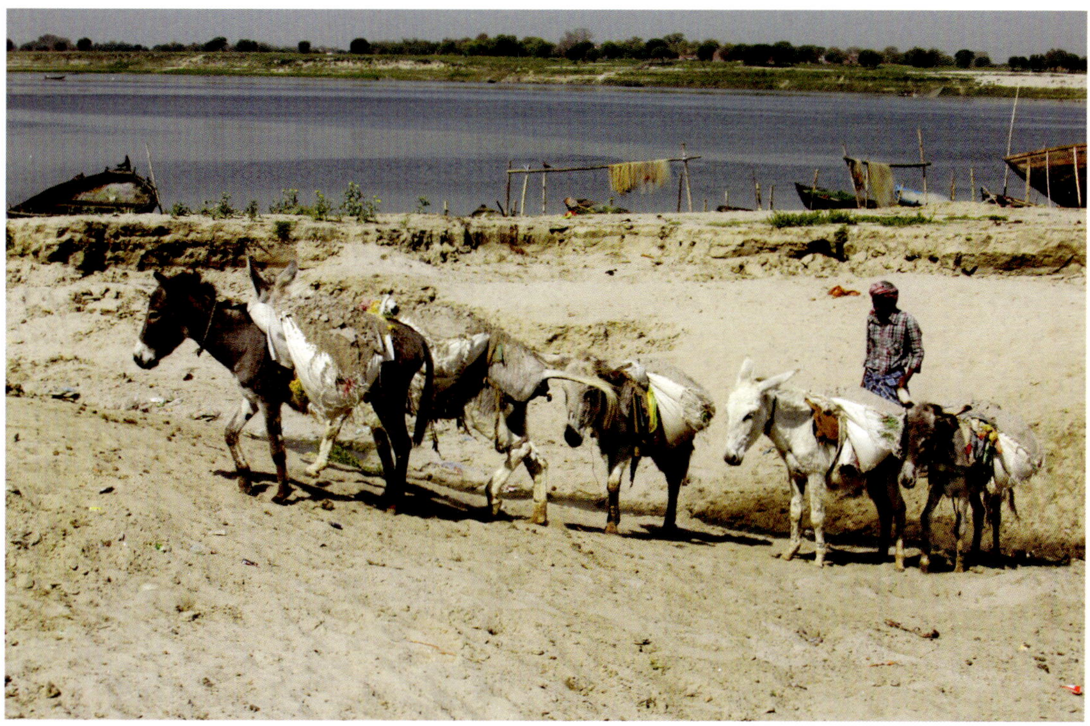

ABOVE: Donkeys carrying sand on the riverbank at Chunar
FACING PAGE ABOVE: *Fortress of Chunar of the Ganges* by William Daniell
FACING PAGE BELOW: Young boys getting ready for a swim, Chunar

and observe; so I kept walking. Everybody seemed to move towards the Ganga, and I merely followed their footsteps. Suddenly I found myself floating in the relative warm water of the river Ganga. I was practically in a trance. Ladies were bathing beside me but I hardly felt like glancing at them. Our bodies touched at times but we were not bothered. All of us seemed to move towards one goal – cleanse yourself of all sins.

CHUNAR

Famous for its fort, picturesque surroundings and salubrious climate, Chunar, a small town, is forty kilometres away from Varanasi, located on the banks of the Ganga. This town has developed on a hillock, with the Ganga flowing in the form of a half crescent, with open spaces all around it. There is no record of who built this town, but according to legend, Bhartrihari, the elder brother of King Vikramaditya, used to meditate

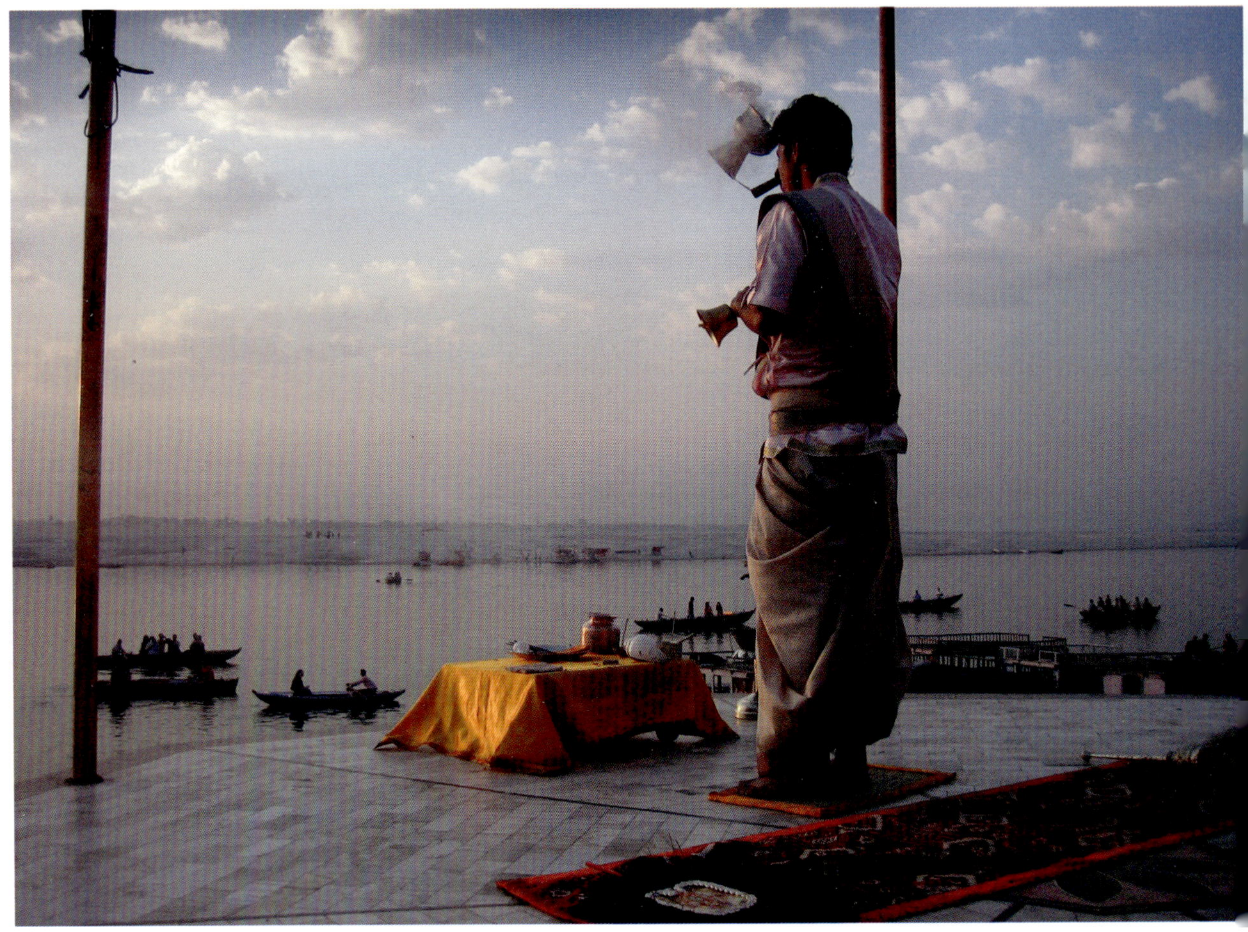

Ganga *aarti* ceremony at dawn

here and after his death he was cremated at the same place. His cremation ground is respected by people of all religions. The main occupations of the people of Chunar are carpet weaving and making stone utensils and idols.

VARANASI

Varanasi is said to be the oldest city in the world. From time immemorial this world of ours has witnessed the rise of so many cities and so many civilisations, but with the onslaught of time most of them have died a natural death. But the city of Varanasi, like the continual flow of the river Ganga, has permanently featured itself on the world map. Analogous to the descent of the Ganga from heaven, it is said that Varanasi too was created by Lord Shiva to be his and Parvati's permanent abode. Indians believe that Lord Shiva resides here. Descending from the Himalayas, the river Ganga sometimes flows

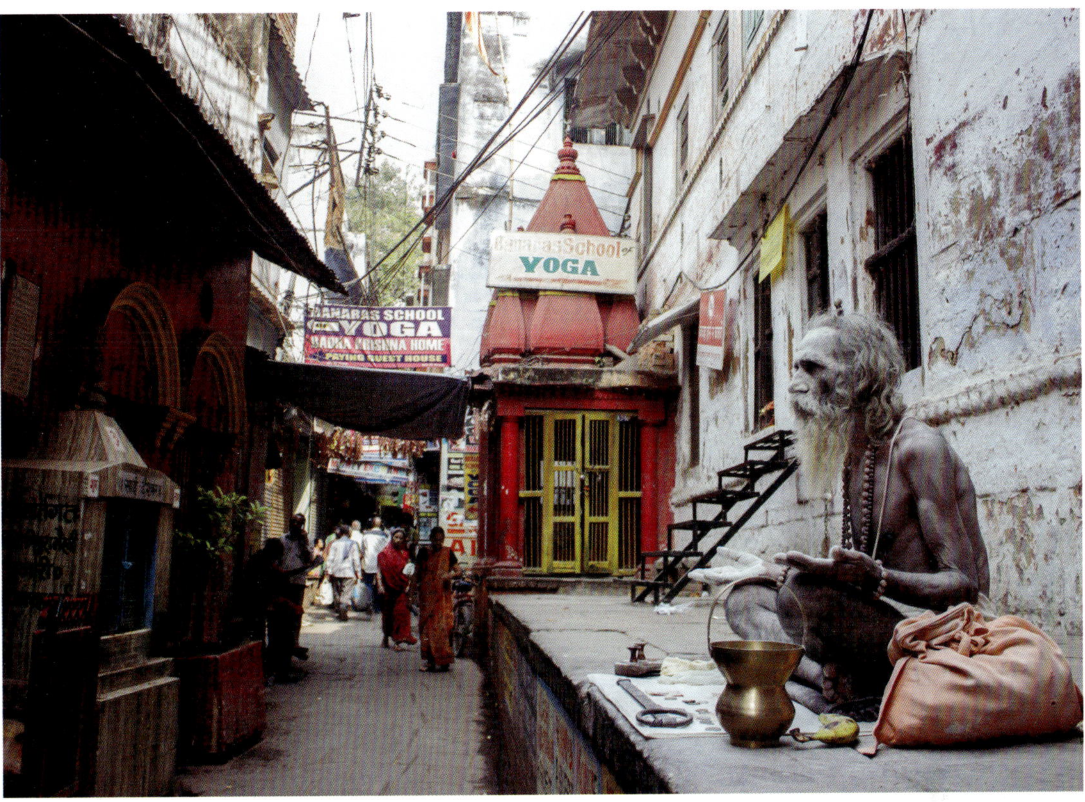

One of the numerous narrow and congested lanes of Varanasi

southward and sometimes northward. Here in Varanasi the Ganga flows northward. According to the *Purana*s, Lord Vishnu's incarnation *Baman* avatar had once stopped the flow of the Ganga and had redirected its course northward.

One legend about Varanasi is that it was established three thousand years ago by King Suho's son Kashya. From Kashya was derived the name Kashi (another name for Varanasi). Another story says that because of the confluence of three rivers, Ashi, Varuna and Ganga, this place came to be known as Varanasi. In the ancient times the incessant flow of the two rivers Ashi and Varuna had supplied Varanasi plentiful water, but now due to constant dumping of human refuse they have become almost non-existent.

Both the Indian epics the *Ramayana* and the *Mahabharata* record the existence of Varanasi. In fact Sumitra, the third queen of King Dasaratha (*Ramayana*), was the

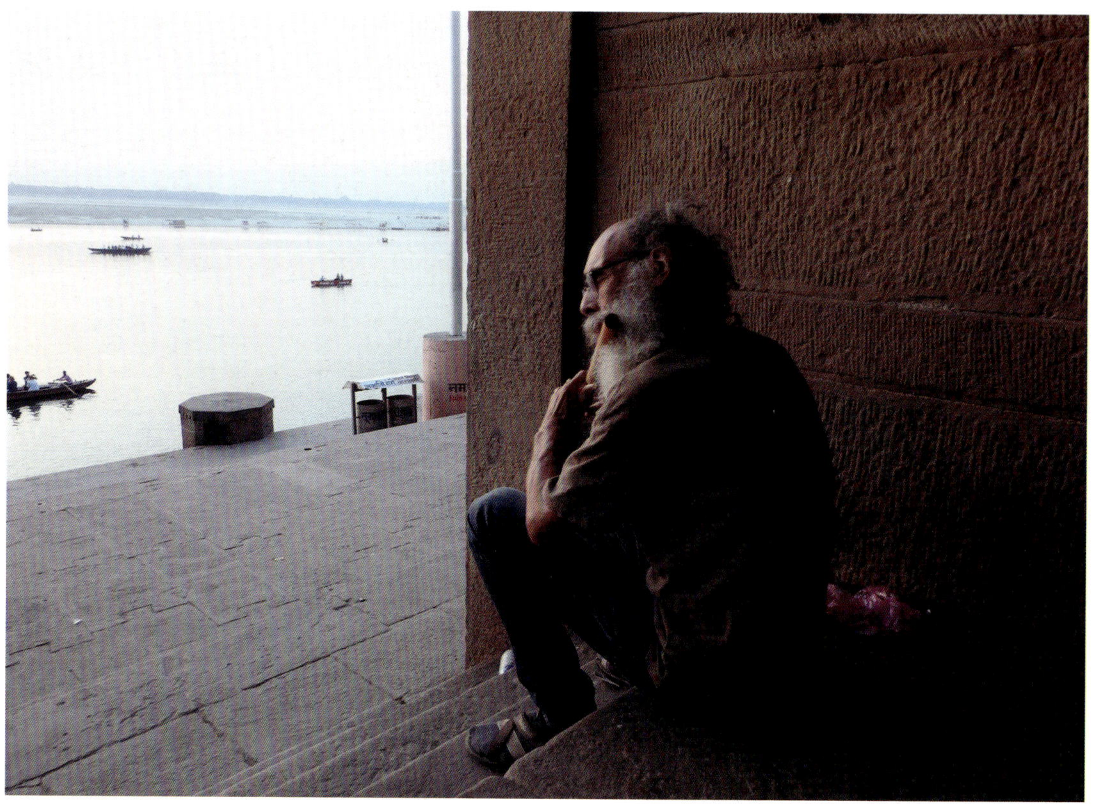

An Italian artist trying his hand at the Indian flute

princess of Varanasi. *Skanda Purana* talks about Varanasi as a pilgrimage. We learn of King Suho and his son Kashya, the first king of Varanasi, from the *Skanda Purana.* In 1600 BCE out of the sixteen important cities of our country Varanasi was considered to the prime one. Right from its inception Varanasi has been the principal centre of learning in India. People from different parts of the country would come here in pursuit of higher learning. Even Gautama Buddha after attaining nirvana, chose Sarnath, situated near Varanasi, to be the prime centre for preaching his doctrines to the people. His disciples would thus frequent Varanasi to preach the doctrines of the Buddha.

Yet initially Varanasi was not considered to be a holy land. The Aryans rather disliked the city and were actually scared of it. The first tribe that settled here was known as Kasi or Kasaite, from which was

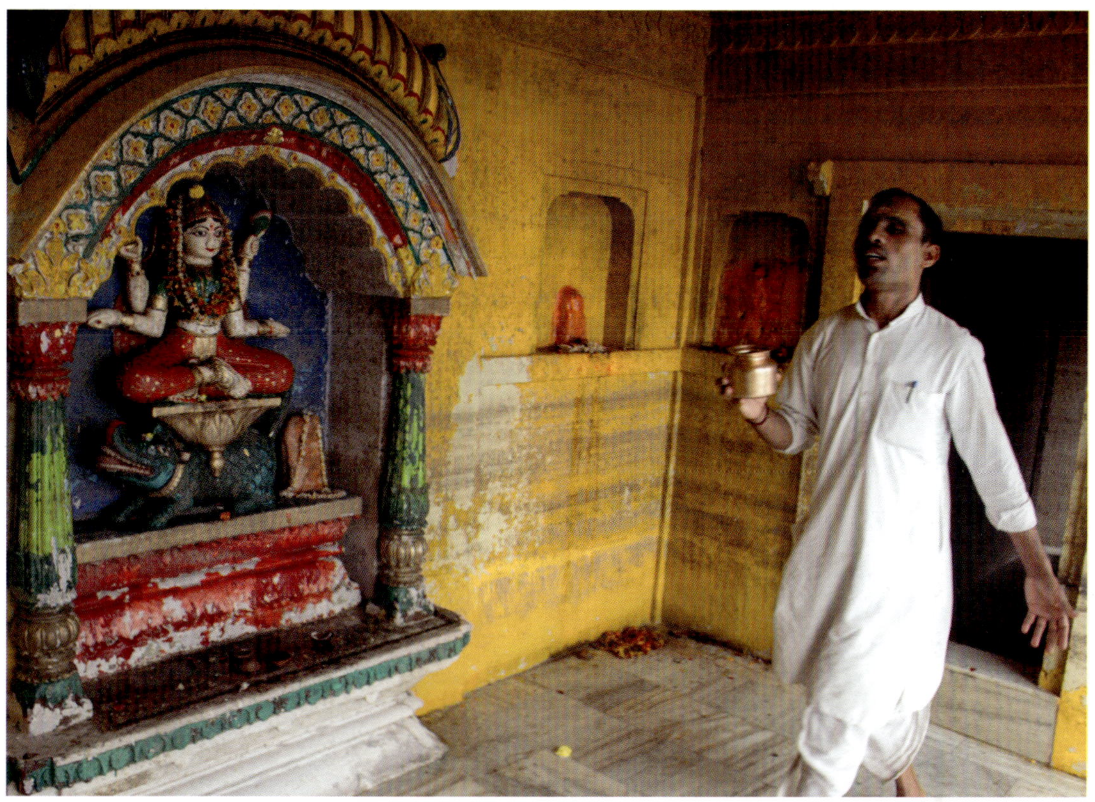

A priest preparing for puja at a Ganga shrine

derived the name Kashi. Neither the Vedas nor did Sage Manu consider Varanasi to be a sacred land. It was only after the second century BCE when Varanasi became a flourishing business and trading centre was it considered a sacred land. Various commercial articles were shipped to different parts of the world from Varanasi.

According to Reverend M.A. Shering, in the remote past when European countries like Babylon and Ninevi were fighting against each other, when Athens was gradually accumulating political power, and when Rome did not even exist, Varanasi was flourishing in full glory. To embellish his palace, even King Solomon imported valuable goods from Varanasi. Varanasi was famous for many other achievements as well. Later on Macaulay too described Varanasi as a flourishing trading centre where ships loaded with different goods anchored round the clock. Palaces both at Versailles and St

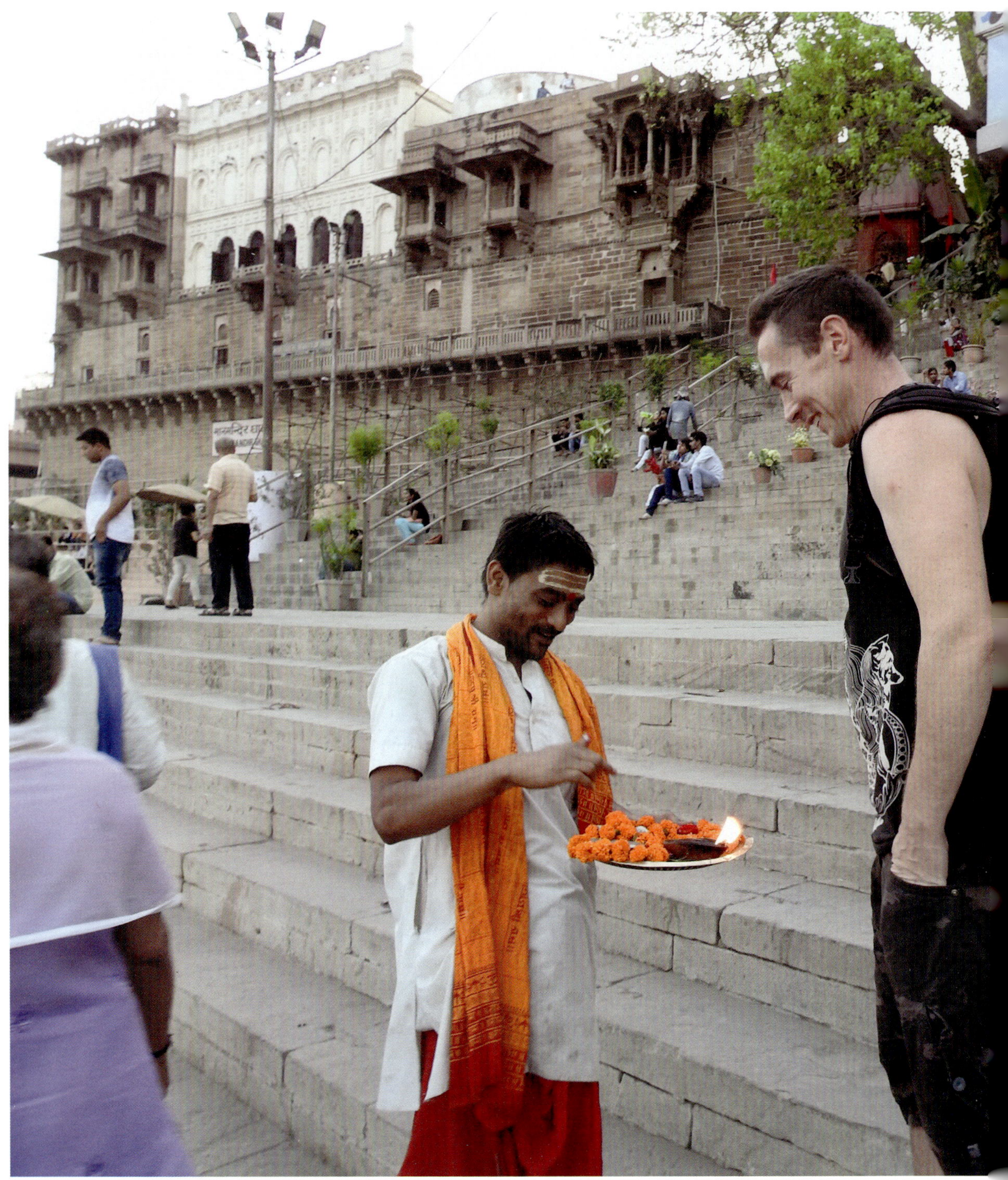

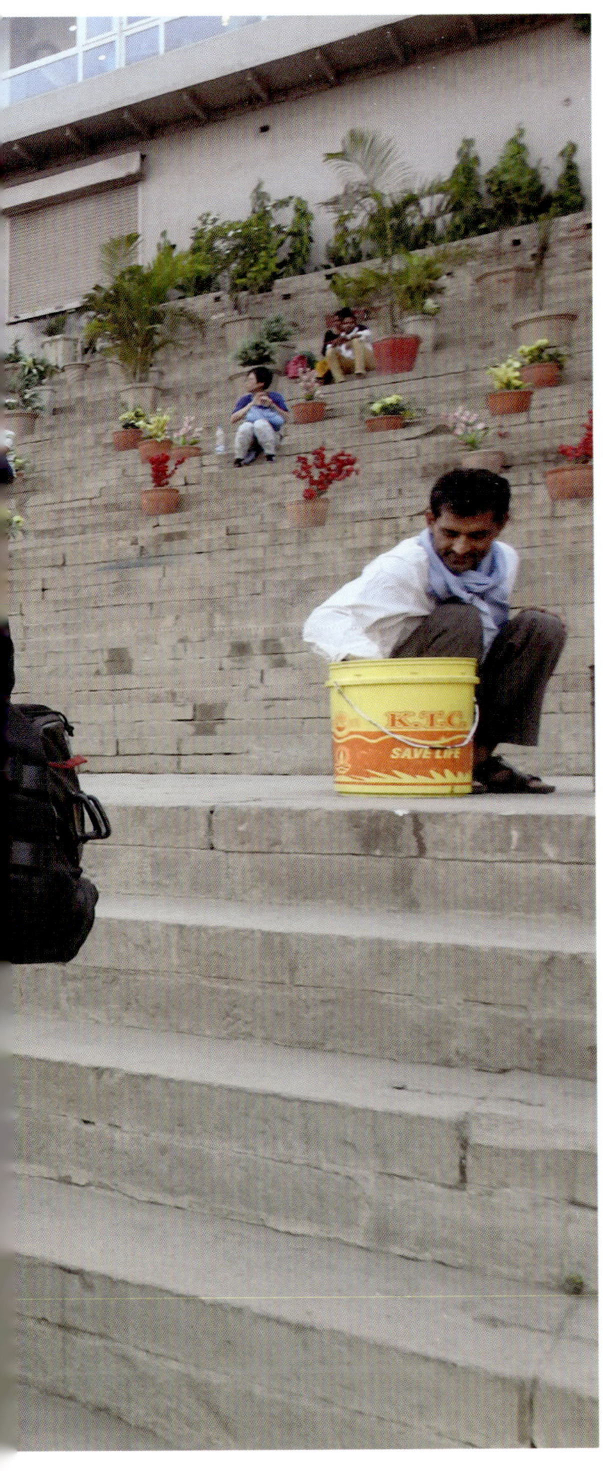

James were decorated with expensive saris imported from Varanasi.

Situated on the banks of the river Ganga, Varanasi is a sacred land for all religions – Buddhism, Hinduism and even Jainism. Innumerable temples have been constructed here. Some say Varanasi is a land of thousand temples while some prefer to double the number, i.e. two thousand at the least. The chief temple however is that of Lord Shiva familiar as Lord Viswanath. Devotees keep flocking the temple right from dawn till late night. For Hindus, this is the holiest of holy temples on earth. As mentioned earlier, people believe that Lord Shiva abounds here. The topmost peak of the temple, which is fifty-one feet high, is encircled by many other smaller peaks as well. Ranjit Singh had wrapped all these peaks with 880 kilogrammes of gold. According to various records, the initial Shiva Lingam was more than fifty metres high. During the reign of Emperor Akbar the temple was once renovated but Emperor Aurangzeb, being totally against Hindu religion, destroyed it and constructed a mosque there. The present Shiva Lingam and the temple were built by Rani Ahalyabai of Indore.

The most striking feature of Varanasi is its religious tolerance. People following

Different worlds merge on the ghats of Varanasi. Here a priest and a student bond over their love for the river

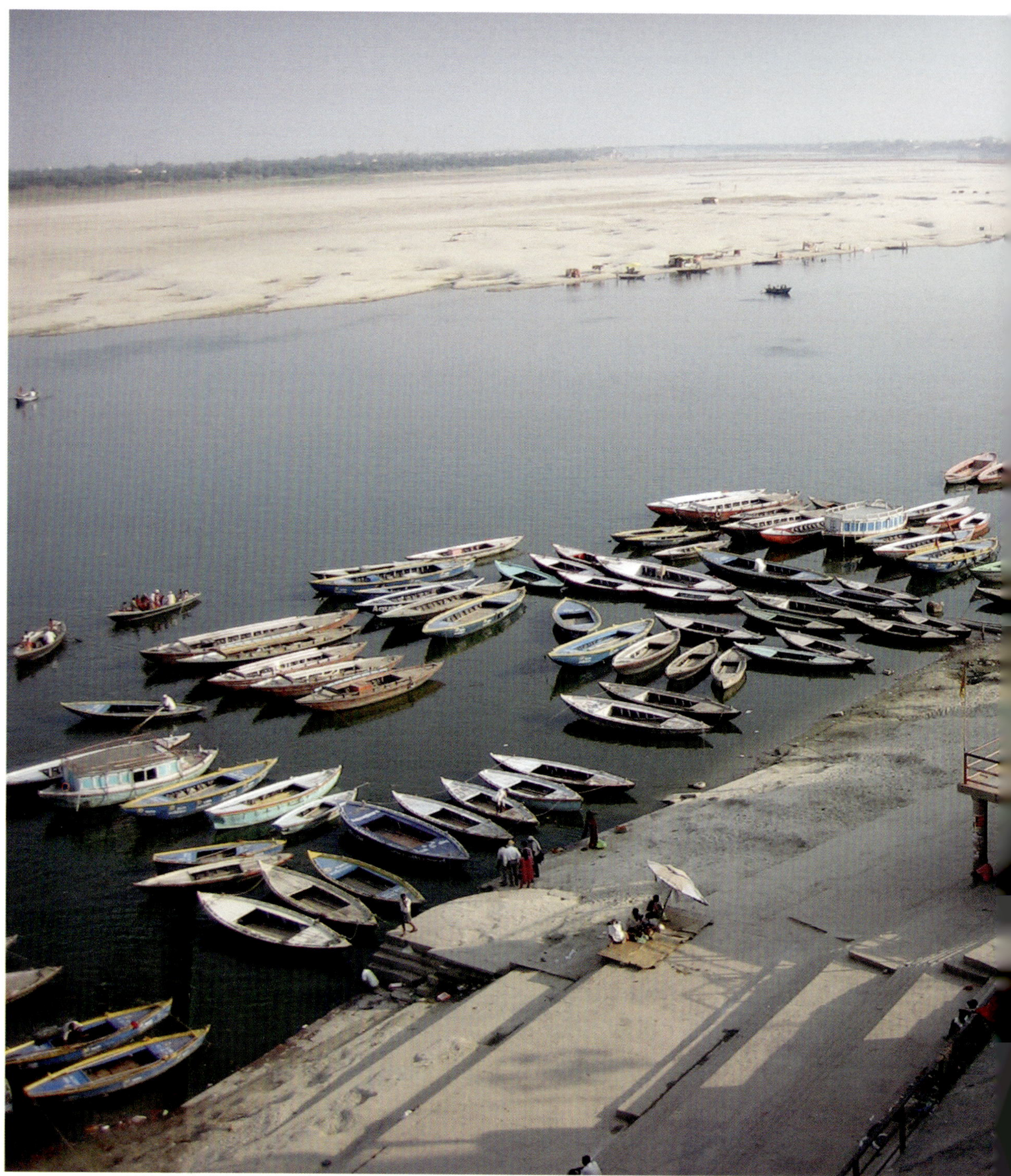

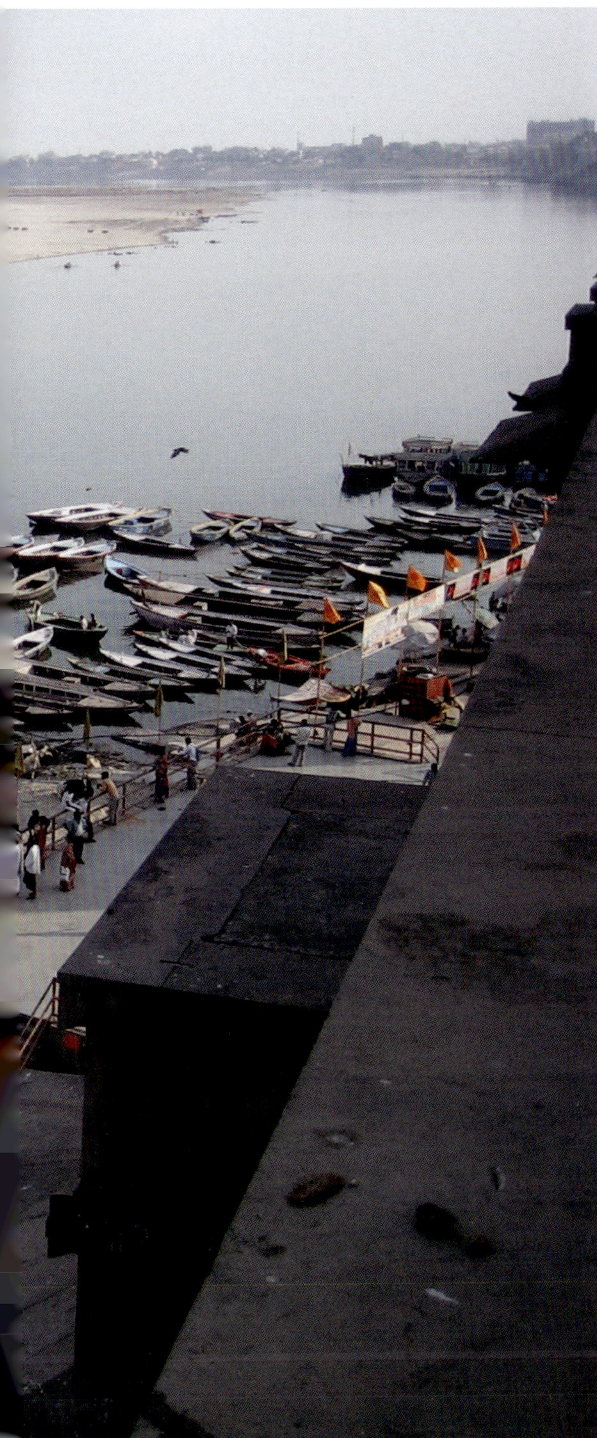

different religions come to live happily in Varanasi. The mosque and the temple of Lord Viswanath exist side by side. And this has been happening down the ages. Unfortunately present-day politicians have introduced strict security vigilance both at the Viswanath temple and the adjacent mosque. Yet, even now one can hear simultaneous chanting of Vedic slokas and Azan. Even on the streets one comes across almost naked monks carrying rudraksha rosaries walking unconcernedly with foreigners. The entire city is a unique conglomeration of the ancient and the modern. Despite all changes, the age-old spirit of the city is still palpable everywhere. But the central attraction of Varanasi is the river Ganga. People come here for holy dips in the Ganga to cleanse all their sins. Unfortunately, even here, like at Kanpur and Allahabad, the pollution level of the river water is pretty high. Steps are being taken to cleanse the river.

The Bathing Ghats of Varanasi

The real spirit of Varanasi seems to exist both in the river Ganga and on the bathing ghats or wharfs dotting the bank. There are numerous wharfs throughout Varanasi. Right from prehistoric times the river

Lined up boats creating a pretty pattern. Boat rides are very popular here with both pilgrims and tourists

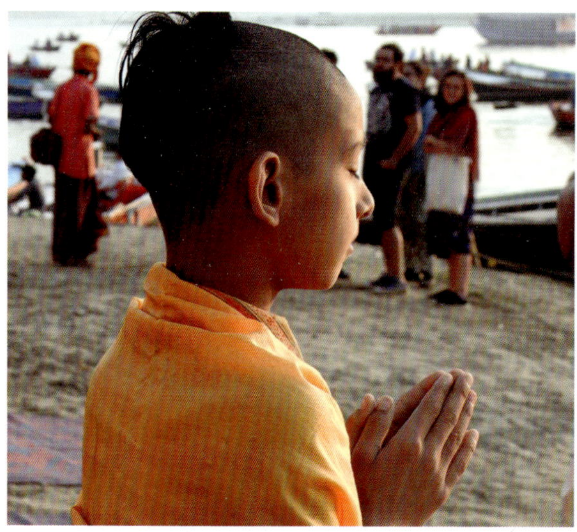

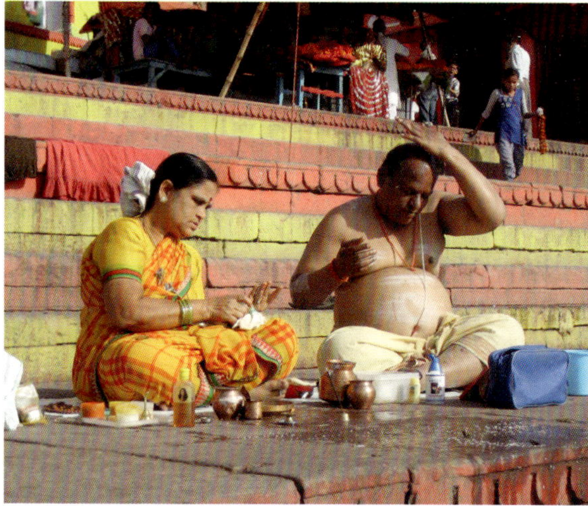

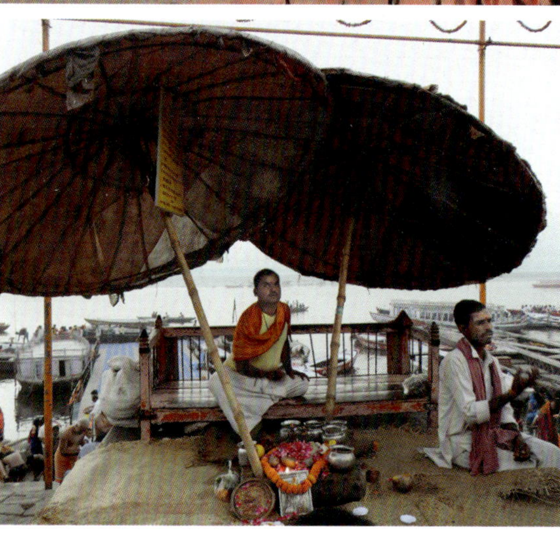

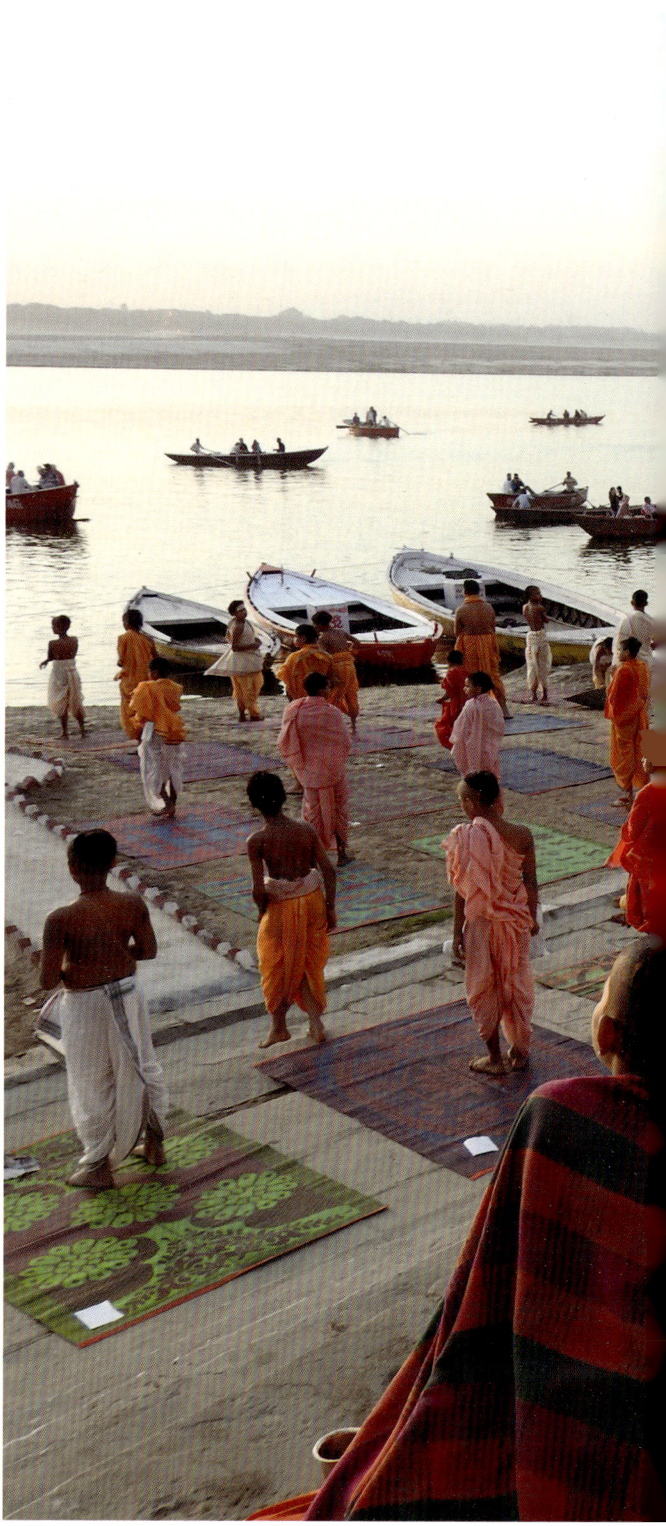

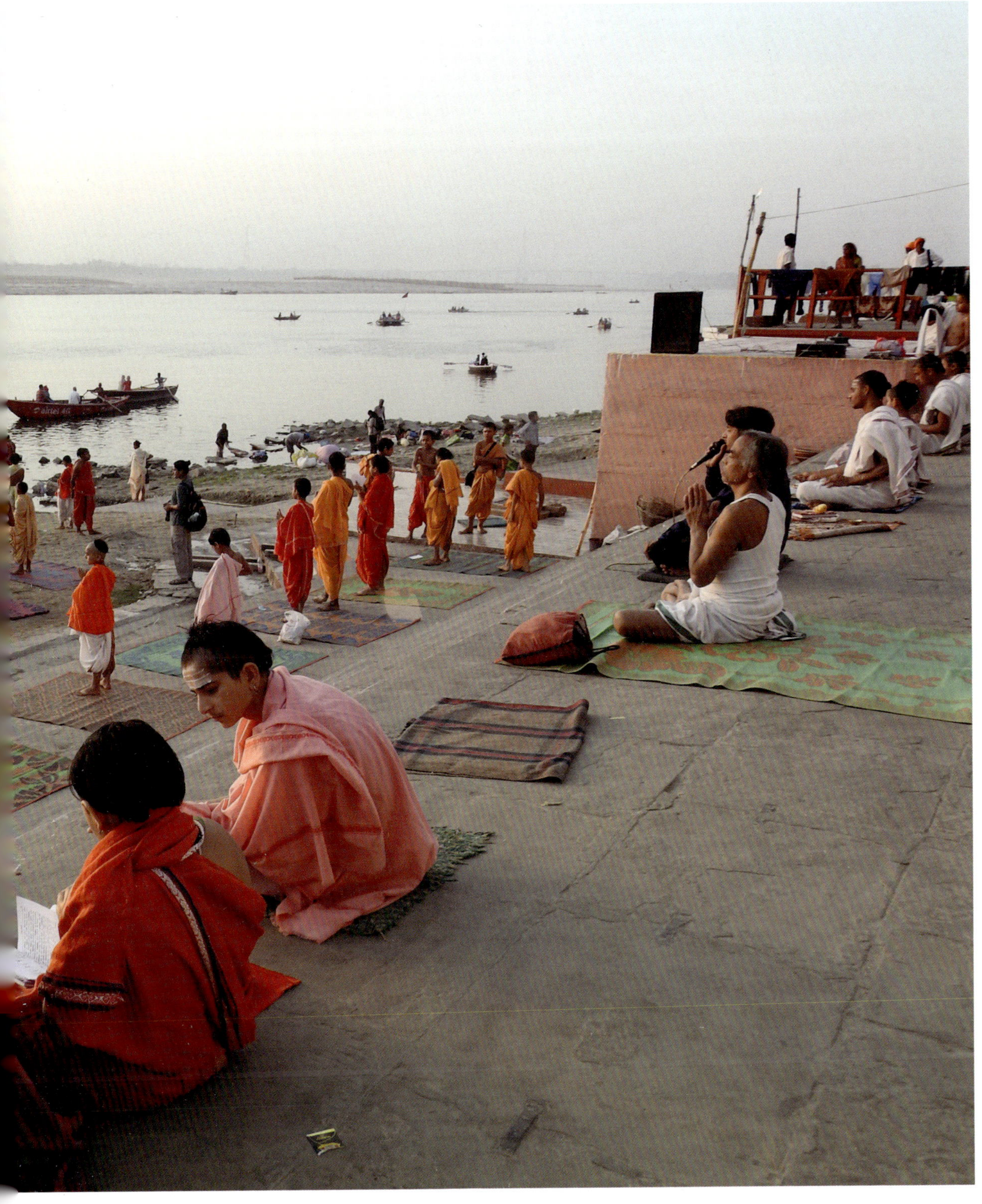

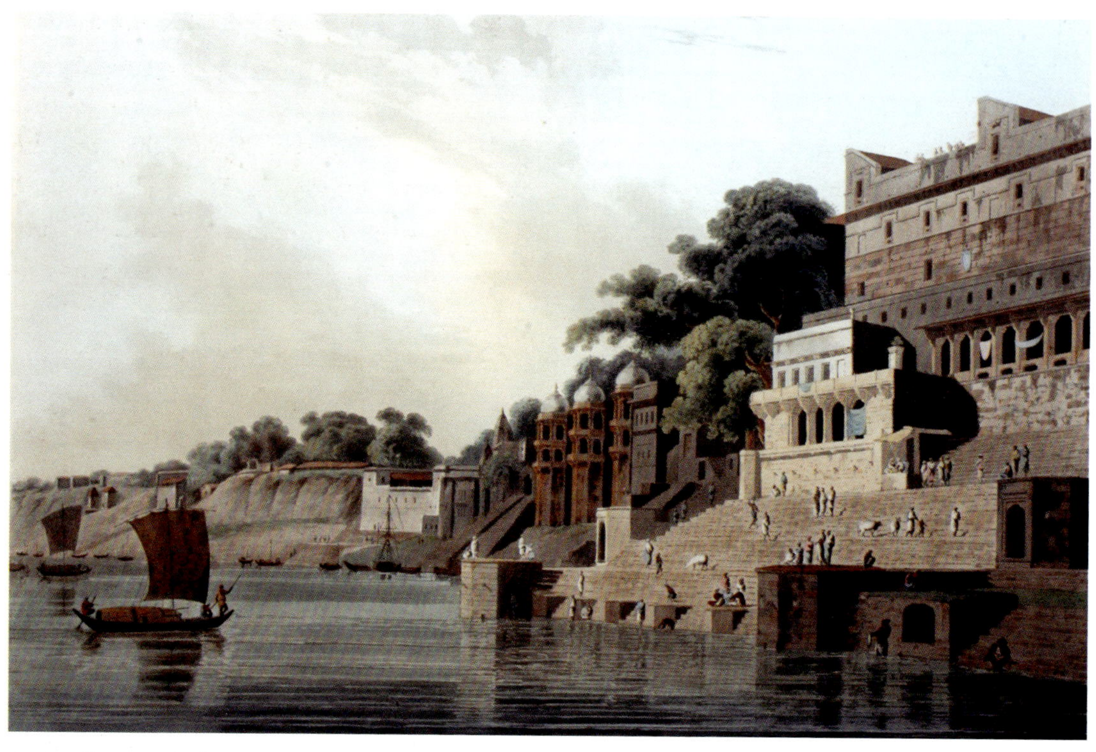

ABOVE: *Dusasumade Gaut, Barnares on the Ganges* by Thomas Daniell

PG. 168 ABOVE: A child draped in a saffron robe, head partially shaved, is deep in meditation

PG. 168 CENTRE: A couple from south India preparing themselves for a holy dip in the Ganga

PG. 168 BELOW: A priest sitting under two huge palm-leaf umbrellas waiting for his clientele

PG. 168-169: Children meditating on the bank of the Ganga

Ganga has been the centre of heritage and culture of Varanasi. Nowhere else in the world does one come across such a unique phenomenon. As mentioned earlier, the river Ganga is both the container and carrier of Indian civilisation and culture, and the Ganga of Varanasi manifests it all the more clearly. Each of these wharfs constructed by different people at different points of time indicates this rich Indian heritage. There are in fact eighty-four wharfs in Varanasi. Among them the important ones are – the Tulsi ghat, the Asi ghat, the Anandamoyee ghat, the Jain ghat, the Hanuman ghat, the Harishchandra ghat, the Kedar ghat, the Rana ghat, the Dasaswamedh ghat, the Rajendra ghat, the Mir ghat, the Lalita ghat, the Manikarnika ghat, the Ram ghat, the

Panchganga ghat, the Gai ghat, the Pralhad ghat and the Raj ghat.

The Dasaswamedh ghat happens to be the most important one. The folklore associated with this ghat is as follows. Once Devadas, the then king of Varanasi, had driven off all the gods from the city. After sometime Lord Shiva wanted to return to his old home in Varanasi, so he went to Lord Brahma for assistance. Lord Brahma approached the king in the guise of a Brahmin and suggested he should conduct ten *Ashvamedha* (horse sacrifice) *yajna*s. His intention was clear, if the king committed any mistake while conducting the *yajna*s he would drive him out of Varanasi and bring back Lord Shiva to his old home. But the king made wonderful arrangements to conduct the ten *yajna*s at this ghat. This is how Dasaswamedh ghat (literally, ten *Ashvamedha yajna*s) got its name. The gods then devised another plan to drive off the

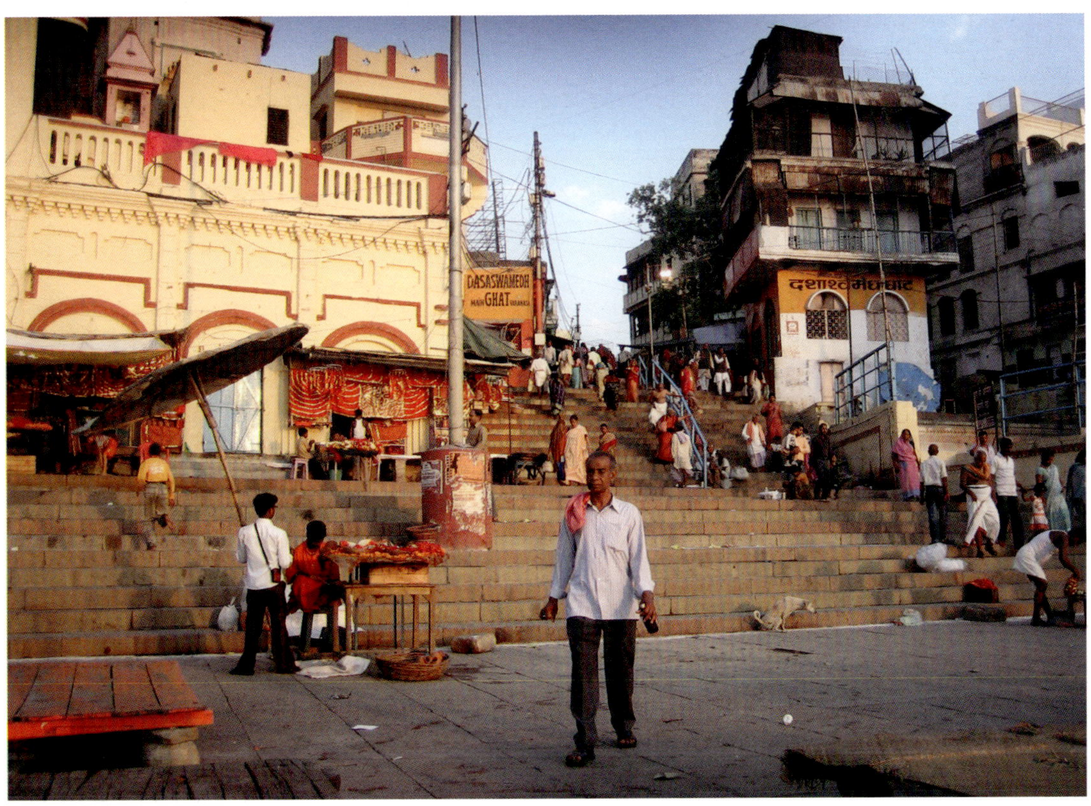

Dasaswamedh ghat is Varanasi's most famous ghat

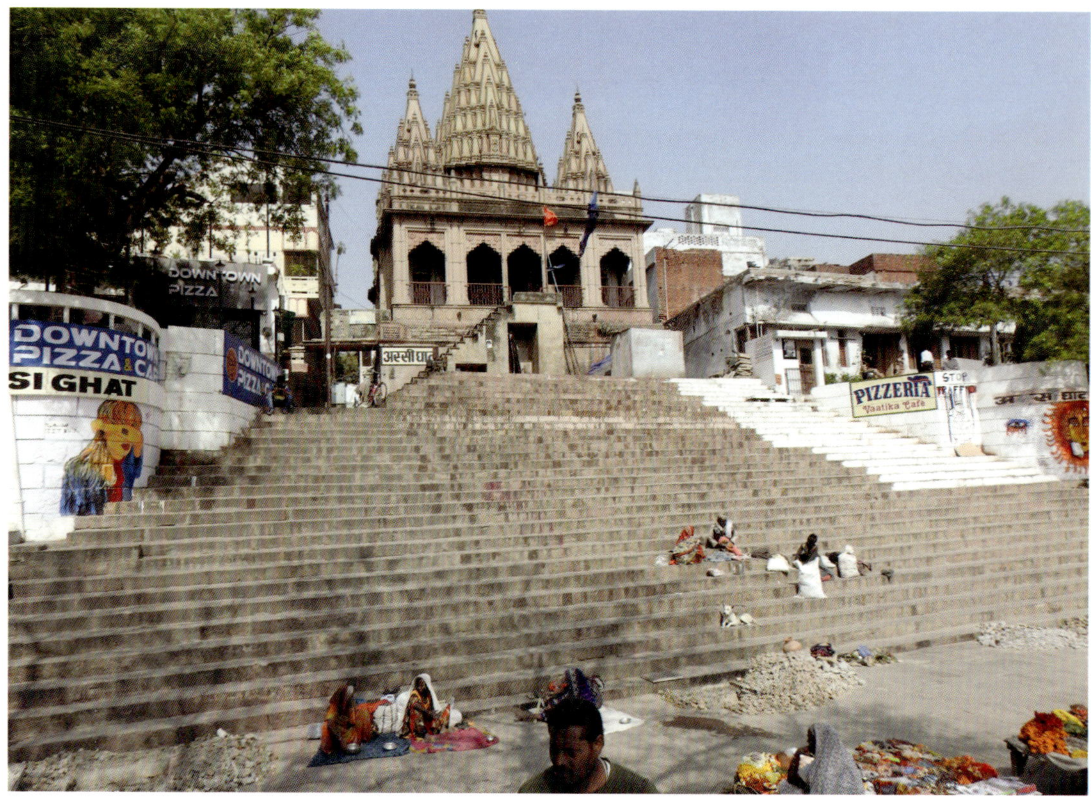

A temple at Asi ghat, Varanasi

king from Varanasi and reinstall Lord Shiva here. People believe that if a person takes a dip in the Ganga at Dasaswamedh ghat with utmost sincerity and devotion he will live a blessed life. No wonder throughout the year the place teems with visitors round the clock. Series of country-made boats anchor here awaiting passengers. Likewise series of priests sit on the pavements of the ghat awaiting devotees. Adjacent to the wharf stands a temple constructed by the queen of Putiya. And in one corner of the ghat is the Ganga temple. The broad stairway of the wharf leads one straight to the Ganga.

Harishchandra ghat is supposedly the oldest wharf of Varanasi. According to a story in the *Purana*s, King Harishchandra in order to fulfil his vow had sacrificed his wife and son here. This ghat even now is serving as a cremation ground.

On the north of the Ganga where the river Asi meets the Ganga is the Asi ghat.

Asi ghat has been mentioned both in the *Matsya Purana* and *Agni Purana*. According to the *Purana*s, Goddess Durga after beheading both the demons Shumbha and Nishumbha had thrown away the sword at this place. Instantly a spring had sprung up, which later on turned into a river – river Asi (which means sword). But unfortunately river Asi now has turned into a filthy canal. The filth of the entire city accumulates here and then is released into the river Ganga. Yet during festivals people come to bathe here because of the pleasant ambience. We found a few boats anchored near the bank and plenty of washermen washing dirty clothes in the water.

We crossed Peshwa ghat, Gangamahal ghat and Rewa ghat to reach Tulsi ghat. The ghat is named after the ancient poet Tulsidas (1540-1623) because he built a cottage and lived here. He was the author of the famous *Ramcharitmanas*. Near the ghat is a cottage where stands an idol of Rama. At the foot of the idol is laid a manuscript wrapped in red cloth. It is supposed to be the original manuscript of the *Ramcharitmanas*. Nobody

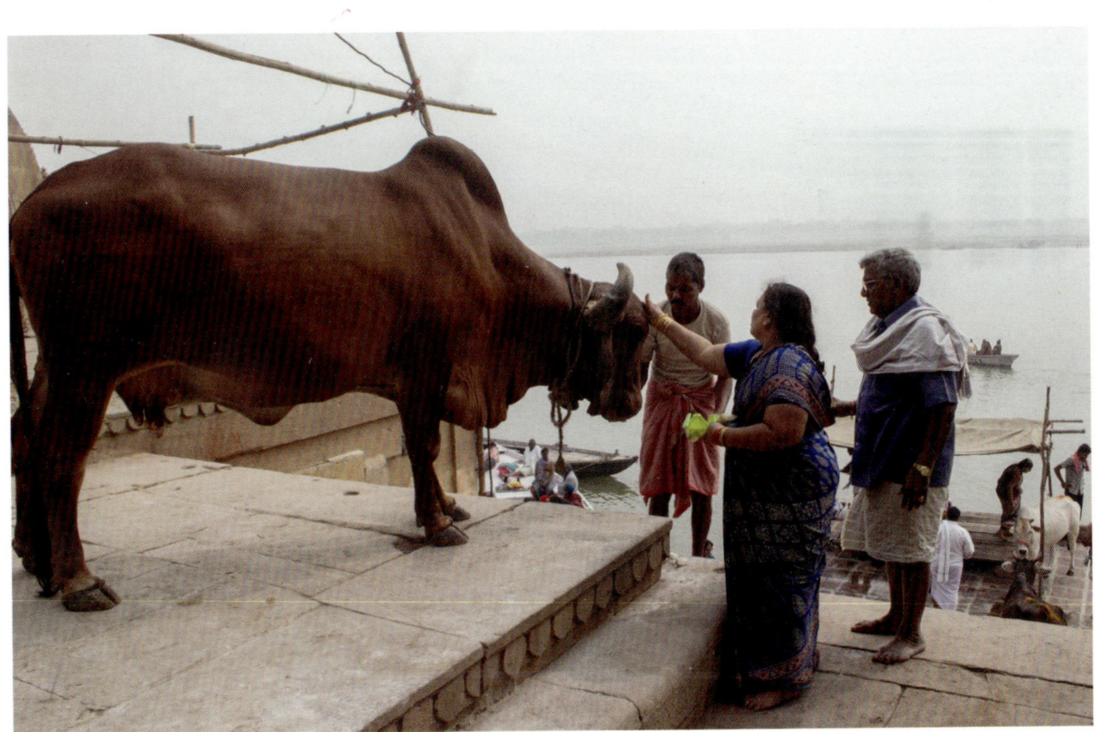

A lady worshipping and feeding an ox as a sacred ritual

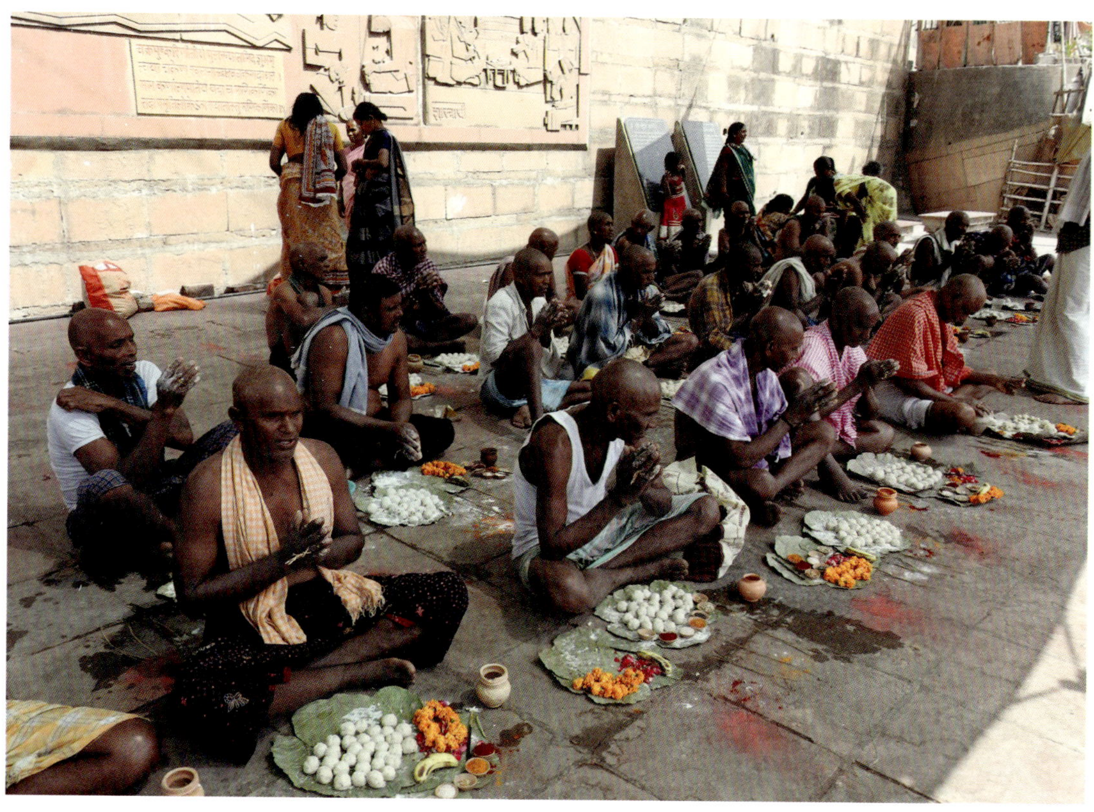

A group from south India observing elaborate religious rites

seems to have verified the authenticity of the claim. Other than the manuscript there is a pair of wooden sandals and a woollen shawl. Slightly away from the cottage is the Lolark kund (or gorge) which is both ancient and deep. At one point of time the *kund* was connected to the river Ganga. The story of the *kund* is very interesting. Sambya was the son of Lord Krishna. Cursed by his father, Sambya once contracted leprosy. In order to cure himself Sambya started visiting places and practising asceticism. But everything failed. Finally he came here and took a bath, and was instantly cured. Since then this *kund* is worshipped as Suryatirtha Lolark kund. People keep coming here to worship the sun god.

Beside Lalita ghat is the Manikarnika ghat and *kund*. Manikarnika kund is supposed to be the most ancient pilgrim spot of Varanasi. Lord Vishnu had dug this gorge and his sweat had filled the gap. Then he

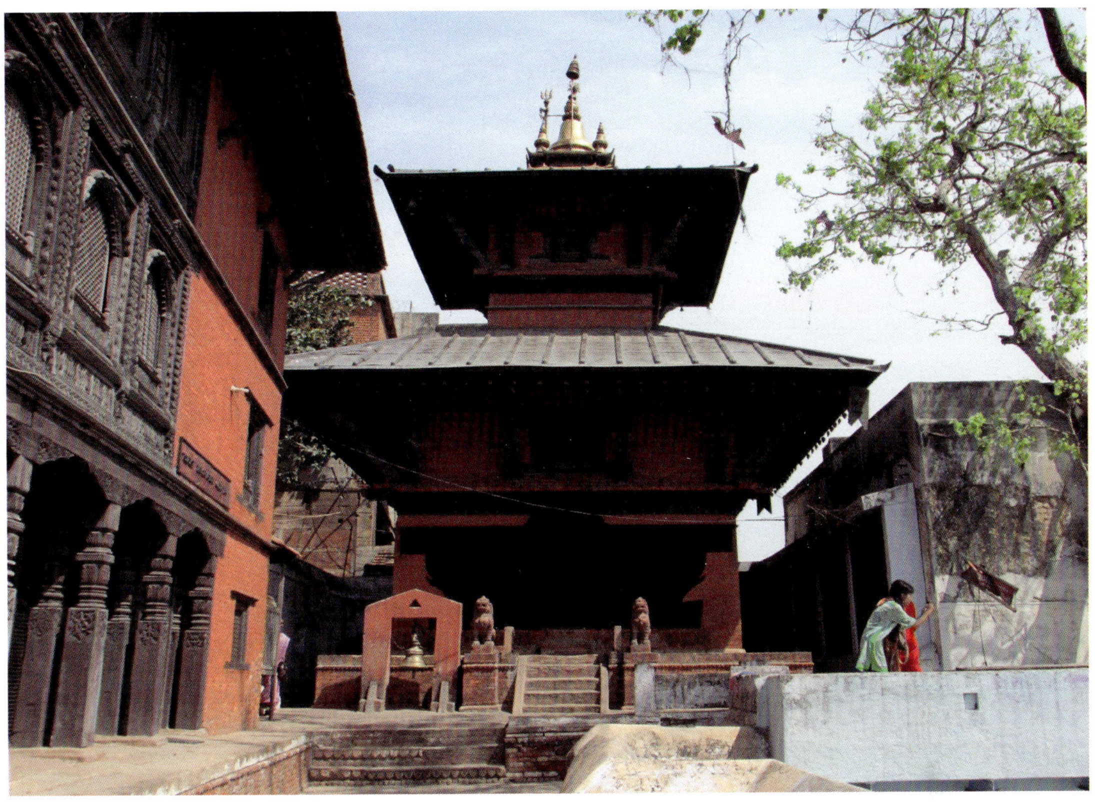

Nepali temple at Lalita ghat is one of Varanasi's oldest and famous temples

sat to meditate. Lord Shiva who happened to cross the place saw the radiant figure of Lord Vishnu and was so awestruck that he started trembling all over. The tremor tore off one of his earrings and it fell inside the gorge. The earring called Manikarnika thus became immortal in the form of Manikarnika kund. It is considered to be a holy place by the Hindus.

There is however another story behind the name Manikarnika kund. Once, Goddess Parvati while flying over Varanasi with Lord Shiva lost one of her earrings in a pond below. Since then the pond became famous as Manikarnika kund. But Manikarnika ghat is famous for round-the-clock cremation. It is said that cremating fires are never extinguished at Manikarnika ghat. Bits of charred wood, flowers, corpses and broken bedsteads are strewn all over the place. Hindus believe that a person cremated at the Manikarnika ghat is released from the

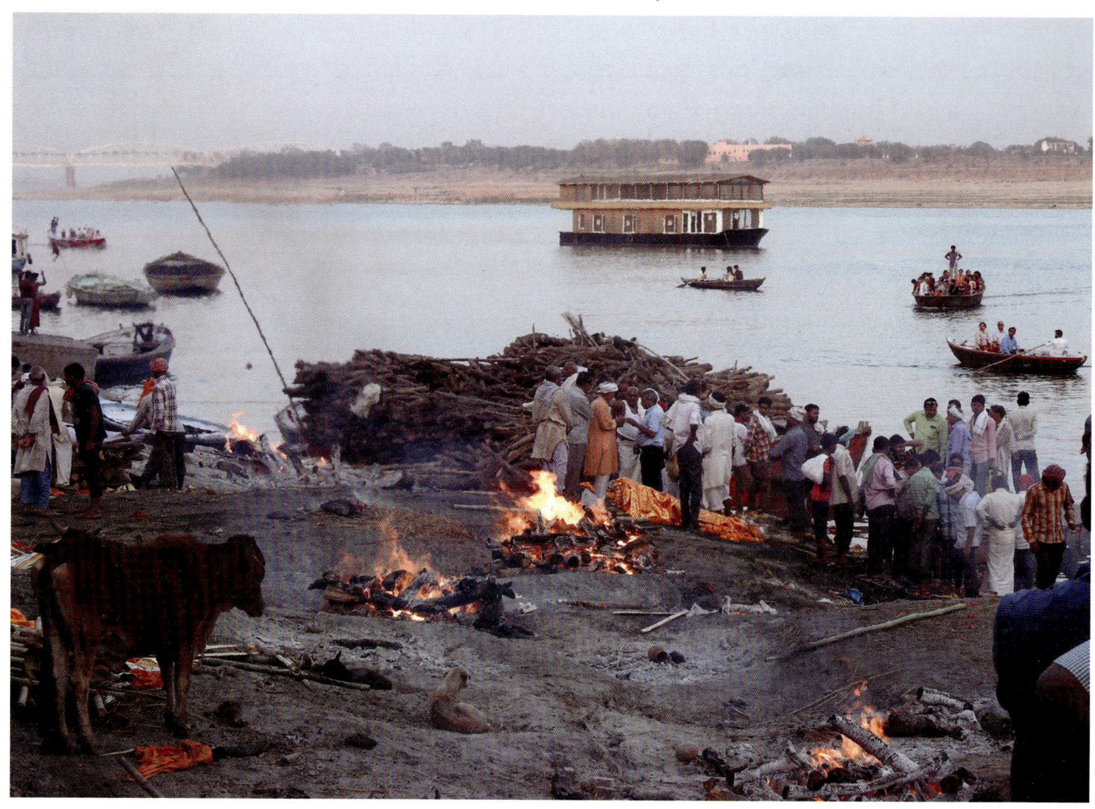

Burning pyres at Manikarnika ghat. It is believed that a human soul finds Moksha if cremated here after death

endless cycles of birth and death. Apparently Lord Shiva personally ensures Moksha for the soul of the deceased.

This is Manikarnika,
Where death is auspicious,
Where life is fruitful
Where one grazes the pastures of heaven,
There is no tirtha like Manikarnika.

(Translated by Diana L. Eck)

From a Pilgrim's Diary

I first visited Varanasi when I was six years old. A friend of my father used to reside at Mughalsarai (a little distance away from Varanasi) and we had put up there. Later we went to Varanasi to my aunt's house. It was a two-storeyed building, and we stayed on the first floor with my aunt. On the ground floor I frequently came across a few old ladies clad in white. I did not know who they were or where they came from. With time I had

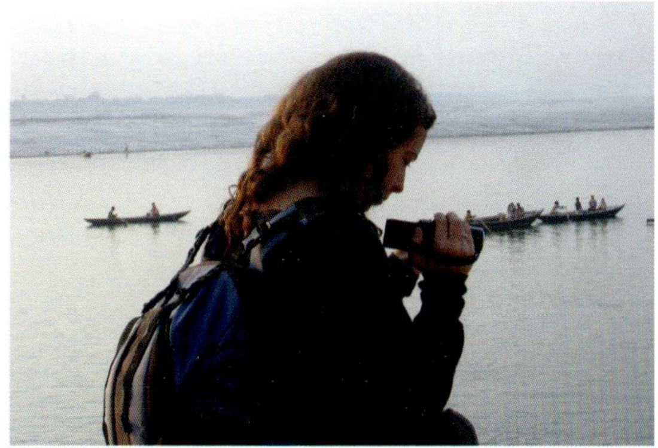

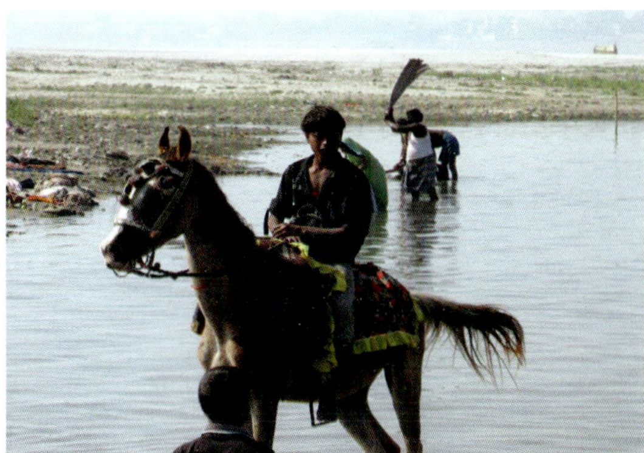

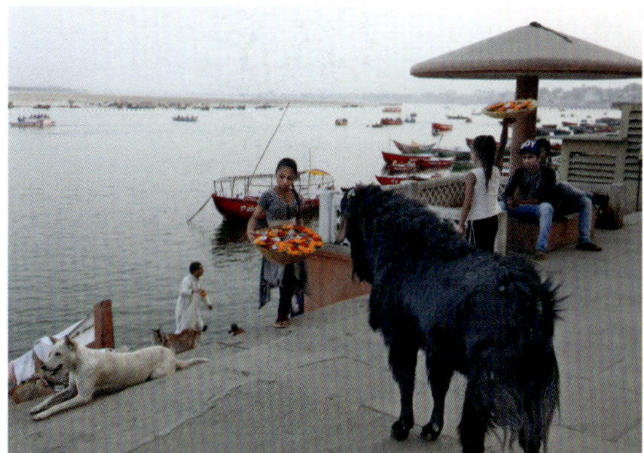

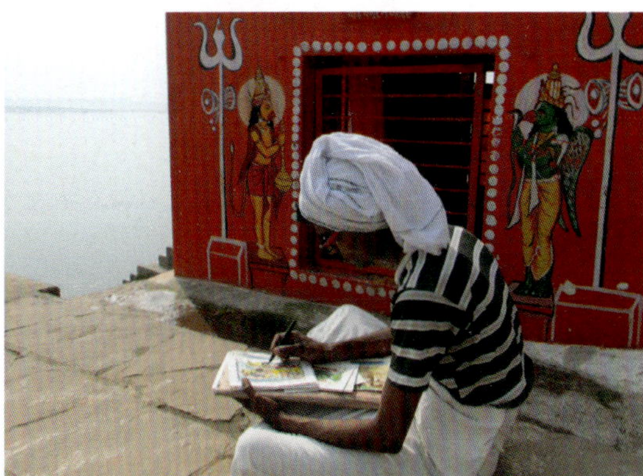

TOP LEFT: A foreigner checking her camera. The ghats of Varanasi are very popular with foreign tourists who come here for a glimpse of the culture and heritage of this ancient city

TOP RIGHT: A man on horseback by the bank of the Ganga

ABOVE LEFT: A flower girl and a goat, locally known as *ram chhagol*

ABOVE RIGHT: An artist drawing inspiration from his surroundings

forgotten all about them. Years later while viewing Deepa Mehta's film *Water* I realised who they were – they were old widows abandoned by their families.

My next visit to Varanasi was from Allahabad. This time I stayed at the guesthouse of Ramakrishna Mission. I had ample time to spare so immediately after lunch I strolled out of the campus to get a firsthand experience of Varanasi. Strolling across the city I landed up at the Dasaswamedh ghat. The place was extremely crowded. Rickshaws, human beings, cycles and automobiles congested the entire stretch leading to the Dasaswamedh ghat. Yet the strangest thing about the place was human tolerance. There were no traffic police to control the crowd. People kept jostling with one another to walk ahead, but nobody seemed to mind! There were garbage strewn all around but people did not seem to notice them. Just ahead of me a group from south India with shaven heads and bare feet chattered their way to the Dasaswamedh ghat, completely oblivious of the noisy surroundings. I just couldn't relate this Varanasi with the picture I had already formed in my mind. I had just crossed the lane that led to the Viswanath temple when suddenly the road met a dead end. And lo, there was the Dasaswamedh ghat. The world I was viewing a few moments ago simply simmered away. There flowed the Ganga, whose other bank was not visible to my mortal eye. In fact the other side of the river seemed to merge with the horizon. Such is

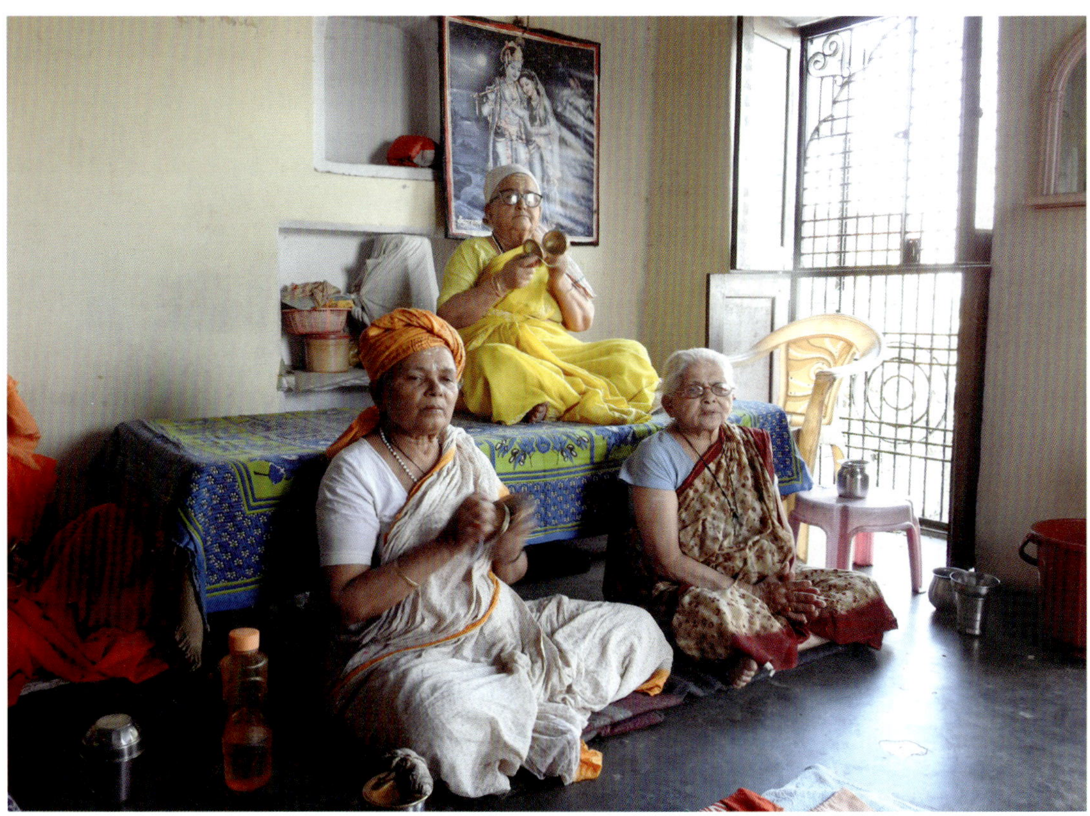

ABOVE: Hindu widows chanting devotional songs at an old-age home. After Vrindavan, Varanasi has the highest number of widows living in ashrams and homes meant for widows

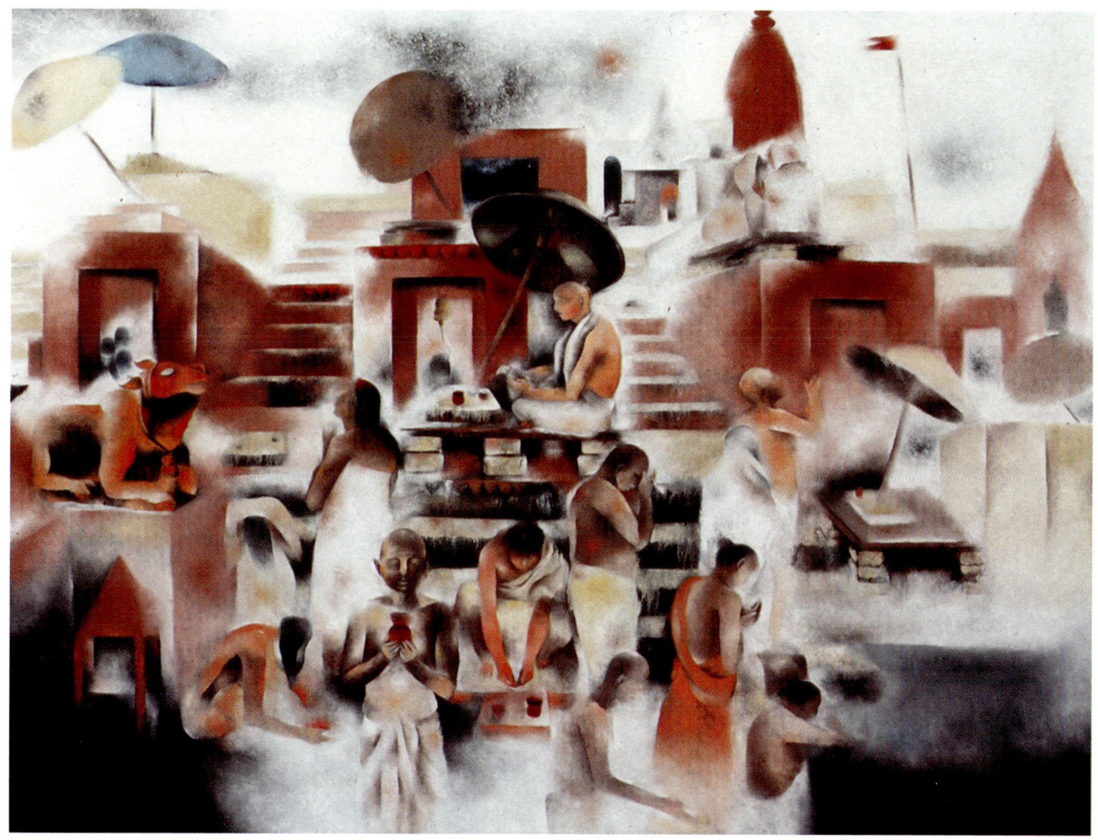

Varanasi Ganga ghat by Siddhartha Sengupta

the vastness of the Ganga in Varanasi. The Dasaswamedh ghat or wharf consists of several stairs leading to the river. A series of palaces dots this side of the bank.

I stood fascinated. The group who was ahead of me at the Dasaswamedh ghat glanced at my stupefied face and climbed down the stairs to bathe in the river. Regaining my composure after a while, I joined them.

The rest of the afternoon was spent in ambling round the different bathing ghats. Interestingly, unlike the other cities, river Ganga here flows much below the land surface. Furthermore, the river turns northwards from Varanasi; possibly because of the growing silt deposits. Strolling aimlessly for quite some time I finally reached the famous Asi ghat situated at the extreme northern end of the bank. There

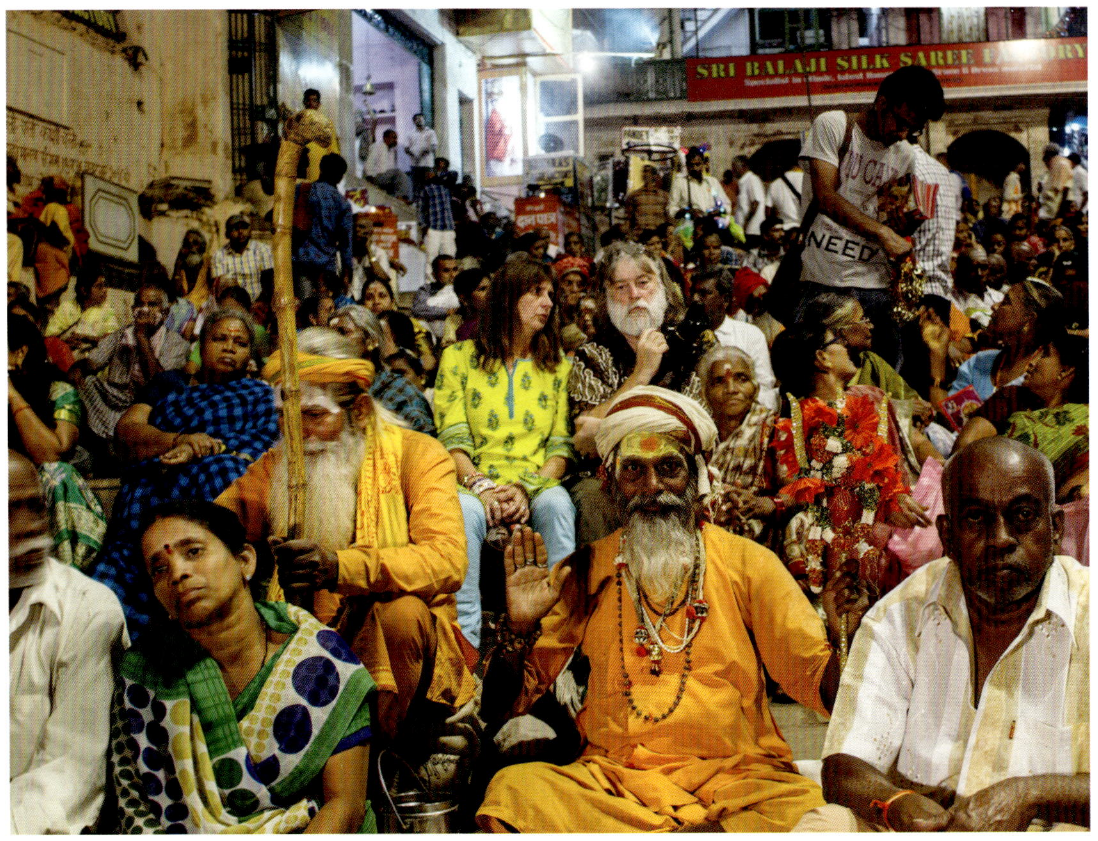

Motley crowd of devotees waiting for Ganga *aarti* at a ghat in Varanasi

are no stairs here because the river runs almost parallel to the land surface. Since I had grown quite tired by then, I decided to sit under a tree. An elderly gentleman too was sitting there. He looked at me and asked, 'Where from?' 'Kolkata,' I replied. Within a few minutes we were friends. He told me his name, Mahesh Prasad Sharma, and I told him mine. He was a clerk at the Banaras Hindu University. His permanent home was fifty kilometres away from the city. Here he stayed at a mess. 'I had got a teaching assignment in one undergraduate college,' he continued. 'But I decided to stay back.' 'But teaching assignment meant higher salary and higher social status. Then what made you refuse that?' I asked quite surprised. He looked at me for a few minutes and then slowly said something which took me by surprise. 'Yes, initially I used to get

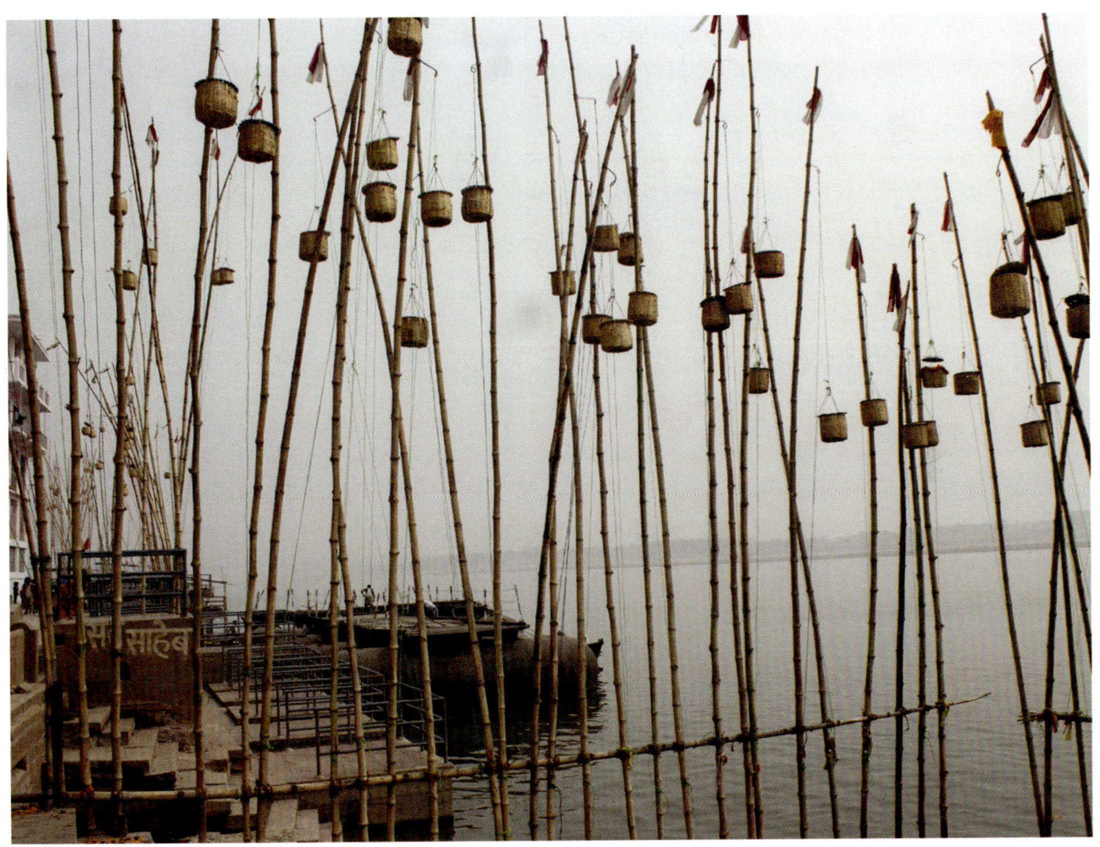

Skylights at the Panchganga ghat

very bored, staying alone. After office I used to come here and spend my time. Eventually I was interested in observing everything around me, right from the visitors from distant lands to commercial boats plying to different places. Gradually I fell in love with the Ganga. The various forms of the river at different hours fascinated me and I couldn't go away. Now I can't stay away from her for long. In fact during vacations I return here sooner than expected.' 'But what will you do after you retire?' I asked. 'I'll stay back, spending the rest of my life here on the banks of the river.'

I heard an echo of the same sentiment during my next visit to Varanasi. This time the speaker was none other than Sehanai maestro Ustad Bismillah Khan. Crossing a filthy congested lane I had reached his house one morning. Unfortunately I could not meet him in person, because he had died just a year ago. Instead it was his grandson, a handsome young man, Nasir Abbas, who welcomed me to his house. We spoke at length and I came to learn many untold stories about the great artist. There was an American lady, a fan of the maestro, narrated Nasir, who had invited the Ustad to shift his base to the United States of America. The Ustad had refused, saying, 'How can I go there leaving my family behind.' The lady had promised to relocate his entire family to the USA. Then the Ustad told her, 'But here I visit the mosque every day to say my prayers. What about that?' She promised to build a mosque for him. 'But what about my Mother Ganga; can you replicate her in America?' he had finally asked. Shaking her head in disappointment, the lady had left crestfallen. Ustad Bismillah Khan always referred to the river Ganga as 'Ganga Maiya' (mother Ganga) and would practise his art on the banks of the river.

Nasir Abbas narrated another interesting story about the maestro. Ustad's teacher had warned him once, 'Here in Varanasi you will have many supernatural experiences. You are not to talk about them to anyone.' It so happened one day as he was practising, he suddenly felt the fragrant presence of a human being. As he opened his eyes he found a tall, handsome monk smiling at him. Looking at the Ustad he said, 'Remain eternally happy, my son,' and vanished. The Ustad was extremely surprised. The door of his room was tightly shut, so how could someone enter it? Scared out of his wits the Ustad ran to his teacher and narrated the entire incident. His story however angered his teacher. Instead of explaining anything to him he slapped the poor child. 'Didn't I tell you not to talk about these experiences? Then why did you come to me?' he retorted angrily. 'Even I have had many supernatural experiences, but I never talk about them. Remember, my son, this is Varanasi and these things keep happening here.' Possibly it is this mystery of the place that binds people living here.

The Balaji temple is close to the Ustad's house. One has to climb almost four storeys to enter the temple. I was however a bit disappointed to see a brand new edition of the temple. My next destination was the Panchganga ghat. Panch means five and the place was actually the confluence of five rivers – Ganga, Yamuna, Sarasvati, Dhutpapa and Kiran. The ancient Bindhu Madhva temple was located here. At one point of time it was considered to be the tallest temple of Varanasi and every night a

RIGHT: Jain temple at Jain ghat, earlier known as Vaccharaja ghat

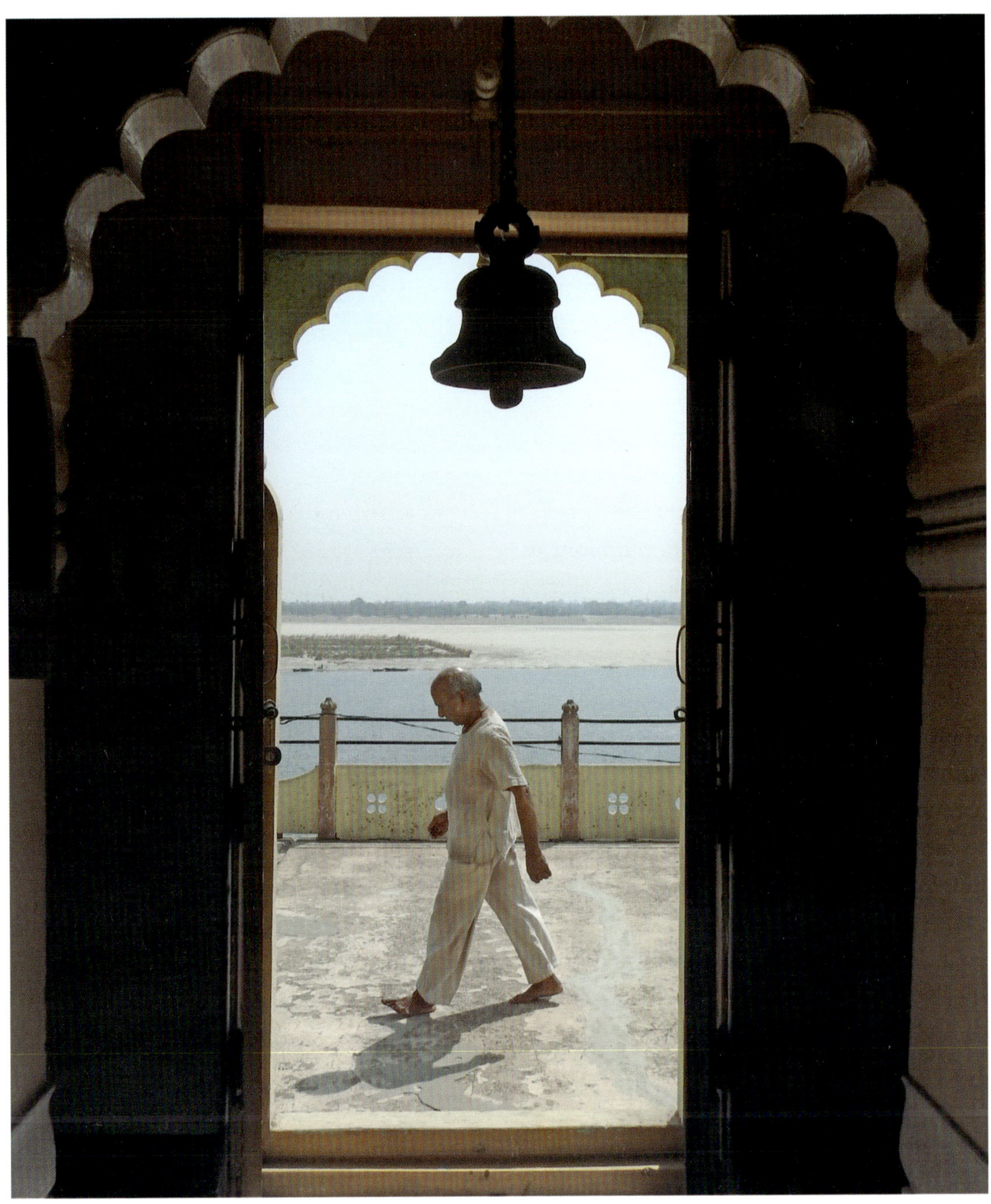

lighted lamp used to burn bright on its peak. But the Mughal Emperor Aurangzeb, unable to stand this symbolic superior status of the Hindus, destroyed the temple in 1669 and constructed a mosque there. Ironically the present mosque is now closely guarded by a group of policemen.

The serenity of the place at once captivated me. To me the Panchganga ghat looked like a lonely planet surviving on the bank of the Ganga. There is a beautiful story of a poet attached to this wharf. The poet was none other than Pandit Jagannath, the court poet of Mughal Emperor Shah Jahan.

Pandit Jagannath was a Tamil Brahmin and a renowned scholar. Under Shah Jahan's patronage he wrote many books of which the most famous one was *Ganga Lahari* (a collection of poems). Unfortunately at one point of time Pandit Jagannath fell in love with a Muslim princess and married her. The act enraged the conservative Brahmin pundits to such an extent that they not only expelled him from his caste but also threatened to kill him. Tormented by ostracism and a sense of guilt, Pandit Jagannath and his wife reached the bank of river Ganga in Varanasi and started reciting slokas from *Ganga Lahari*. According to legend, with the recital of each sloka the height of the river kept increasing and after he had completed reciting all the 53 slokas from *Ganga Lahari*, the river mounted the wharf and swept away both Pandit Jagannath and his wife, providing them ultimate shelter. The following four slokas are from *Ganga Lahari*:

> May your waters, the inexpressible treasure of good fortune for the entire world, which possess the purity of nectar, which are the essence of all Srutis, which are the expression of the merits of the Gods and the great glory of Lord Siva who has created this world through play, put to rest all our inauspiciousness.

> It is because of counting on your support, O Mother, that all the Gods have been disrespected by my displaying thoughtlessly not a small arrogance. Now, If you become indifferent, O Bhargirathi then tell me in front of whom, here in this world, shall I cry.

> May the world Ganga sweet to hear, which even if brought to memory only once makes one's internal sense – organs spontaneously calm, and which pronounced with intensity removes quickly the sin and the suffering of transmigration, shine in my lotus like mouth at the time of my last breath.

> Those who meditate on You do not experience disrespect. (You) who are while like the autumnal moon and whose crown is in the form of a white serpent associated with the crescent moon, (you) who in your two hands hold a jar and the lotus and maintain (your other two hands) in the posture of granting boons and welfare (and you) seated on an alligator whose clothes and ornaments possess an appearance identical to the flow of nectar.
>
> (Translation by Boris Marjanovic)

Such stories abound the city of Varanasi. Some of them are folklores while some narrate supernatural experiences. But to be candid I could not disbelieve any of them. The ambience of Varanasi is such you feel like believing all that you hear. The following verse beautifully sums up the charm of Varanasi.

> Are there not many holy places on this earth?
> Yet, which of them would equal in the balance one speck of Kashi's dust?
> Are there not many rivers running to the sea?
> Yet which of them is like the River of heaven in Kashi?
> Are there not many fields of liberation on earth?
> Yet, no one equals the smallest part of the city never forsaken by Shiva.
> The Ganga, Shiva and Kashi: where this Trinity is wonderful,
> No wonder here is found the grace that leads one on to perfect bliss.
>
> (*Kashi Khand* 35.7-10)

I kept touring the city throughout the day, with just a short respite at night. One day I left my hotel early in the morning to continue my explorations. There were just a few people ambling around. I reached one of the bathing ghats and sat there silently watching the effervescent flow of the river Ganga. Several palaces stood silently dotting the bank of the river and as I looked I had an ethereal experience. Here were the silent palaces, and there flowed the dynamic river. It appeared to be a wonderful fusion of past and present. It recalled to my mind the Hymns of Dawn from the *Rig Veda:*

> Arise! The breath of life hath come back to us – the darkness is gone, the light approacheth! Ush as hath opened a path for Surya, the Sun, to travel; now our days will be lengthened. Singing the praises of the brightening morn, the priest, the poet, ariseth with the web of his hymn. Bounteous maiden, shine

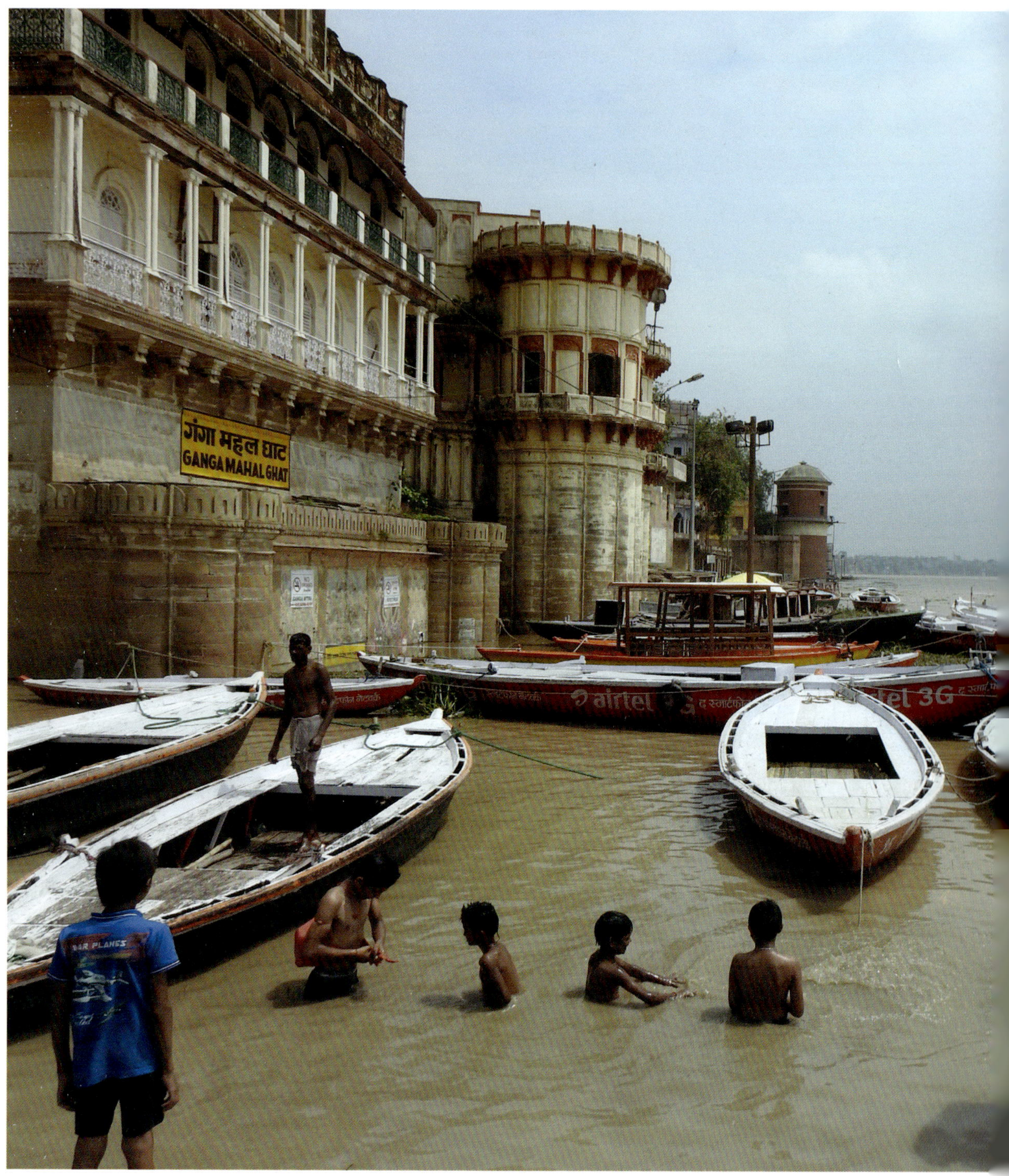
गंगा महल घाट
GANGA MAHAL GHAT
airtel

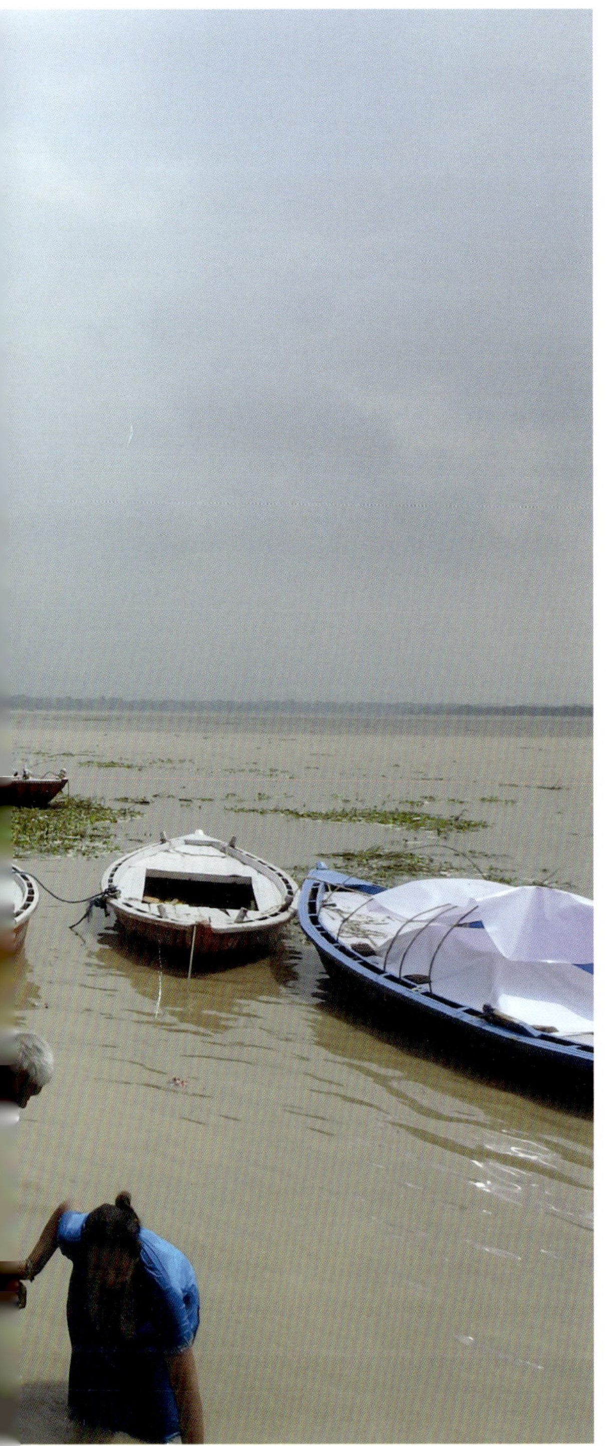

> upon him who praiseth thee; spread upon us the gift of life and children, those who givest heroic sons and wealth of kins and horses.... Mother of the gods! Revelation of the glory of the Infinite! Banner of sacrifice, magnificent Ushas, shine forth – arise! Shower thy blessings upon our prayers, and make us chief among the people.
>
> (Translation by Ralph T.H. Griffith)

A monk was sitting in one corner of Kedar ghat and meditating. There was a country boat anchored at the ghat. I asked my two roommates from the Ramakrishna Mission accompanying me, 'Would you like to tour round the Ganga on that boat?' Both agreed instantly. The helmsman was a youth, who after a little bit of bargaining agreed to take us around for a paltry sum of hundred rupees. So off we went sailing on his boat. We toured for an hour and had a panoramic view of the city. Numerous palaces and bathing ghats dotted the bank of the river. And each of these palaces and ghats had a different story to tell. The declining moon was about to vanish behind the palaces and we looked at its fading beauty. Slowly, the engulfing darkness started fading. Most of

Ganga Mahal ghat during the rainy season

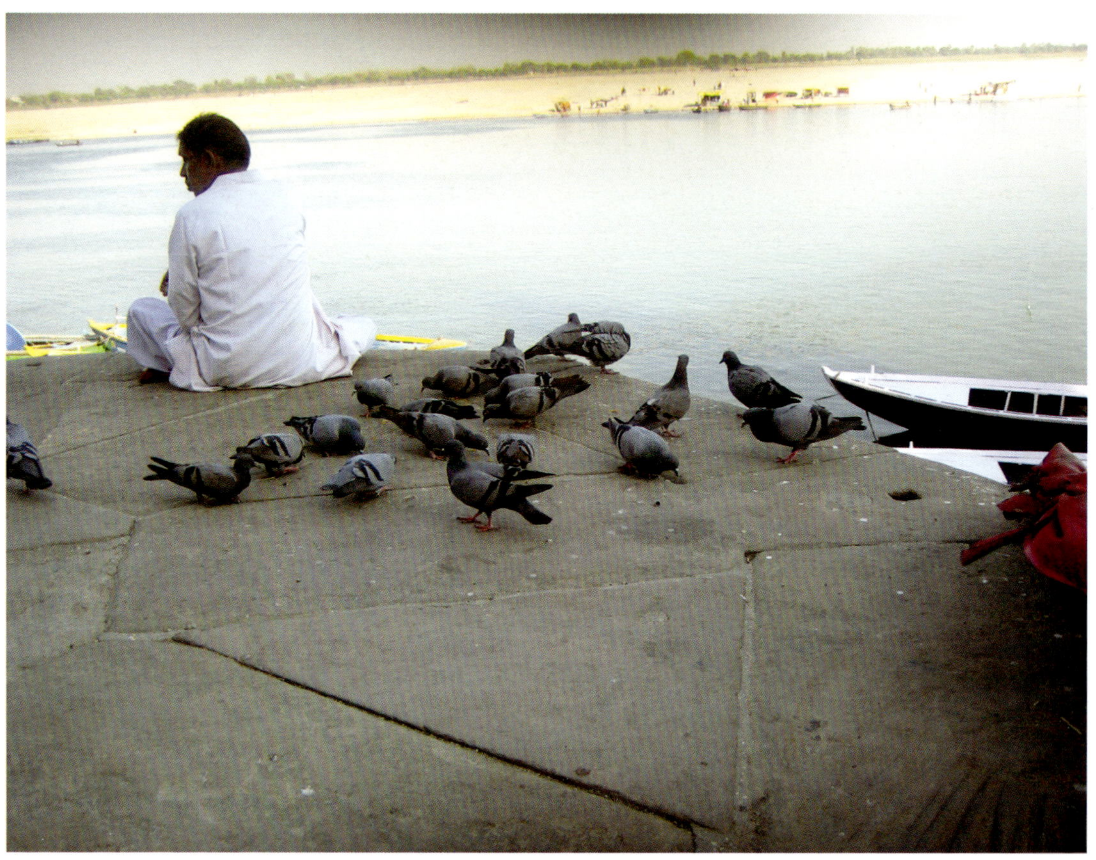

A man sitting at a ghat surrounded by pigeons

Facing page above left: Submerged Shiva temple at Scindia ghat

Facing page above right: A young girl looking upon the Ganga with dreamy eyes

Facing page below: Villagers performing a puja in the holy city of Varanasi

the bathing ghats were still empty except the Dasaswamedh ghat where the ritual worship was being held. There were a few onlookers looking at the morning *aarti*.

Gradually the radiant hue of the sun started bestowing colours all around, as we continued sailing from south to north. Pigeons were flying overhead. More boats were now floating. Finally we returned to the Panchganga ghat where a few early risers were bathing. As we alighted from the boat a young couple came to the bathing ghat. Clearly they too had come for an early morning dip. The poor girl appeared visibly

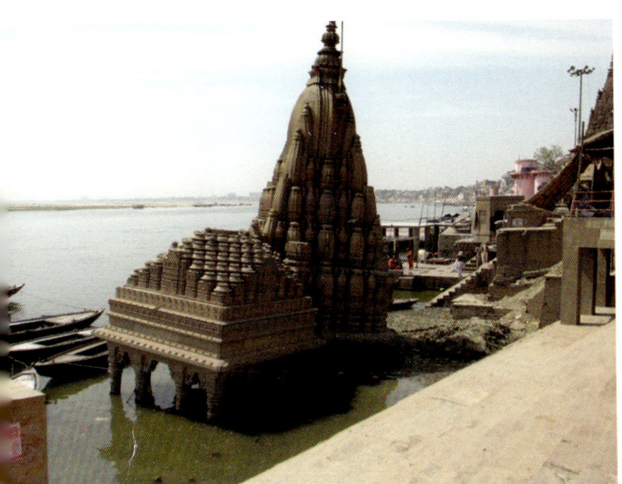

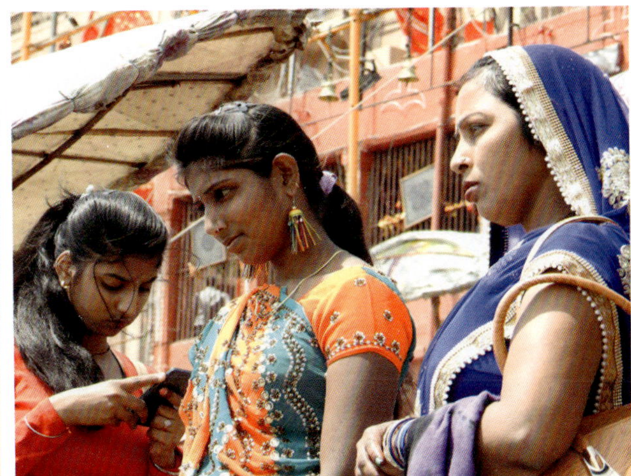

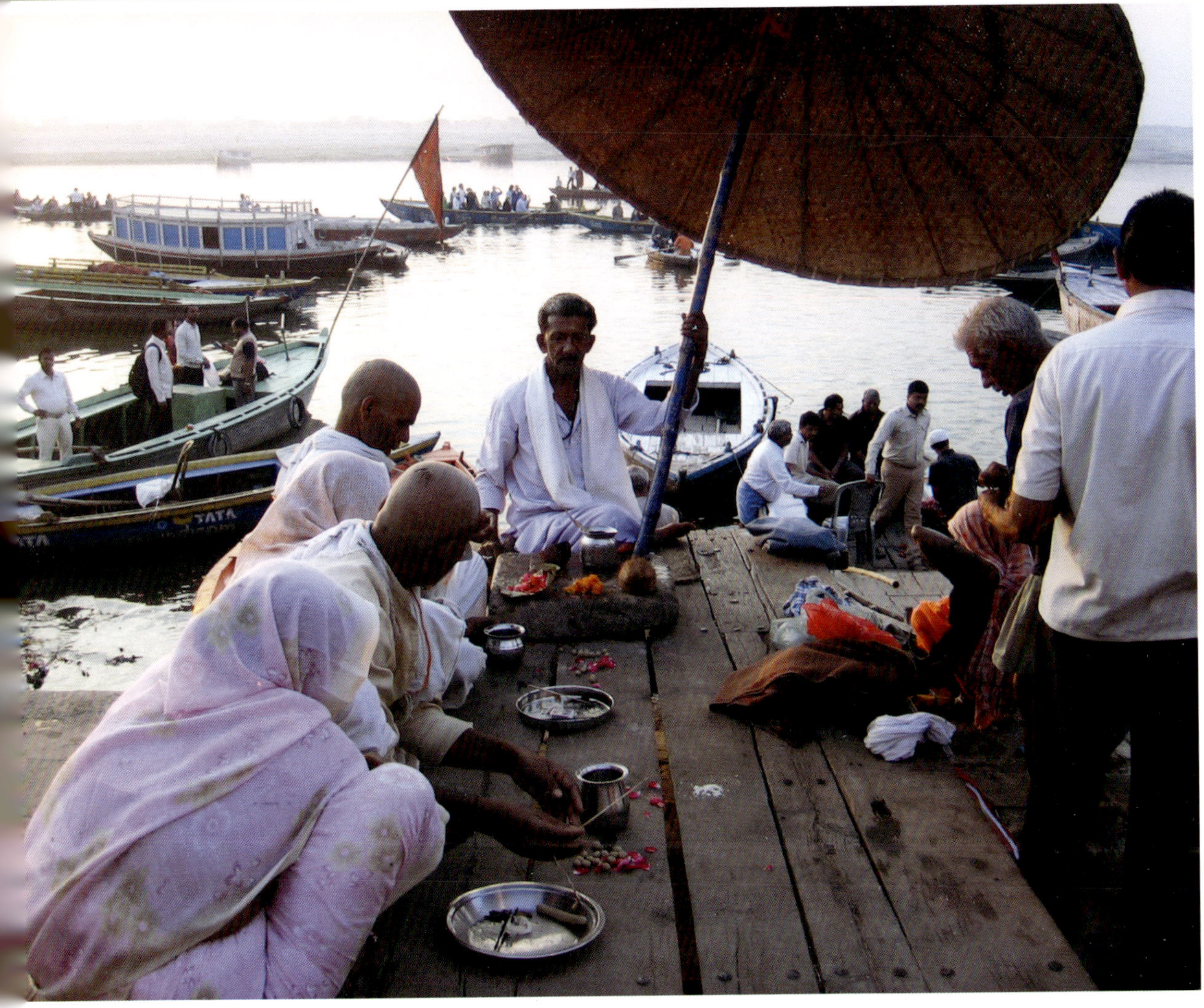

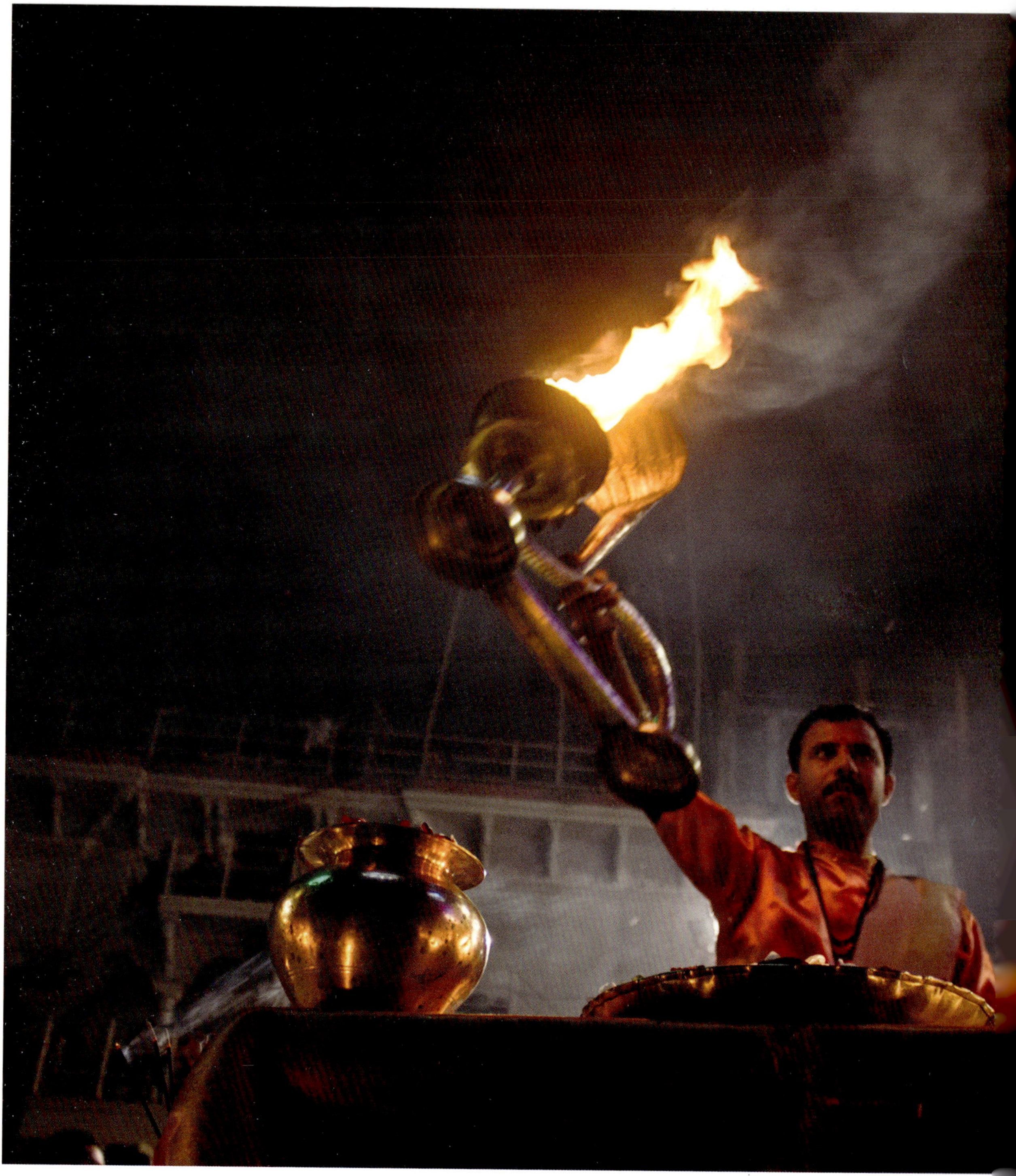

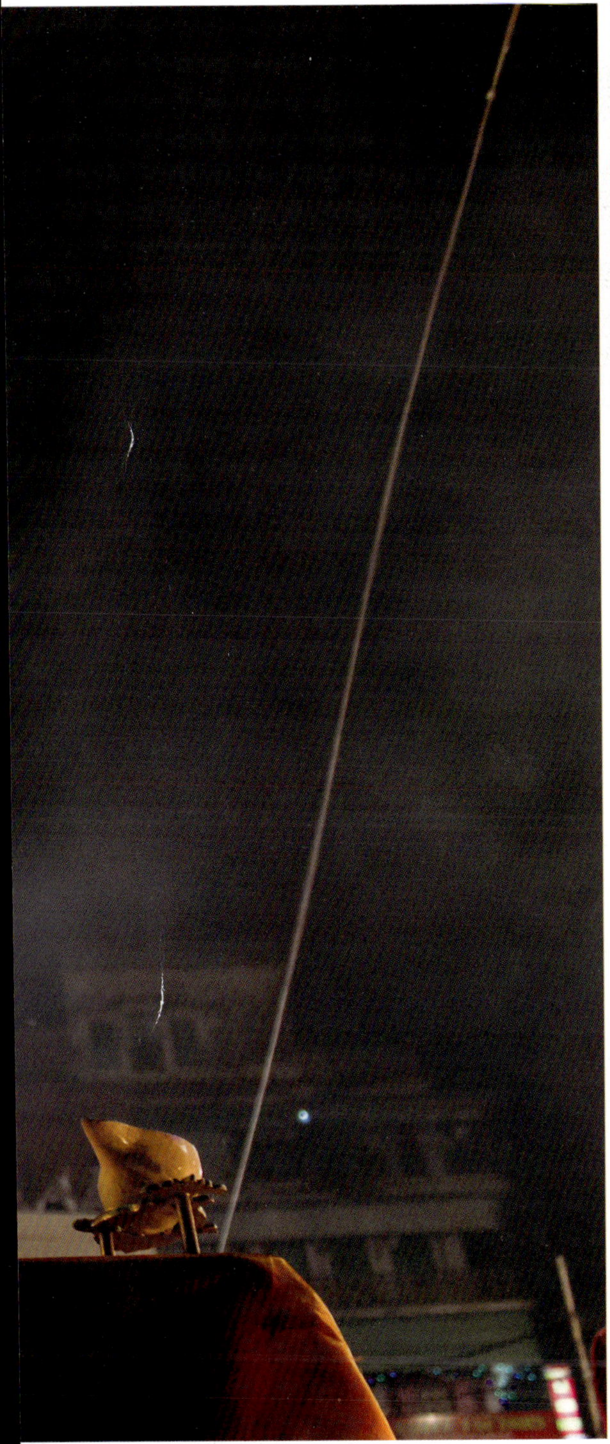

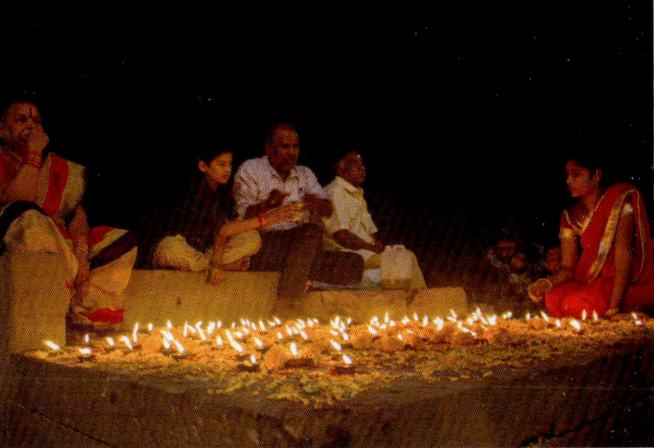

ABOVE: In the evening devotees light oil lamps at the ghats
LEFT: Thousands of devotees gather at Dasaswamedh ghat every evening to watch the Ganga *aarti*

scared to go down into the river. Holding the offered hand of her husband she trod down into the river very carefully. But once inside the river she flashed a million-dollar smile.

Walking along we reached the Manikarnika ghat where pyres were being lit to cremate people. There was a group of people sitting on the ghat looking at a pyre. Despondency was written large over their faces. Suddenly an elderly lady burst out, wailing aloud. Three pyres had been lit and looking at one of them she could not hold back her tears. It was really difficult to see the gradual disintegration of one's beloved, in the raging fire of the pyre, we all realised. Most of the bathing ghats were now being infested with devotees. There were several priests sitting under the protective umbrellas, waiting for their clients. Some of the pilgrims were chanting aloud different slokas from the scriptures.

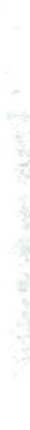

As we walked towards Lalita ghat we heard a mellifluous voice singing a devotional song. I looked back and recognised the singer, an old lady with whom I was acquainted. She was a resident of an old age home near Lalita ghat. Renounced by her family, she had been living in Varanasi for the last thirty years. Singing her way down to the river, she completed her morning ablution and then walked up to us with a pitcher full of the sacred water. '*Pranam,* Mother,' I called out. 'How are you?'

She looked at me absent-mindedly and distinctly mumbled, 'Waiting for my turn to be one with Mother Ganga.'

I was silenced. The Ganga flowed on.

SARNATH

Sarnath, ten kilometres north-east of Varanasi, was the first place the Buddha visited for his sermon after attaining Enlightenment at Bodh Gaya. It was from here that the Buddha's popularity and his teachings spread to other parts of the

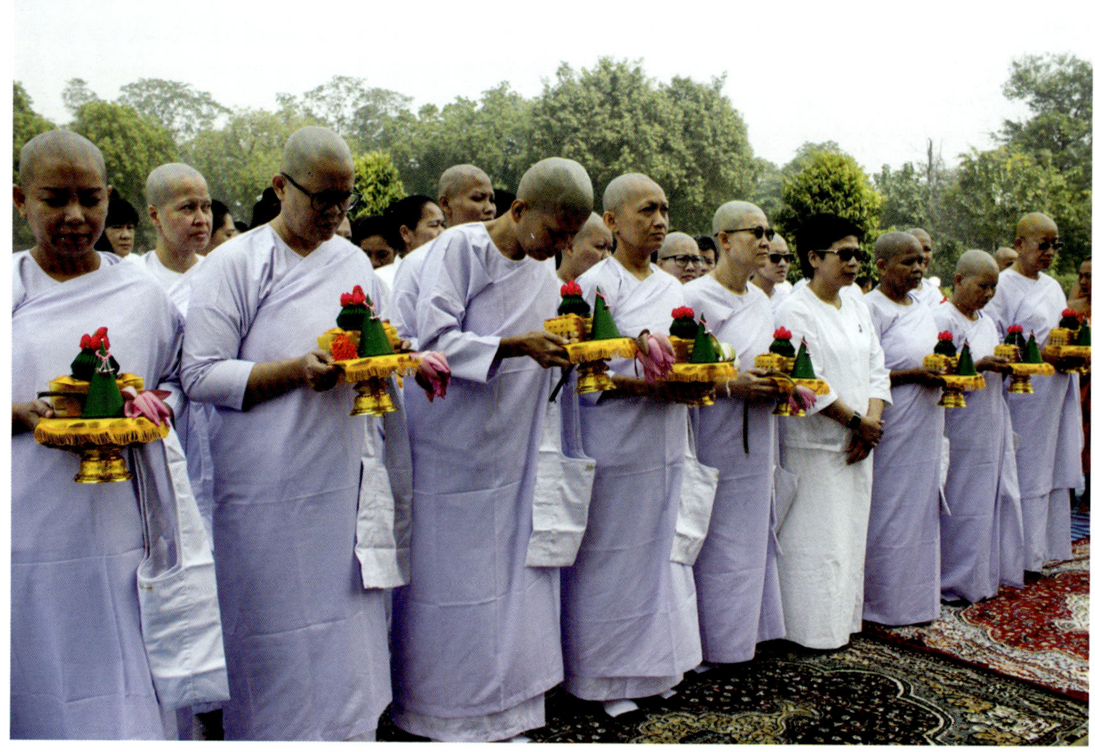

A group of Buddhist monks meditating in front of Dhamek stupa at Sarnath

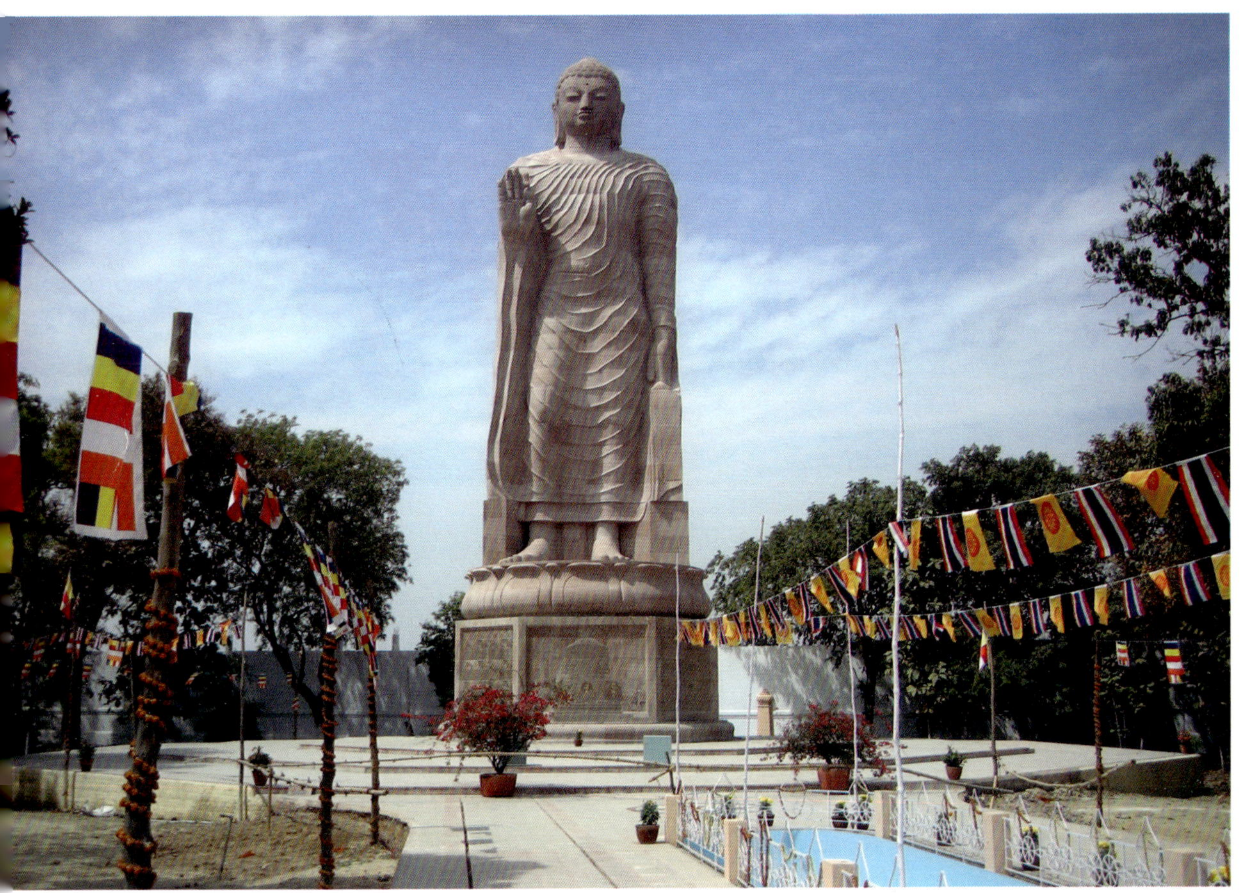

Statue of the Buddha at Sarnath

country. Emperor Ashoka, after becoming a follower of the Buddhist religion, built the Ashokan Pillar and the Stupa here. This place is thus considered sacred by all Buddhists.

GANGA AND THE CULTURAL HERITAGE OF INDIA

Generally a man's status and worth are assessed both by his affluence and his culture. In fact, these parameters were fixed right from the inception of civilisation. Certain features however keep varying with time and place with shifting paradigms. For instance, when assessing the worth of a westerner, one considers her cultural background which is very different from that of Indian culture. Hence, to assess her worth we keep in mind her cultural background and not ours.

Indian culture, for instance, is primarily based on three parameters – renunciation, spiritual and ascetic practices – which are miles away from material comforts or physical

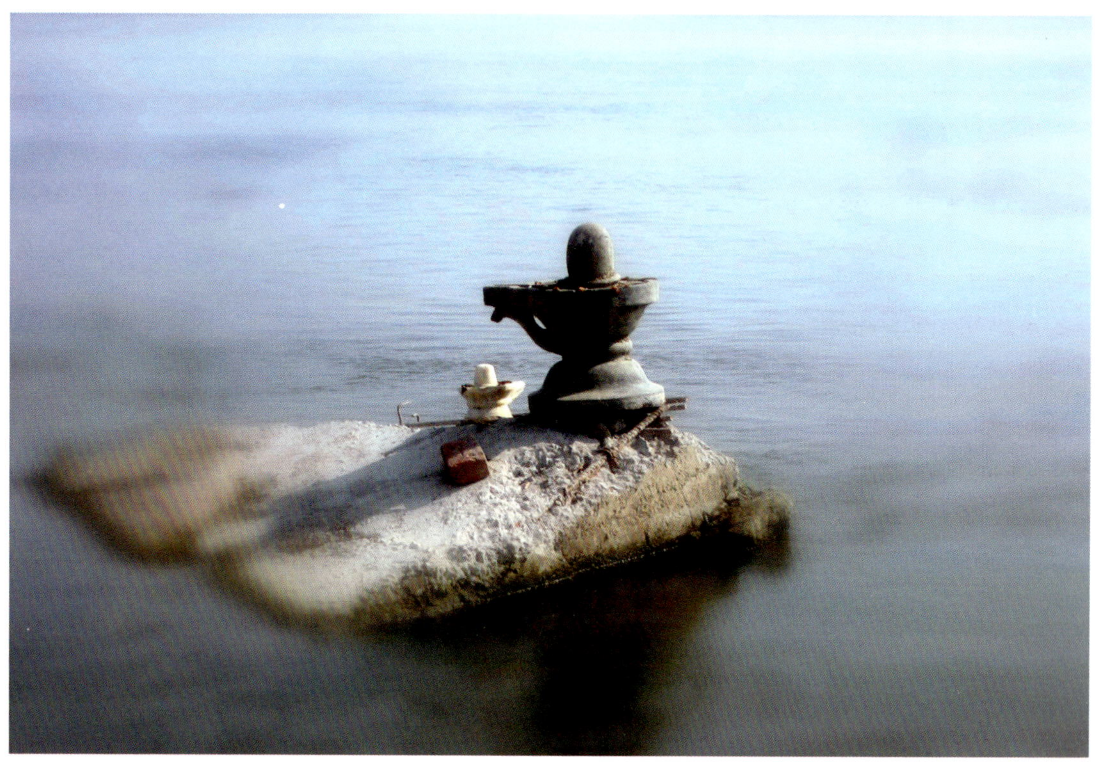

Shiva Lingam in the middle of the Ganga

enjoyment of the westerners. And this has been our heritage for the last five thousand years. No wonder we hear Sage Yajnavalkya's wife Maitreyi categorising material knowledge as something mundane and not worth pursuing. 'Why should I pursue a knowledge that does not provide me the key to spiritual liberation?' she had questioned her mentor. Her words actually echo the quintessence of our cultural heritage.

River Ganga forms an intrinsic part of the aforementioned cultural heritage of our country. The river that flows down 2,525 kilometres has not only homogeneously blended with our lives but has also succeeded in changing our views of life. True, different races and different tribes with varying tastes, culture, language and outlooks live on its banks; but ultimately by some mysterious ties, all of them are bound together to form a homogenous whole – Indians. Rivers like the Sarasvati have flown down the Indian plains, nourished human lives for centuries and then have dried out leaving a void. But the

Ganga has been there with us throughout, nourishing, protecting and helping us to prosper and propagate. Therefore to talk about Indian culture devoid of the Ganga is an impossible proposition. Poets from the past, contemporary poets and poets of the future had, are and will keep praising the river like poet Valmiki: 'Mother, you are the sequel to Parvati (the consort of Lord Shiva). You represent the beauty of the world and you are the stairway to reach heaven. This is my prayer to you, let me live on your bank, drink your nourishing water and keep thinking about your attributes till I die.'

Ganga therefore occupies an important position in the cultural heritage of India. There are innumerable rivers in our country which serve us in different ways. Men use the water of these rivers to bathe, to irrigate lands, to commute from one place to another but none of these rivers are deified as is the Ganga. Ganga inspires love and reverence in the minds of Indians at large, irrespective of their caste, creed, religion, social status, language or geographical distinction. I have personally seen such sights – a rich man while bathing in the Ganga, remains oblivious of the social status of his co-bather; an unthinkable proposition in a caste-obsessed society like ours. That means once you are in the river such petty distinctions are simply washed away.

Right from Gaumukh, the origin, to Gangasagar, the final destination of the Ganga, this phenomenon is visible everywhere. Elucidating this observable fact a traveller once wrote:

> The respect billions and billions of Indians have for river Ganga, right from the Himalayas to the southernmost tip, is something unique. Nowhere else in the world will you be able to see such deification. They recite slokas for the river Ganga, worship Ganga through different rituals, pray to Ganga, manifest their love and respect for Ganga – in fact all the riches that are to be found in the human heart are offered to Ganga. Whosoever has missed this singular sight will never be able to grasp the Indian psyche.
>
> Look at the river from the beginning till the end – i.e. right from Gaumukh to Gangasagar – a distance of almost two thousand miles, you will realize nowhere else in the world, no race on earth, no culture in the human civilization has manifested such love and reverence for a river. Visit Kanyakumari, Madurai, Rameswaram, Mount Abu, Puri, or Panhyavati – everywhere the water of Ganga is

> treated with same reverence and is considered equally pure and holy. And as is the case, it is this river that has bound the nation into one whole. (Translated from *Debatmya Himalaya* by Prabodh Kumar Sanyal)

This deification of the Ganga and its water began several hundred years ago. In fact it began years before the Chinese traveller Xuanzang visited India. Xuanzang while visiting Prayag noted this reverential attitude of the Indians and wrote about it. He had marvelled at the sight of kings coming all the way from their capital cities to the banks of this river just for bestowing wealth upon the poor. They considered neither their kingdom nor their state capital to be as propitious as the confluence of these three sacred rivers: Ganga, Yamuna and Sarasvati. As per Xuanzang's account, even King Harsha Vardhana had stayed here for a month and distributed all his worldly assets, including his rich personal wear, among the poor. After giving away his personal clothes he had gone to his sister Bhagyasree and begged for a piece of cloth to hide his nakedness. Till date, every twelve years Kumbh Mela is celebrated on the bank of the river Ganga to mark this occasion. Previously kings came to the Kumbh Mela to generously donate riches to the poor while the poor came to receive their munificence. But now people come neither to bestow nor to receive anything; they come to bathe in the Ganga expecting liberation from the cycle of birth and rebirth and enjoy momentary bliss.

The river Ganga flows through four northern states of the Indian subcontinent. But the states which do not enjoy the munificence of the Ganga do have alternative rivers to supply them the required water. These rivers too occupy singular positions in the minds of the people living on their banks. For instance, Godavari, the most famous river of southern India, is held in high esteem by Indians residing in the southern part of India. Godavari has been mentioned in the *Ramayana* as well. It is said that when Rama was exiled to the forest, he had gone to the bank of river Godavari and built a cottage there to live with Lakshman and Sita. The famous Panchavati forest too was near the river. Godavari thus can be called a sequel to Ganga in southern India. It is even referred to as the Ganga of the south. Despite this the people of south India prefer carrying a pitcher full of Ganga water, to pour into the river Godavari to sanctify it. It is clearly a symbolic representation of the admixture of two distinct cultures.

Besides the Godavari several other rivers of south India too have been both connected and associated with the river Ganga. For instance, two tributaries of river Godavari have been named after the Ganga: Penganga and Wainganga. In Maharashtra too there is the river that has been named after Ganga: Damanganga. Kings of states not blessed by the presence of the river Ganga were equally respectful about the river. And this has been the trend right from the beginning. Even the Chola kings while constructing their temples felt it necessary to carve out scenes of the stories of Ganga on the temple walls. Such is the status of Ganga in India. Even their victorious kings often assumed the title Gangaikonda to pay their homage to the river. It is said that King Rajendra Chola had once dug a large pond in his capital city for the defeated kings. The punishment meted out to these defeated kings was to pour gallons of Ganga water in it and fill it up.

Since the entire population of our country considers Ganga to be the most sacred river on earth, people of different states, where the river does not flow, like to associate their rivers with sacred Ganga. That possibly generates in them a kind of connection with the regions where Ganga is present and also enhances the sacredness of these rivers. In the entire Himalayan range there are the Kedar Ganga, Janhavi Ganga, Hari Ganga, Vil Ganga, Rishi Ganga and Bhrigu Ganga. Significantly, even Sri Lanka has two rivers named after Ganga – Kelaniganga and Mahavaliganga.

I have seen so many instances of reverence and devotion for the Ganga. For example once while visiting the chilly region of the Gangotri glacier I found young ladies standing in the ice-cold water of the river, praying for her benediction. Likewise, I came across many impoverished families who have spent their lives' savings to visit the Har-Ki-Pauri of Haridwar and pay their obeisance to the river Ganga. Indians even on their deathbeds thirst for a few drops of the Ganga water, because they believe that these few droplets will liberate them from the cycles of birth and rebirth. Thus for Indians the river Ganga is a living deity, a replica of the Divine Mother.

Talking about the river Ganga, Swami Vivekananda had once observed:

> When Hindus visit foreign countries, they carry two things with them – The *Gita* and the water from Ganga. Last time I too carried a little quantity of the Ganga water with me. And occasionally I would sip in a drop or two. A strange kind of tranquility would over sweep me, and I would instantaneously become calm. Maddening crowd, manifestation

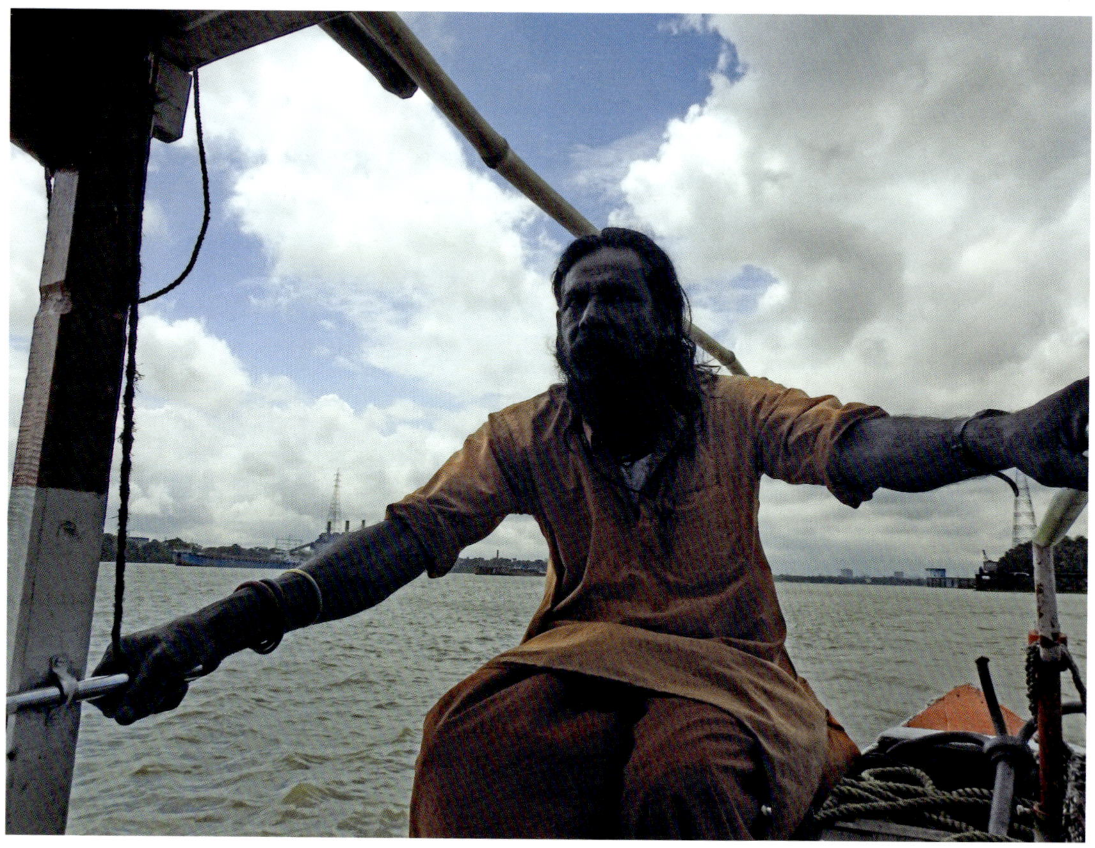

A boatman ferrying passengers from Belur Math to Dakshineswar

> of the Rajaguna, constant strife for supremacy, show of opulence, Paris, New York, Berlin, Rome – all would vanish immediately. And I would be overwhelmed by a strange beckoning from my mother land 'Har Har Har'. I would clearly visualize the river emanating from the lap of the Himalayas and merrily flowing down the arteries of my country with one single call of liberation 'Har Har Har'.
>
> (*Complete Works of Swami Vivekananda*)

A similar prayer was heard from a Muslim poet – Daraf Khan – 'Water means the water of Ganga, let me drink this water before I die. In case I am reborn, then I will have a divine existence.'

In his *Discovery of India* Pandit Jawaharlal Nehru wrote,

Ganga the sacred river of India, has laid the foundation of the heart of our country. Right from the inception of Indian history, we have observed how billions of Indians have built their homes on the banks of the river and lived there happily. The history of its birth from Gangotri to its history of merging with the sea at Gangasagar, is in reality the true history of India and Indian civilization. She is our Mother, who has witnessed the various courses of our lives – creation of cities, destruction of kingdoms, cowardice of men, valor of our heroes, tears and laughter, joys and sorrows. The name Ganga resonates in the Indian psyche.

As Nehru points out, the river is a true torchbearer of Indian culture and heritage. Thus on its banks we witness the wonderful co-existence of different cultures and religions – the Hindu priests chanting the Vedic slokas by the side of their Muslim brothers who are praying to a different god. Jains and Buddhists too, without confronting one another, peacefully follow their distinctly different spiritual paths to achieve nirvana. On the bank of the river Ganga in Varanasi we hear the mellifluous note of Ustad Bismillah Khan's sehanai along with Anup Jalota's Hindi bhajans.

Deification of the Ganga happened, is happening in this age of science, and will continue to happen in future as well. None of the Hindu rituals are complete without using the water of the river Ganga because it symbolises holiness. The river is like an Indian mother, bearing within her all our good and bad deeds. We love her, we hate her, we pollute her, we cleanse her, yet she never complains. She tends us like a true mother.

PATNA

Pataliputra, situated on the banks of the river Ganga, is an ancient Indian city. When Gautama Buddha attained nirvana and started spreading his message of love and non-violence, Patli was just a small village situated near the confluence of two rivers – Sone and Ganga. However, King Ajatsatru, ruler of Magadh, in an effort to protect his kingdom against the onslaught of the powerful Lichhavi kings constructed a fort in Pataliputra. Later his grandson established the present city of Pataliputra.

Greek traveller and ambassador of Seleucus (the ruler of Western Asia after the death of Alexander the great), Megasthenes had visited Pataliputra in 302 BCE, to meet King Chandragupta Maurya. Marvelling at the sight of the city he wrote a graphic account of the place. According to him

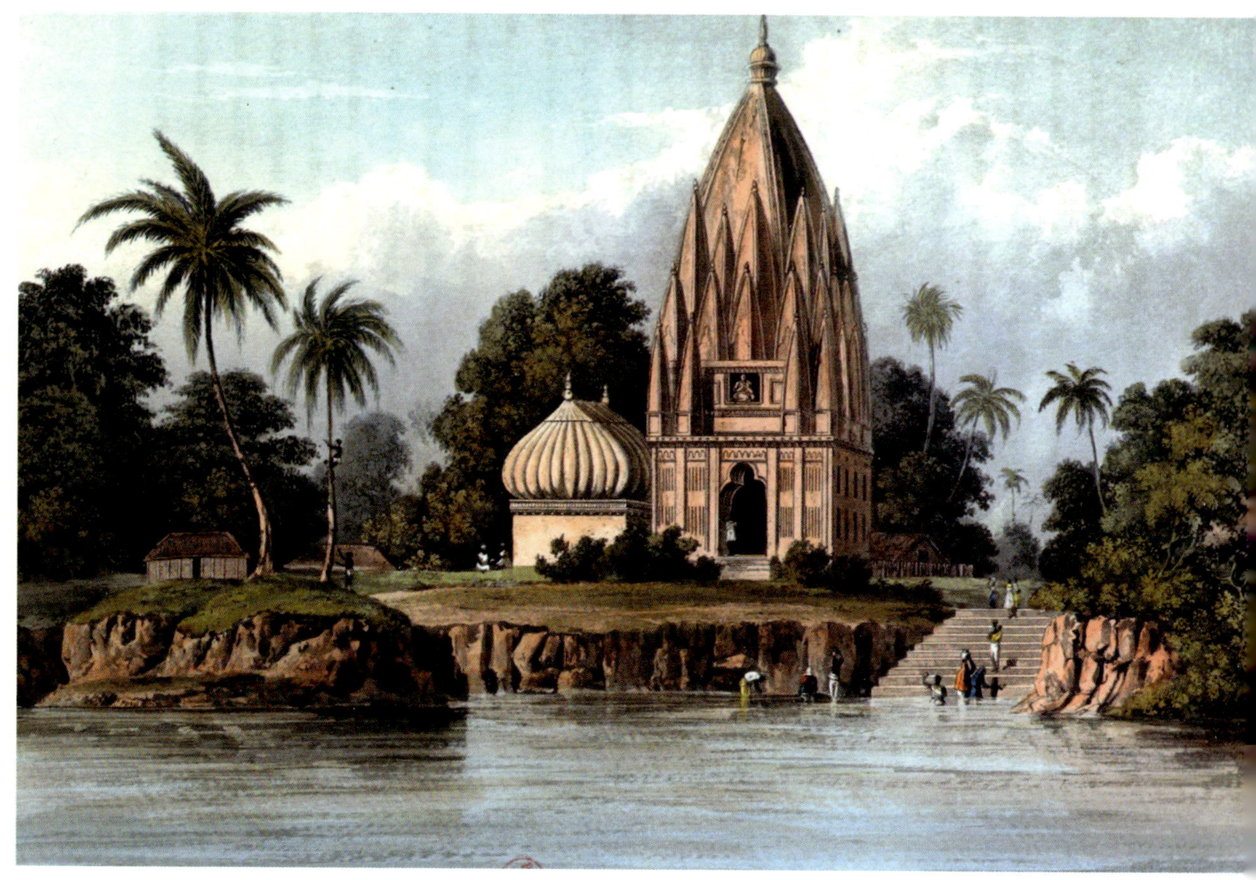

ABOVE: *A few miles below Patna a village with its Pagoda* by Lt Col. Forrest

FACING PAGE ABOVE: Devotees gather on the bank of the Ganga for Chhat puja, the festival of the Sun God, at Patna

FACING PAGE BELOW: A carpenter building a new boat, Farakka

the city, situated on the bank of the river Ganga, was nine miles long and two miles wide. There were 570 boroughs and 60 main entrances to the city. The palace of the king was centrally located. It was an architectural marvel. He also left behind an account of the administration of the country which clearly indicates the capability of the ruler. With time, both politically and commercially, Pataliputra became extremely influential. It became an important trading centre with ships and boats arriving and plying to distant lands for the purpose of trade and commerce. It also became the gateway to travel overseas. It is believed that Emperor Ashoka's son and daughter commenced their journey from Pataliputra and sailed across the Ganga to reach Ceylon via Tamluk. They went there as the emissaries of the emperor to preach the doctrines of Gautama Buddha. The place of

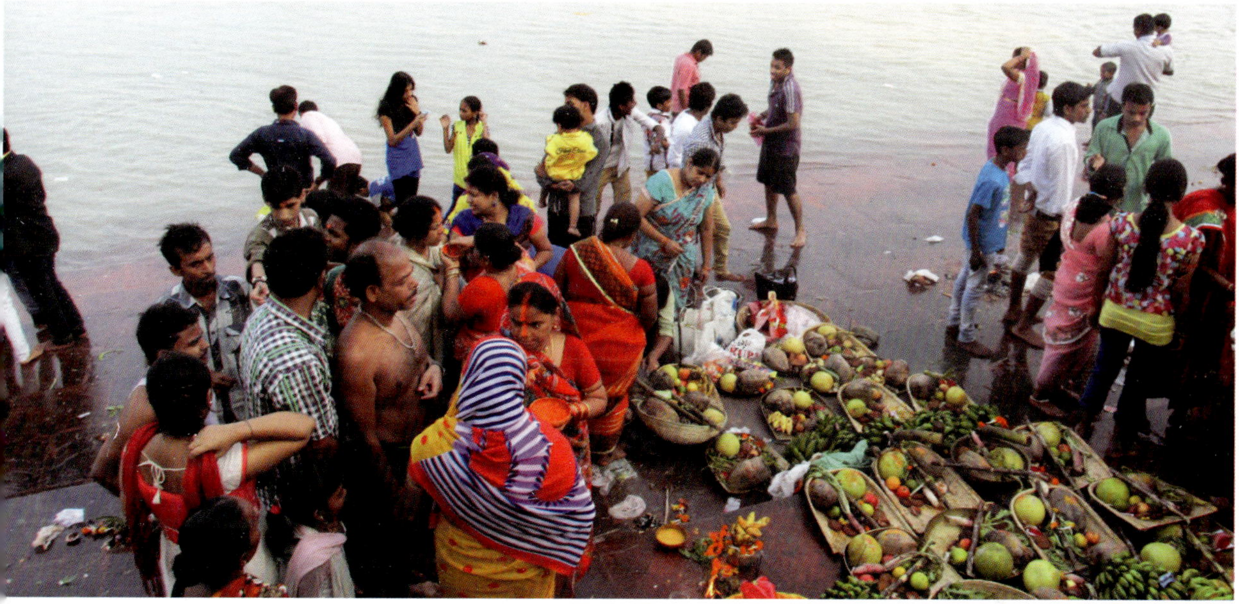

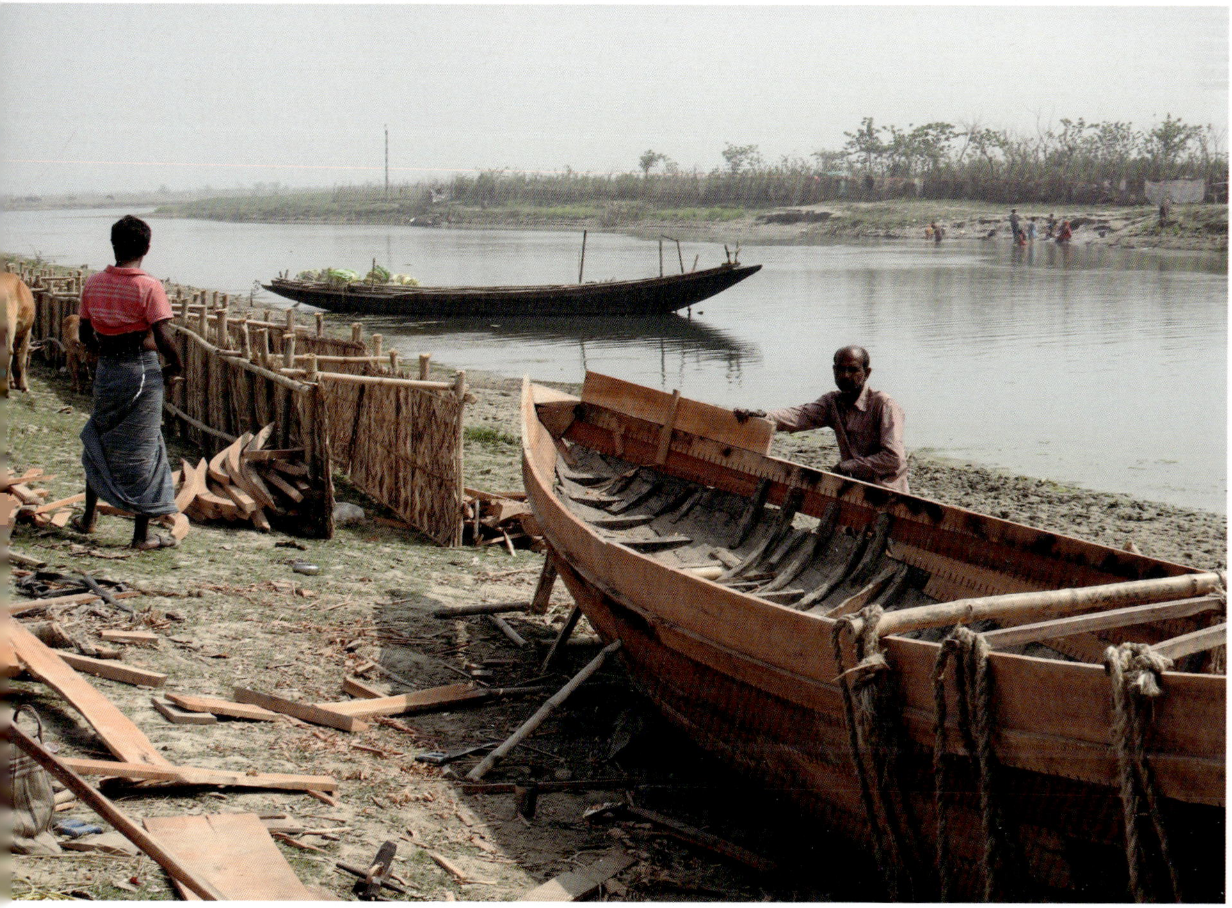

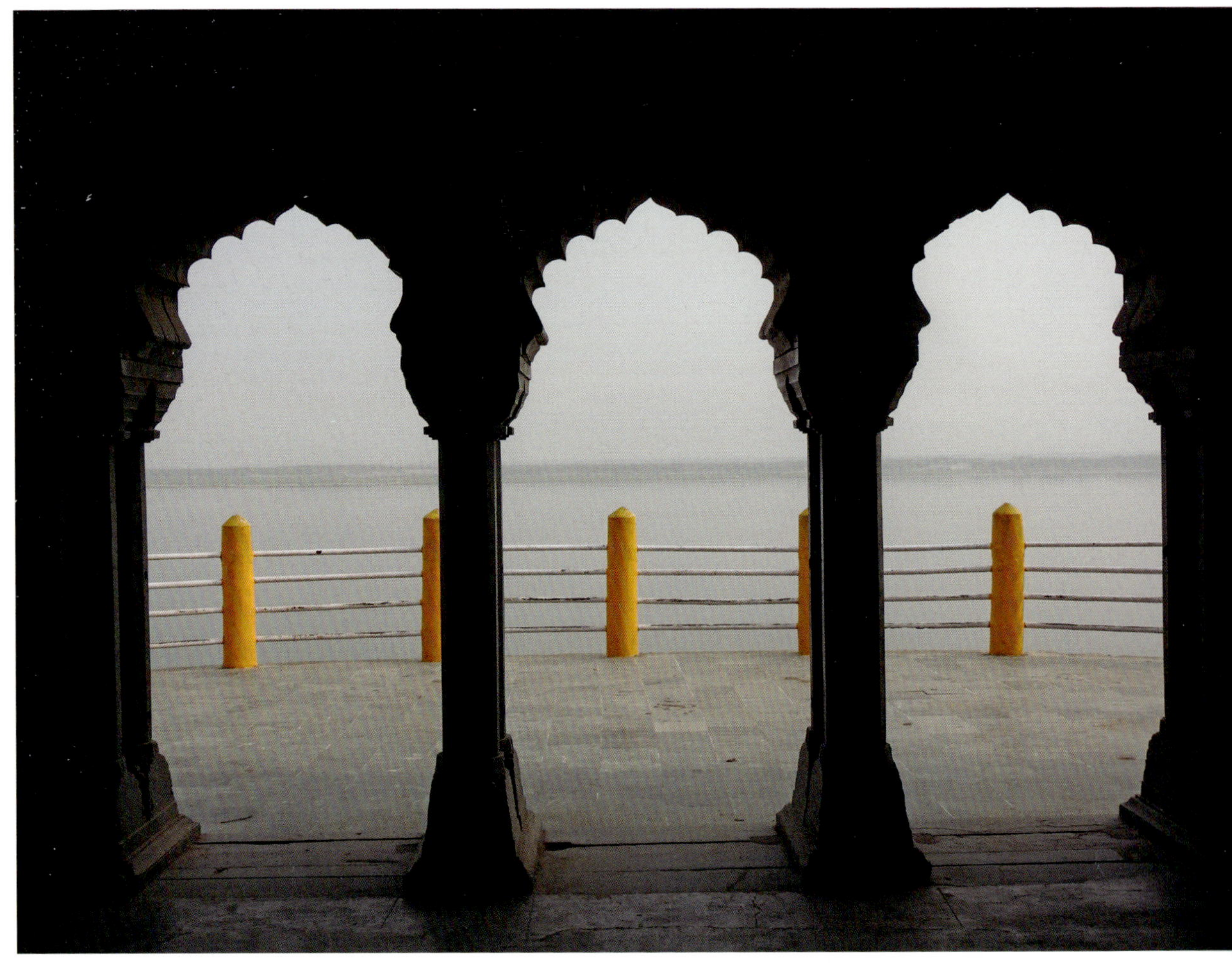

Sangi Dalan (marble pavilion) erected by Man Singh, Emperor Akbar's viceroy in Bengal (c. 1580-1600)

their departure was later commemmorated by a wharf named Mahendra ghat.

According to a Chinese travelogue, Fan Chen, a Cambodian king, had sent an ambassador to Pataliputra. The ambassador had travelled across Bay of Bengal and finally reached the estuary of the Ganga. From there he again journeyed down the river to reach Pataliputra. But by the time Xuanzang visited Pataliputra, the city had lost its lustre due to repeated foreign aggressions.

Sher Shah conquered Bihar and shifted the capital from ancient Pataliputra to a

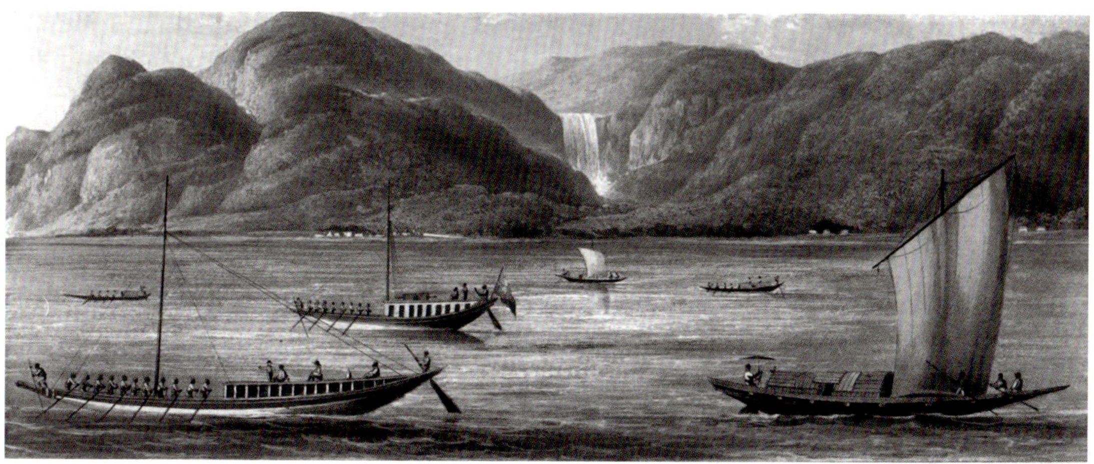

Rajmahal Hill by Lt Col. Forrest

place called Pattan. Possibly the present name Patna has been derived from the old Pattan. In 1669, the tenth Sikh Guru, Govind Singh, was born here in Patna. At present Patna is a busy city down which flows the Ganga. There are several wharfs on the bank where people come to bathe during various festivals.

RAJMAHAL

After crossing Bihar, the Ganga flows into Rajmahal, a city in Jharkhand. Once upon a time in the past, this place had played a very important role in history. During Muslim rule, this place was called Damin-i-koh. King Man Singh had his capital here at Rajmahal. Along the banks of the Ganga were his palace and a Shiva temple. Although the former has been destroyed, the latter is still standing.

Rajmahal had also been the abode of Shah Suja (second son of Shah Jahan), Mir Qasim (Nawab of Bengal) and Shri Chaitanya Mahaprabhu (the Vaishnava spiritual leader).

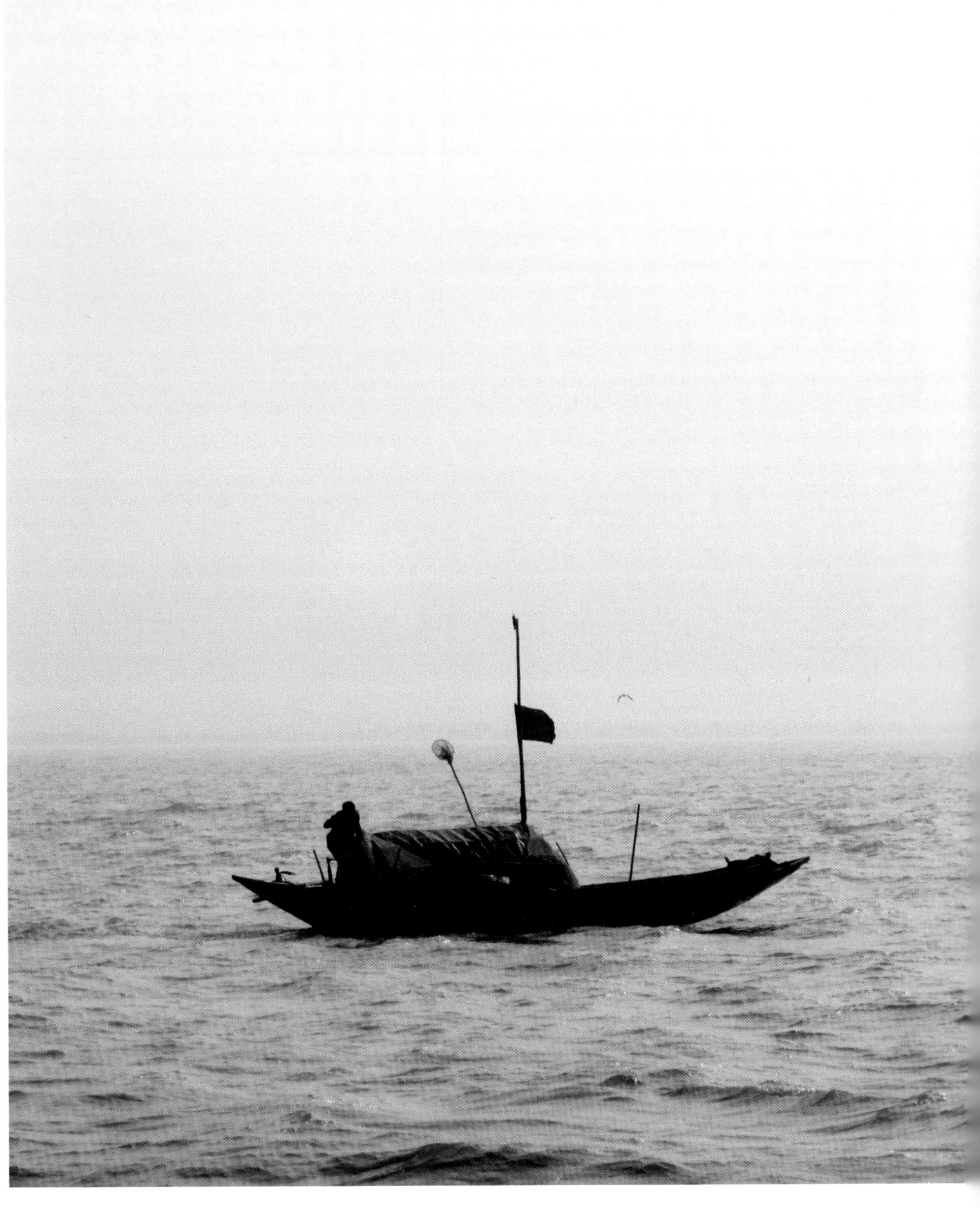

JOURNEY'S END

GANGA IN BENGAL

The story of the Ganga in Bengal is slightly different from those of the other states in India. As mentioned earlier, Ganga starts its course from the Himalayan range and then flows down to merge with the Bay of Bengal at Gangasagar. On its way it traverses five Indian states – Uttarakhand, Uttar Pradesh, Bihar, Jharkhand and then finally reaches West Bengal. All the states have flourished because of the benediction showered on them by the river. Both cultural and economic development of nearly all the states of northern India can be attributed to the river Ganga. The rich silt deposit of the river has benefitted these states and enabled them to fill their stores with abundant harvest. But for Bengal Ganga has a different assignment. Playing the role of a mother, the Ganga has created the distinct land of West Bengal.

FACING PAGE: A fisherman on the Ganga in Bengal

Billions of years ago large parts of West Bengal lay under the sea. The present districts of 24 Parganas, Howrah, Hooghly, and Kolkata were immersed under seawater. And the northern part of Murshidabad district was covered by swampy land and forests. Over time with gradual deposit of silt the river saw the emergence of this new-found land – Bengal, primarily West Bengal. It so happened that after Rajmahal the river divided itself into two parts: the Padma (presently in Bangladesh) and the Bhagirathi which flowed southward in the districts of Murshidabad, Nadia, Hooghly and 24 Parganas before finally flowing into the Bay of Bengal.

After crossing the present state of Bihar, the river Ganga helped Gour, Pandua, Rajmahal, Cossimbazar, Murshidabad and Nabadwip, the ancient state capitals of Bengal, to emerge gradually on its banks. However, the route of the river was starkly different when compared to the present

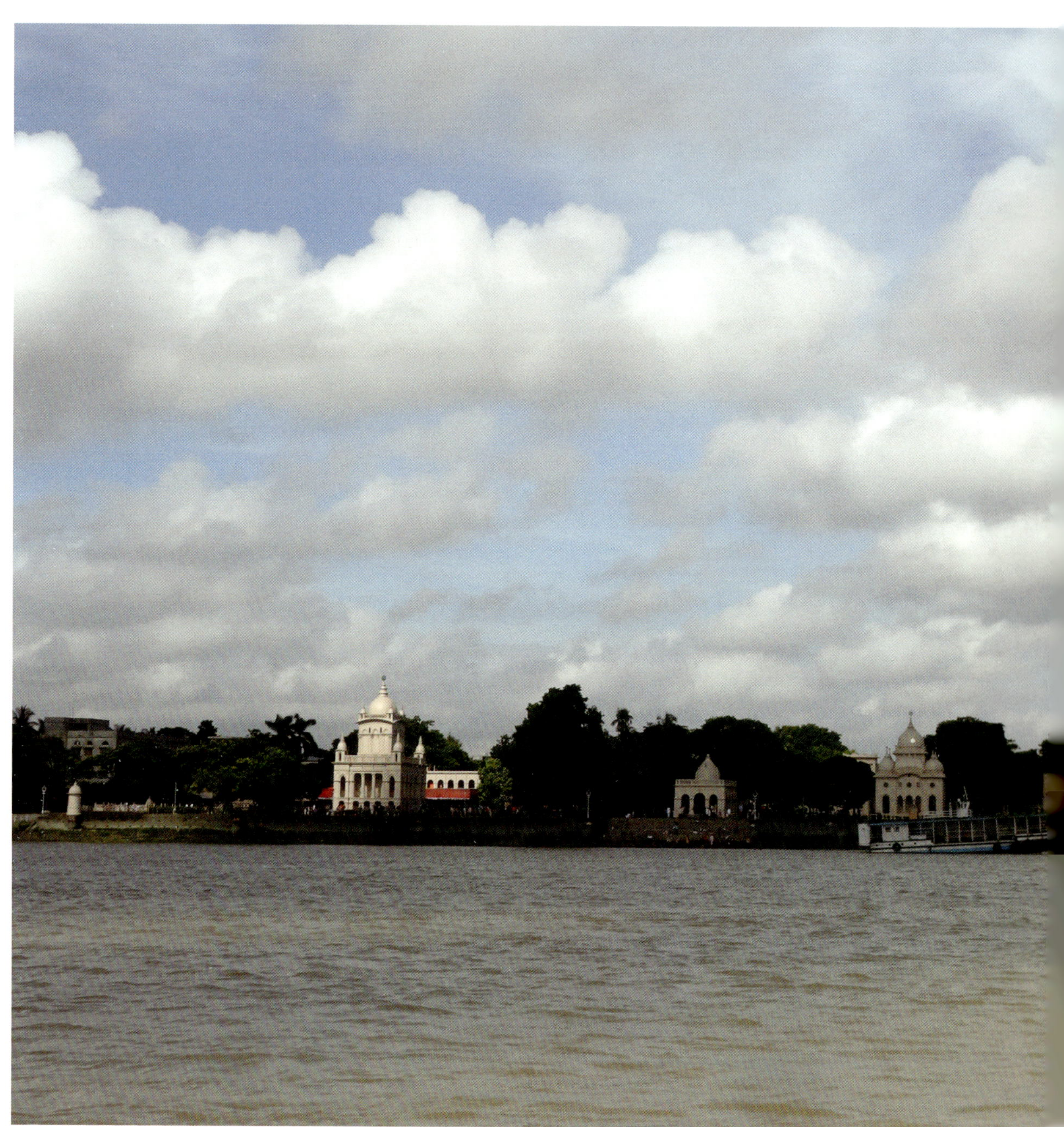

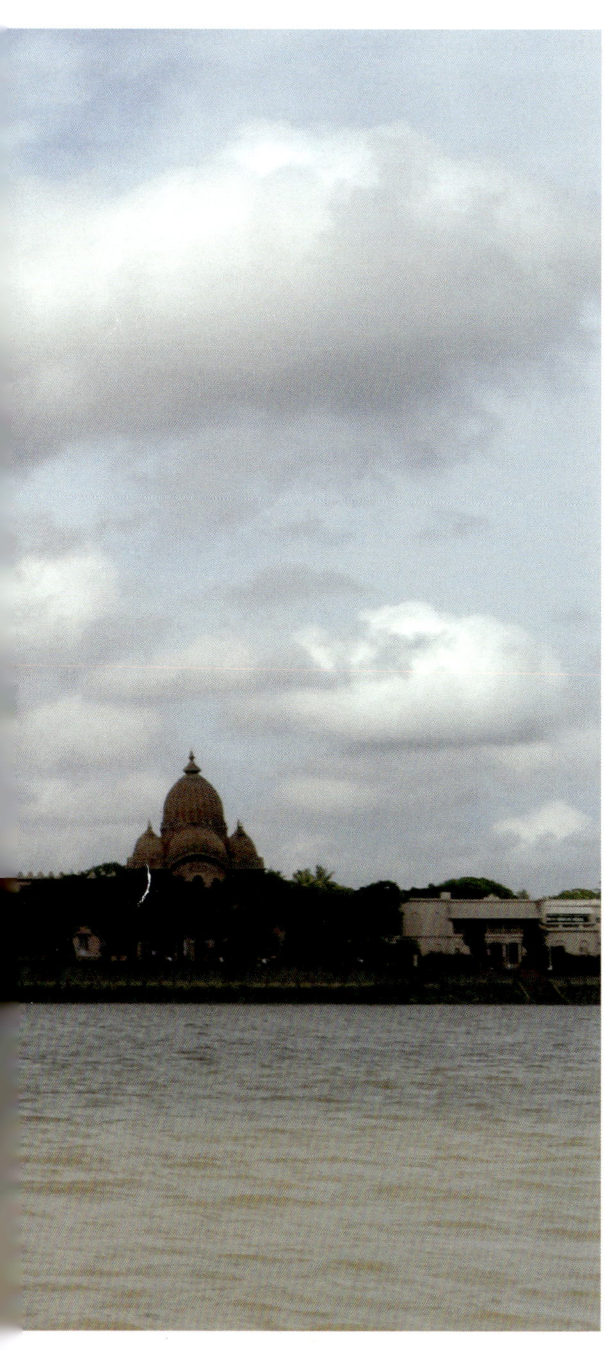

one. For the foreigners though, the Ganga flowing eastward was Padma and not Ganga. Incidentally even though the width of Padma was greater than that of Ganga, to the Indians the Padma, despite being a part of the Ganga, was qualitatively inferior and hence did not qualify to be called either Bhagirathi or Janhavi. To them, Padma was merely a river whose destructive power at times called for such names as 'Kirtinasha' (destroyer of all creations) and 'Bhayankari' (dangerous). Not an iota of the sacredness of Ganga was to be found in Padma. The river Ganga is associated with a spiritually cleansing power and is also the propagator of human culture, history, affluence, social life, agriculture, trade and commerce, fine arts, music and folklores. All these aspects of Ganga were thus deified by the people of West Bengal. But the Padma never evoked this response.

In the *Mahabharata* we come across the present state of Bengal through the conquests of Bhima (the second Pandava). The epic recounts Bhima killed King Jarasandha, King of Pundu, Kings Chitrasena and Samudrasena, the kings of Banga, and the king of Tamralipta. Even Kalidasa mentions Bengal in his *Raghuvamsha*. Furthermore, historians claim that even

Belur Math, located on the west bank of the Hooghly river, is notable for its architecture that uses different religious motifs as a symbol of unity

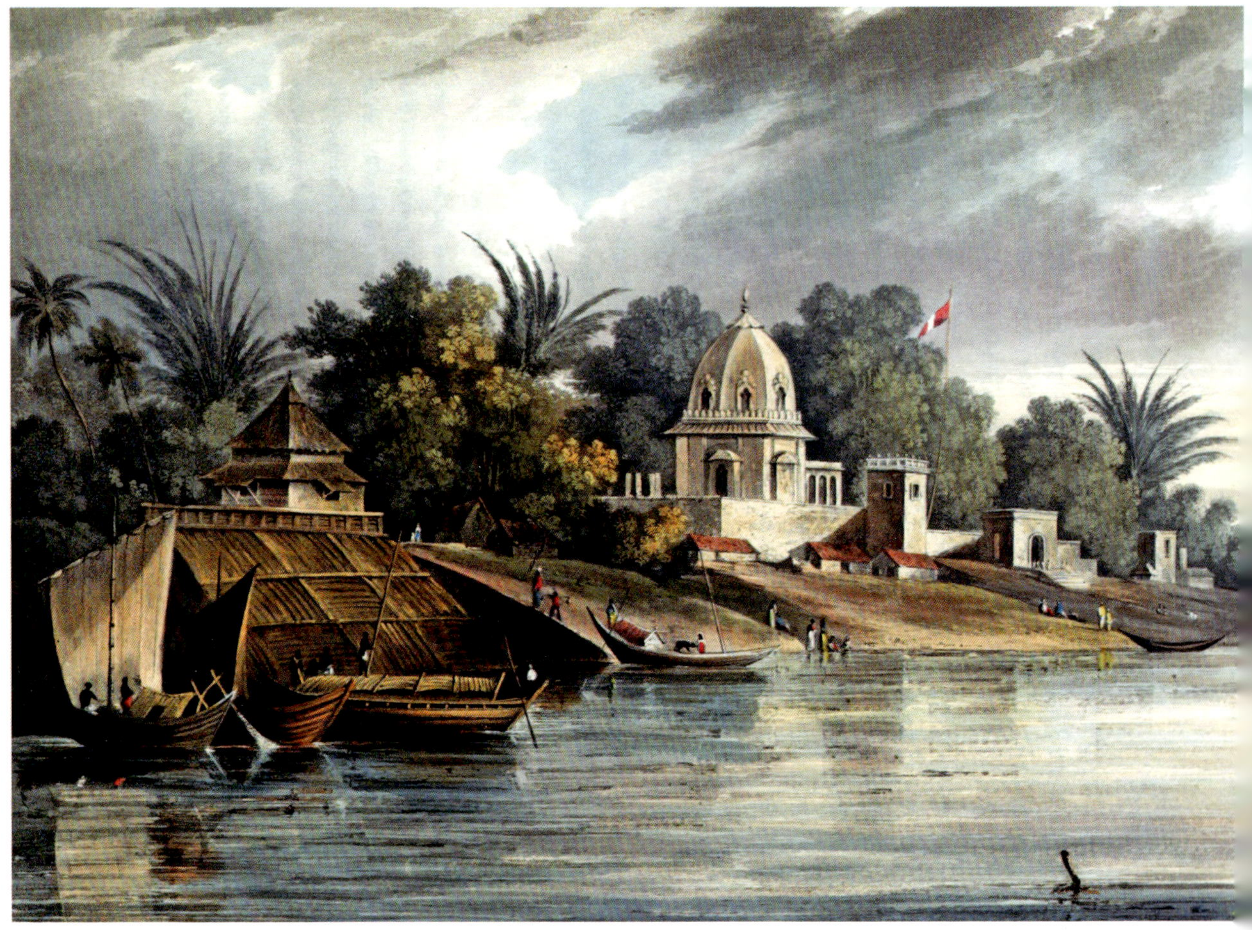

Moorshedabad by Lt Col. Forrest

Alexander the Great while conquering the north-western part of India had heard about the 'Gangaridai' culture. In fact Gangaridai is a Greek term. Later Megasthenes, the Greek ambassador, reached Pataliputra, the capital city of King Chandragupta Maurya, and wrote in his historical treatise *Indica* about the conquests of both Prasioi and Gangaridai. Prasioi refers to Magadh and Gangaridai refers to Bengal. In the first century BCE Greek historian Diodorus Siculus in his *Bibliotheca Historica* mentioned the north-flowing Ganga which merged with the sea. East of Gangaridai flowed the river Ganga, he wrote, which was a land full of elephants, and feared by most conquerors. An Egyptian traveller came to India around 60 CE and went back to his country to write about Gangaridai civilisation.

In the second century CE Greco-Roman scholar Ptolemy in his work the *Geographia* wrote about the five estuaries of Ganga.

All the five estuaries finally merged with the sea at a point near Tamralipta. Tamralipta at that point of time was the largest port of India. Trade flourished between Alexandria, countries of eastern Asia and also Europe. Ships came to Tamralipta from these distant lands. But from eighth century onwards, with heavy deposits of silt, commercial transactions started dwindling. Ships could no longer enter the port of Tamralipta. So, with time, Tamralipta lost its prestigious position and receded into oblivion.

Another important commercial city of ancient Bengal was Gour. Its strategic geographical location, near the confluence of Padma and Ganga, helped it flourish. That there was a flourishing port here has been established by the historians. Small canals from the river flowed throughout the region, which helped small boats to ferry goods to the river. Ancient texts indicate many Arab traders settled here. The Arab traders would sail across Padma and Meghna to reach Chittagong port to trade with Chinese tradesmen. Plenty of foreigners visited the region at that point of time. And some of them even recorded that 'more than fifty ships ply from here with silk and cotton

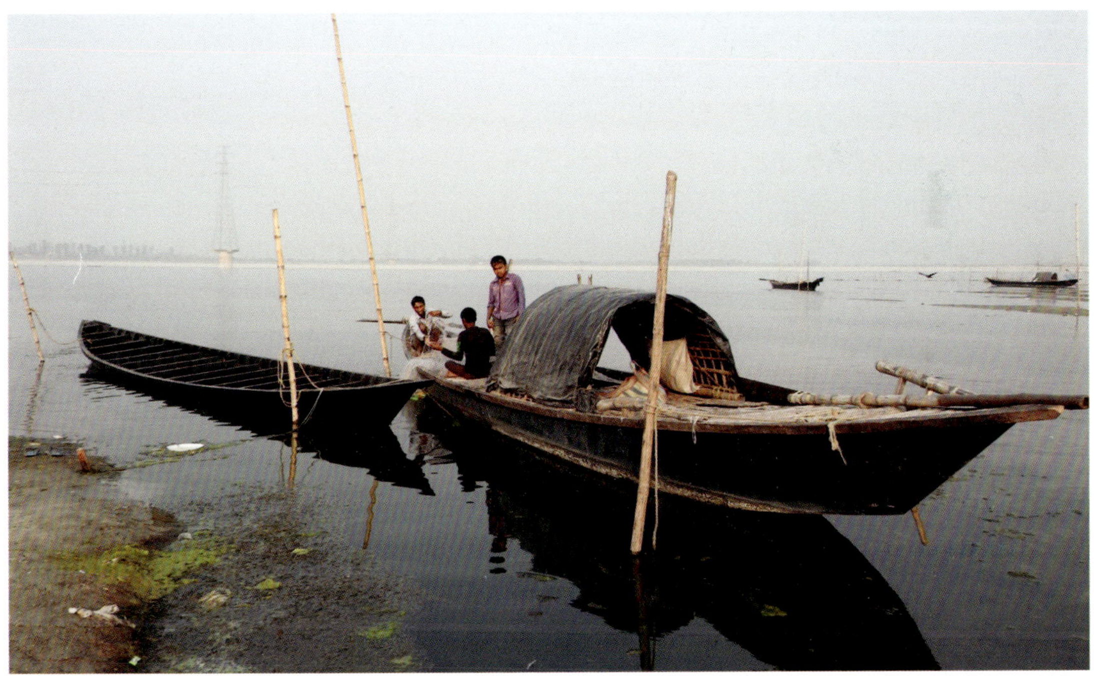

Fishermen trying to eke out a living, Farakka

to different countries'. But the situation changed dramatically with the coming of the Mughals in 1576. Mughal Emperor Akbar took over the reins of Bengal and diverted the ancient route of the river Ganga, leaving Gour to perish as an unhealthy swampy land. In fact, Gour's affluence and fame declined with the diversion of Ganga. The subsequent capital cities of Bengal were Rajmahal, Dhaka and finally Murshidabad.

In 1713, that is nearly at the end of the Mughal rule, Murshid Quli Khan was appointed Subedar of Bengal. He decided to shift the state capital from Dhaka to Murshidabad. Accordingly he left Dhaka with his royal entourage, followed by affluent citizens and the aristocrats and set up a new capital at Murshidabad.

The primary reason for shifting base however was the bank of the river Ganga. It was observed that many of the foreign traders who had settled in and around Cossimbazar, Farashdanga, Chandannagar and Chinsurah (parts of Bengal) were not only successfully trading with foreign countries, but were also growing increasingly rich and politically powerful. So in an effort to check their growing powers and to keep an eye on their movements this shift was essential. Murshidabad proved to be the ideal place to control the growing powers of these traders.

Ironically, along with Murshidabad, another city was gradually and silently gaining importance, and that was the present city of Kolkata.

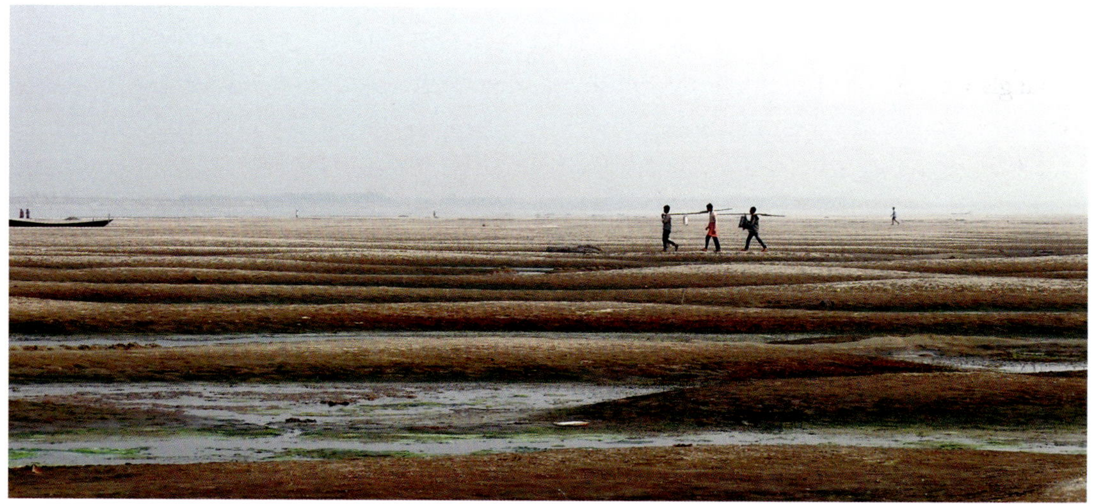

Fishermen walking on the shimmering sand behind the Farakka dam

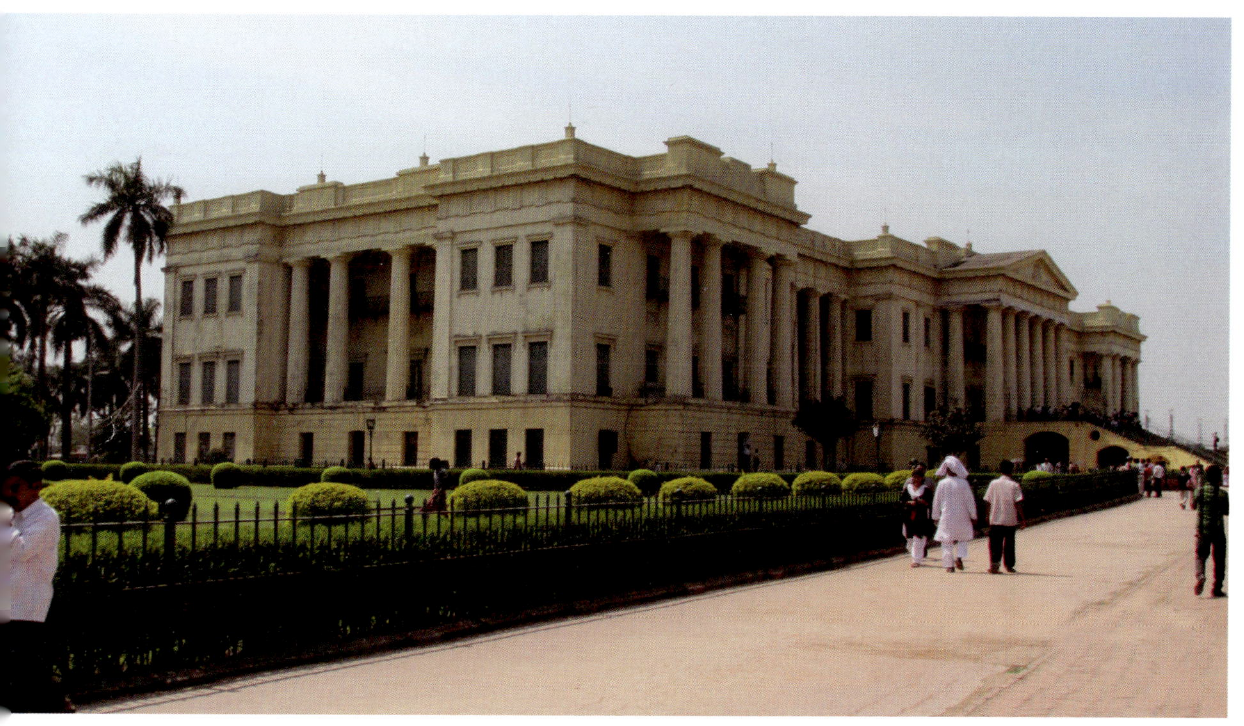

A palace with a thousand doors at Murshidabad – the Hazarduari palace

MURSHIDABAD

Murshidabad was an extremely important city in the past. North of it is the Malda district and east of it is the Rajshahi district, now in Bangladesh. River Padma flows down the fringes of the city while on its north flows river Ganga through the Burdwan district. At one point of time Murshidabad was the capital of three Indian states – Bengal, Bihar and Orissa.

Rajmahal, a part of present Jharkhand, is the actual entry point of the river Ganga into Bengal. As mentioned earlier, once the river enters Bengal it divides itself into two distinct parts – the Padma (in Bangladesh) and the Ganga. Finally of course both these courses merge with the Bay of Bengal. Murshidabad thus remains a mute observer of all these changing courses of the river.

Legend has it that Mukhsudan Das, a renowned doctor of Gour, once treated Sultan Hussain and cured him of a critical illness. The sultan was extremely pleased with the doctor and gifted him the district of Mukhsudbad. In 1704 Nawab Murshid Quli Khan of Bengal shifted the state capital from Dhaka to Mukhsudbad and named the city after himself – Murshidabad. It was under him that Murshidabad started flourishing. Murshid Quli Khan was followed by Nawab Sujaudullah Khan and Nawab Sarfaraz Khan. But unfortunately neither of the two

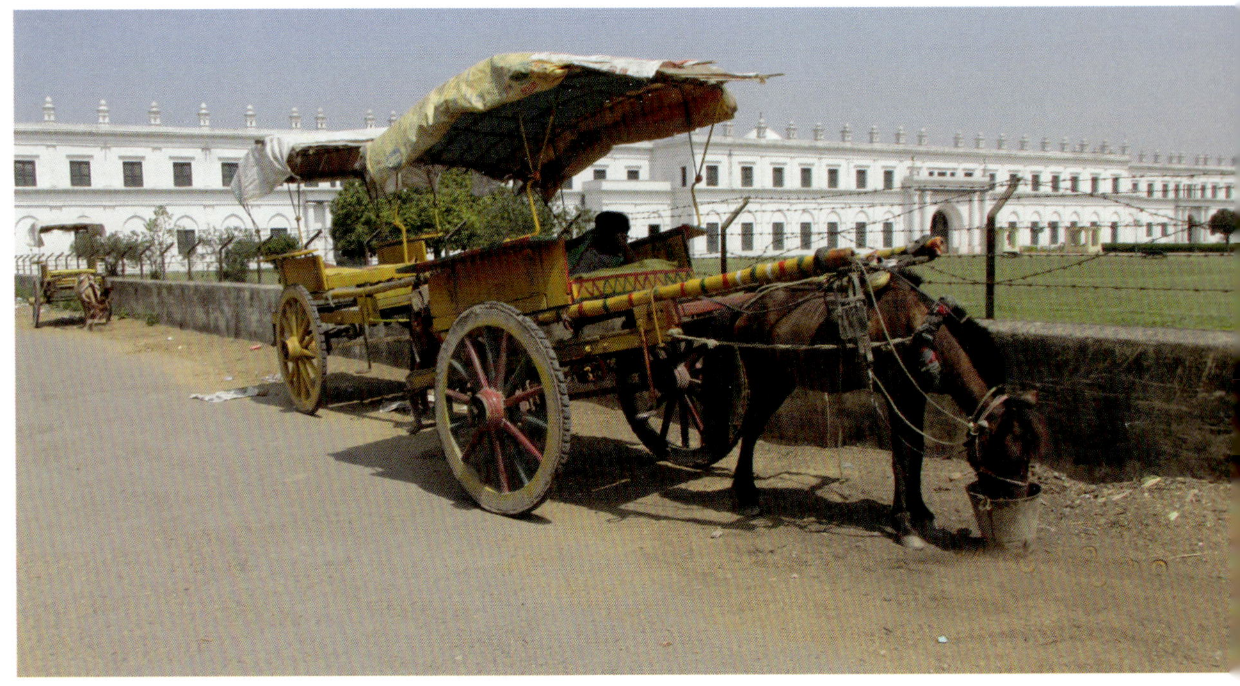

The Nizamat Imambara is situated opposite the Hazarduari palace, just a few feet away from the Bhagirathi river

could reign for long. In the battle of Giriyar, Sarfaraz Khan was killed by Alivardi Khan, who then captured Murshidabad. Alivardi Khan was succeeded by Nawab Sirajudullah, his grandson. In 1757, when in the Battle of Plassey Sirajudullah was defeated by the British, Murshidabad's fortune gradually started declining. And since the British imperialists concentrated their efforts in developing the present-day Kolkata, the city started flourishing. Then with the passage of time it became the capital city of the Indian subcontinent.

From a Pilgrim's Diary

Dhuliyan is a small town in Murshidabad district situated on the bank of the Ganga. It takes hardly two hours by bus from Baharampur to reach Dhuliyan. The road route lies parallel to the bank of the river.

I met Radheshyam Das during my journey to Dhuliyan. Radheshyam is a native of Dhuliyan. He was on his way home. On reaching Dhuliyan we parted ways with a promise to meet after lunch. Therefore in the afternoon when both of us met again, our destination was the riverbank. Crossing the local market we reached the bank of the river. But to be candid the very sight of this bank shocked and actually unnerved me. Could this be the same Ganga I had seen so far – I tried to rationalise.

In fact, before reaching Dhuliyan, I was aware only of the benign aspects of the

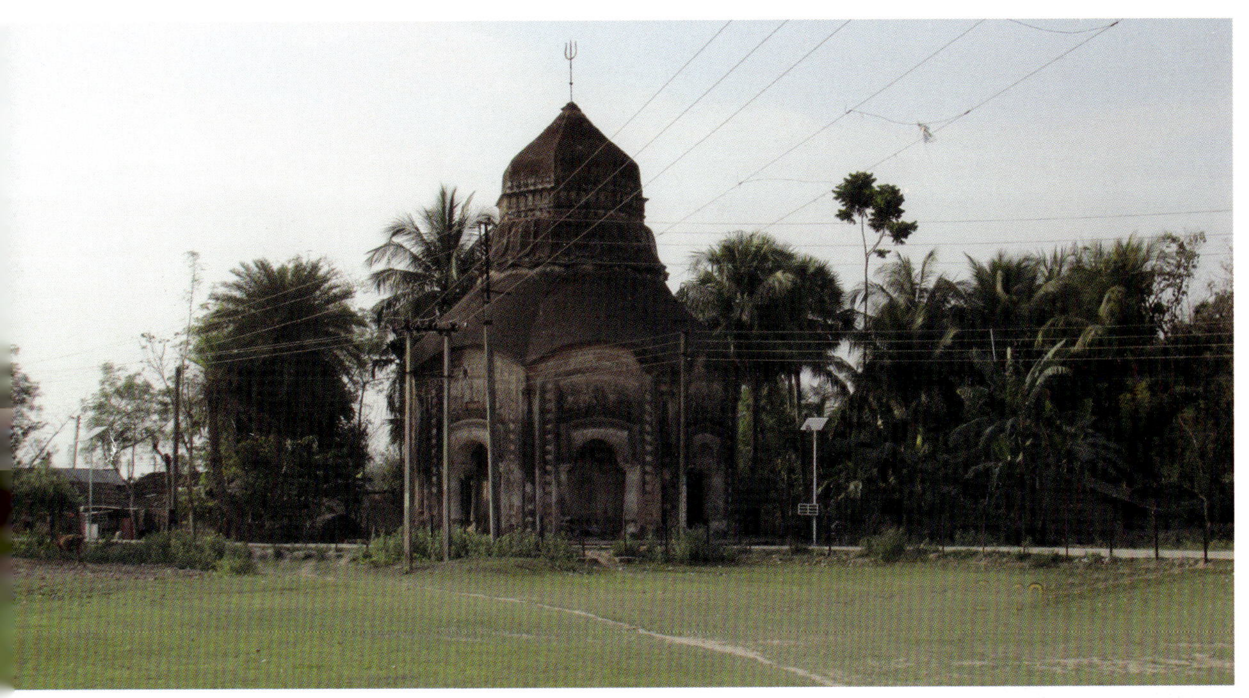

Shiva temple at Barnagar near Murshidabad. It was built by Queen Bhavani of Natore (now in Bangladesh)

river and had deified her as an earthly form of Divine Mother. But the sight of the riverbank at Dhuliyan shattered me. That the river could also be so devastating and overwhelmingly cruel had never crossed my mind. There was hardly any bank left here. Other than bits of broken lands here and there, and deep gorges created by the river, there was nothing in front of us which could be called the riverbank. On one edge of the receding bank line, stood a two-storeyed house which could topple over into the river at any moment. I looked at the other side of the river and to my horror found similar traces of receding bank lines. It was indeed a depressing sight for both of us.

Utterly depressed we went to the nearest tea stall for a cup of tea. Looking at our gloomy faces the owner Somnath Barui, a middle-aged gentleman, said, 'Don't be disheartened, babu. We have learnt to live with this deadly river. When we were young the river ran its course some half kilometre away from here. My father was a renowned doctor and had constructed a three-storeyed house there. We were quite affluent then. We used to swim in the Ganga and my mother and aunts would go to the river to worship her. Things started deteriorating from 1975 onwards when the Farakka Barrage came up. Ganga, refused her natural route, started depositing silts everywhere. During monsoon when the water level kept rising

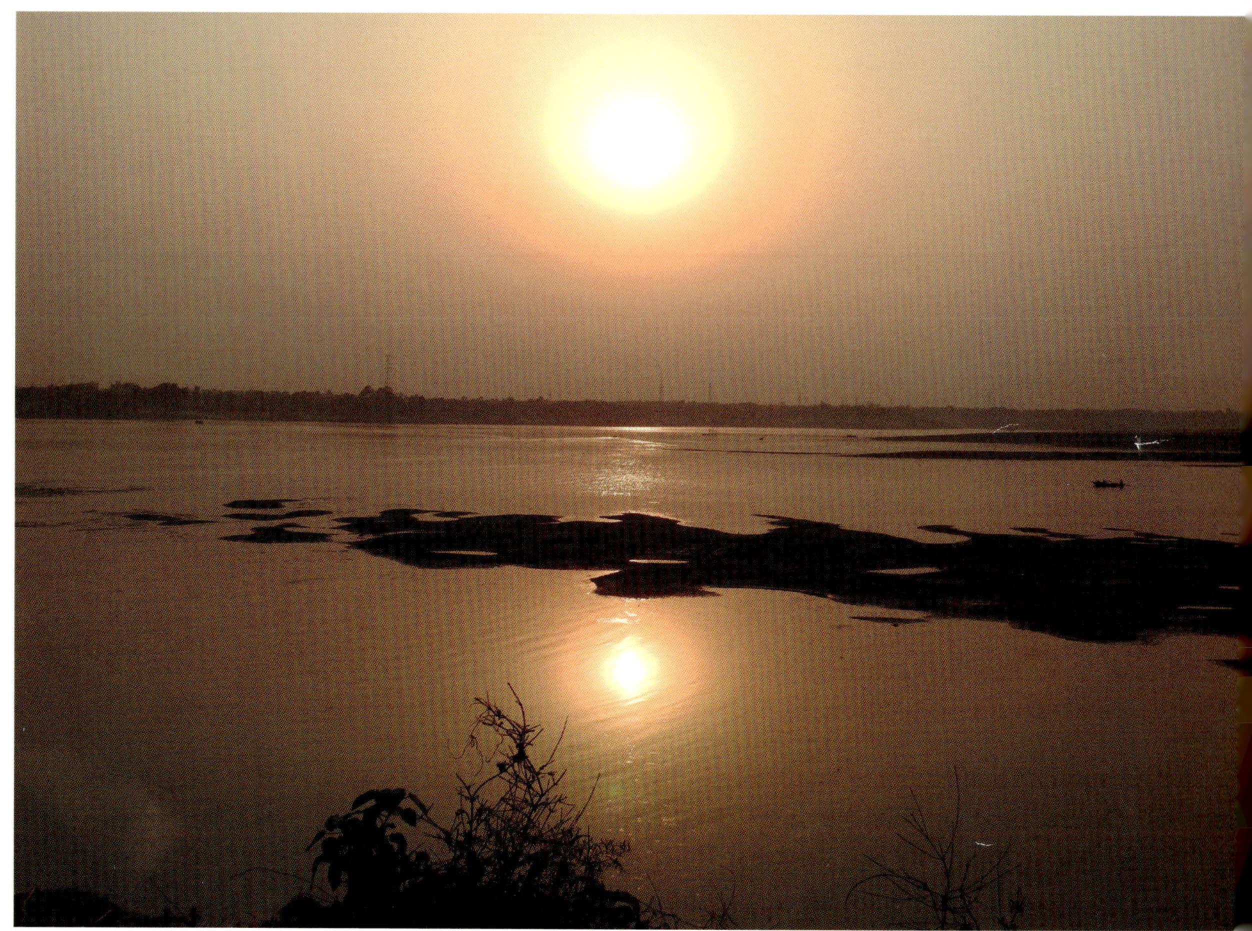

Dusk at Nimtita, Murshidabad

and reached unmanageable heights the bank lines started receding. One morning the river would assault the bank line on her left, and sweep away everything that came her way, and the next morning she would attack the bank line on the right and wipe it out of existence. Everything that was there on those banks was simply whisked off at one stroke. One morning we found the river just a few furlongs away from our house. The message was clear; it would now wipe out our house as well. Immediately we started collecting our belongings to vacate the house. Within a few hours the river struck the three-storeyed house and it simply disappeared into the river. We left the place and hired a house to stay at. My father was unable to absorb the shock and died soon after. We had no money to continue our studies hence started working at an early age. After years of struggle I have now finally set up this tea stall and am somehow managing to survive.'

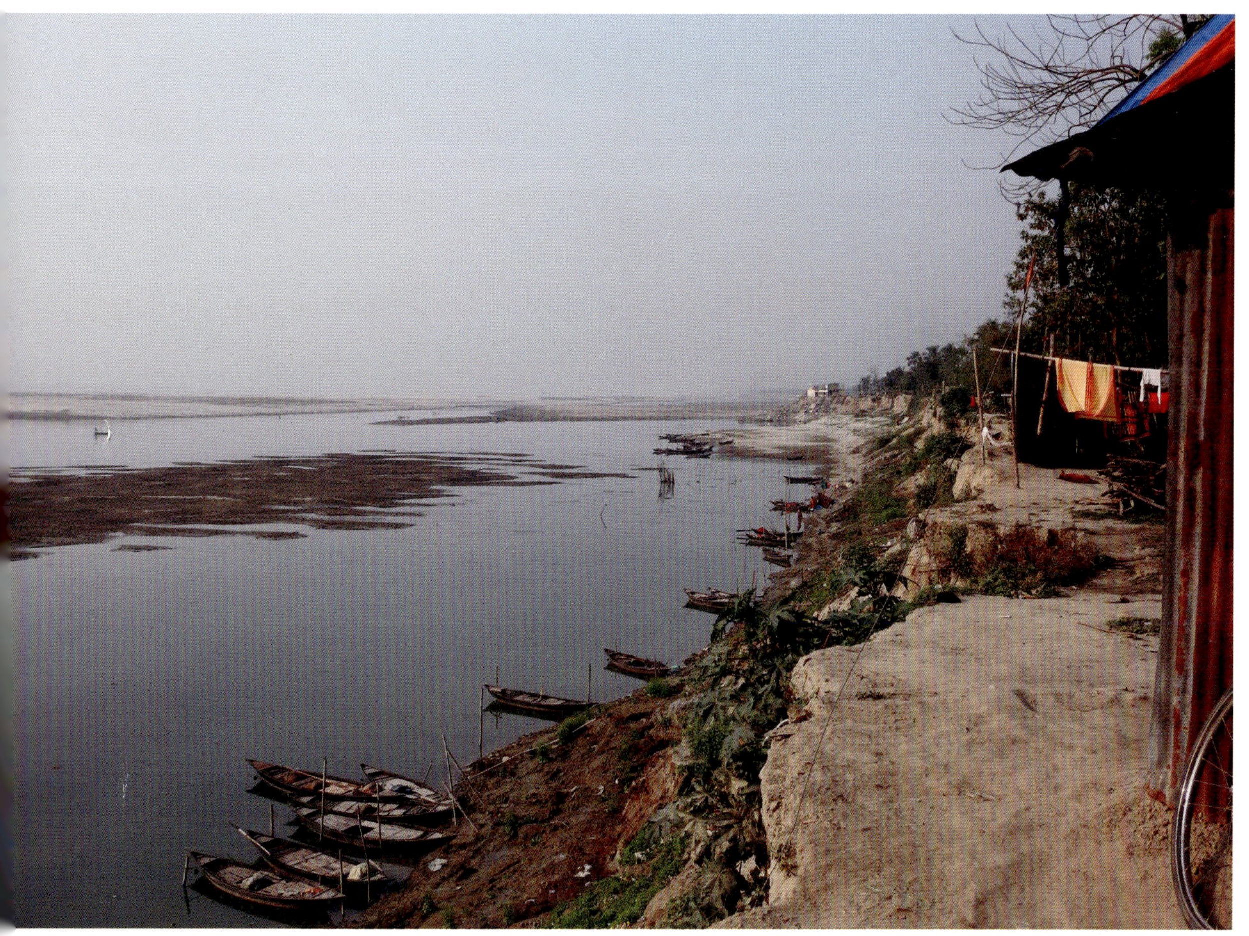

At Dhuliyan half the village has been swallowed up by the Ganga

The story made me very sad. I walked away from the tea stall and loitered along the bank that was still intact. After some time I reached Harinagar village. Most of the people in the village are Vaishnavites. A small temple stood in the middle of this small nondescript village. An elderly gentleman, Haripada Roy, was sitting on its porch. I approached him and asked, 'How is the condition here?' The gentleman sighed and said, 'We are mortally afraid of the river Ganga. She plays havoc with our lives. Particularly in the months of July, August and September, she terrorises us. We spend sleepless nights listening to the roaring waves of the river which keep inundating every bit of land that comes her way. Days are spent worrying about our fates – would we or would we not survive the onslaught of the river? The existing roads get inundated and we can hardly venture out of our houses.'

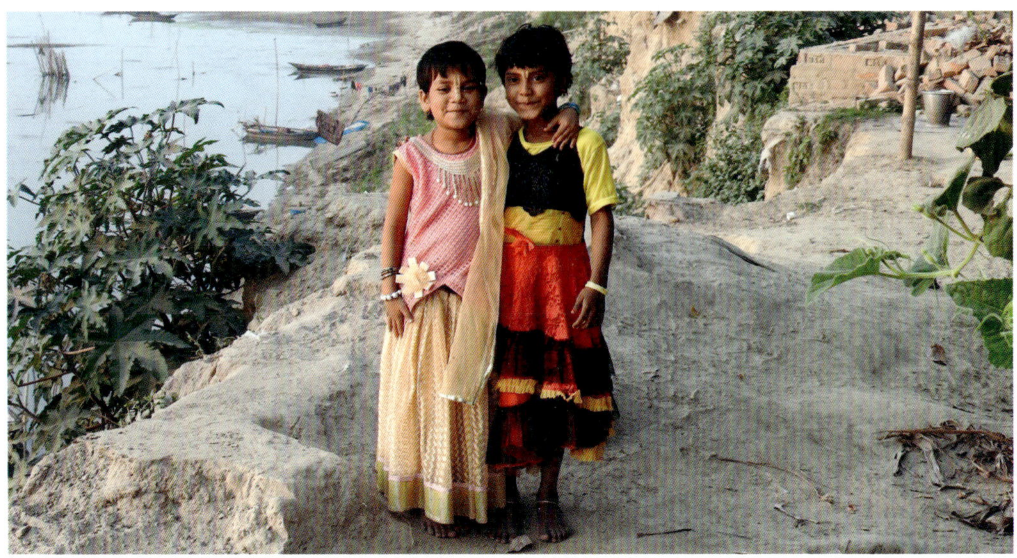

Life amidst destruction at Dhuliyan

Haripada's uncle, who was sitting beside him, recounted a nerve-shattering story to us. 'It happened during the monsoon last year. It was about nine pm and we had all gone to sleep. A shattering noise suddenly woke us up. As we looked out, we found the gushing waves of the river at our doorstep. It had already swept off our boundary wall and was fast approaching the house. We knew it was just a matter of time before the water engulfed our family. It would devour our house and drown all of us. Instantly we left the house and within half an hour the entire building collapsed before us. Just a few days prior to this incident we had witnessed how an entire kitchen, where our neighbour's pregnant daughter-in-law was cooking a meal, was suddenly washed off by the Ganga – so we knew our fate if we tarried longer.'

'But what has happened to that lady?'

'No trace of her. She was simply washed away by the river.'

'Oh God! Where have you put up now?'

'We have set up a temporary structure now to live in, because we don't know how long Ganga will allow us to live here.'

'Don't you receive any assistance from the government?'

Haripada Roy frowned at me and said, 'Yes, government representatives come to us before the elections, with promises of a rosy future. But after the elections everything is forgotten and our conditions remain unchanged. At times we look at the river and wonder why she is worshipped as the Divine Mother. To us she is a demon devouring everything that comes her way. She is nothing but an instrument of annihilation and destruction.'

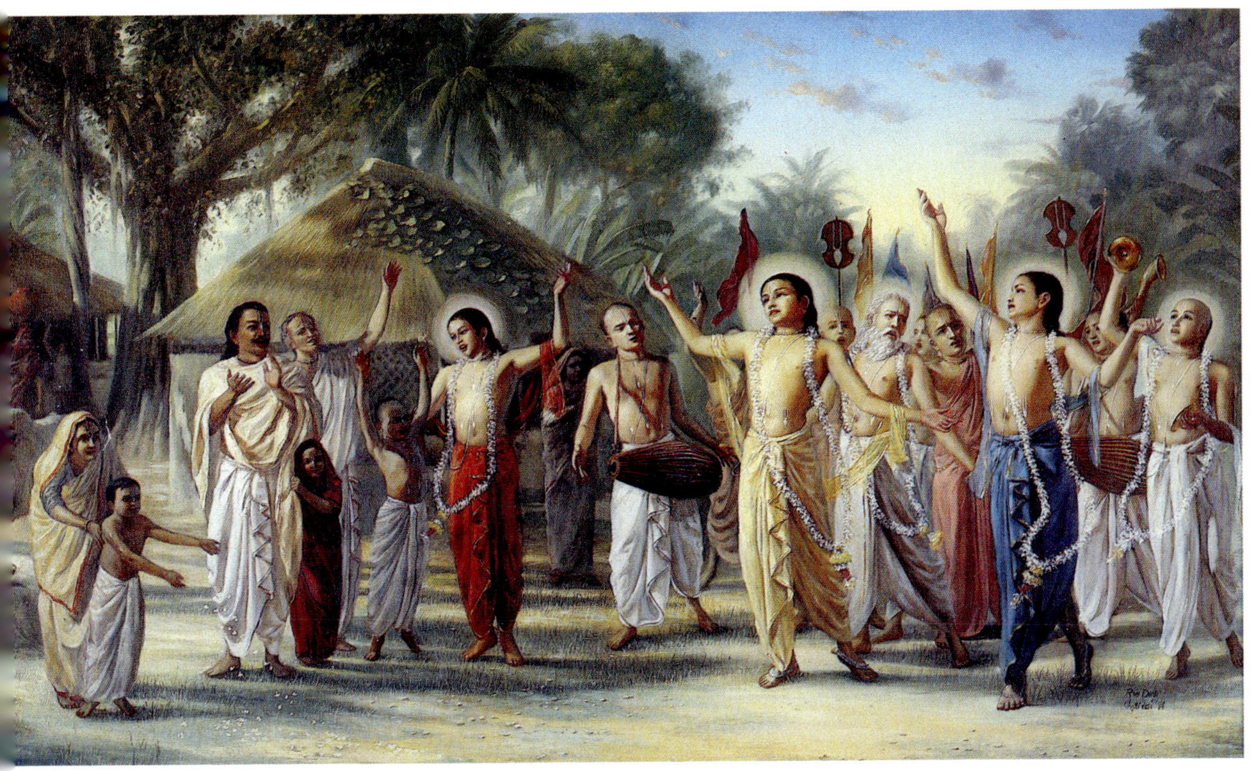

An old painting of Sri Chaitanya Mahaprabhu (1486-1534)

NABADWIP

Nabadwip is an old district town of West Bengal. It is also an important pilgrimage for the Hindus. Other than the Ganga, Nabadwip is also famous as the birthplace of Sri Chaitanya Mahaprabhu (1486–1534).

The origin of the name Nabadwip is however shrouded in mystery. No scholar till date has been able to ascertain why the place was named Nabadwip. 'Naba' means new and 'dwip' stands for island. Maybe at one point of time the place was born from the silt deposits of two rivers, Ganga and Jalangi – hence the name Nabadwip or New Island. Or maybe it was named after a sage who lit nine (naba also stands for number nine in Sanskrit) lamps (dwip also means lamps) regularly to perform his ritual worships. Some even claim that since in the remote past the entire area comprised nine islands, it was named Nabadwip. Whatever may be the origin story, historically Nabadwip is an important place in West Bengal.

Even though with time the river has shifted its course from the ancient town of Nabadwip, and presently flows far away from the birthplace of Sri Chaitanya, the memories of the great spiritual leader still loom large throughout the present-day Nabadwip. There are numerous temples here,

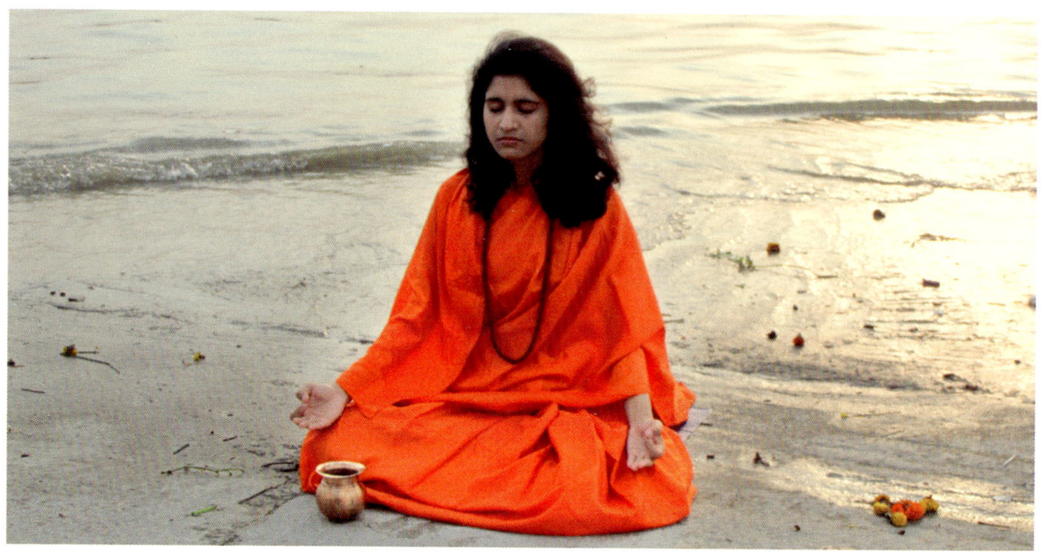

A young lady meditating on the riverbank, Mayapur

where local people worship different deities. According to government records there are 186 temples in and around Nabadwip. Among them the most important one is dedicated to Sri Chaitanya Mahaprabhu. The other important temples are Adwaita temple, Nityananda temple, Sri Govindaji temple, Golden Gauranga temple, Swarabhuj Mahaprabhu temple, Buro Shiva temple, Harishabha, Poramatla, and Bauro Akhra. From the architectural viewpoint none of these temples are really outstanding. Yet, there is no dearth of devotees visiting them.

Nabadwip was a famous learning centre in ancient India. Scholars from different parts of the country used to come here for higher studies. Recently Nabadwip has once again attracted the attention of the world because of the ISKON temple, which is situated at Mayapur (near Nabadwip town). ISKON stands for International Society for Krishna Consciousness, an organisation established by AC Bhaktivedanta. Members of ISKON come from different parts of the world to pay homage to their spiritual guru Bhaktivedanta at the ISKON temple of Mayapur.

KOLKATA

Kolkata (formerly Calcutta), the City of Joy, is nearly 300 years old. Originally it was an innocuous and uninhabitable marshy land, on the bank of the Ganga. It comprised only three villages running north to south – Sutanati, Gobindapur and Kalikata. The socio-political scenario of India was not a very happy one at that point of time. There were many foreign traders visiting the country and settling at random. One amongst them was Job Charnock, the chief administrator of the English East India Company at Cossimbazar, a place situated on the bank of the river Hooghly. Unfortunately soon after his arrival Charnock got into trouble with the Nawab of Bengal, Shaista Khan, over the imposition of customs duty. According to Job Charnock the ruling was in violation of the deal between them and the Nawab.

Consequently, on 24 August 1690, Charnock fled from Cossimbazar and reached Sutanati, to settle there permanently. Prior to his escape he managed to gather all the goods of the East India Company, and also convinced thirty army men to accompany him. Soon, after his arrival, Charnock personally became involved in developing Sutanati and making it habitable. Gradually a small civilisation started sprouting in and around Kolkata.

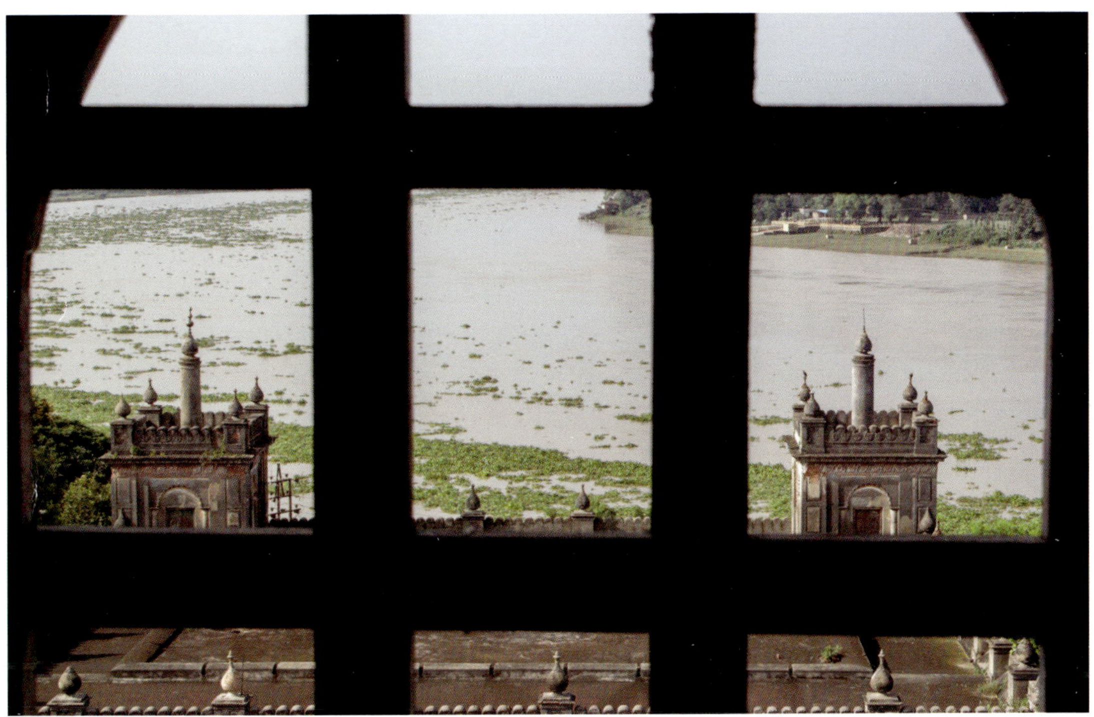

A glimpse of the Ganga from Imambara palace, Hooghly

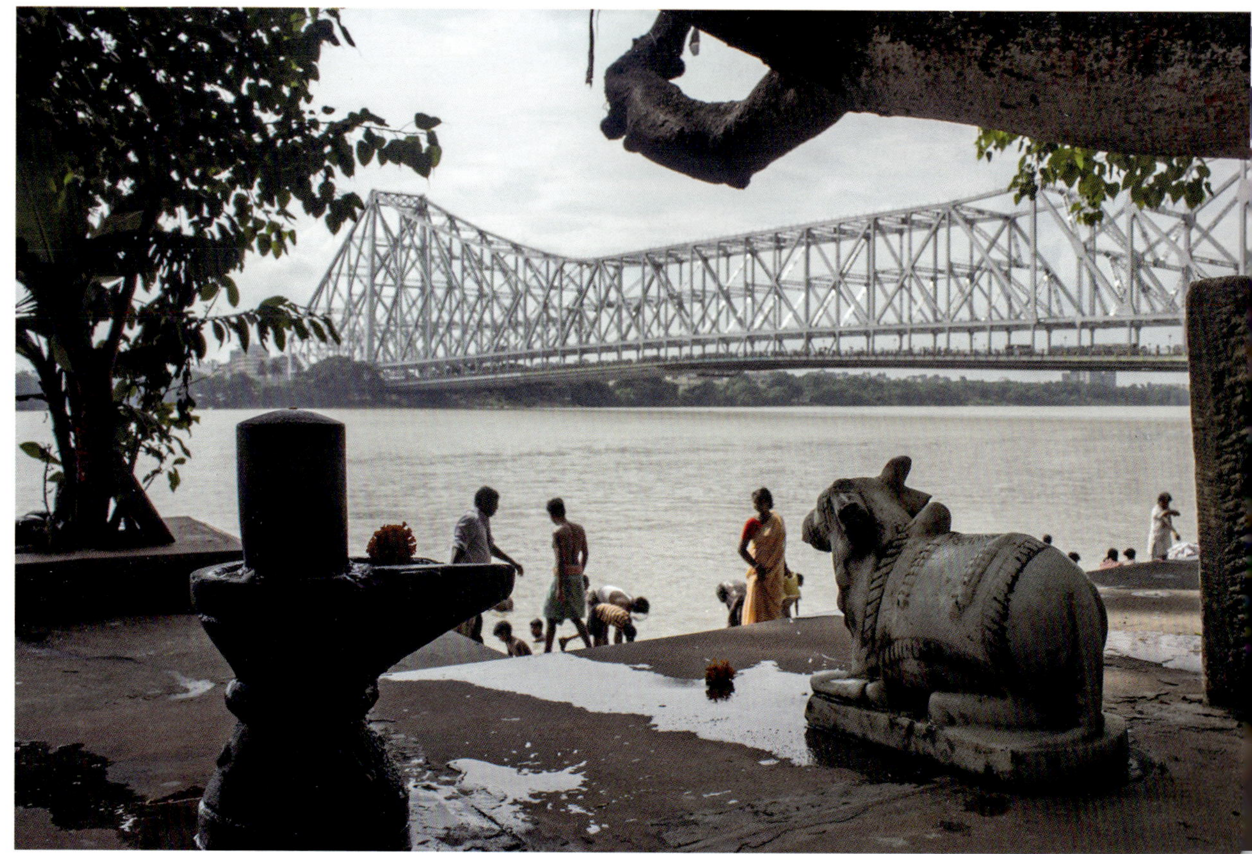

ABOVE: Mullick ghat, Kolkata. The Mullick ghat flower market here is over 130 years old
FACING PAGE ABOVE: The iconic Howrah bridge, one of the city's landmarks, links Howrah with Kolkata
FACING PAGE BELOW: Dusk at Ahiritola Ganga ghat

On 10 November 1698, Charnock bought three villages from the zamindar Saborno Choudhury for a sum of 1300 rupees and slowly started developing it. With time residential areas, marketplaces, Saheb Para (residential areas for the English) and Desi Para (residential areas for the Indians) started emerging. Soon Kalikata or Calcutta became the most important trading port for the Company. An army was deployed since it was the most important requirement to carry on trade. Forts too were built within the now fast-emerging city to provide shelter to the army men. However, the then Nawab of Murshidabad destroyed these forts. Yet the English remained undeterred.

At this point of time Lord Clive assumed power and started planning the defeat of the Nawab. Accordingly on 22 June 1757, Lord Clive crossed the Ganga with his army to reach the battleground of Plassey, to fight the Nawab. And on 23 June 1757 began the

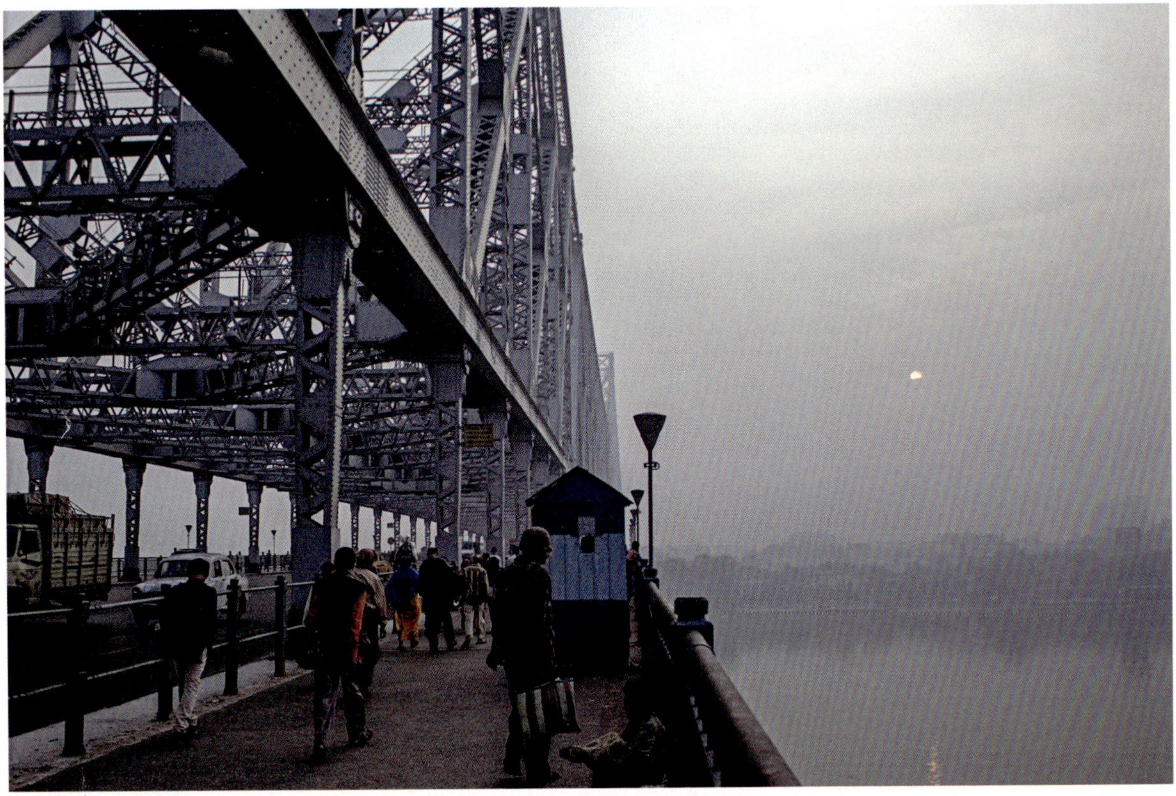

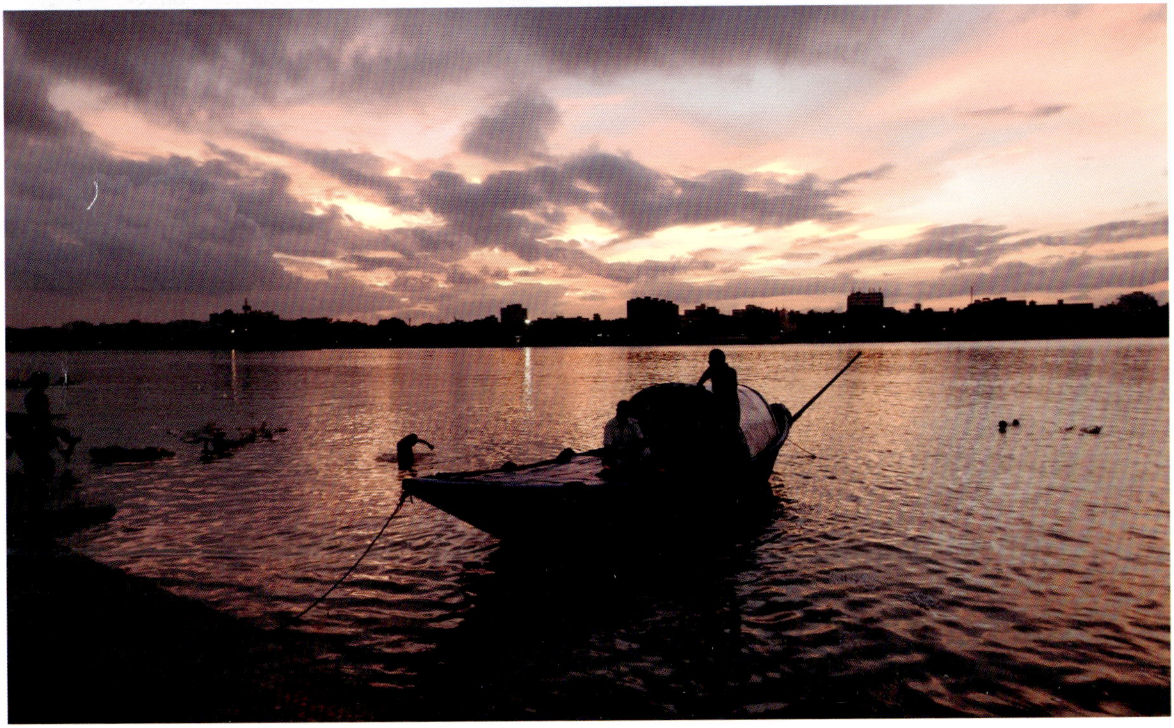

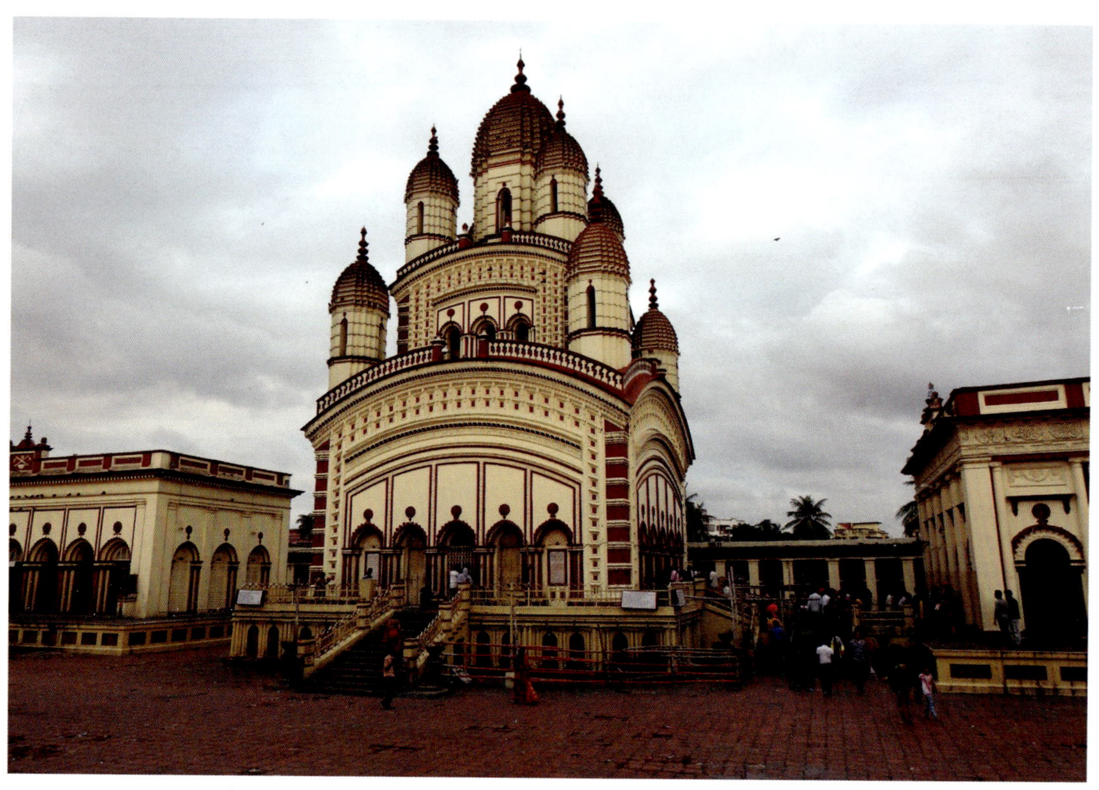

Above: Dakshineswar Kali temple on the right bank of the Ganga

Facing page above: Goddess Durga on a boat in the middle of the Ganga

Facing page below left: An artisan with her creations at Kumartuli

Facing page below right: A Kumartuli artist drawing the eyes of the idol

famous Battle of Plassey where the Nawab (betrayed by Mir Jafar) was defeated. Soon thereafter the entire domain of India came under the purview of British rule.

The victory at Plassey encouraged the English and helped them to concentrate on their developmental works in Calcutta, their headquarters. In 1773, the British Parliament permitted Warren Hastings, the Governor, to declare Calcutta the capital of British India and develop it as the largest and most important city of India. Interestingly the English were paying attention to this once small village only because of the river Ganga. They needed the river for carrying on their trade.

A trade route from Calcutta to Allahabad was established immediately followed by

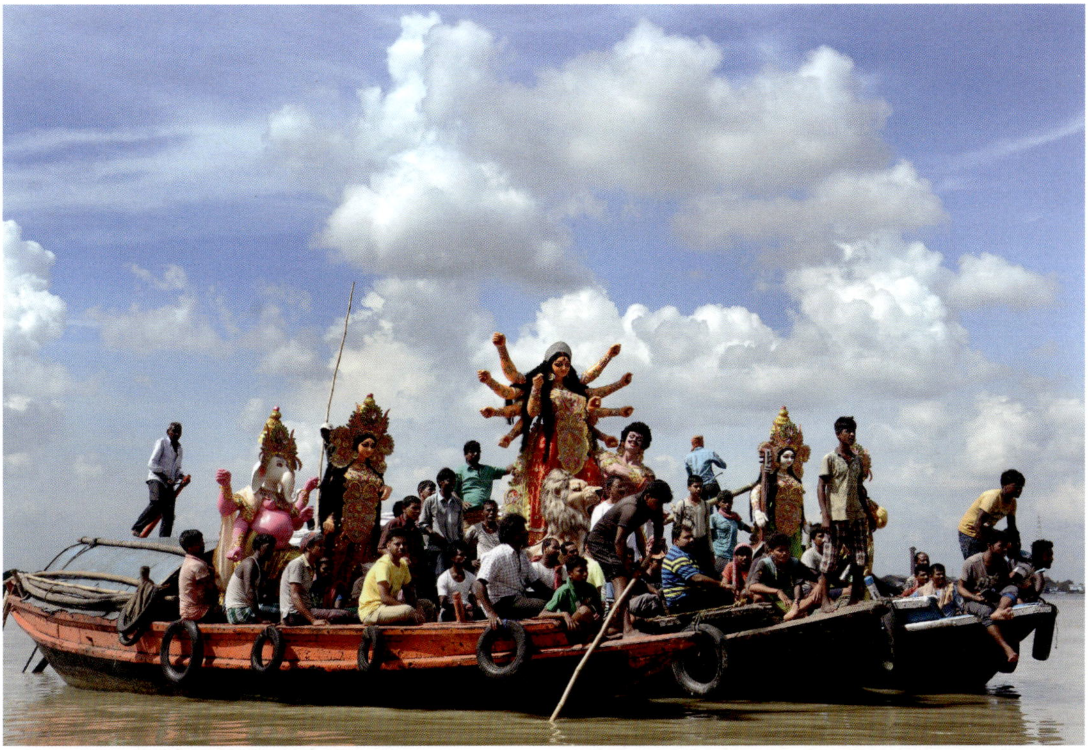

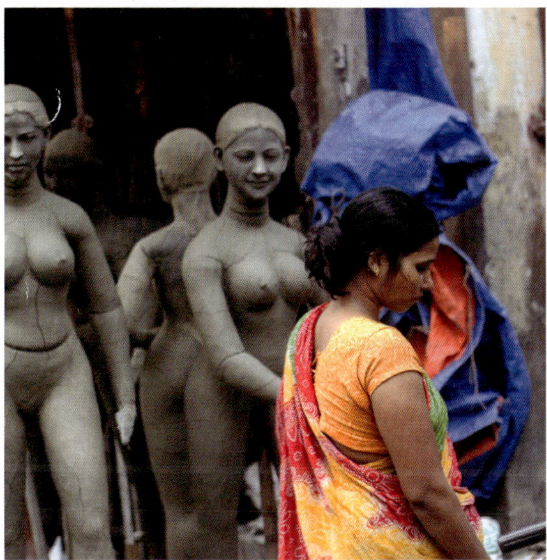

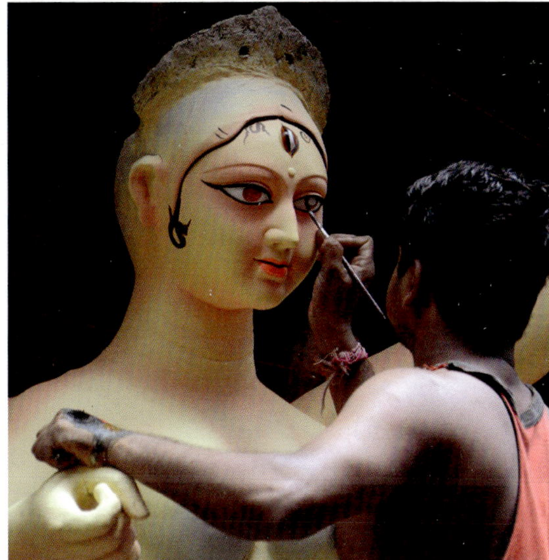

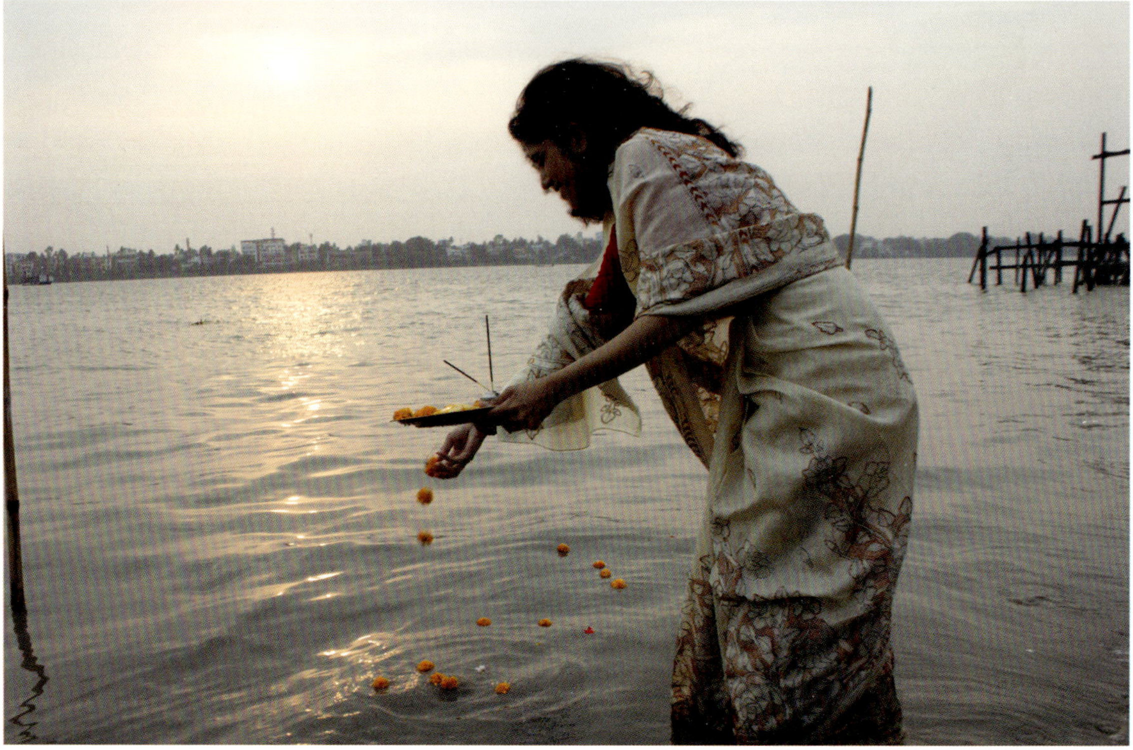

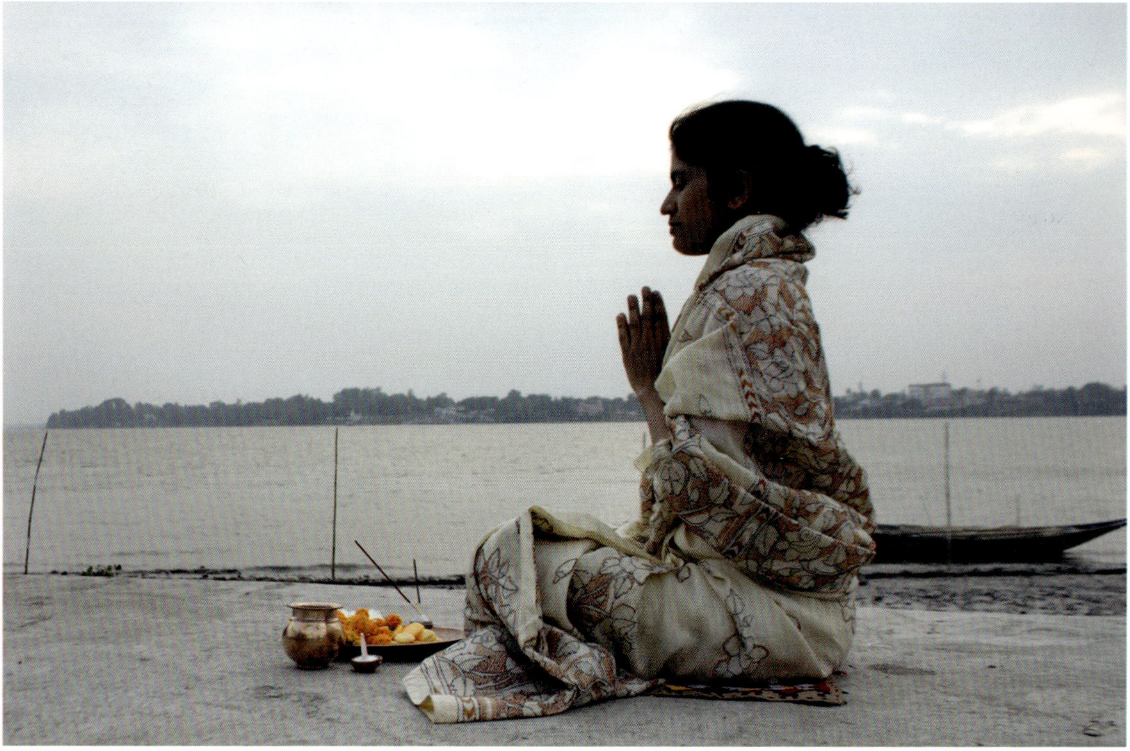

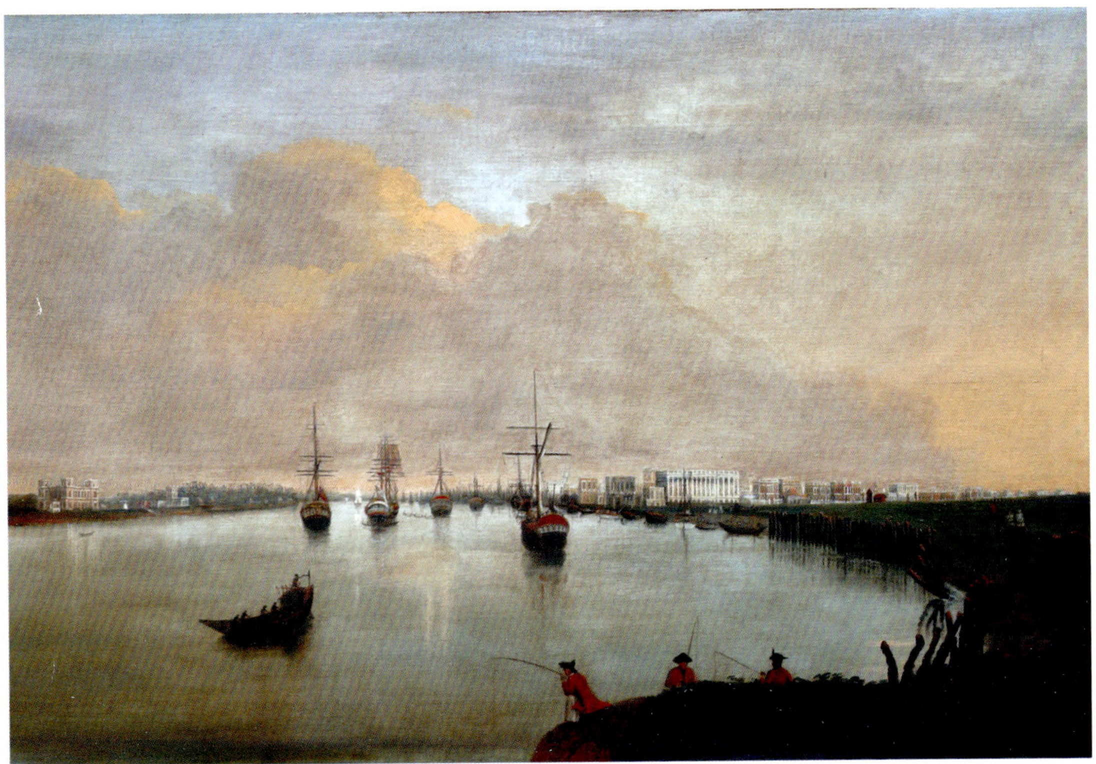

Above: *View of Esplanade, Calcutta before 1800* by Thomas Daniell
Facing page above: Flowers offered to the Ganga after the puja
Facing page below: Ganga puja

sporadic construction of different factories on the riverside. The river proved to be an ideal pathway for exchanging goods. Raw materials were brought to these newly developed factories dotting the cityscape of Calcutta, while finished products were carried away to distant lands – and it was the river Ganga that bore the brunt of it all.

Indian history is replete with instances of British imperialist excesses. And significantly, just a hundred years after the historic defeat at Plassey, it was here at Barrackpore, situated on the bank of the river Ganga, that the first sparks of rebellion were ignited. The Sepoy Mutiny of 1857 was triggered by this spark and it spread across the country, especially in northern India. It was not only a war cry against the imperialists, but also a clarion call for the Bengal Renaissance. Spiritual leaders and social reformers like Raja Rammohan Roy,

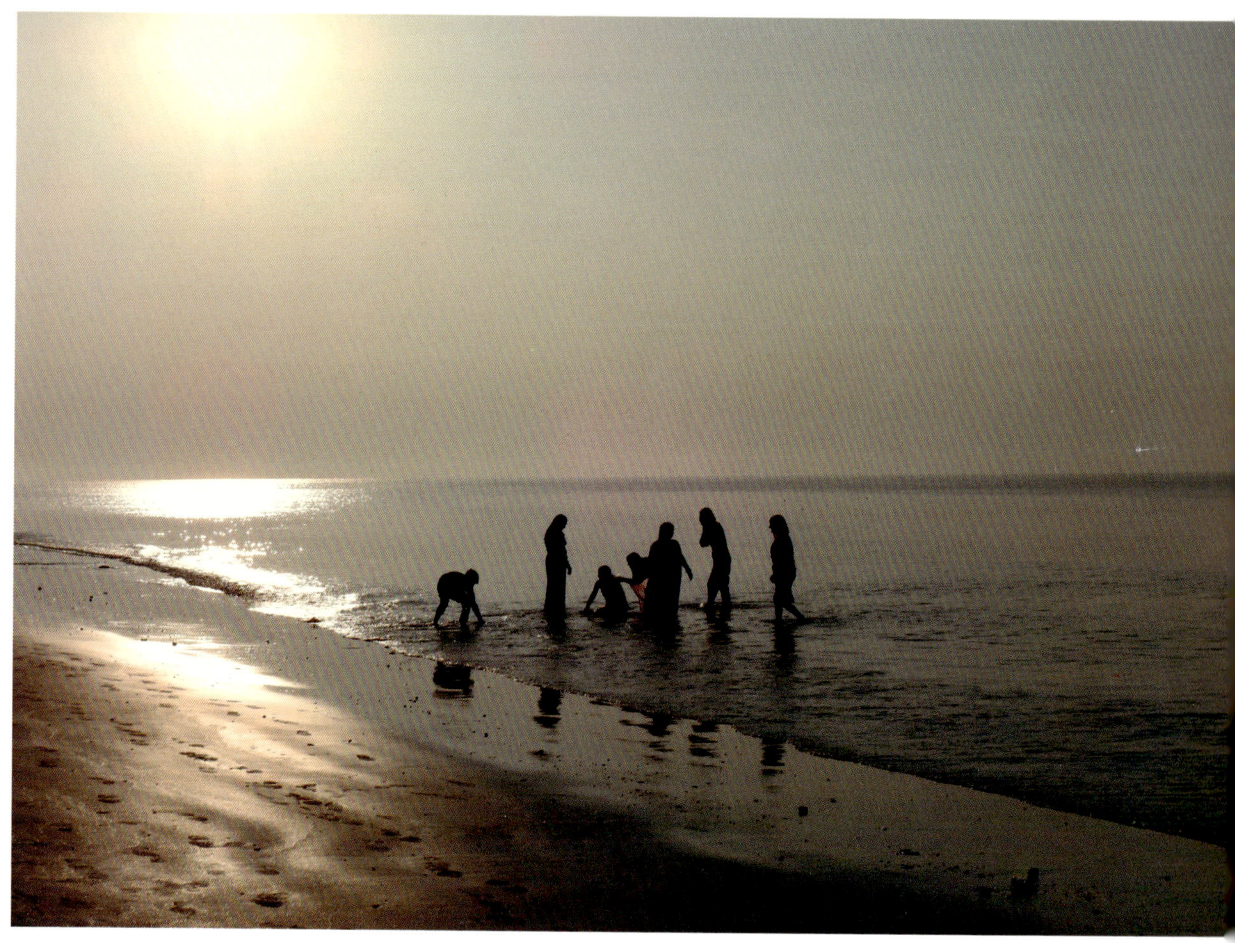

Golden rays of the sun shimmering on the water

Vidyasagar, Bankimchandra, Ramakrishna, Vivekananda and Rabindranath rose in unison and spoke against the corrupting and degenerating medieval social practices. The Bengal Renaissance was not restricted to Calcutta alone; it spread far and wide, spearheading a new social awareness in our country. Thus it was on the bank of river Ganga that Indians were first initiated into the world of modernity, social consciousness and free-thinking.

GANGASAGAR

Originating from Gaumukh, the Ganga travels a distance of 2,525 kilometres before finally flowing into the Bay of Bengal. The confluence of Ganga and Bay of Bengal is known as the Sagar Island. This is a sacred place for the Hindus. It is said that Sage Kapil was at his hermitage here when the sixty thousand sons of King Sagar unknowingly insulted him. Their disrespectful words had so infuriated the sage that he cursed them and burnt them alive. Finally the cursed souls were liberated at this very place by the river Ganga. And it is at this point Ganga finishes her journey and unites with the sea.

In the ancient times this place was uninhabited. During the British Raj a few rebellious hilly tribes from Arkan district decided to come and settle here. Gradually people started coming in and the place became habitable. However before independence the approach road to the Sagar Island was entirely neglected. It was only during Makar Sankranti, when a fair used to be held, people came here by country-made boats. But the journey was very hazardous. Frequently the boats would capsize drowning hundreds of pilgrims. Hence there was a popular saying about Sagar Island – 'Visit other pilgrimages a number of times / But visit Gangasagar only once in your lifetime.' But things have improved now. Arrangements have been made to accommodate at least three million people on this little island. Schools, proper roads, a hospital and conveyance to commute to and from the mainland have been arranged for these three million residents. During Makar Sankranti a large fair is held on the bank of the confluence. Temporary thatched rooms are built to accommodate millions of visitors. Even the temple of Sage Kapil is illuminated beautifully.

It is said that the original hermitage along with the temple has long been devoured by the sea. The present buildings are their replicas. The new structures came up in 1947, the year of our independence. The presiding idol of the temple is Sage Kapil, holding a small pitcher in his left hand and a rosary in his right hand. On his right side are the idols of four-handed *Makarvahini* Ganga and Lord Hanuman. On the left side of the temple statues of King Sagar, God Indra and Goddess Vishalakshi are to be found. The priests worshipping the deities are all from Ayodhya. This has been their ancestral profession down the ages.

Monks and sannyasis from the remotest parts of the country keep visiting Sagar Island during Makar Sankranti. They even set up temporary shades for a week's stay. Other than them there are pilgrims from West Bengal, Bihar, Uttar Pradesh and Rajasthan who come every year and stay in the thatched rooms, set up by the government. The entire place appears like a cauldron of human beings. They all come to bathe in the confluence on the auspicious day of Makar Sankranti. After Makar Sankranti however the bank becomes desolate once again. The island becomes quiet with only the sound of waves thrashing on the sandy banks audible.

Sage Kapil keeps staring at the sights without batting an eyelid. The rest of the

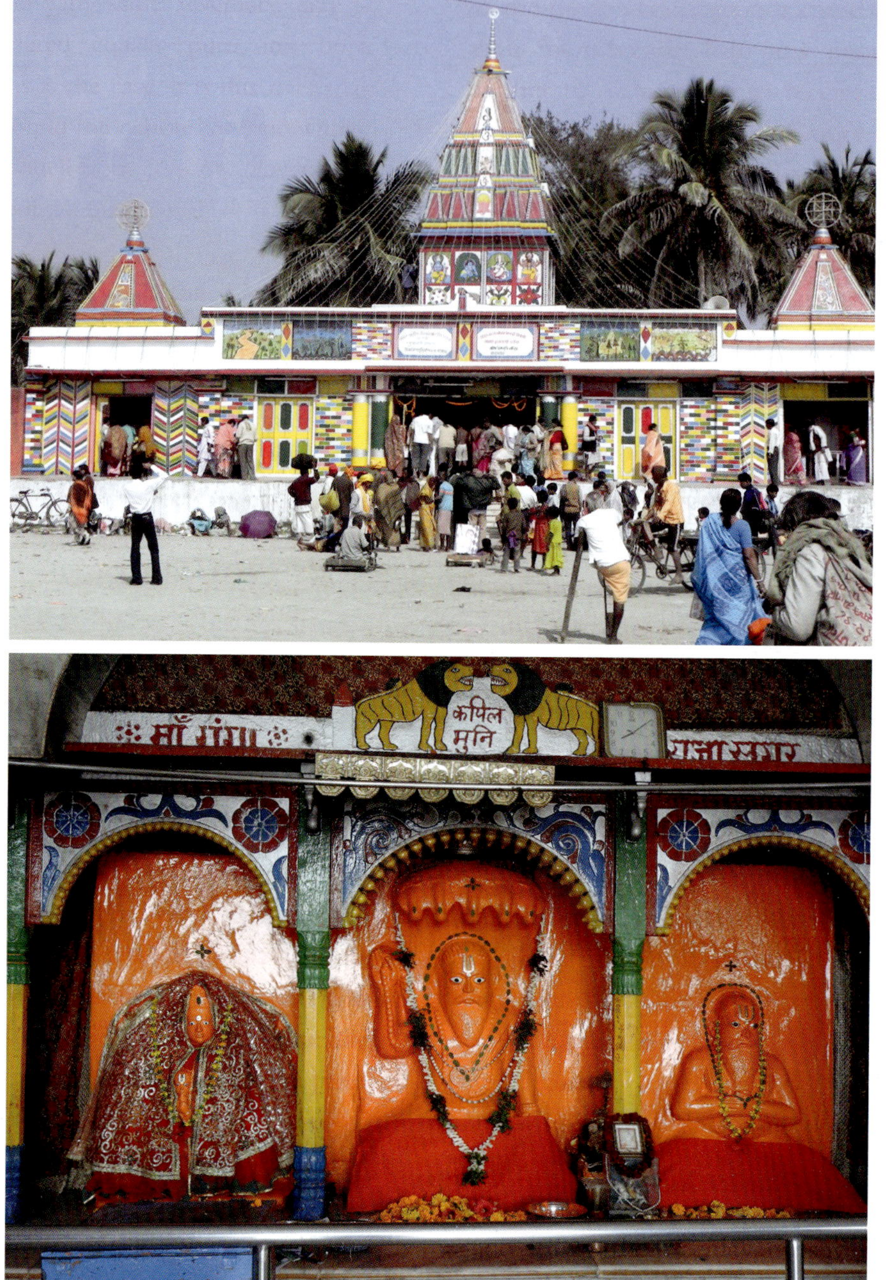
माँ गंगा
कपिल
मुनि

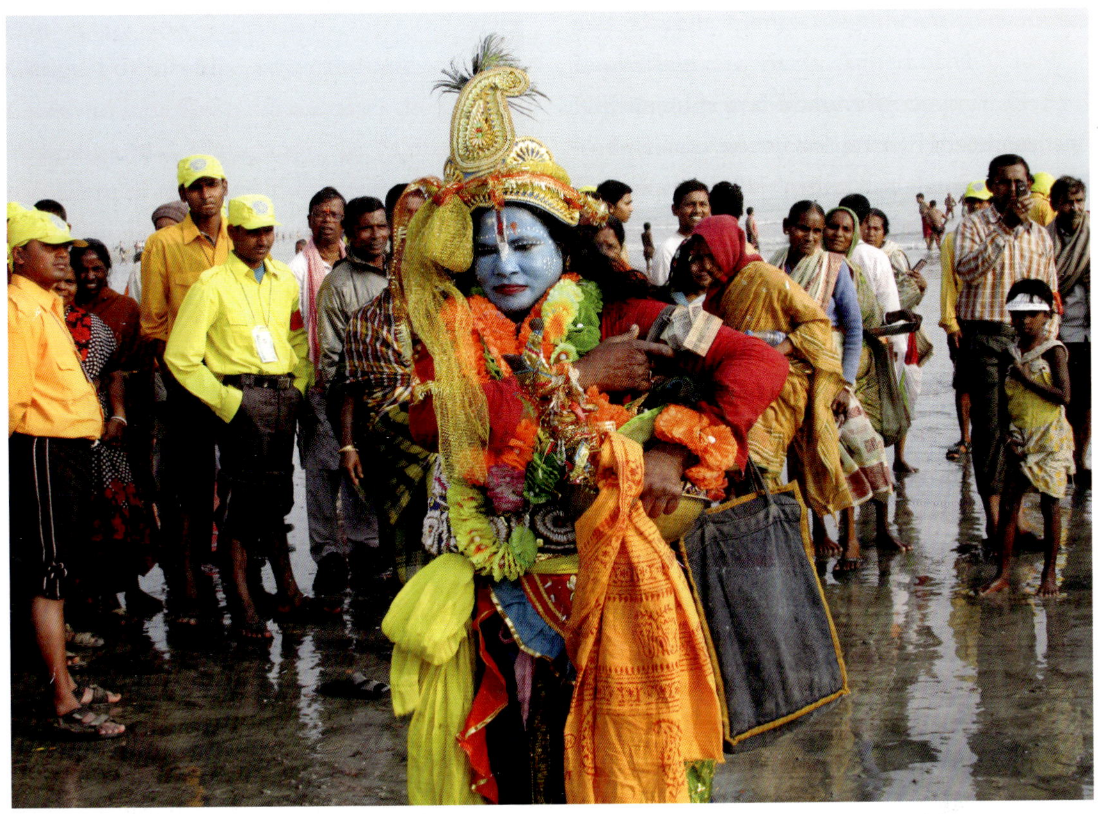

ABOVE: A woman dancing dressed as Krishna. She is headed to Gangasagar just like the others
FACING PAGE ABOVE: Temple of Kapil Muni at Sagar Island
FACING PAGE BELOW: Image of Kapil Muni

year he remains busy meditating with eyes tightly closed. Yet, billionaires and religious leaders who come here to seek his blessings, prefer landing up at Hanumangadi Math at the end of the fair, instead of staying back in the island to offer homage to the sage year round. But to a detached soul like him, these lapses hardly matter. Or maybe he had voluntarily renounced the material world while seeking this isolation. It's a world of eternal peace throughout the year.

From a Pilgrim's Diary

This is a story narrated to me by my paternal grandmother. She had visited Gangasagar almost seventy years ago. As mentioned above, the journey to Sagar Island then was not only perilous but also very time

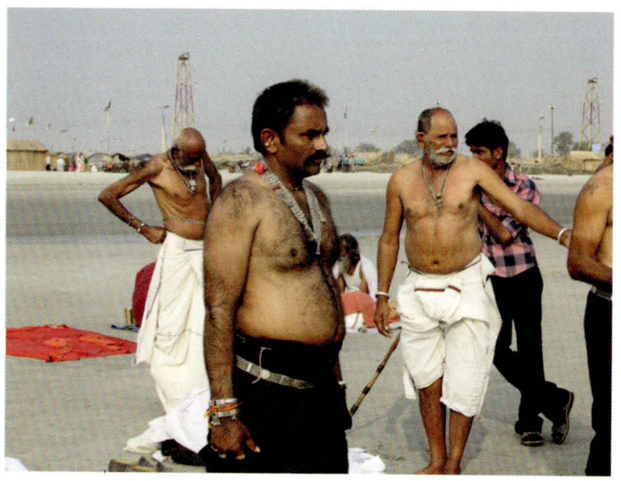

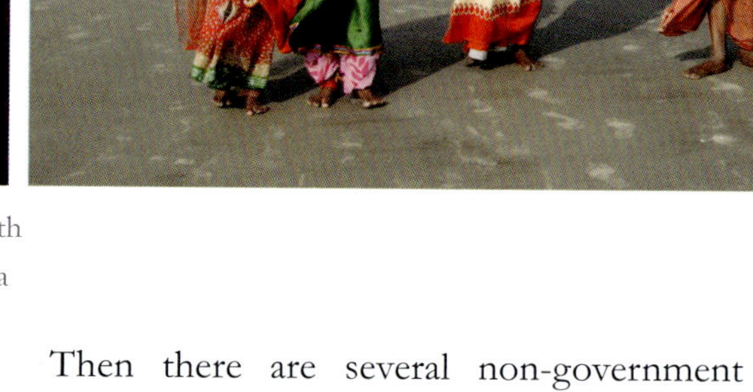

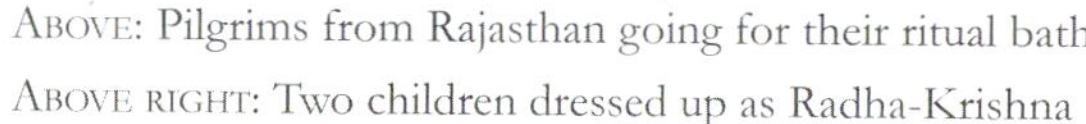

ABOVE: Pilgrims from Rajasthan going for their ritual bath
ABOVE RIGHT: Two children dressed up as Radha-Krishna

consuming. There were no motorboats or steamers to ferry pilgrims to the island. So one had to risk one's life to visit the island and return alive. To worsen matters there were no proper boats to look after the basic comforts of the passengers.

Previously, sailing on country-made boats, it took almost two days to reach the island. And most of the time the overloaded boats ran the risk of capsizing. My poor grandmother, despite being a devout Hindu, could not help recounting to me the trouble she had to face while going to Gangasagar.

But things are different now. If a pilgrim now decides to visit the Sagar Island, she is spoilt for choice. There are steamers and motorboats ferrying people to the island. Moreover, it takes just a few hours to reach the destination. Government agencies, too, arrange proper rooms and restrooms keeping in mind the comfort of pilgrims. Then there are several non-government organisations working round the clock to help people make their stay a happy one.

I am recounting below a first-person account of the ghastly experience my paternal grandmother had while visiting Gangasagar during Makar Sankranti:

'Om Jaya Ganga Mata', 'Om Jaya Ganga Mata', the cry of a thousand pilgrims filled the air of Calcutta as they boarded country-made boats plying to Gangasagar from Strand Road. As we started sailing women threw coins and coconuts into the water for a safe journey to and from Gangasagar.

The boat I boarded was sufficiently large to accommodate a lot of passengers. A part of it was covered with a thick cloth, especially segregated for women, while the rest of the open portion was allotted to men. Not an inch of the boat seemed vacant. Men, women, bags and baggage practically filled

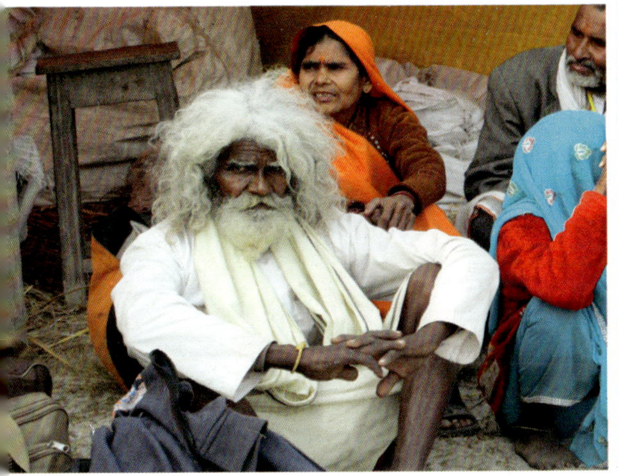

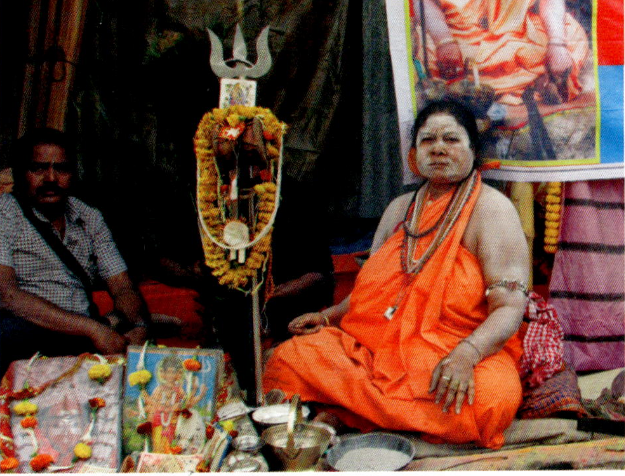

ABOVE: Old man from Bihar with his wife

ABOVE RIGHT: A sannyasini resting at Gangasagar

the entire area of the boat. Most of the bags and baggage comprised warm clothes as it was very cold. Most of the passengers were from Bihar and only three ladies were from Bengal. They were all widows and practically renounced by their families.

As the boat started sailing, I found a place in a corner to view everything that came our way. On two sides of the banks I saw fleeting glimpses of trees and houses while on the right bank two large ships stood anchored. It was almost afternoon and all of us were enjoying the natural beauty of the river.

After sometime the ladies from Bihar started singing in praise of the river Ganga. Since the words were in Hindi, I could not follow what they were actually singing. Yet, the melody of the song touched my heart. Within half an hour we reached the Kidderpore dock and found ships both large and small lined up – ready to sail far and wide. Dusk was fast approaching and the air was already quite chilly. People started huddling together in different corners of the boat. Gradually with the light fading, land and river both disappeared from sight. The swaying of the boat made most of us sleepy. An old man from Bihar had two wives with him. I found him sitting stiffly to support both his sleeping wives on his shoulders. It was already pitch dark by now. The boatmen lit four petro-maxes to illumine the interiors of the boat. Although most of us were feeling extremely sleepy, none of us could find a place to lie down. So we sat and dozed.

After an hour or two, a loud gushing sound of water woke us up. The river was in spate, the boatmen informed. Suddenly the boat started swaying dangerously. It was as if the rising water would throw us off the boat. Men started screaming and the ladies started crying. Since the boat was

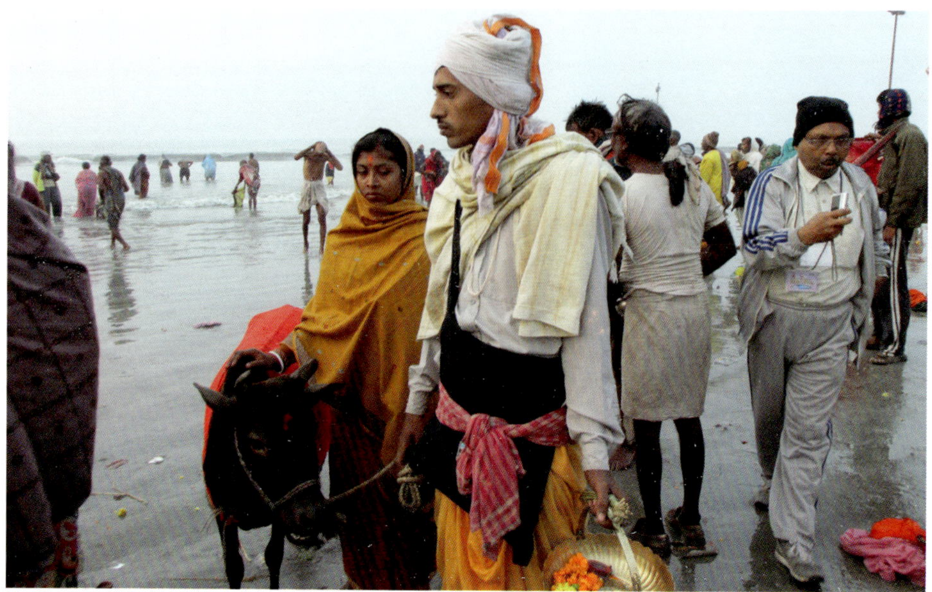

Holy cow – 'Gau Mata' worshipped by Hindus at Gangasagar

overcrowded there was every possibility of it capsizing.

The helmsman however tried to pacify our growing fear. 'Don't worry,' he kept repeating. 'This happens with the rising tide. The boat will not capsize. But now we cannot proceed forward, because of the rising tide. So it is best to anchor it.' His words however did not convince anyone till he and his assistant boatmen jointly directed the boat towards the bank and finally anchored it. On reaching the bank some of the male passengers alighted both to relieve and stretch themselves, while we ladies decided to stay back – huddled in our places. By dawn we resumed our journey. But dense fog prevented us from seeing anything around. The boatmen however knew their way and steered us forward.

With the rising sun, the surrounding dense fog gradually started melting. It was time for morning ablutions. The boatmen arranged temporary toilets for both men and women. On the right side of the boat a cage-like structure made of tough cords was hung down into the river to serve as temporary toilets for men. While on the left side of the boat a similar structure was hung down for women to use. It was a tough going I must admit. If you missed a step while alighting into the cage you would fall straightaway into the river. Miraculously nothing really happened and all of us were back from the ordeal, safe and sound. Many of the passengers however appeared quite ill. Among them were two nuns, who unable to bear the ordeal any more, lay down and kept counting the beads of their rosaries.

Most of us were carrying food with us. There were a few however who not foreseeing such a situation hadn't got anything to eat. So sharing breakfast with them was mandatory for the others. Out of sheer boredom people started chatting with one another. There were several other boats accompanying us to Gangasagar. So there was no dearth of subjects to talk about. At times a large ship would pass by and our boat would start swaying with the onslaught of mighty waves. Cries would then reach the sky. The second night on the boat was no different from the first one. The only difference was our hope to reach the bank at Kochuberia by dawn.

On the second morning, we reached Kochuberia. Chants of '*Om Jaya Ganga Mata*' and '*Jay Kapil Muni*' from the boatmen woke us up. After disembarking from the boat we had to board a bus to reach the confluence. But boarding the boat was a cakewalk compared to disembarking. Our limbs had gone stiff and walking down the narrow gangway to reach the bank appeared to be the toughest job on earth. However, we collected our bags and baggage and somehow scampered our way down the gangway. On the bank the aroma of food stalls almost attacked us. They were all temporary structures made of bamboo and tin built for the purpose of the Makar Sankranti fair and would be dismantled at the end of the fair. Since all of us were famished we decided to breakfast properly and then proceed to the bus stand. As we sat for breakfast we saw streams of pilgrims alighting from different boats and rushing towards the bus stand. After some time we too joined them.

Though a few furlongs away from the shop where we had our breakfast, the crowd that had gathered there was beyond our imagination. Millions of people were waiting for the bus to arrive. And the moment a bus arrived, within a spilt second it overflowed with passengers. We kept waiting for an empty bus for quite some time. Finally a bus arrived and I managed to get in. Kochuberia is situated on the southernmost tip of the Sagar Island. Since the bus was overflowing with passengers, it moved at snail's pace. Meanwhile most of the passengers who wanted to bathe and visit the Kapil Muni temple were getting increasingly impatient. All the rituals had to be completed before early morning. So the bus journey proved to be a hindrance to them. We kept crossing places like Bamunkhili, Phooldubi, Harinbaari, Rudranagar, Chayargheri and Kalibazar, till we reached our destination. And what a destination it was. Even though men kept hailing '*Om Jaya Ganga Mata*' and '*Jay Kapil Muni*' their voices had already turned quite feeble. A long stretch of silted land lay before

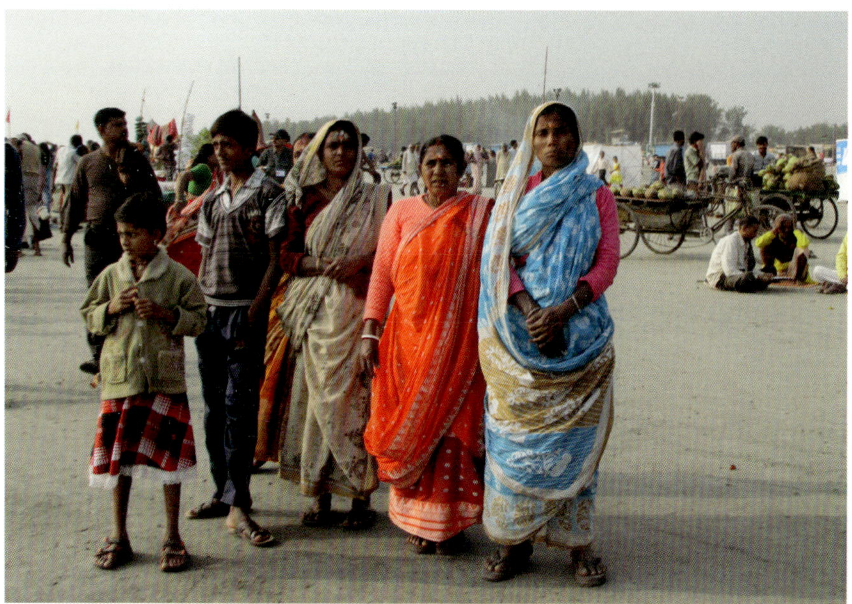

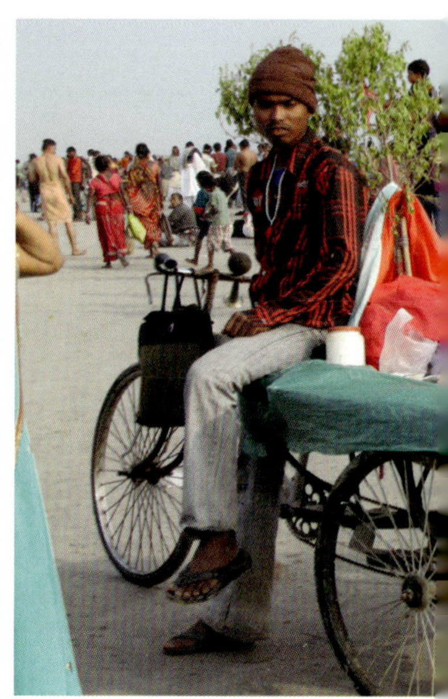

Above left: Pilgrims from Assam at Gangasagar
Above centre: The Gangasagar mela provides livelihood to vendors selling wares for puja
Above right: A woman in dripping clothes after the holy bath

us, and we were expected to stay there. A few concrete buildings stood scattered around, but they were all government offices.

Yet people who had arrived before us seemed undeterred. They had already taken their bath and were proceeding towards the temple of Kapil Muni. We saw a long procession of mixed crowds. Finally I found a few thatched rooms to put up for the night. I quickly scampered into one of them. The ceiling of the room was so low that it was impossible to enter it with my head upright. I deposited my bag and walked out. Just a few steps away the fair was on. It was dotted with numerous shops and food stalls, and beggars, lepers and even monks wandered around the fair.

I walked up to the temple of Kapil Muni. No less than a million men and women had already gathered there. Everyone wanted to view the idol and offer flowers. A glimpse of the great sage who had demolished a brigade of sixty thousand young warriors with just a glance was a must for all. The shops lining the temple and supplying flowers and sweetmeats to be offered for worship were naturally doing brisk business. Images of gods and goddesses too were being sold. I looked at the sight in dismay and turned my eyes towards the confluence. A long stretch of sandy land lay before me. I decided to walk down. But the walk proved quite laborious. First of all the sandy soil proved to be a deterrent for a brisk walk. Secondly, in the absence of

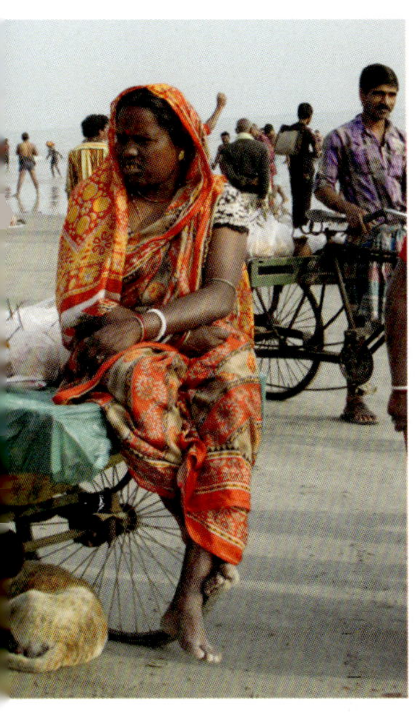

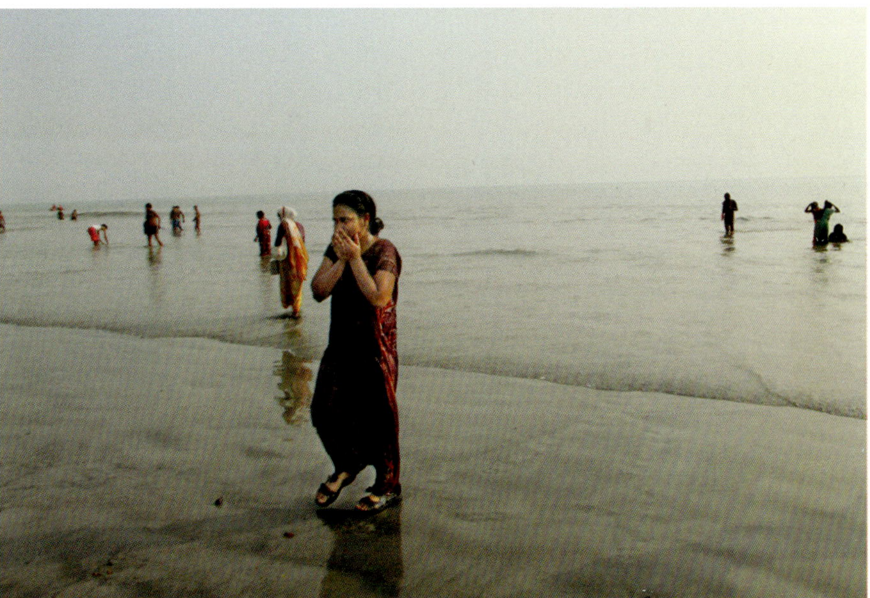

proper toilet facilities, men had unthinkingly left their night soils wherever they pleased. So I had to watch each step of mine.

On my way I came across a series of thatched rooms allotted for the naked monks, popularly known as Naga sannyasis. Some had long matted hair while most of them smeared ashes on their bare bodies, possibly to hide their nakedness. Somehow the sight did not really appeal to me. I kept walking. Suddenly I came across a monk who had submerged his head and torso inside the sand. In front of him lay a cloth where people were throwing coins of all denominations. How is he surviving, I wondered. Isn't he feeling suffocated? There was another naked monk who was resting his body on bits of broken glasses. He too wanted money. And people were throwing coins before him. So just for a handful of coins both these monks were undertaking so much suffering, I mused.

The day progressed but the crowd kept swelling. As night descended, petro-maxes and lanterns were lit all over the fair ground. Everybody seemed to wait eagerly for dawn because that was the most auspicious moment to bathe in the confluence.

A loud noise woke me up much before dawn. Before sunrise people had to finish their baths and visit the temple, so they were all getting ready to go to the confluence. I decided to join them. On reaching the confluence I was really surprised to see the

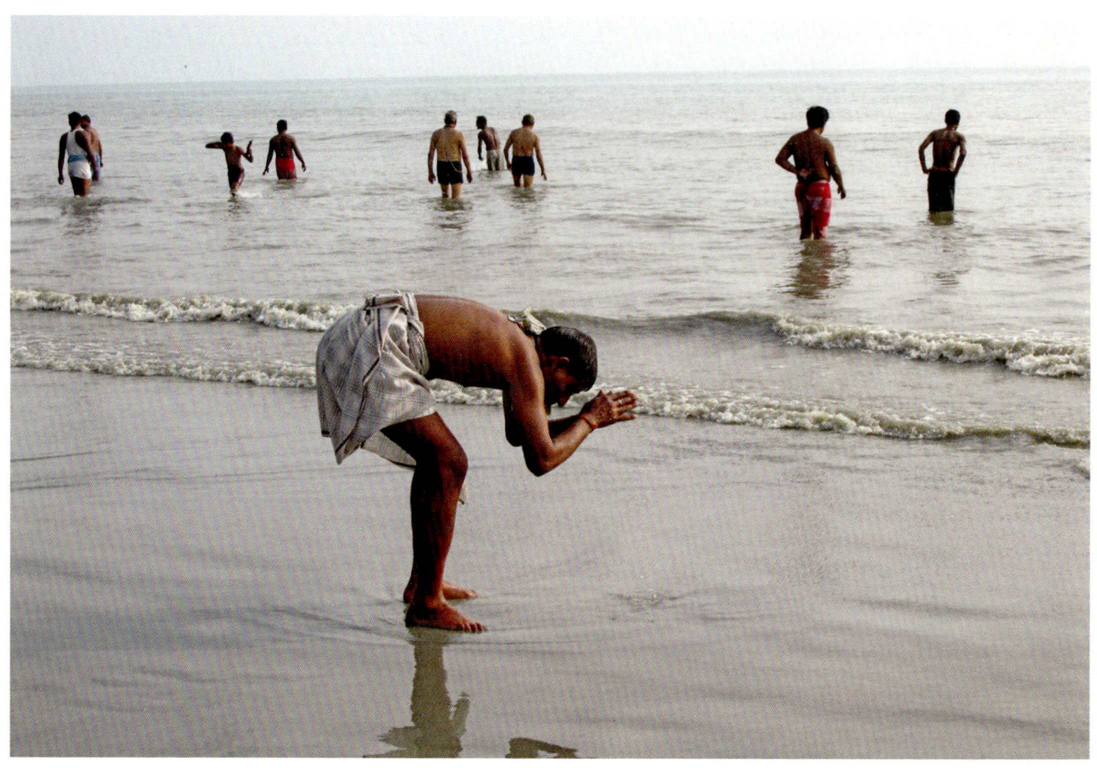

Offering obeisance to Mother Ganga

transformation of the ocean. It was high tide and huge waves were constantly hitting the sandy bank with great gusto. Yesterday what appeared to be a calm water body had now changed into a roaring ocean. Men and women were already undressing themselves to bathe in these waves. Nobody seemed to be ashamed of their own nudity. Men and women were bathing together and cleansing themselves of all sins.

Hailing Mother Ganga and Kapil Muni the ritual continued for hours. After ablutions some walked to the temple making way for others to follow, while some waited on the shore for their turn to bathe. I completed my bath after offering a palm full of holy water to my departed ancestors, and then followed the procession heading towards the temple of Kapil Muni. There was a long queue in front of the temple to enter the sanctum sanctorum. I stood patiently for my turn. Finally I entered the temple and offered my prayers.

When my life's little day, O Mother, comes to an end
And wistful, I wait upon eternity,
May thine unfailing Grace on me descend
On the eyes in sleep, on the ears in melody.
Redeem my restless soul with thy deep peace
And my limbs, O Ganga, with
Thy nectarous bliss.

(Song: Dwijendralal Roy;
translated by Dilip Kumar Roy)

I felt really happy.

THE ENDLESS JOURNEY OF A PILGRIM

Our scriptures and epics have taught us that rivers are the real sustainers of the universe. They function as mothers, rearing human beings to grow and propagate. Therefore, we can never treat the Ganga as a mere river. To us she is the universal mother, who generates lives and also sustains them. As Hindus we love the Ganga, deify and worship her.

What need of expensive sacrifices
Or of difficult penances?
Worship Ganga, asking for happiness
And good fortune,
And she will bring you heaven and salvation

(*Padma Purana* - V60.39;
translated by A.L. Basham)

I too was brought up with these feelings for the Ganga. And my journey too was based on the above stated sentiment. Yet my journey down the Ganga was slightly different from either the adventurists or the wandering monks. Most of the adventurists or the wandering monks prefer to follow a definite route while journeying down the river. Normally both begin their journey by visiting either Gaumukh or Haridwar and then follow the river's course down the five states of our country. Or else they start their search from Gangasagar, the end point of the river, and then travel all the way up to Gaumukh. But I am neither an adventurist nor a wandering monk. Hence I had neither a definite plan nor a definite route to follow. I tried to trace the course of the river according to my inclinations and conveniences. In fact, I have visited a few places several times while I have left out some. But the entire journey has enriched me in a number of ways. In reality, I have not merely witnessed the course of a river, I have actually seen from close quarters, the pulsating lives of Indians. And my conclusion is this – common Indians are by and large honest, religious, helpful, benevolent, large hearted and spiritual.

I really don't know why I had begun my journey from the city of Kanpur. Maybe because a relative of mine residing in Kanpur

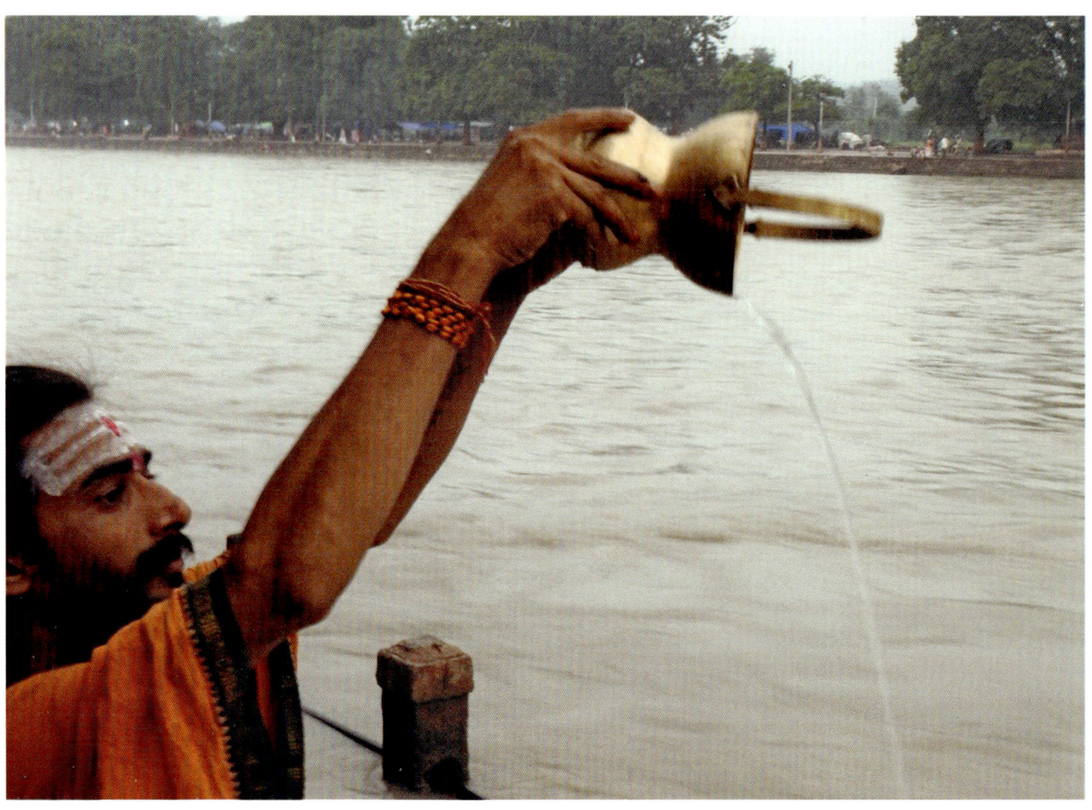

Ganga puja with Ganga water

had once invited me to visit him. But before I set out, my friends and acquaintances had warned me about Kanpur. 'Kanpur is not a nice place. People are all crooks out there, so beware,' they said. However, impervious to all warnings, I boarded a train for Kanpur one fine evening.

Just before the train reached Kanpur, a policeman boarded our compartment. Since I was not really interested in talking to a policeman I remained tight-lipped, answering in monosyllables. But as I disembarked and walked out of the station, I found my new-found friend, the said policeman, waiting for me. 'I was waiting for you,' he said with a smile. I was really scared – why should a policeman wait for me? After all I am not a criminal so why this benevolence? His reassuring smile however set me at ease. He called a rickshaw puller and asked him to take me to my destination. 'Pay him twenty-five rupees only,' the policeman told me.

'Since you are a tourist they will charge you double the amount; so I waited for you and fixed up this fellow. Have a good day,' he said and walked away. So my first experience of Kanpur was not really as scary as it was made out to be!

Indeed Kanpur is a strange city. The roads are infested by men walking on foot, cars, cows, buffaloes, cycles and vans – all proceeding at their own pace towards their destinations. The river Ganga flows on one side of the city and then proceeds forward. Kanpur, I was told, has defiled the Ganga beyond redemption. In fact the pollution of the river begins in this city and the trend follows. The information disturbed me to such an extent that I was compelled to curtail my stay to two days only.

My next destination was Bithoor. So one fine morning I boarded a bus in Kanpur and travelled twenty-five kilometres to reach Bithoor. At Bithoor my sole destination was the riverbank. A brisk walk to the bank left me charmed. On one side of the bank I found an ancient wharf used by the people residing in the nearby palace, while on the other side of the bank was a long stretch of empty land. Quite afar was a piece of cultivated land. The entire scenario pleased me immensely. A priest who was sitting on the steps of the wharf greeted me. We instantly struck a chord of friendship as he started narrating a lot of old stories of Bithoor. After several hours when it was time to return to Kanpur I started walking towards the bus stop. After a few minutes, I started feeling thirsty. In fact, extreme thirst prevented me from proceeding further. There were no shops or houses nearby and I didn't know where to go for a glass of water. There was only a doctor's dispensary nearby. But I was full of misgivings. Should I approach a doctor and instead of consultation ask for a glass of water – I kept asking myself. Out of sheer desperation I decided to walk in. Fortunately for me the doctor was of an amiable disposition. Since the dispensary was empty, I dared to ask for a glass of water. The doctor himself offered me a jug full of water. I was overwhelmed. After I finished my second glass of water, to my utter amazement, the doctor invited me home. 'Come, let's go home,' he said and led the way. Once home, he called his young daughter and asked her to serve me lunch! It was too good to be true.

I was really hungry by then. So after gobbling my food and satisfying my belly I decided to be polite. Turning to the girl I politely asked, 'Whose lunch did I consume dear?' 'Nobody's,' she answered smiling. 'Papa often brings home guests like you and asks me to serve lunch. So every day we prepare some extra dishes, so that nobody returns unfed.' Till now I had merely heard about Indian hospitality but never had the fortune to experience it personally. But that day I had a firsthand experience of it and was simply overwhelmed.

Allahabad was my next destination, a place famous for the confluence of three rivers: Ganga, Yamuna and Sarasvati (a Rig Vedic river that had dried up long ago). I reached Allahabad one morning and found the city full of colours. Holi, the festival of colours, had arrived. Outside the station I found an auto-rickshaw which I thought would take me straightaway to the confluence. But after a few furlongs the driver informed me that I would have to board another auto-rickshaw to reach the confluence. 'But, Sir, I hardly know the way to the confluence. I have come from Kolkata and am planning to write a book on Ganga. Please can you guide me to reach the confluence,' I pleaded utterly dismayed. The driver shook his head and said, 'It's just two kilometres from here. Walk straight ahead and you will reach the confluence.' I started walking. What could I do other than walk the distance? After a few minutes I heard a tinkle from behind. On turning round I found the same auto-rickshaw. The driver on second thoughts had decided to give me a lift! 'Get in,' he invited me. After a while, when I could almost see the confluence, the auto-rickshaw stopped. 'There lies the confluence, Sir, go ahead.' 'How much do I pay you,' I asked gratefully. 'Nothing, you don't owe me a pie. Just remember to send me a copy of the book you are planning to write on Mother Ganga,' he smiled. 'I am Bhajanlal. Just mention my name at the auto-rickshaw stand and you will find people leading you to me.' With that he waved his hand and left.

It was a sandy path, and I trudged on in a happy frame of mind. The soft morning sun lent a multicoloured hue to everything around me. An old man was standing right in the middle of the confluence and saying his morning prayers. After some time when he came up to me I was curious to know what he was praying for. 'Whom did you address your prayers to?' I asked.

He replied, 'To the two gods I believe in: one is the Sun in the sky and the other is the Mother of Earth, Goddess Ganga. I offered my prayers to Sun above and Mother Ganga below.'

From Allahabad I travelled to Vindhyachal. The temple of Vindhyavasini stands right on the bank of river Ganga. My plan was to spend the whole day seeing Vindhyachal and then return to Allahabad in the evening. Accordingly, in the evening when I reached the bus stop I found several over-crowded buses plying to Allahabad. It was quite impossible for me to board any one of them. Suddenly two youths appeared out of nowhere. On hearing my problem both unanimously declared, 'Uncle, no problem. We will take you to Allahabad.' Though not exactly reassured I waited to see what they were actually planning. Suddenly I found them running towards a moving car. Both were desperately waving their hands and trying to stop the driver. And the poor fellow unable to overlook them decided to stop in the middle of the road. Without another word both of them dragged and shoved me inside the car and became my accomplices in the mission. Poor driver, he could not refuse us either, so off we went towards Allahabad. As promised by the duo, the journey was indeed a comfortable one. But as ill luck would have it, just a few kilometres away from Allahabad the car refused to go further. We were right in the middle of a highway. 'This is a mechanical failure and the car will not be able to move even an inch,' announced the driver ominously. It was late in the evening and we were stranded on a deserted road. To make matters worse, I did not know my way to the ashram where I had been staying. The youths however appeared quite confident. 'Don't worry, we will take you to Allahabad,' they repeated. And I must say they kept their promise. I was there at the ashram within an hour. Before waving them goodbye I asked, 'Where will you go now?' 'Just ten kilometres, bang opposite to this place, uncle,' replied one of them. 'We came here just to drop you safely. Bye.' I found no words to thank them enough. They had come as saviours to bail me out of a crisis.

From Allahabad I proceeded to Varanasi. I had boarded a passenger train which halted at every station. And the transient views I had from the train convinced me that the traditional ambience of Varanasi hadn't really changed. But when I walked out of the station, I was in for a shock. The modern urbanity of Varanasi left me disappointed. The city was so different from the one Mark Twain had written about!

> The history of the city is older than the oldest historical records of the world; perhaps, even older than fairy tales. A glance at the life style of the people living here convinces us of its ancientness. The city often reminds us of a beehive – comprising of small pockets. Each of the pockets has either a temple or a mosque lined up. It's a magnificent combination of heaven and earth. But the best part of Varanasi is the river Ganga. (*Following the Equator*)

As I travelled across the city, I realised that today's Varanasi is nowhere close to the one described by Mark Twain. It's a modern metropolitan city with broad commutable roads, expensive cars, shopping malls, offices, hotels and newly built apartment buildings. Varanasi and modernity is such a contradictory concept! I crossed the city on a rickshaw to reach the bank of the river Ganga.

Visitors often complain that Varanasi is perhaps the filthiest city on earth. 'But never think of the filth of Varanasi. Then you will miss out on its beauty,' a friend of mine had warned me. After reaching the riverbank I realised how prophetic my friend was. My short stay in Varanasi was so eventful and satisfactory, that when it was time for me to leave, I felt really sorry. The entire stretch of the river was full of country-made boats waiting for passengers. I spent most of my time in Varanasi, sitting on the wharfs and enjoying the beauty of the Ganga. The river keeps changing her form with changing hours. But the only aspect that remains unchanged throughout the day is the processions of devotees. Devotees from different parts of the country and also different parts of the world keep visiting the river, unmindful of time. Some visit Varanasi intending to stay just for a few days, but the allure of the Ganga is so strong, that most of the time they tend to overstay. What is that inexplicable pull? I really had no answer.

Among the Indian visitors, I found most of them came from south India. They visit the temples and then go sailing across the river Ganga. Some of them, however, prefer entering the temples after shaving off their hair. The priests sitting on the bank then lead them to the temple premise. 'Most of the priests of Varanasi are not Brahmins,' a friend had told me once. Interestingly, an old person at the wharf substantiated this information. 'What difference does it make, my son?' he asked me. 'After all, these devotees have come here not to worship the Brahmins. Have they? They have come to worship the deities. The priests leading them to the doorstep of the gods are functioning as postmen. So why malign them on the basis of caste?'

One day, during my daily visits to the bank, I came across Azad Kapoor, a young artist, sitting on the steps of a bathing ghat. He was a second-year student of an art school. In his free time he visited the banks of the Ganga and sketched human figures. Where else would he find such a collection of variegated human beings? It was he who first spoke about the changing forms of the river with changing hours. 'At dawn the river looks gorgeous,' he said, 'like a newly wed bride. All decked up in fineries. As the day advances, the number of devotees keeps decreasing. Except a few travellers like us the wharfs remain almost empty. Ganga looks forlorn, like a widow, who has recently lost her husband. In the evening when the devotees flock back, Ganga smiles joyously as if happy to reunite with her lost mates.' I simply loved the way Azad described the river.

I was keen on visiting the Manikarnika ghat, because I had heard that this ghat is the only place in Varanasi where the fires of the crematorial pyres are never extinguished. I came across several corpses either being cremated or waiting for cremation. Truckloads of charred wood were scattered over the place while another truckload was being thrown into the Ganga. Heaps of flowers accompanied the charred woods and found their way into the river. The sight horrified me. It is sinful, I felt, to pollute the river in the name of religion.

Haridwar was my next destination. There are no historical records of Haridwar. Only our epics and our *Purana*s tell stories about the holy land of Haridwar. In the pre-historic era the place was identified by different names – Brahmapuri, Mayapuri, Haridwar, Gangadwar, Kapilkshetra, etc. The land has always been blessed by the presence of the river Ganga. Attracted by its spiritual ambience, monks and spiritual leaders have kept visiting Haridwar, making it the holiest of the holy land.

The central attraction of Haridwar is its main wharf – Har-Ki-Pauri. Till date, Har-Ki-Pauri is always crowded with devotees. Therefore to avoid the surging crowd I decided to visit the Vishnu ghat in the evening. The ritual *aarti* (worship) was about to begin and devotional songs were being played aloud on the microphones. Four priests arrived at the riverbank with four tall lamp stands, full of numerous little lamps. The lamps were all lit and were burning brightly. Many more devotees arrived at the bank to view the *aarti*. A musician with a huge cymbal accompanied the priests. Turning towards the Ganga the priests started worshipping the river. It was a magnificent sight. The crowd was watching the scene with bated breath and now hailed the river in unison – '*Om Jaya Ganga Mata*'. The songs that were being played for *aarti* were popular devotional songs and I had heard them before. Yet, today, when I heard them all over again, I was transported to a different world. It was a divine experience for me. I returned to the hotel almost in a trance.

The incessant chattering of the unending crowd of bathers woke me up next morning. In fact it was still quite dark when I peered out of the hotel balcony. Apart from the long line of bathers, I espied something else which I had never seen before in my city Kolkata; a bright starlit sky and a shining moon. As I looked down from the balcony I saw long processions of people walking towards the Har-Ki-Pauri. Sporadic hailing of Mother Ganga was also heard from afar, as bathers dived into the river at Har-Ki-Pauri. What amazed me was the zeal of these devotees. Braving the cold they not only bathed in the river but remained practically naked till they completed their prayers; which incidentally is a time-consuming affair. Inspired by their enthusiasm I too decided to visit Har-Ki-Pauri and off I ran down the staircase of the hotel and walked out. I found a narrow footpath beside our hotel which I knew would take me to Har-Ki-Pauri. But before venturing towards the bathing ghat I looked at the hotel courtyard. A group of people was sitting there. I looked at the eldest member of the group and said, 'Namaste ji.' 'Namaste,' he answered. 'Where have you come from?' I asked. 'Doyelgano, a remote village in Meerut,' he replied. 'When did you reach Haridwar?' 'Yesterday night ji,' he answered. 'Since we could not afford a hotel room and found no place to put up for the night, we decided to sit here the rest of the night. We will bathe in the river, offer our prayers and return home today.' I looked at their rustic attires and simple innocent faces and wondered – what is it that has driven these simple folks to undertake such a tedious journey.

My astonishment was possibly quite visible on my face, because a young man shifted a little and made way for me to sit with them. 'Sit down, Babuji,' he invited. Unable to refuse I sat amidst them. 'Do you have some landed property in your village?' I asked. 'No, Babuji, we are day labourers. We go round places in search of work,' answered the young man.

An elderly lady in the group who was looking at me for quite some time suddenly turned towards an old man sitting beside her, and whispered something. The man nodded his head in approval and then turned to me. 'My wife wants to offer you some sweets. Will you accept it, Babuji?' I hardly knew them and, to make things harder, they themselves appeared quite impoverished. Yet here they were, generously offering a complete stranger a portion of their food! I simply couldn't believe my ears. Neither could I refuse. So when the lady drew out a small packet from her bag and offered me two pieces of sweets I gratefully extended my hand and accepted them. Back home in Kolkata I could not ever dream of such a scenario!

The distance between Haridwar and Rishikesh is approximately twenty-five kilometres. Rishikesh is the first plain land where the river alights from the Himalayas. Unlike Haridwar, Rishikesh is peaceful and tranquil. You feel a palpable spiritual presence in the ambience of Rishikesh. It is via Rishikesh people head towards the Himalayas. I really loved the atmosphere of

Rishikesh. But the best part of Rishikesh was the old man whom I met on the riverbank. He had come with his wife from Bhagalpur, a place in Bihar. He was a retired professor. After retirement he has been spending a large part of his time visiting various pilgrimages. Talking about the Ganga he said, 'There is no historical record about the river's descendance from the Himalayas other than stories and folklores.'

Then he went down to the river for a bath. After his bath he looked at me and said, 'This is my third bath today. I feel rejuvenated after every bath in the river. According to our scriptures the more a person bathes in the Ganga the more he is cleansed off his sins.'

'But do you really believe in this theory?' I asked in surprise. 'Being a man of science, do you think a mere dip in the Ganga can negate the effects of all your misdeeds? If that is the case, then men will keep committing crimes and bathe in the Ganga, to cleanse their sins.' He was quiet for a few minutes looking afar as if reflecting upon my words. Then slowly he answered, 'Listen, child, our ancient sages were wiser than us. They knew that men have a natural propensity to commit sins. But their aim was to lead men to the correct path of life. And to affect that, mere preaching of holy and noble words are not enough. So they had devised a simple method which men would readily accept. Hence the concept of the cleansing power of the river was devised. Since we believe in the cleansing power of Ganga, a criminal while bathing in it will at least momentarily repent for his wrongdoings. And once he repents, psychologically he will be cleansed, like Ratnakar, the dacoit in the *Ramayana*.'

I realised the depth of his faith. And possibly it is this deep faith ingrained in the Indian psyche which compels people to come here. People come here from all parts of India – north, south, cast and wcst. Irrespective of their social status, or their economic conditions, they all come here driven by this faith in the river Ganga. Thus the bank of the river is the true meeting point of Indian culture and heritage.

The old gentleman then turned to his wife and said, 'Come, let's return. It's already late and we have to traverse a long distance.' 'But where will you go now,' I asked. 'We will go to Haridwar and from there take a train for Patna tonight. Tomorrow evening we will reach Patna station, and then again travel two hours to reach our village. It's a very poor village, son. I have been trying my best to improve our economic condition. But what can an old man like me do? We need a contemporary Bhagirath who can bring down heaven on earth. Only then can our country arise and prosper. I don't know when that will happen. The degradation of our society at times scares me. Where are we heading?'

Bidding them goodbye I walked on.

Another interesting person whom I happened to interact with at Rishikesh was Bangshidhar Pokhriyal, a former schoolteacher. He too had retired and was popular as the universal Guruji. He had narrated many stories to me about the river Ganga. The incident I am going to narrate now took place during my second visit to Rishikesh. It was during *Shivaraatri* (the auspicious day to worship Lord Shiva) that I reached Rishikesh. Much to my dismay I found all the hotels, motels and inns filled to the brim. Suddenly I was reminded of Guruji. I called him up. 'I want to put up here for the night – can you arrange something?' I asked. 'Walk straight to Darsan Mahavidyalya. I am the secretary there. Introduce yourself and tell them that I have asked you to stay there. You will have no problem getting a room.'

Darsan Mahavidyalya is a beautiful two-storeyed building situated near Ram Jhula, on the bank of the river. I walked in and found it chock-a-block with visitors. Most of them were foreigners. Yet, the authorities allotted a very comfortable room to me. But the amenities of the room worried me. Since my pocket was almost empty, how would I pay the rent for this room? Anyway without a second thought I decided to stay there for the next three days. On the third day Pokhriyal came to meet me. 'Guruji, I will be leaving tonight. How much do I pay you for having stayed here for three nights?' I asked.

'Who pays whom, Sir?' he asked me in return. 'Do I pay you, or do you pay me?'

'Guruji, I ought to pay you.' He shook his head and said, 'No, you are not to pay a single pie, Sir. Since you have undertaken the sacred task of writing about our mother Ganga, it is our moral duty to assist you in all possible ways. This room will be reserved for you in future. Come over whenever you feel like it.' Words could not express my gratitude so I bowed my head in reverence and left.

The narrative will be incomplete if I do not recount the story of another person – Sri Sundarlal Bahuguna. When I visited his home in Dehra Dun, I was simply overwhelmed. Setting aside all formalities, his wife, Smt. Bimla Bahuguna, had opened the door for me and asked me in. Almost seventy-five, she appeared more dynamic than a young girl. She had spent half of her life supporting her husband's efforts to preserve the purity of river Ganga.

After sometime Sri Bahuguna walked in. His very presence radiated a kind of spiritual serenity which captivated me. Dressed in immaculate white he appeared to be a contemporary edition of an ancient Indian sage. We spoke at length, for more than two hours to be precise, about the vitiating effects of the Tehri dam and his tireless efforts to prevent its construction, the Chipko movement et al. It was time for lunch and I stood up to bid them farewell. But the moment I said, 'Mataji, it's time for me to return,' Bimla Devi replied, 'Son, wait, you will have lunch with us today. Though the meal is meant for two of us, I will be happy to share it with you.' I could not refuse. She served us and like a doting mother looked after my comforts.

Before I left them, Sri Bahuguna said, 'Come over again. I feel a strange kind of kinship when I come across a Bengali gentleman. You may not know, we Bahugunas originally hail from Bengal.' I was taken aback. 'Sir, I didn't know that you are a Bengali.'

'It's a long story,' said Sri Bahuguna. 'Originally our family name was Banerjee. But our ancestors had renounced the original family name and assumed the title of Bahuguna. Yes, three hundred years ago, three of my ancestors had visited the Garhwal district on their way to Badrinath. All three of them were not only well versed in scriptures but were highly proficient physicians as well. On their way to Badrinath they reached Srinagar and heard that the king of Srinagar was suffering from an incurable disease. The king's men heard of the three brothers and took them to the king. They treated him and cured him. Pleased with their skills the king then offered three villages to each one of them and requested them to settle down in Srinagar. It was the king who conferred the surname "Bahuguna" (man of multiple qualities) upon them.'

It was a revelation to me. External division is overridden in view of internal integration – and that is the true spirit of our country.

From Rishikesh, I was on my way to the Himalayas – to trace the origin of the Ganga. For Hindus, the Himalayan range is not just a series of mountains; rather it's a holy place where gods reside. Nearly all our religious leaders, in order to worship God in peace, have spent a large part of their spiritual lives in the Himalayas. Geographically too the Himalayan range is very important because from it originates many of the Indian rivers. Chief among them is the river Ganga. But when I reached Tehri, my first point up the Himalayas, I was really very disappointed. The lifeless flow of water down Tehri via Deoprayag did not match the picture I had in my mind. It resembled an enclosed water body and not a river at all. When I spelt out my disappointment to my co-passengers in the bus I was travelling in, they all started abusing me in unison. 'Had there been no dam here, we would all die. There would be no agriculture, no electricity and no development. For you the appearance of Ganga is important because you have never faced the hardship we faced before the dam came up.' I did not answer, but silently asked myself, *what if this dam finally destroys the river*? I knew it was useless arguing with the local people about the pros and cons of Tehri dam since most of them appeared very shortsighted. In fact most of us are! We hardly care to think beyond our personal interests. Here the Tehri dam stands as a monumental example of our shortsightedness.

Finally we reached Uttarkashi. As we alighted from the bus, it started raining. Fortunately for me there was an inn just opposite the bus stop. I practically ran into it. Originally the inn was meant to house only the pilgrims visiting Uttarkashi. But now with changing times visitors like us too are accommodated. The beauty of Uttarkashi moved me. Surrounded by mountain ranges on all sides, the little town is both peaceful and quiet. Nature has poured all her bounty upon this little town. On one side of the town flows the river Ganga with all its force and glory.

I visited the largest temple of Uttarkashi and met a strange monk. Unlike other monks who believe in total renunciation of material objects here was a person who being an ex-army chief, did not consider it necessary to renounce worldly objects to worship God. So there was an air-conditioned car waiting for him along with other luxury items like an expensive camera, a laptop and what not. He had just exchanged his army uniform for an ochre robe and nothing more. What surprised me was the number of disciples, sitting in the courtyard of the temple, listening to his lecture. He was talking about renunciation – the irony of it all.

My journey to Gangotri had already begun. I spent three days at Uttarkashi, and then travelled 100 kilometres to reach Gangotri. In the past people would have to walk from Uttarkashi to reach Gangotri. But now there are frequent buses plying to Gangotri. So one morning I boarded a bus to Gangotri and reached there in the afternoon. In the evening I visited the Ganga temple. I met Varshram Semwalji, an old villager, in the temple courtyard while coming out of the temple. A long chat with him proved very useful. He spoke at length about the origin of the Ganga, how it flowed out of the matted hair of Lord Shiva, and also about the deep conviction of the Hindus in the sanctity of the river. Gangotri, he further pointed out, is actually the meeting point of heaven and earth. I was really impressed.

'God cannot be bounded in the enclosure of a temple,' he said. 'He keeps moving among His creations – whether be it a human being or nature. And river Ganga at Gangotri is a living example of God's activity.' One of his opinions that profoundly influenced me was, 'Son, Gangotri is possibly the only pilgrimage on earth where you realise how God has broken the barriers of His temples and manifested His enormity. Here standing on the bank of the Ganga you can perceive His palpable presence.'

Next pointing at the five domes of the temple I asked, 'But, Sir, what about these five domes at the top of the temple? Don't you think it indicates Islamic influence?' 'You are possibly right, my son. People keep asking me about them. You know what I feel? The temple was built by a group of artisans from Rajasthan. Maybe their long association with Islamic architecture influenced them to build the temple in this manner. Or maybe the architect himself was a Muslim. Whatever may have been the reason, one thing is for sure, all of them were most certainly inspired by their deep reverence for Mother Ganga.'

It grew dark and it had started snowing when I walked back to the hotel. Yet, with the onset of dawn, ignoring the severe cold, people started flocking to the temple. They bathed in the ice-cold water of the river and walked to the temple to offer their prayers. As the sun rose, a palanquin arrived at the temple gate. The temple door finally opened, for public viewing. The wicker lamp that was lit six months ago stood intact, still bestowing light on the goddess! Could it be a divine intervention? I really had no answer.

I came across a family of herdsmen from Ujjain, in central India. Theirs was a four-member family: the gentleman, his wife, his nine-year-old daughter and his octogenarian mother. The man had come all the way to Gangotri to fulfil the last wishes of his deceased father. Even the old lady who had lost her husband years ago was eagerly waiting for this journey. Before his demise the gentleman had expressed his wish of visiting the Gangotri and offering a puja to Ganga Maiya. Paucity of funds coupled with many other problems had prevented them from undertaking the journey. So now, after all these years, his dutiful son had come to Gangotri both to fulfil the last wishes of his father and honour his old mother. He had incurred a debt to make it happen, but that didn't seem to bother him much. He was carrying an urn with him which contained the last mortal remains of his father. After completing the ritual he washed away the urn in a gesture of offering the river the soul of his deceased father. The sight left me speechless.

Other than this humble family, the other interesting person whom I happened to meet at Gangotri was a middle-aged monk – Vedatmananda. He lived in a small hut, situated a mile below the glacier. His love for the Ganga had prevented him from going back to his native village in Bihar. After attaining the highest degree from his university he had visited both England and the USA for higher studies. Upon returning, instead of pursuing academics, he had joined the Ramakrishna Mission. The strict regimented life of the mission had left him dissatisfied; hence he undertook a journey across India. Finally when he reached Gangotri he was at ease. Without a second's thought he decided to set up his humble abode here. His daily routine was to visit the river and silently pray to the divine Ganga Maiya. And what did he offer? 'Nothing, my son,' he said. 'I look at the river and offer my heartfelt tears to her. That's my way of worship.' The bathing ghat has now been named after his offering – Krandan ('crying') ghat.

After my three days' stay at Gangotri I found a companion-cum-guide in Dilip who encouraged me to visit Gaumukh. 'It's eighteen kilometres from here,' he said. 'The road to Gaumukh has been cleared and we can walk our way there. The scenic beauty is unparalleled, Sir,' he added. So one fine morning we set out for Gaumukh. It was a heavenly experience. There was the Shivling peak on one side of the road bestowing golden-coloured light on the world; while on the other side merrily flowed the crystal clear Bhagirathi. Finally we reached Gaumukh. It was simply an unbelievable sight to behold; out from the snow-clad cave gushed the river Ganga. Despite the hazardous path I couldn't resist reaching the actual spot. It was dark inside the cave and nothing was visible. Yet I continued standing in a trance, trying to visualise the scene in my head.

After about an hour Dilip's words brought me back to reality. 'Sirji, come up, it's time to return,' he was shouting. I gingerly stepped back and started walking my way back to Gangotri. It was a bright sunny morning and I found a few visitors around. There was an old sannyasi on the riverbank reciting Shankaracharya's *Gangastotram*.

As I listened to his chanting I was transported to a different world. I could actually feel the presence of the Almighty, who like us had arrived there to worship the goddess Ganga. Before I could talk to him, I found him disrobing for his bath. Filling a small pitcher with the water of the Ganga he first sprinkled the holy water all around. And then he poured another pitcher full of water upon his head. The very sight of him pouring the ice-cold water on himself sent shivers down my spine. But he seemed impervious. After he had finished the entire process I walked up to him and asked, 'How could you do that, Baba?' My amazement seemed to tickle his sense of humour. 'It's the blessing of Mother Ganga,' he answered laughing. 'Is this your first visit to Gaumukh?' I kept on talking. Reflecting for a while he answered, 'My first visit to this place was fifty years ago, son. Since then I have been visiting it regularly. In fact, I have lost count of my visits. My love for my mother keeps drawing me here.'

I could not ask him anything more. What can possibly inspire a person to bathe in this ice-cold water? But then he was not a deviation; there were many more like him, who kept visiting the place down the centuries. What was that driving force, I wondered.

It was time to return. I had already covered a long distance: Gaumukh, Gangotri, Dharali, Mukhba, Tehri, Deoprayag, Rishikesh, Bithoor, Kanpur, Allahabad, Vindhyachal, Chunar and Varanasi. Now it was time for me to call a halt to my journey. But I could not. An irresistible force kept me moving ahead. *The Ganga hasn't stopped flowing, so why should you* – someone kept whispering into my ears. Bihar and Bengal had to be covered – so off I went.

My next destination was Patna. A friend of mine invited me to his home in Patna. He arranged everything for me. But what a drastic change after the Himalayas! To my dismay the bank of the Ganga in Patna appeared like a large garbage dump. Added to that, constant silt deposition from the river was also obstructing its natural flow. Sprouting of unplanned houses here and there were further deterring its flow. It will not be long before the river will meet an end here in Patna. Completely disillusioned I sat on the bank steps. A Kali temple was near at hand, just adjacent to Patna University. I looked at the scattered images of women bathing, washing their clothes and also worshipping the river. Suddenly I found a group of school children approaching these polluting agents. 'You should not do that,' they told the ladies. 'Don't pollute the river any more. Stop washing your clothes here. Don't pollute the place by throwing your garbage,' they kept repeating. Their appeals and slogans were not heeded by many, yet they persisted undeterred. For me it was a ray of light in the otherwise surrounding darkness.

From Patna I reached Kolkata via Bhagalpur. In between I had also stopped at Murshidabad to get a glimpse of the river. Historically Murshidabad is very important, because it stands as a living relic of the transitional period of Indian history – end of Islamic rule and beginning of

British imperialism. Despite the historical monuments I did not really like Murshidabad. Rather Barnagar appealed to me because of the story of Natore and Queen Bhavani. The queen was on her way to Varanasi once. Her ardent desire was to spend the rest of her life in Varanasi. As she reached Barnagar she received a divine instruction in her dream. A Divine Being came to her and said, 'You ought to stay here and recreate a miniature Varanasi. Build a replica of the temple at Varanasi here.' Queen Bhavani couldn't proceed further. She developed Barnagar. Now at Barnagar stand numerous temples and a palace with wonderful engravings upon it. Even though the palace is now in a dilapidated condition, some of the engravings draw our attention. In the evening sitting in the courtyard of the main temple I was listening to the old stories of Barnagar. The narrator was a ninety-year-old man, of Queen Bhavani's lineage. It transported me to a different world altogether.

I kept on moving. From Murshidabad I went to Nabadwip, Barrackpore, Dakshineswar, Belur and then finally to Nimtola crematorium. So many of my near and dear ones had left behind their mortal remains at this Nimtola crematorium! Childhood memories came flooding back. I recalled how as a child I would accompany my mother when she visited the bank of the river Ganga for a holy bath. On one such visit I was amazed to see the otherwise empty bathing wharf full of people. When I asked my mother the reason behind it, she replied that this day being the Ganga Dussehra, it was auspicious to bathe in the Ganga. 'What is Ganga Dussehra, Maa?' I asked her. 'It's the birthday of river Ganga,' she answered. 'So a river too has a birthday to celebrate like me,' I was really surprised. 'Yes, only if you believe,' she had smiled affectionately. 'If you believe her to be your mother then why not,' she added.

I did not want to know anything more. The bank was crowded with bathers. Some were collecting the holy water in small pitchers, some swimming in the river, while a few having finished their baths were offering their prayers to the Sun god. 'Why do people bathe in the Ganga?' I had asked my mother while returning home. 'To cleanse their sins and be liberated from the cycle of rebirth,' she replied. I had full faith in my mother and, hence, believed what she said.

This was the Ganga I have been seeing since my childhood. After having traversed almost the entire stretch of northern India I finally reached the bank of Ganga in my native place – the city of Kolkata. The Ganga here is very different from the Himalayas, Haridwar, Varanasi, Patna, Dhuliyan and even Nabadwip. Here the presence of the river is more of a necessity than mere deification. People here depend on her more for commercial purposes than as a site to exhibit their devotion. This difference of approach is possibly born out of urbanity – a utilitarian approach of a city-bred man. Unlike the inhabitants of the Himalayas, the Ganga for the people of Kolkata is merely a river, a means to fulfil their requirements.

Undoubtedly there are deviants, but they do not exactly belong to our world. They seem to have landed accidentally in this ever-congested materialistic world of ours. One such person whom I had met was Sadhu *majhi* (monk helmsman) who was ferrying me across the Ganga one evening. His route is restricted – from Belur to Dakshineswar only. Dressed in an ochre robe he keeps ferrying people from morning to night. His smile seems everlasting. 'How long have you been ferrying people?' I had asked while on my way to Dakshineswar. 'For about fifty years.' 'Haven't you ever faced any danger?' I had insisted. 'If you really love mother Ganga she will never betray you. If a danger approaches she will warn you in advance to be cautious. So that way I have really never encountered any danger,' he answered simply. 'Does the river ever talk to you?' I kept on. 'Yes, she does. At the dead of night when the humdrum of the city dies off, she talks. You too will be able to hear her if you care to.' He had gone on and on recounting many of his rich experiences. Finally before I disembarked he came up with a profound statement. 'Son, our lives are like rivers, ever flowing towards eternity.' I had marvelled at the wisdom of an illiterate helmsman. We had reached Dakshineswar.

I could almost visualise the scene unfolding at Dakshineswar in the year 1855. Queen Rashmoni had just inaugurated her temple complex. The central temple was dedicated to Goddess Kali. On the left and right side of the main temple stood six temples each – twelve temples dedicated to Lord Shiva. Today was the day of the festivity. People had come here to attend the gala inaugural ceremony. They were being treated to a sumptuous lunch. But one little boy stood on the bank of the river, having refused the lunch that was offered to him. His elder brother was standing beside him, coaxing him. 'Come on, don't refuse the food. You are hungry, so am I. Let's go and have our lunch,' he kept repeating. 'I cannot touch the food served by a low-caste person,' the little boy was firm. Queen Rashmoni belonged to a lower caste and Brahmins of the time were strictly prohibited from even touching food served by low castes. So the little boy was right in a way. But his brother

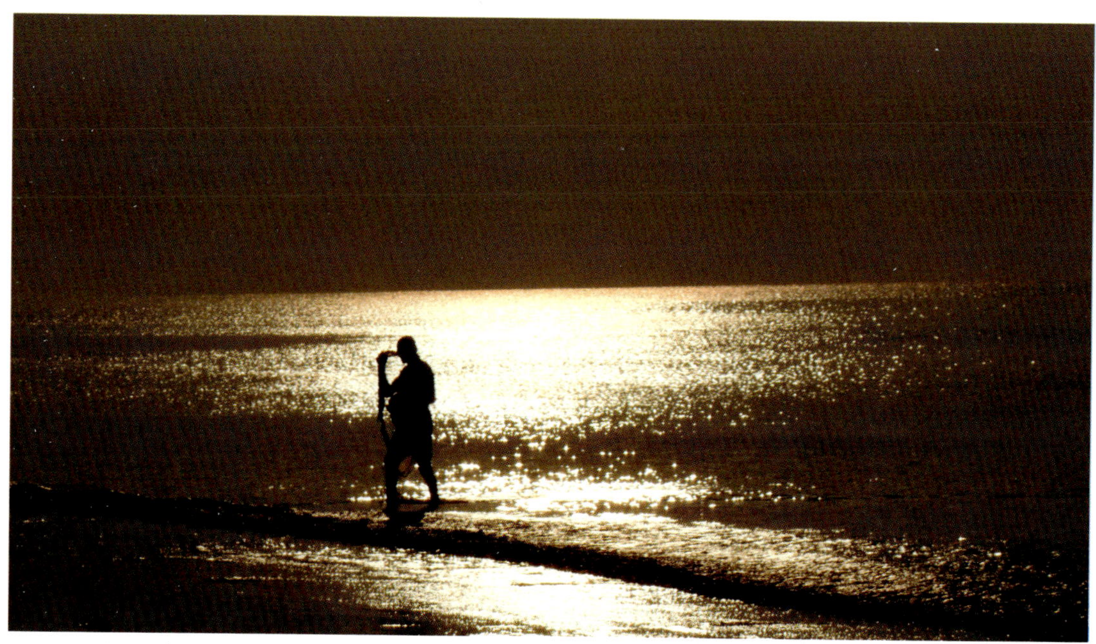

Silhouette of a devotee at Sagar Island

seemed annoyed at this obstinacy. 'So go and cook your own meal on the bank of the Ganga,' he said finally. The word 'Ganga' had a magical effect on the little boy. He appeared completely transformed. 'Ganga – okay fine,' he said, 'I am ready. Ganga is all holy and cleanses everything. I will have lunch with the crowd.' So off went the two brothers for a sumptuous meal.

This little boy was none other than Sri Ramakrishna, the most famous and most revered saint of modern times. Not only did he have his lunch at the temple, he spent the rest of his life worshipping Goddess Kali at the temple built by low-caste Queen Rashmoni. It was the river Ganga which changed his entire perspective. Later on, his wife Sarada Devi too joined him.

For Sarada Devi a bath in the river Ganga was mandatory. And she would unfailingly bathe in the Ganga every day. But after Sri Ramakrishna's demise when Sarada Devi returned to Kamarpukur, the village of her in-laws, the very thought of missing her holy dip in the Ganga depressed her. However, after a few days, as she was proceeding towards the local pond for her bath, Sri Ramakrishna appeared before her in a vision. Sri Ramakrishna, followed by his disciples, was walking right in front of her.

Suddenly water started gushing out from the feet of Sri Ramakrishna and flowed towards the pond and then merged with it. To Sarada Devi, it appeared to be a sequel to the proverbial water gushing out from the feet of Lord Vishnu. She realised at once that the water of the pond had been sanctified by the presence of Sri Ramakrishna. She plucked some hibiscus flowers and placed them on the spot where she had seen the vision.

She had a second vision of Sri Ramakrishna in Calcutta. Sarada Devi had gone for her usual bath in the river Ganga. Once again she saw Sri Ramakrishna walking with his disciples on the bank of the Ganga. Next she saw him going down into the river and gradually melting in the river water. Sarada Devi stood transfixed. A little later she saw Swami Vivekananda collecting the water from that sacred spot and sprinkling it all over the place. It convinced Sarada Devi of Sri Ramakrishna's over-reaching influence over the human race, both present and future.

Finally I reached the end point of the Ganga, the Gangasagar. It was in the middle of January, the auspicious day of Makar Sankranti. Millions of believers had gathered at the Sagar Island, to bathe in the confluence of the Ganga and Bay of Bengal. The temple of Kapil Muni is here. The legend about Sagar Island is that the sixty thousand sons of King Sagar being touched by the river Ganga were finally rid of their curse here.

Journeying across Ganga on a motorboat I finally reached the Sagar Island on the auspicious day of Makar Sankranti. The first person I met on alighting was a physically challenged youth. He was using his hands to move about. I went to him and asked, 'Where have you come from?' 'Giridih,' (a remote place in Bihar) he replied. 'Why have you taken all this trouble to come so far?' 'No trouble at all, Babuji,' he answered. 'I have come to Mother Ganga,' he added smiling.

I also met an old lady, Girija Devi, from Jaunpur who appeared to me equally unfortunate. A little over eighty years old, Girija Devi had begged her way to the Gangasagar just for the final liberation from the endless cycles of rebirth.

I looked at the crowd mesmerised. Thousands were bathing in the confluence and then visiting the temple of Kapil Muni. Standing beside me was a cloth merchant, Badrinathji from Agra. 'This is my seventh visit to Sagar Island,' he said. 'Do you intend to come again?' I asked. 'Of course, I will come again if I am alive. If I fail, my son will come. And in case he fails, my grandson will come.'

It seemed to me like a continuous cycle of waves which had no beginning, no end and has remained so since ages.

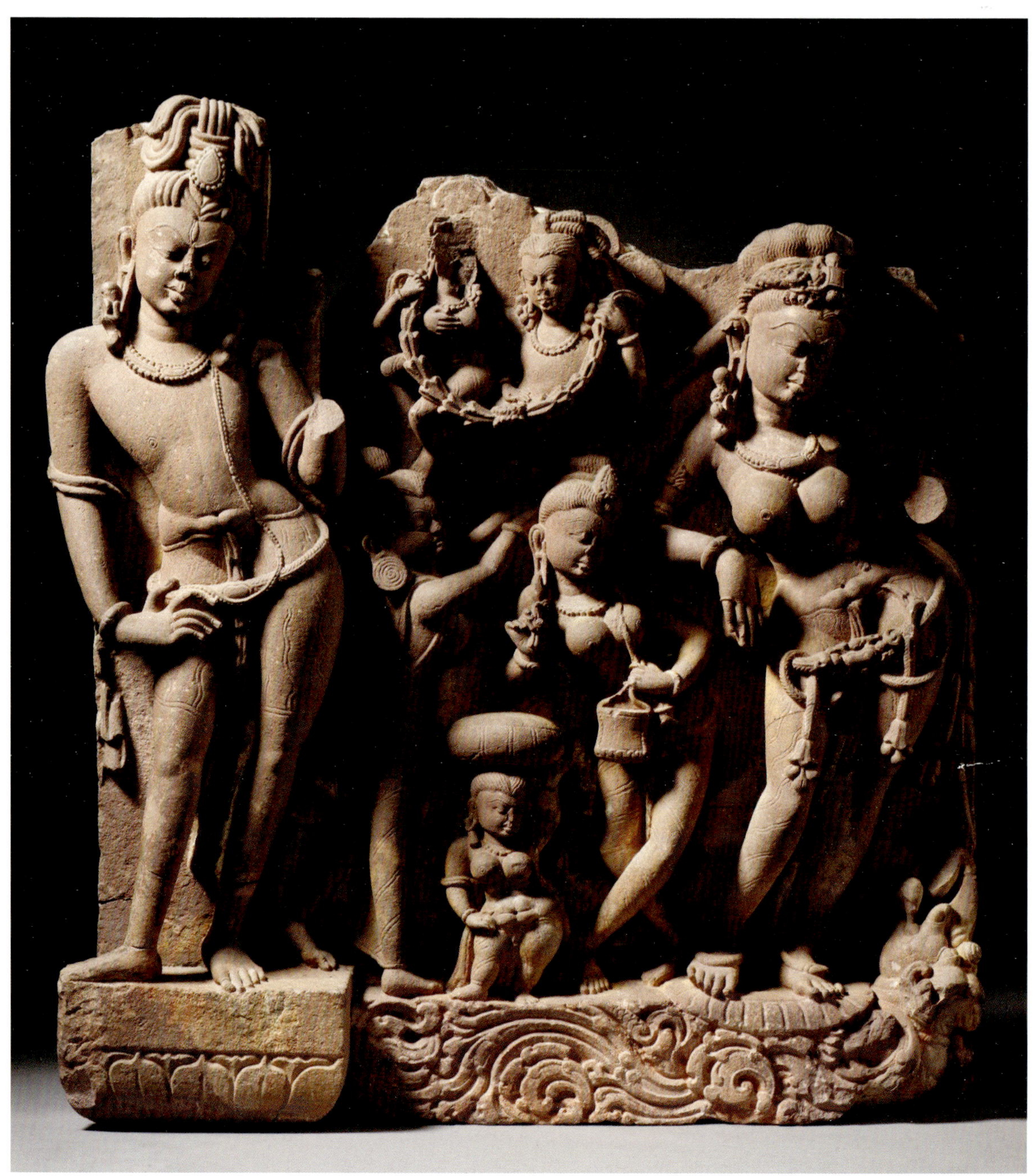

The River Goddess Ganga and Attendants, c. 800, Rajasthan, red sandstone sculpture. *Courtesy of Wikimedia Commons*

APPENDIX

IN QUEST OF ART INSPIRED BY THE GANGA

To Indians, the Ganga is not just a river among the many others in the country. She is not even earthly and it is by a special grace that she flows on earth. She is the heavenly stream brought to the earth by Bhagirath, who is stepping ahead blowing his conch. Ganga, the goddess, follows him on her carrier (*vahana*), the capricorn. She carries a pitcher and her face glimmers with happiness.

The poets of our ancient books, the *Puranas,* imagined this picture of Ganga and that imagination found its way into the creations of artists through paintings and sculptures for thousands of years.

People tend to love beauty and these beautiful creations inspire them to set out on their journey in search of salvation. This beauty does not satisfy the bodily appetite, but calms the mind. Its vision fills the mind with pleasure. This art has spread to the corners of India – from the ancient sites of Mohenjo-daro and Harappa to the temples of modern times. The eternality of this art has been bewitching the human race for a very long period.

The names of the artists have been lost in the passing of time. Their names do not appear in the papyrus of history or in the writings found inside ancient caves. Mentioned are the names of those royal personalities who sponsored the artists in their artistic pursuit. The identities of these great artists have remained in darkness like the dark place under a lamp. They went on creating and establishing their genius with little expectation of name and fame. They are the creators who create for unconditioned mirth – the mirth of creation.

I set out one day in search of that mirth. The editor of a magazine sponsored my travels. 'I want an article on "Ganga in Indian Art".' The editor wanted it to be a first-person account, not information gathered from books. He was willing to bear the cost of my travel and was in a haste to get the article, and therefore I had to leave in no time. 'Do not waste time, start the job as early as you can,' he said.

I stumbled. All starts have a beginning. I was a bit bewildered about where to begin. In the words of *Kabiguru* Rabindranath, the work of preparing the wick before lighting the lamp.

I went to see a learned friend of mine before setting out for the journey. After listening to my dilemma, he gave me a fat book and said, 'You need to know the history before you start.'

'So big a book!' I was nervous.

'Just go through the first chapter. You don't have to gobble the whole,' my friend encouraged me.

'But time is so scarce, when will I read this?' I added clumsily.

'Going by train, right? You'll have plenty of time on your hands,' he said smiling luxuriantly.

My train started from Howrah station on the scheduled date. The destination was Chennai. From there I planned to visit the pilgrimage of art – Mahabalipuram. The train left the station and gradually accelerated leaving the town behind. I, after finishing the primary to-dos, opened the book. The pages were filled with pictures of the goddess in different poses and styles. The pictures were pretty engaging and I started ruminating on the beginning of the concept of these pictures of the goddess. I went on turning the pages. I was transported thousands of years back, perhaps to the period of Mohenjo-daro and Harappa – two populous and extremely prosperous cities. They were built with a certain planning like the cities we live in at present. The common folks undertook different occupations for their sustenance, although most of them were involved in agriculture. Besides earning their livelihood, they used to practise different religious rituals.

Did they worship idols? Scholars have different opinions in answer to this question. A group of them says that idol worship had started in that period. The other group thinks that although they had made idols, their worship had not started till then. Actually it is difficult for common people to think of god without any shape. So they imagined an idol of *Param* (absolute) *Brahma* and started worshipping it. Research suggests that the sages of the Vedic period described the shape of god, but no proof has been found that they made idols adhering to that description and then worshipped them. They performed *yajna*s, in which they summoned their gods and goddesses and offered *ahuti* (offering) in holy fire. Some idols were made here and there but idolatry was not introduced as a custom.

In the Vedic period, after *Kriya Kand,* there was *Gyan Kand.* The sages of the Upanishads perceived the existence of shapeless and bright Brahma. There is no reference to sages worshipped sitting in the jungle or *Tapaban* in the Upanishads. After this came the epoch of Buddha. In the religious books of the Buddhists also, there is no mention of idol worship. If idol worship had any existence before this era, the influence would definitely have been there in the Buddhist period.

Idol worship began in India during the reign of the Gupta dynasty. The different *Purana*s were written during this period. The shapes of different gods and goddesses were imagined around this time. There were two reasons behind starting idol worship as a socio-religious act. The first reason was to diminish the Buddhist influence in society and the other was to establish the *Bramhanya* religion and to attract people to it. Temples for different gods and goddesses were built. The idols of gods were placed in them. With this change, a new thought was born. That was the creative spark which gave rise to so many paintings, engravings, cave paintings and more.

At the very primary level, the creative thinking started on the bank of the river Sindhu. Like all the other civilisations of the world, artistic thought was oriented towards religious belief. The people of that age used to perform religious activities at home. No temple or altar has been discovered but it is quite certain that the people were believers in the concept of God. Evidence has been found in support of this conviction. The symbols of Hinduism such as trees, animals, birds and snakes were usually worshipped. Apart from this, numerous mother figures made of burnt clay have been found, which tell us that they worshipped the mother goddess. Historians have also found seals. One of them shows the image of *Trimurti* sitting in a yoga pose. He is wearing a three-horned headgear and is surrounded by animals. It is believed that this picture is the first version of *Pashupati* Shiva. The shape of some rocks suggests that Linga was also worshipped by the people of those days.

Sindhu civilisation was destroyed but the artistic thought survived. From Sindhu to Sarasvati, from Sarasvati to Ganga. Ganga is the primary and the longest river in north India. Gangetic civilisation took birth on the banks of the Ganga. Therefore, in the epics, *Purana*s or ancient stories, the river Ganga has been apotheosised to

Goddess Ganga. Her divinity is completed when she is assimilated with heaven, the Himalaya, Shiva, Brahma, Vishnu and the great sages. Indians consider Ganga to be the symbol of holiness and salvation. This symbol not only found its place in ancient literature but also in thoughts of the artists. Ganga took her exquisite form in the hands of the artists and started to appear in the outer and inner walls of the temples, and inside caves and on rocks.

One of the best examples of Ganga engraving is her descent to earth from Mahadeva's locks. It is like the assimilation of earth and heaven, the copulation of the feminine Nature and the Divine male figure. This theme of Ganga descending has been engraved in Mahabalipuram.

After travelling a 36-hour-long distance, the train stopped at the station in Chennai. Mahabalipuram is 58 kilometres from here. Buses are quite frequent. I bought a ticket and acquired a seat in the bus. Most of my co-passengers were local people. A few tourists like me were also seen sitting here and there.

The bus set off and lush green fields were visible on both sides. A few cottages dotted the landscape once in a while. The road was almost clear. After one-and-half hours we reached Tirukalikunram. The mile post showed '3 kilometres from Mahabalipuram'. The bus stopped at last at Mahabalipuram. Some small shops and houses were spread over the place. But looking around I was transfixed by the grand artistry of Mahabalipuram. People from every nook and corner of the world had come to see this creation with their own eyes. I started approaching the monuments.

The world famous bas-relief was in front of my eyes! I had been looking at its pictures for all these years and now, to my wonder, it was just before me! Two grand rocks had been cut into whale-shaped pieces standing beneath the open sky – 98 feet long and 49 feet high. Numerous images of gods, animals and birds had been engraved on the rock. The liveliness of the sculptures was truly remarkable. I identified Nagraj with a big hood spread over its head. Just under it, the Nagrani is standing with joined hands. On the left, the yogi Bhagirath is meditating on one foot. He seems to be quite thin, probably due to the drudgery of his position. It is said that Bhagirath meditated for a thousand years.

Within these enormous rocks, the idols seem to be floating on air. All the sculptures here are so balanced that it is like a great imagery of art. We know from the *Mahabharata* that Ganga has flowed in heaven, on earth and in hell. The idols here finally gave me a chance to appreciate what I knew. On the right-hand side, there is the sun, the moon and other celestial bodies; the Himalayas are seen overhead. This signifies that Ganga is coming down from there. A lion is standing with his mane in full splendour. On the left, some people are moving towards Ganga. Four singers of heaven (*Kinnar Kinnari*) are flying through that place. I was completely immersed in it. Nothing else was visible. It seemed that I was standing in a no-man's land and all alone in this universe. I came out of the trance with the touch of a human hand on my shoulder. Turning around, I saw a middle-aged man smiling at me. Before I could respond, he said, 'I am the oldest guide of this place. My name is Krishnan. I noticed from a distance that you were watching this relief for a long while. You seemed to be lost in your thoughts. So I came to you. Otherwise I don't approach tourists myself.' I perceived that nothing can be known without the help of a guide and said, 'I have come here to write on these monuments. This is my first visit and I know almost nothing.'

'Let's sit down in the shadow of the rock and let me remove the darkness from your mind. First I'll tell you about the history of this place and then show you each and every corner of it,' Krishnan said.

The sun was burning overhead and it was extremely hot. There was a cave adjoining the Bhagirath relief. We both sat there in the cool shade. It was an artificial

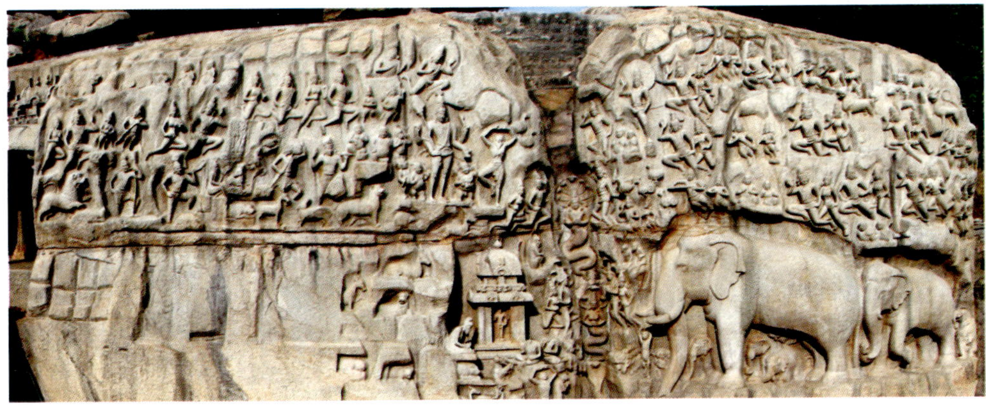

The Descent of Ganga at Mahabalipuram, a giant open-air rock relief, is an outstanding work of craftsmanship

cave. It was really strange to think that artisans had carved it out of the mountain with just chisel and hammer.

'Please tell me something about this place.' I was trying to feel the rhythm.

'The Pallavas were the most powerful kings of south India. They acquired worldwide fame for their bravery, vigour and their love of art and culture. The Bhagirath relief was built by the kings of this dynasty. According to the historians, this temple had been built by 700 CE; the approximate time period of the making of it is 635 to 645 CE. One of the Pallava kings was Raja Narasingha Burman. And Narasingha Burman is said to be the creator of Mahabalipuram. Today's name Mahabalipuram or Mamallapuram has come from the old name Mahamallapuram. The most significant engravings of Mahabalipuram are nine chariots made from a single rock, a cave temple carved by cutting through twelve hills, Saikat temple and the famous bas-relief named Meditation of Bhagiratha or Meditation of Arjuna.'

By then the sun had grown milder. Krishnan said, 'Come, let me show you the place.' After walking a few yards, there was a cave, the Krishna Mandapam. The cave walls were filled with engravings – an idol of Krishna and a cow being milked in one of the engravings; *Gopini*s are everywhere going about their work, the cow is licking her calf – a heavenly sight.

I was following Krishnan, wherever he took me. Rows of hotels were spread over the seashore. In the distance, my eyes caught sight of the famous Panchrath. An enormous rock has been hewn to create five completely separate temples. The amount of rocks engaged in this work is less than the amount that has been wasted. The chariots of the Pancha Pandava are seen standing in their regal splendour. They amaze the spectators with the enormity of the creation. It is quite evident that numerous artists had spent their entire lives in creating these works. There are statues of elephants and lions in front of the chariots. They seem to be the sentries of the five great chariots. They have been keeping watch on this precious Indian creation for thirteen hundred years. Apart from these there is the Saikat temple. Although not as magnificent, its presence on the seashore bewitches the mind.

We spent the whole day looking at the artistry of Mahabalipuram. Darkness was creeping in at a slow pace. I was completely oblivious to time and space, when Krishnan brought me back to reality. It was time to say goodbye to Mahabalipuram.

I paid Krishnan his fees and smiled at him. He silently departed without saying a word. I stood alone at the shore watching him walk away. After having covered some ground, Krishnan suddenly turned around and ran towards me.

'Please come again. Won't you?' He seemed so close to my heart. This is probably the mesmerising effect of art!

I held his hand, 'I'll definitely come again and you have to tell me more about it the next time.'

Finally, I departed with a heavy heart.

Now it's time to move towards Pattadakal in Karnataka. I had read about Pattadakal before but had never seen it. India has so many beautiful temples that it is impossible to visit them all in one lifetime.

The train was leaving the station. I took out my friend's book and started turning the pages. Suddenly I discovered an article about the antiquity of the Ganga. It says that in the Vedic period when the people arrived at the bank of the Ganga from the bank of the Sarasvati, they did not consider Ganga as a goddess. They had great reverence for her but only as a river. In later periods, when *Ramayana* and *Mahabharata* were written, the Ganga was shown to be the sacred wave coming down from heaven. It was then that Ganga was perceived as a goddess and she was assimilated with Indian life and culture.

The poets borrowed the description of Sarasvati while delineating the Ganga. There is no clear image of Sarasvati in our ancient literature. Only it is said that, 'Hey *Subhre* [White Lash], you extend and prosper. You offer your breast to feed me.'

The Ganga took the place of the Sarasvati when it dried up. The *Padma Purana* has a beautiful description of the Ganga. It says, 'She has two hands. She is carried by capricorn. She is as white as flower *Kunda*, the moon and conch. She is garnished with all the ornaments and holds white lotus and *Abhay Mudra* in her hands. She wears white clothing and is very good looking. Ganga has a filled pitcher in her hand.'

My train reached Hoppet. It is a very small station. A few rented cars were waiting at one side. These cars are pretty expensive if rented by one person. I was looking for co-passengers to make my travel a bit cheaper and found them quite easily – a professor of history and his young student, a girl of tender age. The master and the disciple had set out for research work. They had come from Hyderabad. I extended my hand to the professor and exchanged pleasantries. The professor's name was Srinivas Reddy and the girl was named Krishna. They were going to Vadami, Pattadakal and Aihole – the three major temple-cities of Karnataka. Amongst those, my destination was only Pattadakal.

We got into the car and it started rushing along the road. On both sides were deserted fields. A few small villages could be seen on the way between those fields. It takes two hours to reach Pattadakal from the station. A strange dryness overwhelmed the whole place. The graceful greenery of Bengal was completely absent. My mind was out of tune with the grave aridity of the environment. But soon it was compensated for by the amiable nature of the professor. After hearing what I had to say about the Ganga, he started talking. 'The people of north India are more fortunate than that of south India at least in one aspect; they have the Ganga. There is no Ganga in south India.'

'But you people have the Godavari, the Ganga of the south,' I protested smiling.

Professor Reddy remained silent for a few moments and then said, 'That is like satisfying your desire for drinking milk with *ghole* [a drink made by diluting curd with water]. But one thing is obvious. The inhabitants of south India respect the Ganga far more than the inhabitants of north India. The proof of this statement can be found in the engravings. The temples of south India are filled with statues of Ganga and Lord Shiva. But why just south India? Western and central India also have statues of Ganga. If Ganga herself is absent in some of them, her *vahana*, capricorn, is definitely there.'

'May I ask you a question?' I interrupted him.

'Definitely. I'll answer your query if I know the answer.' Srinivas was unexpectedly earnest.

'Where did the concept of capricorn come from? Does it have a history?' I questioned. The professor kept looking at me for some time. He was probably contemplating the answer. Then he said, 'The statues of Ganga we see now came into being in the age of the Gupta dynasty. But capricorn as the *vahana* of Ganga used to be found in olden times. We first witnessed capricorns in the seals of the Sindhu civilisation. It is possible that people saw crocodiles in the Sindhu river and that inspired the myth of the capricorn. The people of that period went abroad through sea routes to transact business. It is not impossible that they saw crocodiles in the seas. They used to make the prow of their boat resemble the face of a capricorn. In Buddha's time also, people did business in Malay and Indonesia. In the long sea route, they had to cope with different difficulties. In one of the *Jataka tales*, we see that a capricorn overturned a ship. This devastating form of capricorn was given shape in the weapons too. Among the statues of Mathura, we see a statue of Kanishka. He is standing with a maul in his hand engraved with a picture of a capricorn. It finds mention in all the *Purana*s. We can see a capricorn-shaped boat in the *Chandi Mangal*.

'In later times, when the Gangetic civilisation grew, the Ganga used to be infested with crocodiles. Abu'l Fazl wrote that a man was thrown to the mouth of a crocodile at Prayag at the confluence of Ganga and Yamuna.

'There is no certain information about how the capricorn became the *vahana* of Ganga, but if we consider the great heritage of India, we see that the capricorn was referred to as a dangerous aquatic animal in the *Rig Veda*, who hinders man's travel through the river. So the king of the gods, Indra, killed it. Afterwards, when the Sarasvati dried up and people migrated east towards the banks of the Ganga, the image of the crocodile as a dangerous creature was slowly wiped out. In a sloka, it is said that the sages are offering prayers to the fish of the water and the crocodiles of the river. Amongst the aquatic animals of the Ganga, the crocodile is the most powerful. There is a royal demeanour in its movement. That is probably the reason why it was chosen to be the *vahana* of the most powerful Goddess Ganga. Everywhere in Indian art, wherever Ganga is seen, the capricorn is also seen along with her. The oldest image of the capricorn was found on a hill near southern Patna in the cave of the sage Lomos. It was created approximately in 350 BCE. In the Jain sculptures of Mathura we see the capricorn too. At the entrance of Amaravati, there are two pictures of capricorns on two sides. It was believed that the capricorn symbolised rivers. The other opinion is that the capricorn is the symbol of good countering evil forces. This is why these images are found at the gates of temples or doors of houses, so that no evil power can enter them.'

Srinivas had been talking for a long time. Krishna was listening to him sitting by my side. As soon as the professor paused, she said, 'There is one more thing, Sir, apart from the capricorn. In most of the pictures of the Ganga, we can see a pitcher in her hand.'

Srinivas said, 'Right you are. Capricorn is the *vahana* of Ganga and the brimming pitcher is her symbol. The goddess sits on a capricorn with the pitcher in her hand. This full pitcher is used in different Hindu religious rituals. This pitcher is almost everywhere filled with water from the Ganga. In some places, where Ganga water is not available, the pitcher is filled with water considered taken from that sacred river. Other than this, there is another reason for considering the full pitcher as the symbol of Ganga. Our *Purana*s say that Ganga was born from the *Kamandali* [a pitcher-like water container used by the sages]. Its water is not only the symbol of holiness but also of youth. The *Mahabharata* says that the sage Chavan got back his youth by bathing in the Ganga's water. The pitcher is also compared to the womb, where life is created. In the *Ramayana*, Rama is offered a golden pitcher containing Ganga water during his coronation.'

Professor Reddy was going to say something further but stopped. Our eyes caught sight of a small river by the side of the road through the window. A few palm trees gave a touch of green to an otherwise dry region. A series of mountains could be seen in the distance.

Srinivas said, 'We have reached. The village Pattadakal is just beside this river called Malprava.' Our car stopped after covering a little more distance. The group of temples of Pattadakal was just in front of us. Green grass and gardens of flowers of different colours surrounded the place. The temples were in the middle standing in rows. In spite of being so scenic this place was not crowded. We entered it after buying tickets. The path to the temples were made up of marbles. We were proceeding silently. I requested the professor to tell me something about these temples. Srinivas said, 'The three temple cities – Vadami, Pattadakal and Aihole – are famous for the beauty of their temples. The founders of these temples were the Chalukya kings. The city of Vadami was their capital. There are cave temples in the city. Pattadakal was a small village, twenty-nine kilometres away from the river Malprava. The placed used to be called Raktapur in the past. The coronation of the Chalukya kings took place here. The Chalukya king Vikramaditya II and his two queens were connoisseurs of art. They brought artists from Kanchipur and commissioned these temples. There are ten temples in Pattadakal. Among them four have been made in the north-Indian style and the remaining six are in the Dravidian artistic style.'

'Is there any statue of Ganga in these temples?' I enquired.

'Yes, in the temple of Virupakshya. Let us visit temple Virupakshya first. Then we will see the others.' Srinivas guided us towards the temple. The whole place was covered with green grass and the colossal temple stood in the middle. The architecture was the life of the temple. There was a sculpture of Shiva in the *Garva Griha.* I bowed my head as a mark of respect and proceeded further. The whole temple has numerous *khilan*s or pillars with unparalleled sculptures.

'You have seen the sculpture of the transformation of Ganga at Mahabalipuram. Here Ganga has two forms – one is the descending Ganga and the other as the mother figure,' Srinivas remarked while moving slowly.

'What is the mother figure of Ganga?' Krishna asked curiously.

'Ganga as a mother figure is there in the *Mahabharata.* King Santanu while loitering by the riverside saw a lady of peerless beauty. He was bewitched by the magic of her charm and fell in love with her and asked for her hand in marriage. The woman agreed but on one condition: that Santanu would not ask any questions about her actions. They got married and she later gave birth to a son. But she drowned the child. Santanu could not question her act because of his promise. One by one, seven sons were born to them and were drowned. When the queen was about to drown the eighth son, Santanu could not restrain himself and stopped her from drowning him. As soon as the promise was broken, the queen disclosed her real identity as Ganga, the goddess. She came on earth for the salvation of the seven Vasus. Her eighth son remained on earth. He was Bhisma. Gradually the mother of Bhisma became the mother of all Indians.'

We reached a pillar that depicts the story of Ganga and Bhagirath on its entire surface. In the first panel Bhagirath is meditating; he is praying for the salvation of his predecessors. Ganga is sitting on the right side. Eight Vasus are standing before him in a series. They are also praying for salvation.

In the second panel, a sage is depicted engaged in divine pursuit. He is the sage Kapil, who cursed the sixty thousand sons of King Sagar to be turned to ashes. The imagery shows a man angrily saying something to the sage while pointing at him. He is probably one of Sagar's sixty thousand sons.

In the third panel, Ganga is descending to earth from heaven. Lord Shiva has given her refuge in his locks. Nandi and Parvati are standing by his side. Water is gushing out of Lord Shiva's hair.

The fourth panel shows the sage Janhu drinking the water of Ganga. King Bhagirath is praying to him for the salvation of Ganga. And the final panel shows the wave of Ganga following King Bhagirath.

It is a magnificent work of art. I kept looking at it. When I emerged from my trance, I brought out my camera and took some snaps. I was silently doffing my hat to all those artists whose magical touch had infused life into the rocks. I wandered there the whole day and set out to catch the train in the evening.

Srinivas and Krishna would now move towards Aihole. Numerous temples were waiting for them there. They insisted that I accompany them. In Aihole there is a famous cave temple. At the entrance of that large temple, there are images of Sapta Matrika, Lord Shiva and Ganga.

Unfortunately I could not go with them. I had to leave for Mumbai and my train was leaving that very night. After reaching Mumbai, my schedule dictated a visit to the Elephanta Caves to see another statue of Ganga.

When the launch started from the Gateway of India, the morning had become very bright. I was absent-mindedly sitting in a deck chair watching the deep-blue seawater and its waves. A group of seagulls were playing with the waves. The Elephanta Caves are ten kilometres from Mumbai. It was visible after approximately an hour's travel. It seemed like the tortoise of the fairy tale that suddenly emerges from water.

I bought a guidebook before boarding the launch. It contains information about this island and the history of the engravings of the caves. In the past, there was an island named Gharapuri or the 'island city'. The caves here are the creation of mankind. In all probability, these caves were made in the years between 450 and 750 CE. At that time the inhabitants living here also performed religious rituals. The island is a couple of kilometres in length. Within this small area, there are two villages.

In the *Purana*s it was said that the cave was built by Vanasura, a devotee of Lord Shiva. No cave writing has been found inside it. Dissension exists regarding the founder of these cave temples. But the scholars agreed on one point. They affirm that Pulakeshi II, a king of the Chalukya dynasty, built most of the caves here. Some opine that the famous Trimurti cave was built by the kings of the Rastrakut dynasty. But all these creations reflect a singular idea – that their founders were all *Shaibya* or the devotees of Lord Shiva.

This island was uninhabited for a very long period. At one point, the Portuguese captured the island. This island had statues of two elephants on one side. So the Portuguese called it 'Elephanta'. During target practice they destroyed one of the eyes of the elephants. The caves of this island can be divided into two categories. On one side, there are the Hindu caves. Their number is greater. Buddhist caves are the other kind. The Hindu caves carry instances of splendid sculpture. These caves are presently a UNESCO World Heritage Site. It is said about these cave temples – from Gateway of India to Elephanta Caves – that they take you away from the commotion and hustle bustle of Mumbai to a time when faith, mysticism, artistic thought and creation were at their peak. Long-cherished beliefs and the emotions of Indian thought have been transformed and assimilated in the works of the artists here. It is truly a remarkable expression of human creation.

Most of the sculptures at Elephanta Caves are of Lord Shiva. There are eight caves here.

- First cave: The marriage of Shiva and Parvati. The priest is Brahma. Vishnu, Himalaya and Chandra are also present.
- Second cave: *Nataraj* (Lord Shiva while dancing).
- Third cave: Shiva and Parvati embracing one another.
- Fourth cave: *Ardhanariswar* Shiva. In this statue, one half is Shiva and the other half is Parvati.
- Fifth cave: Ravan trying to lift Mount Kailash. Shiva and Parvati are present.
- Sixth cave: *Chaturbhuj* Shiva – Shiva with four hands.
- Seventh cave: The descent of Ganga on earth. Shiva has given her refuge within his locks. Rivers Yamuna and Sarasvati are standing by.

- Eighth cave: Here we see Shiva in the form of *Maheshwar*. A *trimurti* has been created by cutting a single piece of rock. This statue is twenty feet long. The three faces of Lord Shiva symbolise *Sristi, Sthiti* and *Pralay* respectively. On the right, the face expresses life and liveliness (*Sristi*). He holds a bud of a flower, which is the symbol of creation. He is Brahma. On the left, the angry-faced statue with a large moustache is of Shiva. This is the Shiva who brings *Pralay* or destruction. His other name is *Rudra* Shiva. The face in the middle is in meditation. He is *Sthiti*, the symbol of Lord Vishnu, also known as *Jogeshwar* Shiva. At a little distance is the statue of *Gangadhar* Shiva.

The launch I was travelling in reached the dock. We all got down from the launch one by one. A small train took us near the caves. To reach the top, one has to climb 120 steps. The caves and sculptures have been hewn by cutting a single rock on a hill. The roof rests upon a series of pillars. I could not resist roaming about the place the entire day and seeing the wonderful relief work on the rocks. Most of it is based upon Lord Shiva.

My eyes were overwhelmed looking at the Trimurti cave. I kept on looking at it for hours on end thinking about the creators of this unparalleled art. They were not only the makers but also the devotees. They must have completely dedicated themselves to this work. Looking steadily at the eyes of these sculptures, my mind went back in time thousands of years. The sculptures began to talk inside my heart. Millions of pages are written in their eyes! The stories do not end and continuously go on and on.

Unfortunately I was compelled to return to the real world. Besides Trimurti cave, there is the *Gangadhar* Shiva. This Shiva holds Ganga in his hair. This sculpture has faced severe damage. Parvati is there along with Lord Shiva. It is a beautiful image. Shiva has four hands but two of them are broken. He has three feminine figures caught in his hair. They are Ganga, Yamuna and Sarasvati respectively. Together they symbolise the flow of water. The great king Bhagirath is laid at the feet of Lord Shiva. Looking at the statue I felt that the whole theme was the imagination of the artist who created it. But people now explain it according to their own interpretations.

Daylight began to fade. Time to return. In this short span of time, whatever had been seen was merely a trifle in comparison to the things unseen.

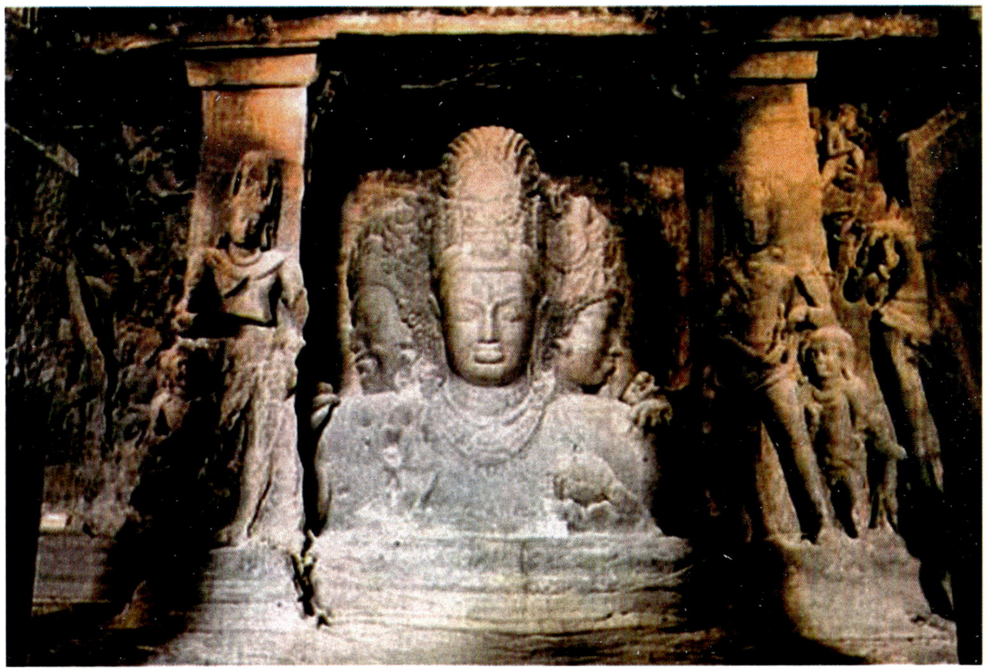

The Trimurti is considered to be the most important sculpture in the Elephanta Caves

Now it was time to move on to the Ellora Caves of Maharashtra. It is considered to be the most exquisite example of Indian art. I caught the train from Mumbai to Aurangabad. Sitting in the train, I recalled the companion of my journey, that book my friend gave which enlightened my path. The caves of Ellora are 28 kilometres away from Aurangabad. It has 34 caves. Out of these caves, the first 12 are Buddhist caves. These were made between the years 500 and 700 CE. The next 17 are Hindu caves. These were created between the years 700 and 900 CE. And the last 5 are Jain caves. The Buddhist caves were made by Buddhist monks. The Hindu caves were made during the reigns of the kings of the Chalukya and the Rastrakut dynasties.

I shut the book when it was almost midnight. I thought I'd take a small nap since the train would reach Aurangabad at dawn. When I got down at Aurangabad, there were very few people in the station. My destination was 29 kilometres from here. No conveyance was in sight till it was nearly noon. At last I boarded a bus which travelled along deserted roads. When I reached the Ellora Caves, I saw that quite a

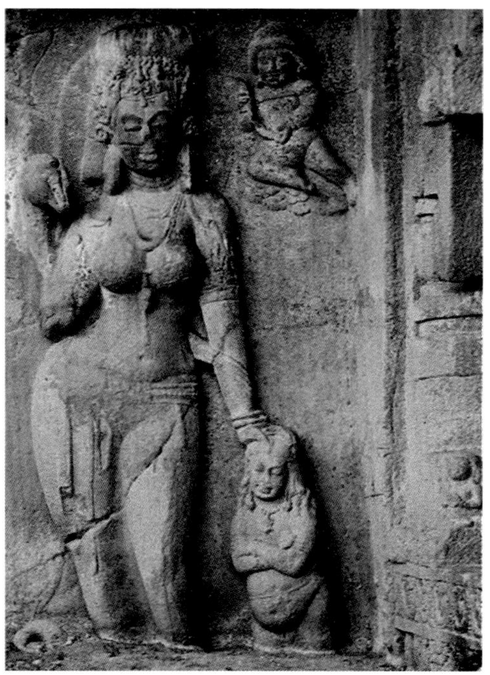

Ganga sculpture, Elephanta Caves

few tourists were already present at the spot. I immediately bought a ticket and entered the caves.

Suddenly a young man came forward. 'Do you need a guide, Sir?' he asked boldly. He cannot have been more than twenty-five. I looked at him for a while wondering whether this young man would be competent at his job. The boy said with a smile, 'You must be hesitating because of my tender age; but do not worry, Sir. We are working as guides for three generations. I know every bit of this place.'

'What's your name?' I asked with a smile.

'My name is Shivram. People call me Shiv.'

'Then let's go. I have the rare fortune of visiting Lord Shiva's cave with Shiva himself!' I said laughing.

We climbed the stairs. The greatest combination of human toil and pursuit opened up before my eyes. I wondered at it. Shiv, the guide, said, 'This cave is the greatest creation of Ellora Caves. It is called the Kailash cave. The Rastrakut kings built it 1,200 years ago. It took 150 years to make. Six generations of artists worked at it.'

'But tell me one thing. What was this place like before the caves were hewn here?' We were standing in front of an idol of Lord Ganesha.

Shivram said, 'A complete mountain was standing by itself here before the caves were made and it was overgrown with dense forests.'

'But how is it possible to transform a complete mountain into this vast work of art?' I wondered.

'There are three steps of cave artistry. First it had to be examined whether the rocks were appropriate for engraving or not. Then the rock-cutting experts were called upon. They started cutting the rocks according to the instructions of the artists and prepared a rough structure of the cave. At that time, there was no concept of exploding rocks. They used to complete the entire thing with the help of a chisel. After the caves were made, a group of sculptors were summoned. They started making the windows, doors of the cave and also the columns and the shelves. They used to give shape to the cave in balance with the types of rocks. At last the artists arrived to provide the cave its final form. With their proficient hands they lovingly engraved the rocks to create stories through sculptures. Most of these stories were derived from our great epics – the *Ramayana* and the *Mahabharata*. A calculation reveals that the amount of rocks used to make this weighs more than two lac tons.'

I kept marvelling at the creation before me. These apparently looked like caves but in reality they were not. The caves had been made in the same way, involving the process of rock-cutting, as humans made their habitations in the olden days with bricks, timber and rocks. The temple was started from the top of the mountain. They used to come down cutting it all the way. The artist's imagination, the maker's technique and the sculptor's dexterity got assimilated in the work. The main temple is placed on a stage-like structure. The sides of the stage are engraved with elephants in such a way that it seems that the elephants are holding the weight of the temple with their trunks.

I asked, 'Shivram, where are the sculptures of Ganga?'

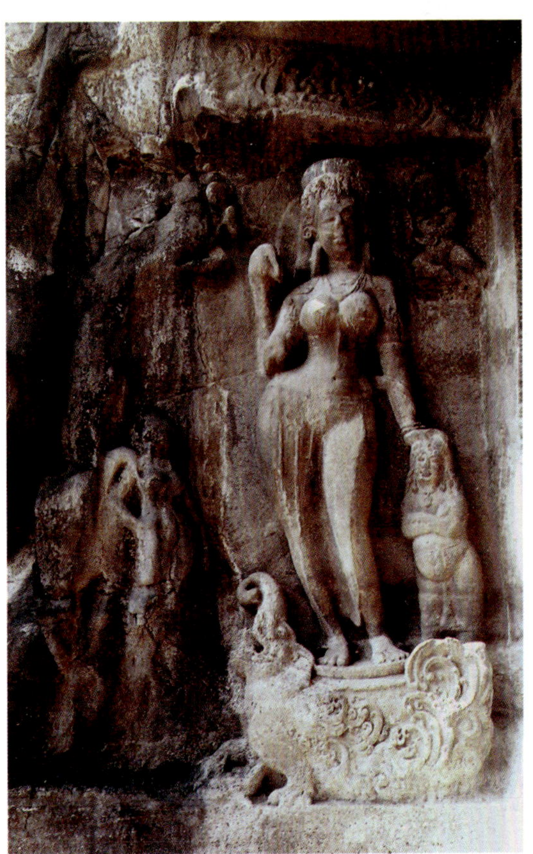

Ganga sculpture, Ellora Caves

'Just to your left,' Shivram replied.

I turned my face and saw the relief of Ganga on the wall where the door of the Kailash cave was. The Goddess Ganga was standing over her *vahana*, the capricorn. One of her hands was resting upon a boy's head. She was standing in her full glory. The sculpture made me stand motionless before it for a long time. On the other side, there was the relief of Goddess Durga in the stance of *Mahishasuramardini* or Durga while killing the demon. And in front stood Lord Ganesha, the god of knowledge.

'Babu, let's go. Many things left to see, babu!' Shivram hastened me.

We entered the Kailash cave. Lord Shiva's sculptures created in different styles decorate the walls of this cave. Shivram made me stand before one of them. Here Ravana has lifted the mountain Kailash with his hand. Lord Shiva is calm but Parvati looks on nervously. Other sculptures are spread all over the place. Such beautiful imagination! It seemed to me that the artists offered obeisance at the feet of the gods through their creation.

Time knows no bounds and flies with its pink wings. We came out of the Kailash cave. In front of us was a monolithic pillar. It was 115 feet high with a *trisul,* a trident, on top.

'Is there any other statue of Ganga?'

'Yes, in cave number 21.'

I stepped forward with Shivram. We entered a comparatively small cave. The outer portion was designed with different images. Three sculptures of Ganga, Yamuna and Sarasvati were visible as soon as one entered the cave. The goddesses can be easily recognised with their emblems and *vahana*s. Yamuna was standing upon a tortoise, Sarasvati upon a lotus and, in the middle, Ganga on a capricorn. There was a *jyotishchakra* behind Ganga's head. She had a crown upon her head and a necklace and many other ornaments adorned her body. Among the sculptures of Ganga, Yamuna and Sarasvati, Ganga's face reflected a tranquil and placid beauty. Her shape and style was unparalleled. It resembled statues of the ancient Greek goddess Aphrodite.

We spent the entire day at the Ellora Caves. The sun started setting in the west. It cast long shadows over the caves. My mind also felt heavy because of the load of art I had been bearing. I turned my face towards the Ellora Caves once more before

I finally left the place. It was the sweetest experience of my life but for some reason a kind of sadness overpowered me gradually.

A question haunted me while coming back. When did the revelation of the forms of Ganga start taking place in Indian art? Once again I opened the book I was carrying with me and found 'The History of Indian Art'. In that section is a chapter called 'Ganga in Sculpture'.

In Indian art and sculpture, works on Ganga had been revealed during the Gupta dynasty. The Gupta reign started in Magadh at the advent of the fourth century CE. During Samudragupta's reign, this dynasty flourished in north India. He was not only a good administrator, he also had a profound love for literature, art and music. After Samudragupta, his son Chandragupta II ascended the throne. His court was bedecked by the *Navaratna* (the nine stalwarts of art and culture). This epoch is known as the Golden Era in the history of India. The administrative service was extremely efficient during this period. The subjects lived in peace and comfort. Trade thrived and the economy flourished. The patronage of the Gupta kings ensured that art and culture scaled newer heights. This climate saw the birth of many new ideas in the fields of art and their ripples could be felt far away, even outside India. These new lines of artistic thought set this age apart from all previous ages. Art now was fused with the intellect. The artists, while excelling in technical finesse, also became conscious of spirituality. This is evident in all the works of this period – they have a numinosity, a tenderness. This characteristic feature was equally evident in Hindu, Buddhist and Jain arts.

The most ancient manifestation of this art can be seen in the caves of Udaygiri in Madhya Pradesh. The Udaygiri mountain is located at a distance of 13 kilometres from Sanchi in Madhya Pradesh. It is reached by crossing the river Betwa. A series of caves are situated here. It is known from a cave inscription that Udaygiri sculptures were created during the reign of Chandragupta II (ca fifth century CE). Apart from the mythological stories, the caves also narrate stories related to the social life of that time. Twenty caves exist in Udaygiri. It is the supreme example of the arts, crafts and engravings of the Gupta period. Among the caves situated at the top of the mountains, cave number five is the most exquisite one. It is engraved with the *Varaha,* the avatar of Lord Vishnu. The *Varaha* image has a human body and

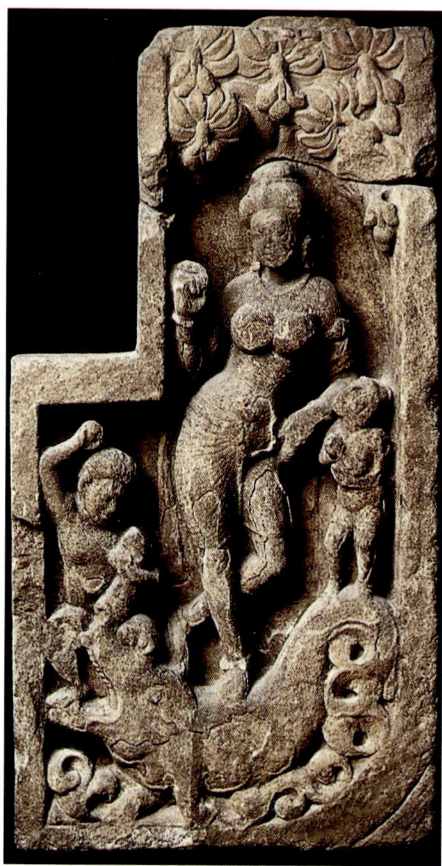
Ganga sculpture, Udaygiri Caves

the face of a pig. The cave depicts Vishnu coming out of the sea in his *Varaha* avatar. He takes the world out from the depths of the sea. Here Ganga has been shown as the wife of Lord Vishnu. In the other caves of Udaygiri too, we can see Ganga and Yamuna upon their respective *vahana*s.

Apart from the pitcher and the capricorn, Ganga is accompanied by a small boy. He is known as *Gana*. *Gana* is the symbol of prosperity and fertility. The capricorn symbolises fear and awe-inspiring objects. Assimilation of these two leads to the fullness of art. *Gana* has been seen first in the Udaygiri Caves. Here the art of engraving found its culmination in Ganga, *Gana* and the capricorn.

Examples of Ganga sculptures are also found in the temple of Dashavatara in Deogarh, Uttar Pradesh and in the temple of Laxmaneshwar in Chhattisgarh. They were built in the seventh century CE and tenth century CE respectively. At the beginning Goddess Ganga used to be seen standing under the shade of a tree (Udaygiri). Later this imagery was modified. From the seventh century CE onwards, artists started adding a lotus-shaped umbrella where the tree was placed and gradually, with the passage of time, the lotus flower started to be seen with Goddess Ganga and the use of the umbrella became extinct. It can be presumed that the lotus was used because the flower blooms in water.

The Dashavatara temple at Deogarh is another peerless creation of the Gupta dynasty. The temple, built in the fifth century, flaunts all the great architectural inventions and high points of the Gupta period. The principal god of this temple is

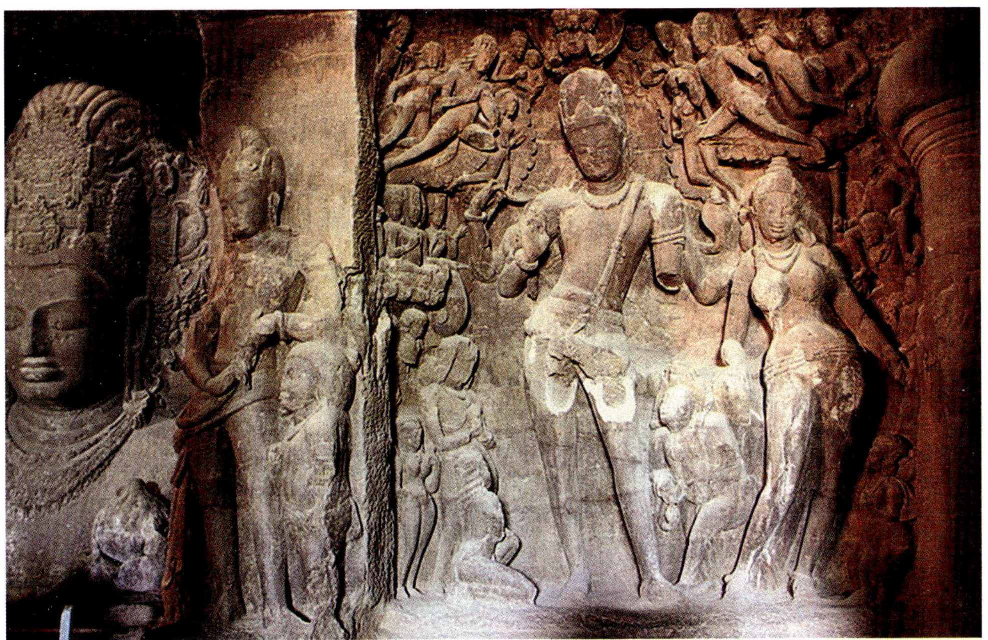

The famous Gangadhara sculpture at Elephanta Caves, depicting Lord Shiva bringing Ganga down on earth

Lord Vishnu, whose statue has been made by subtly cutting rocks. He is recumbent on a large snake. A big snake spreads it enormous hood upon his head. The temple is engraved wonderfully both within and without. The famous critic and art historian Percy Brown commented after visiting this temple, 'Here we see the highest stage of artistic essence.'

A sculpture of Ganga is present in this Dashavatara temple. It is standing at the entrance of the temple. The goddess has her *vahana*, the capricorn, and a tree alongside her. Her form has been engraved in rock. An umbrella shades her head. Yamuna is present too. This style of representation is also found in the Kharod temple at Bilaspur, Madhya Pradesh.

I close the book. Thoughts of Ganga completely absorb my consciousness, my cogitation. Time elapses, art evolves, people change a great deal but Ganga – her charisma undergoes no change and keeps on inspiring artists from time immemorial to the modern age.

REFERENCES

Abhedananda. 1967. *The Complete Works of Swami Abhedananda.* Ramakrishna Vedanta Math.

Alley, Kelly D. 2002. *On the Banks of the Ganga, when Wastewater Meets a Sacred River.* University of Michigan Press.

Basham, A.L. 1964. *The Wonder that was India.* Grove Press.

Darian, Steven G. 2010. *The Ganges in Myth and History.* Motilal Banarsidass.

Eck, Diana L. 1998. *Banaras: City of Light.* New York: Columbia University Press.

Forrest. 2015. A *Picturesque Tour along the Rivers Ganges and Jumna in India.* Niyogi Books.

Havell, E.B. 1905. *Benares: The Sacred City.* London: Blackie and Son Limited.

Hollick, Julian Crandall. *2007. Ganga.* India: Random House.

Kalidasa. *Meghadutam.* Trans Colin J. Holcombe.

Law, Bimala Churn. 1944. *Rivers of India: Historico-Geographical Sketch.* Calcutta Geographical Society.

_______. 1954. *Historical Geography of Ancient India.* Paris: Societe Asiatique de Paris.

Mahajan, Jagmohan. 1994. *Ganga Observed. Foreign Accounts of the River* (selected and edited). New Delhi: Virgo Publications.

_______. 2004. *The Ganga Trail: Foreign Accounts and Sketches of the River Scene.* Varanasi: Indica Books.

Newby, Eric. 1998. *Slowly down the Ganges.* Lonely Planet Publication.

Panditaraja Jagannatha. 2008. *Ganga Lahari: The Flow of the Ganges.* Indica Books.

Roy, Dilip Kumar. 2009. *Kumbha: India's Ageless Festival.* Bharatiya Vidya Bhavan.

Singh, Raghubir. 2003. *The Ganges.* Thames & Hudson.

Tapovan Maharaj, Swami. 2006. *Iswara Darshan.* Chinmaya Prakashan.

The Hymns of Rigveda. 1973. Trans Ralph T.H. Griffith. Motilal Banarsidass.

Twain, Mark. 1989. *Following the Equator: A Journey Around the World.* Dover Publications.

Unknown. 1910. *Prayag or Allahabad: A Handbook.* The Modern Review office.

Vivekananda, Swami. *The Complete Works of Swami Vivekananda.* Advaita Ashrama.

Books in Bengali

Achutyananda, Swami. 2014. *Baranasi Tirtha: Pathe-Pathe Ghaate-Ghaate.* Dev Sahitya Kutir.

Akhandananda, Swami. 2008. *Tibboter Pothe Himalaye.* Udbodhon Karjalaya.

Basu, Ashok Kumar. 1989. *Ganga Pother Itikotha.* Paschimbanga Rajya Pustak Parshad.

Bhaduri, Nrisingha Prasad, ed. 2018. *Purankosh.* Sahitya Samsad.

Bharati, Sibshankar. 2004. *Kumbh Mela O Sadhu Darshan.* Aadi Nath Brothers.

Bhattacharya, Hemchandra, trans. 1978. *Balmiki Ramayan.* Bharavi Publications.

Dutta, Ramesh Chandra. 1976. *Ridveg Samhita*, Vol. 2. Haraf Prakashani.

Ghosh, Chanchal Kumar. 2016. *Ganga: Bharatatmar Praan Probaho.* Gangchil.

Kalelkar, Kakasaheb. 2013. *Jibonleela.* Trans Priyaranjan Sen. Sahitya Akademi.

Mukhopadhyay, Amal Kumar. 1970. *Pouranic Abhidhan.* K.L. Firma.

Roy, Tapan Kumar. 1999. *Baranasir Itikotha.* Kashi Prokashon.

Sanyal, Probodh Kumar. 1963. *Debatmya Himalaya.* Bengal Publishers.

Sarkar, Krishnakanta. 2012. *Bharater Shobhyota.* Shetu Prokashani.

Sinha, Kaliprasanna. 1986. *Mahabharat.* Reflect Prokashani.

Unknown. 2003. *Umaprashad Mukhopadhyay Shotobarshiki Sankalan.* Mitra Ghosh.

Unknown. 2005. *Ganga Bishesh Sankhya.* Aporajito Sahitya Patra.

Books in Hindi

Semwal, Umaraman. 2012. *Gangotri Tirth Kshetra.* Avinab Prakashan.

Unknown. 2010. *Ganga ke Dhar Par.* Uttarkhand Tourism Department.

Unknown. *Kalyan Ganga Ankh.* Year 90, no. 90. Gita Press.

ACKNOWLEDGEMENTS

While writing the book I was assisted by innumerable people, whom I want to thank from the bottom of my heart. I am thankful to Dr Nirmal Kanti Bhattacharjee, Dr Vandana Shiva, Dr Ramram Chatterjee, Pronab Goswami, Dr Soumya Bhattacharya, Avitra Mallick, Saurav Roy Choudhury, Dr Radhyashyam Ghosh (Bithoor), Sri Arup Bosu, Sri Tapash Bandyopadhayay, Sujit Bose, MLA, Salt Lake and Dwijendra Nath Banerjee. Sumati Joshi, Bangshidhar Pokhriyal, K.L. Dewban, Siddhartha Sengupta, Puskhar Rawat, Hemant Dhayne and Umaraman Semwal have assisted me in numerous ways. My blessings to Baishakhi Ganguly, Shruti Singh and my son Pradipta. I am thankful to National Library, Kolkata for their help. Many thanks to the editor, Sucharita Ghosh, and to the entire staff at Niyogi Books. I am also indebted to my three well-wishers – Pracheta Gupta, Kumar Roy and Mangesh Kumar – for their support and encouragement. Other than them countless people of our country have been my true source of inspiration. I am grateful to them all. My family too has been my constant support.

The paintings of Thomas Daniell and William Daniell have been obtained from the archives of Victoria Memorial, Kolkata. Special thanks to the Director, Directorate of Tourism, Uttar Pradesh for providing me with some photographs.

INDEX